D1283836

REVENGE TRAGEDY

REVENGE TRAGEDY

Aeschylus to Armageddon

JOHN KERRIGAN

CLARENDON PRESS · OXFORD

*This book has been printed digitally and produced in a standard design
in order to ensure its continuing availability*

OXFORD
UNIVERSITY PRESS

Great Clarendon Street, Oxford OX2 6DP

Oxford University Press is a department of the University of Oxford.
It furthers the University's objective of excellence in research, scholarship,
and education by publishing worldwide in

Oxford New York

Athens Auckland Bangkok Bogotá Buenos Aires Cape Town
Chennai Dar es Salaam Delhi Florence Hong Kong Istanbul Karachi
Kolkata Kuala Lumpur Madrid Melbourne Mexico City Mumbai Nairobi
Paris São Paulo Shanghai Singapore Taipei Tokyo Toronto Warsaw
with associated companies in Berlin Ibadan

Oxford is a registered trade mark of Oxford University Press
in the UK and in certain other countries

Published in the United States
by Oxford University Press Inc., New York

© John Kerrigan 1996

The moral rights of the author have been asserted
Database right Oxford University Press (maker)

Reprinted 2001

ISBN 0-19-818451-4

in memoriam
Stephen Kerrigan
1929–1994

Preface

EVERY station bookstall shows our fascination with revenge. In the crime section, *Vendetta* rubs shoulders with *A Suitable Vengeance*. Providing more in the way of action is a thriller called *Wild Justice*. Over on the newspaper rack, the theme is equally prominent. Vicious reciprocations are meat and drink to the tabloids, while up-market broadsheets run pieces headed 'Revenge is for losers', 'Getting your own back can hurt'. One purpose of *Revenge Tragedy* is to show that there is nothing new in all this. The pleasures and pains of vengeance have been celebrated since antiquity and a great deal of European literature gravitates towards the topic. Moreover, if revenge has featured in much shoddy and ephemeral writing, it has also inspired the production of recognizable masterpieces. A second, more taxing, intention of this book is to show how well adapted revenge is to literary and dramatic treatment—how its impulse towards structure, its ethical ambiguity and emotional turbulence have helped authors, acting companies, and (in a broader sense) entire cultures produce major works of art.

Revenge is a cultural practice which arouses intense emotion, not only in those who exact or endure it but in those who stand by and judge. Much of its capacity to disturb stems from its paradoxical nature. A destructive impulse, it is mobilized by values and allegiances which would have to be called positive: a proper sense of self-worth, a willingness to strike back in defence of family or other social bonds. Partly because of this, revenge is regarded as 'a kinde of Wilde Iustice' (in Bacon's phrase) even by those who fear its tendency to put 'the Law out of Office'. Arguments about the merits of vengeance quickly become entangled with intractable debates about the validity of retributive punishment and the nature of justice itself. Such paradoxes and complexities make the subject attractive to writers, but they put the student of revenge tragedy in a difficult position because (to simplify distinctions) the raw materials of the genre are already contentious before they enter the literary sphere. To understand the lasting vitality of such works as *The Oresteia* it is necessary to look beyond the usual province of literary criticism. That is why *Revenge Tragedy* is so interested in anthropology and intellectual history, and why it is steadily drawn towards moral philosophy.

The term 'revenge tragedy' was given currency by A. H. Thorndike in about 1900, as a way of labelling a class of plays written by Shakespeare and his contemporaries. It is my contention, of course, that the term can be usefully applied to a great deal of literature, opera, and film produced since Aeschylus. Not all the works discussed in this book will strike the reader as being much like *Hamlet*. Horror fiction, medieval epic, confessional lyric, and GIs' memoirs are all scrutinized in the course of an enquiry which is interested, among other things, in exploring what 'tragedy' might be. Just as the idea of 'revenge' is subjected to clarifying pressure, in order to disentangle its relations with sadistic violence, retributive justice, and the like, so the notion of 'tragedy' is tested. One chapter, for instance, pairs Sherlock Holmes with Sophocles in order to work out why, though detective fiction deals with significant deaths, it does not belong to 'tragedy'. Another looks at plays by Shakespeare, Marston, and Middleton to show how revenge tragedy exhibits a 'comic strain', and how, just across the generic border, in *The Merry Wives of Windsor* and *The Tempest*, family resemblances can be found.

A comprehensive account of the development of revenge tragedy in Europe would be the work of a lifetime, and fill many volumes. This book is necessarily selective. Each chapter analyses texts which are historically related but which have also been brought together for conceptual reasons. The conceptual emphasis is strongest in Parts I and II, where I seek to make accessible the classical roots of Western thinking about tragedy and revenge by setting up a dialogue between Renaissance and modern works on the one hand and ancient texts on the other. Part III, 'Histories and Readings', is, as its title implies, more systematically attentive to the evolution of revenge tragedy, from the Middle Ages to the Romantic period. Even there, however, my account is purposefully episodic, and discriminate rather than schematic in its use of cross-cultural references. *Revenge Tragedy* is, self-evidently, a comparative study. Not least for the sake of being readily understood, though, I have concentrated on texts written in English, and, where I range beyond the familiar, it is usually to discuss those literary and philosophical sources which have mattered most to the Anglophone world. Part III thus starts from twelfth-century French epic and romance (the literature of Roland, King Arthur, and Galahad), and it concludes with chapters which touch on Sade, Laclos, and Schiller. Part IV shares with Parts I and II a tendency to organize discussion more thematically than historically, while following a chronological drift. In it, I think about the writing of those philosophers, poets, and novelists, from Nietzsche to Margaret Atwood, who have shaped, or who vividly reflect, current perceptions of vengeance. A desire to illuminate the present is not limited, though, to Part IV. Repeatedly in this book, contemporary texts and issues are engaged. Though *Revenge Tragedy* offers no single, overarching narrative— because such an account would have to be false—it is committed to the view that certain truths about where we are can only be understood through the long perspective of the past.

*   *   *

This book was mostly written between 1990 and 1994, but it has been in and out of my mind for well over a decade. As a result there are long-standing debts. I am grateful to the Warden and Fellows of Merton College, Oxford, to the Master and Fellows of St John's College, Cambridge, and to the Faculty of English at the University of Cambridge for appointing me to positions which made research possible. Equally important has been the help of Anne Barton. Without her generous support and criticism this book would have languished. At an early stage, Stephen Wall gave valuable advice. When I was only just beginning to think about revenge tragedy in a comparative context, he published, in *Essays in Criticism*, 31 (1981), an article of mine on 'Hieronimo, Hamlet and Remembrance' which is the basis of Chapter 7. At the invitation of Richard and Sylvia Wordsworth, I presented a version of Chapter 10 at the 1989 Wordsworth Summer Conference (Grasmere); it was revised for publication in *Romanticism*, 1 (1995). During my time in Oxford, John Carey, John Jones, Sir Hugh Lloyd-Jones, Sir Keith Thomas, and Nicholas Richardson were open-handed with knowledge and expertise. Since then, many colleagues have pointed me to relevant scholarship. Thanks are particularly due to John Creaser, Simon Goldhill, Jack Goody, Tom Keymer, David Loewenstein, the Revd Andrew Macintosh, Simon Schaffer, and James Simpson. Alan Robson helped me with Old French and J. P. Stern with Nietzsche. Kim Scott Walwyn, at OUP, has been a patient friend of the book.

My first impressions of how *Revenge Tragedy* was shaping up came from audiences of undergraduates in the Cambridge English Faculty. I am grateful for the attention with which they followed my arguments, and also for the blank looks and shufflings of paper which indicated, from time to time, which parts needed revision. Latterly, various friends have read chapters: Hugh Barnes, John Barton, Richard Beadle, Robert Hinde, Neil Hopkinson, Ruth Morse, and Michael O'Neill. Malcolm Schofield was attentive to my philosophical deficiencies. Anne Barton, Colin Burrow, and Adrian Poole gave up a lot of time, during a busy part of the academic year, to read full versions of *Revenge Tragedy*, and they made a number of searching observations which pushed my thoughts forward. Helen Small also read the book, valuably pointed to weaknesses, and was generally a force for good during the months of completion. For last-minute, local adjustments I am, again, indebted to Stephen Wall, as well as to Judith Mossman and an anonymous OUP reader. Jeremy Maule kindly helped me with proofs and Raphael Lyne made the index.

J.F.K.

Contents

List of Illustrations

between pp. 112 and 113

Fig. 1. Eugène Delacroix, *Medea* (1838). Reproduced by permission of the Musée des Beaux-Arts de Lille.

Figs. 2–3. Policoro Painter, *Medea* (*c*.400 BC). Reproduced by permission of the Museo Nazionale della Siritide.

Figs. 4–6. Pasolini, *Medea* (1970). Reproduced by permission of Pandora distribution, Paris.

Fig. 7. 'Two Years for Fan Who Bit Off Police Dog's Ear', *The Sun*, 27 October 1987. Reproduced by permission of *The Sun*.

Fig. 8. Henry Peacham (?), drawing of *Titus Andronicus* (*c*.1595), Longleat Portland Papers, 1, fo. 159ᵛ. Reproduced by permission of the Marquis of Bath.

Fig. 9. From *The Lamentable and Tragical History of Titus Andronicus* (broadside ballad, printed *c*.1655–65). Reproduced by permission of the British Library (Huth 50 (69)).

Bibliographical Note

IT is difficult, when dealing with material written in classical and foreign languages, to strike a balance between accessibility and fidelity. I have made it my rule to provide translation whenever a general reader might be puzzled, putting the original into a footnote, where appropriate, or inserting its key words in brackets. At most points I have been content to follow existing translations, inserting changes (in square brackets) only when questionable renderings would distract from the argument. Unattributed translations are my own. Except where indicated, quotations from Greek tragedy in English come from David Grene and Richmond Lattimore (eds.), *The Complete Greek Tragedies*, 4 vols. (Chicago, 1959), whose line numbers are followed. I have worked with various editions of the plays in Greek, but quote from *Aeschyli septem quae supersunt tragoediae*, ed. Denys Page (Oxford, 1972), *Sophoclis fabulae*, ed. Hugh Lloyd-Jones and N. G. Wilson (Oxford, 1990), and *Euripidis fabulae*, ed. James Diggle, 3 vols. (Oxford, 1981–94). For Scripture I employ the Authorized Version of the Bible, though I have also found *The Oxford Annotated Bible*, ed. Bruce M. Metzger and Roland E. Murphy (New York, 1989) helpful. Quoting Shakespeare is a problem. *The Riverside Shakespeare*, ed. G. Blakemore Evans (Boston, 1974) conflates the early texts of such highly variant plays as *Hamlet* and *King Lear*—a practice now frowned on by informed scholars. On the other hand, the edition is widely available, and the synthesized texts which it conservatively re-edits have enjoyed canonical status since the eighteenth century. Since my arguments are not, in any extended way, affected by textual variation, I have cited Evans's edition throughout; but I urge serious students to consult it only in conjunction with Stanley Wells and Gary Taylor's innovative, though sometimes tendentious, *William Shakespeare: The Complete Works* (Oxford, 1986).

To have catalogued all the sources which have advanced my understanding of European tragedy, or which have influenced my argument by inciting disagreement, would have been to attach a huge tail to an already substantial dog. My policy has been to mark points of specific indebtedness in footnotes and to end not with a guide to further reading or an exhaustive catalogue of works invoked but a Select List of Works Cited. This gives details of all the works from which I quote, but it excludes many items which are mentioned without quotation. The latter can often be accessed through the index, but editors' names (as is the convention) are not recorded there.

Part I

INTRODUCTION

1. On Aristotle and Revenge Tragedy

FOR almost three thousand years, revenge has been a central preoccupation of European literature. Sophocles and Shakespeare, Dostoevsky and Byron, Calderón, Toni Morrison, John Ford—writers as ideologically various as they are historically disparate—have explored the same subject with similar passion, complexity, and concern. Vengeance formatively structures the founding narratives of the West: Homer's *Iliad* and Virgil's *Aeneid*, the *Nibelungenlied* and *La Chanson de Roland*, the last, great books of Malory's *Morte D'Arthur*, Melville's *Moby-Dick*. As I shall stress in this chapter, however, its natural habitat is the stage. Revenge underlies and informs the most fertile periods of our drama: fifth-century Athens, with its Orestes and Electra plays, its *Hecuba* and *Medea*; the Rome of Seneca's *Thyestes*; seventeenth-century Spain, notable for tragedies of honour; the France of Corneille and Racine; the England of Kyd, Shakespeare, and Marston. During the eighteenth century, revenge passed into the world of the novel. But it continued to flourish in melodrama, in Romantic tragedy, and across huge tracts of opera, from *Don Giovanni* to *Wozzeck*, through Verdi, Wagner, and Strauss. My theme is not, then, a negligible one, even if it has become a cliché of gangster movies, pop songs, and pulp fiction.

The long love affair between revenge and drama is readily understandable. Vengeance offers the writer a compelling mix of ingredients: strong situations shaped by violence; ethical issues for debate; a volatile, emotive mixture of loss and agitated grievance. The avenger, isolated and vulnerable, can achieve heroic grandeur by coming to personify nemesis. No less dramatically, groups of characters fuse in vindictive conspiracy through lurid ritual and oath-taking, discovering between themselves a sympathy which can exalt those forms of relationship—such as hold, for instance, between kin—which given cultures find it useful to celebrate.

Revenge can be exacted by omission, or take the paradoxical form (as in Heywood's *A Woman Killed with Kindness*) of mortifying forgiveness; but its characteristic drive towards punishment makes it complicit with the energies of a form whose name, in most European languages, derives from the Greek verb *dran*, 'to do'. When Sartre was looking for a structure in which to explore the philosophical grounds of action, he naturally found himself writing an Oresteian drama, *The Flies*. For the most cerebral and perplexed of revenge plays cannot escape from action as a principle. Shakespeare's *Hamlet*, for instance, revolves around the question, what might action be? Everybody in the play seems to have a different answer, whether it is the prince, the first gravedigger (dividing 'an act' into 'three branches'), or those men who make acting their profession, the troupe of travelling players. And the fact that little of significance is done, or that when it is done it looks disconcertingly like theatrical performance, only gives the more scope for wondering what is meant by 'the name of action'.[1]

There is a sense in which theatrical 'doing' gravitates, quite naturally, towards revenge. Imagine two actors on an open stage, with no props, no text, and, as yet, no character traits. The simplest yet most fraught way to mesh them is through injury and a retaliation. One exchange simultaneously connects the players and sets them in opposition. A dramatic situation emerges: something coherent but emotionally divided. The exchange makes up a miniature play, with unity of time and place, a dramatic tension heightened and relaxed, and a symmetrical structure which is simple but satisfying. Injury breaks a taboo, and disinhibits violence. In the tense phase between assault and riposte, the potential for outrage is awesome. Temporal flow, apparently slowed or suspended, becomes a function of swings of mood. The aggressor recoils to the defensive, his antagonist escalates towards attack. More than in most drama, the bodies of the actors are integral. As an eye is taken for an eye, a tooth punched out for a tooth, both agents have registered upon them what they have inflicted on the other. Under the arc of action, the 'empty space' of performance becomes patched with fields of meaning. Parts of the stage come to signify points where remembered, unresolved acts occurred. This is an Ur-scene for actors because they might better be called 'reactors'. As any director knows, it is easier for a performer to respond

---

[1] *Hamlet*, v. i. 11, iii. i. 87.

to something than to create events *ex nihilo*. Meanwhile, revenge is a building-block, the seed from which something larger can grow, since, one man's vengeance being another man's injury, the single exchange on an open stage will breed others as blood calls for blood and the symmetries of action extend into plot. Revenge tragedies practically construct themselves at this level, and the problem for an author is to prevent the material ramifying endlessly (as in Icelandic saga).

Aristotle is not only the first thinker whose views about tragedy survive: his arguments, in the *Poetics*, point up the radically dramatic power of revenge. When he asserts that tragedy imitates action, that its *muthos* is the *mimēsis* of a *praxis*, he helps explain the drift of writing, across entire periods, towards the subject. Aristotle's guiding interest in the fall of great men, and in the contribution made by knowledge and ignorance to their suffering, leads him to analyse a wide array of texts. Yet he refers with noticeable frequency to plays about Clytemnestra and Orestes, about Medea, Philomela, and Tereus, about the cannibalism of Thyestes and the madness of Ajax. Reading between the lines of his frequently elliptical treatise, it is possible to sense what attracted him. The author of the *Metaphysics* was impressed by the teleology of revenge plots, by their eye-for-eye attentiveness to lucid causal relations, while the social analyst of the *Nicomachean Ethics* found in their mutual violence an instructive obverse to that principle of benign reciprocity which he recommends in his writings about friendship. Above all, in the *Poetics*, Aristotle sounds like the philosopher as natural scientist. He deals with plays as though they were organisms, complexly articulated yet whole. And the tripartite ordering-within-unity which he advocates for tragic plots ('. . . "with a beginning, a middle, and an end"')[2] coincides with the pattern of injury, anticipation, and reaction which structures an Ur-revenge action, played out on the open stage.

Aristotle identifies three elements of the tragic plot: *peripeteia* or surprising reversal, *anagnōrisis* or recognition, and that 'act involving destruction or pain' which he calls *pathos* (1452a–b). The last of these goes far towards generating the 'pity and fear' in an audience which Aristotle regards as essential. Significantly, he illustrates the creation of 'pity and fear' by citing, as an instance of surprise (*peripeteia*), 'the

[2] *Poetics*, 1450b, tr. M. E. Hubbard, in D. A. Russell and M. Winterbottom (eds.), *Ancient Literary Criticism: The Principal Texts in New Translations* (Oxford, 1972).

case of the statue of Mitys in Argos killing Mitys's murderer by falling on him as he looked at it'. This is a shocking event, but it involves things happening 'because of each other', and 'chance events seem more marvellous when they look as if they were meant to happen . . . for we do not think that things like this are merely random' (1452a). After saying that 'such plots will necessarily be the best', Aristotle remarks, 'The best sort of recognition is that accompanied by *peripeteia*, like that in the *Oedipus*' (1452a). This does not rule revenge plays out of the highest class of tragedy. For a drama about the death of Mitys's murderer would show *peripeteia* combining with *anagnōrisis* by virtue of retribution. Like Don Juan being dragged off to punishment by the statue of the man he had murdered, Mitys's killer would experience a moment of recognition as the statue toppled towards him. He would be afflicted (though rather late in life) by the kind of *anagnōrisis* which strikes Oedipus when, at the *peripeteia* of *Oedipus Tyrannus*, he recognizes his oppression by a shocking chain of events which does not seem to have accumulated by chance. Revenge plays specialize in recognitions of this sort. The object of retribution does not just suffer from what is done to him but from perceiving in what is done to him what he did to his victim, and from enduring that knowledge.

Evidently, the structure of vengeance excites more than a visceral thrill. Ethical exchanges are implicit in the simplest plot. In that primal action on the open stage, the symmetry of revenge is inseparable from a dramatic irony which complicates the moral situation of the revenger. This irony takes effect regardless of authors' views; whether or not they approve of vengeance, the complications will register. For when B, injured by A, does to A what A did to him, he makes himself resemble the opponent he has blamed, while he transforms his enemy into the kind of victim he once was. Indeed, the more scrupulous he is in pursuit of retribution, the more exact in exacting vengeance, the more he effects this interchange. In his two-act play *Revenge* (1970), Howard Brenton has one actor play both MacLeish of the Yard and his old criminal antagonist Adam Hepple, until, as the conventionally right and wrong battle it out through a series of revenge actions, it becomes clear that the Assistant Commissioner and the old lag are equally just, equally crooked, and in some ways indistinguishable. No classical or Renaissance play is so extreme, yet it is in response to this ethical irony, as much as to a Christian disapproval of 'private' vengeance, that such protagonists as Chettle's Hoffman and the Vindice of *The Revenger's Tragedy* become as corrupt as their opponents.

These characters stand somewhat apart, of course, from A and B on the open stage. Like most dramatic revengers they are not direct victims of an injury. Hoffman acts on behalf of a dead father, like Hamlet, while Vindice works in a threefold capacity, revenging his and Hippolito's ruined father, his skeletal mistress Gloriana, and, towards the end of the tragedy, the raped wife of Antonio. It might seem a dramatic weakness that, the more disablingly violent an initial attack, the less likely it is that the victim can come up with an appropriate response. Have a character murdered and, unless you are prepared to raise him from the grave—or turn him into a toppling statue—you have excluded him from violence. But this is, in dramatic practice, an advantage since, in the transference of revenge from the dead to those who survive, questions of duty, justice, and loyalty are amplified, while a vibrant and eminently theatrical territory of ghosts, dream-visions, and graveyards opens up. It is here that the stately figure of Old Hamlet appears, and Vindice's 'bony lady', here that Marston's Antonio dreams of a spirit, while Orestes and Electra summon their father's ghost from underground.

The displacement of revenge from one character to another creates a structure of obligation which modifies the economy of vengeance. The promises, debts of honour, and blood allegiances which shape Hamlet and the rest involve systems of feeling which lead beyond the immediate action. It is an observable fact of societies which permit vendetta, as well as a painful feature of much tragedy, that, until revenge is exacted, those close to an injured or murdered person feel the guilt or shame of betrayal. Why were the victims not protected by their loved ones? Was the 'neglect' which allowed the attack even a form of complicity? Such anxieties mean that the assaulted can find it easier to forgive than those expected to revenge, while the latter persuade themselves that the retribution which they exact is taken in the name of the wronged. This has implications for tragic action not least because, while A and B can be regarded as symmetrically equivalent when construed as functions of a *praxis*, once they are endowed with a social dimension they decisively, even if minimally, differ from one another. And when B, or one of his agents, thinks of striking back against A, he must anticipate hurting by association those who are in some way related to his opponent but not guilty of the crime. Revenge tragedy likes to show how the sins of the fathers are visited upon the sons when only the fathers are directly punished.

Nor is the structure of displaced agency free from irony. If the victim of an injury resembles his opponent in the act of vengeance, the revenger who assumes the burden of another person's resentment suspends his own identity. This is plain enough outside drama. When Aeneas, for instance, roused by the sight of Pallas's belt upon Turnus, stabs his killer, he cries: ''Tis Pallas, Pallas who with this strike sacrifices thee, and takes atonement of thy guilty blood!'[3] Theatrical tragedy, however, thrives on such mergings and doublings. Chettle's Hoffman, for example, crowns the son of his father's enemy with red-hot iron because Old Hoffman had been executed in that way, only to be crowned himself, in revenge. As his brains sizzle and boil inside the iron circle, Young Hoffman resembles his father, killed before the tragedy began. He might be his father's ghost, come to show the world his injuries. Or consider an ancient example. In Aeschylus' *Libation Bearers*, Orestes is repeatedly identified with Agamemnon. When the old slave gnomically tells the queen, '[a live man is slain by] the dead' (886), his jest about Aegisthus' murder is secured by the killer's commitment to his father. Disguised as a Phocian, Orestes has returned to Mycenae announcing his own death in exile. But he has also come home as the instrument of Agamemnon's anger. When Aegisthus is slaughtered and Orestes takes his and his father's place at the head of the royal household, two dead men conspire in the taking of one life.

At this point, revenge leads towards some fascinating, if murky, issues. Given the degree to which vengeance incites men and women to act for others within the kin, and given, too, the mental anguish this lets them in for—dreams, hysterical guilt, and antic dispositions not entirely assumed[4]—it is hardly surprising that revenge tragedy should have become a happy hunting-ground for psychoanalysts. *The Oresteia* is a key text for Kleinians; *Hamlet* has

---

[3] 'Pallas te hoc volnere, Pallas|immolat et poenam scelerato ex sanguine sumit'; *Aeneid*, XII. 948–9, in *Virgil*, ed. and tr. H. Rushton Fairclough, rev. edn., 2 vols. (London, 1934–5).

[4] For Renaissance examples see Charles A. Hallett and Elaine S. Hallett, *The Revenger's Madness: A Study of Revenge Tragedy Motifs* (Lincoln, Nebr., 1980), chs. 2–3.

been a prize exhibit from Freud through Ernest Jones to Lacan. The organization of affects within the family is so historically and socially variable that it can hardly be claimed that, in some way that is permanently true, the Prince of Denmark hates his father and longs to sleep with his mother, or that his feelings towards Gertrude and Ophelia are twisted by what Melanie Klein calls breast envy. There is a sense, however, in which the structure of obligation under which Hamlet labours makes him, on a psychologically significant level, a substitute for the father he is out to revenge. It might take a reading c.1900, in bourgeois Vienna, to make the oedipal element explicit, but that does not mean that such a potential was lost on Shakespeare's contemporaries. Certainly the two plays most immediately imbued with the spirit of Elsinore deal in incestuous passion. In the murder of the Duke in *The Revenger's Tragedy* an audience witnesses not only a classic display of Jacobean syphilitic dread, as the old lecher's mouth and tongue and teeth are eaten away by poison from Gloriana's kiss, but the father-displacing tableau of his son Spurio consorting with the Duchess as her husband writhes in death-agony (III. v). Rather similarly, in *Hoffman*, Chettle's hero puts himself in mortal danger by refusing to dispose of the mother of the man whom he has murdered and is now disguised as, because (though he resists the confession) he has fallen in love with her, and cannot bring himself to mark her flesh by strangling her.[5] Clearly the picture of A vs. B antagonism needs qualifying with the thought that motives are often rationalizations, that desires can go in disguise.

Some ways in which the buried plots of revenge tragedy might be retrieved can be grasped by glancing at psychoanalytic accounts of those father/son identifications which run through *The Libation Bearers*. In 'Some Reflections on *The Oresteia*' (1963), Melanie Klein relates Orestes' hostility towards Clytemnestra to the aggression of a child in the 'paranoid–schizoid position', fearful of being devoured by the mother and envious of her capacity to provide warmth and nurture at the breast.[6] Oddly, given her interest in the breast, Klein overlooks Clytemnestra's dream. 'She dreamed she gave birth to a snake', the Chorus tells the newly-arrived Orestes:

---

[5] Henry Chettle, *The Tragedy of Hoffman*, ed. Harold Jenkins (Oxford, 1951), 1742–70.
[6] Repr. in her *Envy and Gratitude and Other Works 1946–1963* (London, 1975), 275–99.

CHORUS She herself, in the dream, gave it her breast to suck.
ORESTES How was her nipple not torn by such a beastly thing?
CHORUS It was. The creature drew in blood along with the milk.
ORESTES No void dream this. It is the vision of a man. (527-34)

Clytemnestra recalls this episode when, just before she is murdered, she exposes a breast to Orestes in supplication ('You are the snake I gave birth to, and gave the breast' (896 ff., 928)). Most likely, Klein suppresses the dream because the phallic quality of the snake points, more strongly than she would like, towards the kind of oedipal reading which the Lacanian, André Green, has set against her own.[7] Certainly, in Stesichorus's pre-Aeschylean *Oresteia*, Clytemnestra dreams about Agamemnon in serpent form. Depending on how the Greek is translated, either this snake turns into Agamemnon or Orestes springs from its blood-stained crest. Writing with Stesichorus in mind, Aeschylus fused father and son in the dream-snake, making Orestes a phallic infant who appropriates his father's claims to the mother. The slave's cry, '[a live man is slain by] the dead', becomes a darkly oedipal riddle.

My intention is not to suggest that, since Klein and Green cannot both be right, the whole tradition in which they operate must be wrong (though it might be). Nor is it to imply that revenge tragedy succeeds in proportion to the readiness with which it delivers a psychoanalytical message—the deadening, manipulated Freudianism of Eugene O'Neill's *Mourning Becomes Electra* sufficiently refutes the thought. My concern is, rather, to indicate how richly articulable even ancient revenge tragedy can be when exposed to the kind of interpretation which looks beyond ostensible motives for evidence of buried desires, and interprets characters as questers after psychic balance as well as ethical equivalence. As Simone Weil once said: 'The desire for vengeance is a desire for essential equilibrium. . . . The search for equilibrium is bad because it is imaginary. Revenge. Even if in fact we kill or torture our enemy it is, in a sense, imaginary.'[8] The equivalencing impulse of B against A cannot be understood simply in terms of *praxis* because the idea of equilibrium-through-action is loaded not only with assumptions

---

[7] *The Tragic Effect: The Oedipus Complex in Tragedy* (Cambridge, 1979), ch. 1. For further, eclectic observations, see George Devereux, *Dreams in Greek Tragedy: An Ethno-Psycho-Analytical Study* (Oxford, 1976), ch. 6.
[8] *Simone Weil: An Anthology*, ed. Siân Miles (London, 1986), 217-18.

about justice as balance but with psychotherapeutic commonplaces about the need for a balanced psyche. The poise of a revenge action can bear intricately asymmetrical relations to the psychic needs and potentialities of A and B, or their agents. One way of thinking about this would be to ponder the extreme case of a tragedy, such as Ariel Dorfman's *Death and the Maiden* (1991), in which it is never finally established whether A actually did commit the wrong (in this case, torture and rape) against the B who now, to recover her own equilibrium, seeks to avenge the injuries inflicted on her. Many revenge texts similarly, if to a lesser degree, put fantasy into action. The loppings, rendings, and cannibalistic ingestions of *Titus Andronicus*, for example, are 'imaginary' even though they happen: pieces of wild fantasy worked out in dramatic play. The heroine of *Death and the Maiden*, of course, avenges specific injuries against a disputable opponent. A and B relate as problematically when psychic disequilibrium is created by factors which have nothing to do with B's grievance. This, again, is a feature of the genre. As Christian Wolff says of Euripides' *Orestes*: 'Revenge . . . becomes an irrational response to the world's failure to render what one imagines is his due. It could be an attempt to force repayment on the loss between what seems and what is.'[9]

A thoroughgoing psychoanalytic approach would extend this principle to the composition of revenge tragedy itself. Since it is now a cliché to say that 'The place where one can wreak vengeance on reality is known as art,'[10] it is not surprising to find works about revenge being construed as fantasy outlets for writers' resentments, nor, even, for creative endeavour in general to be endowed with a reparative function. In her 1929 paper on 'Infantile Anxiety-Situations Reflected in a Work of Art and in the Creative Impulse',[11] Melanie Klein finds in the sudden emergence of a depressed and anxious woman's ability to paint, and especially to paint her mother, the operation of a vengeful dynamic which meshes with a desire for creative atonement. Using an argument already half familiar to us from her account of Aeschylus, Klein says that Ruth Kjär experiences 'the desire to make reparation, to make

[9] 'Orestes', in Erich Segal (ed.), *Euripides: A Collection of Critical Essays* (Englewood Cliffs, NJ, 1968), 132–49, repr. in Erich Segal (ed.), *Oxford Readings in Greek Tragedy* (Oxford, 1983), 341–56, p. 354.
[10] Terry Eagleton, 'Angry 'Un', *London Review of Books*, 15/13 (8 July 1993), 16.
[11] Repr. in her *Love, Guilt and Reparation* (London, 1975), 210–18.

good the injury psychologically done to the mother . . . The
daughter's wish to destroy her mother, to see her old, worn out,
marred, is the cause of the need to represent her in full possession of
her strength and beauty' (p. 218). This is a relatively sophisticated
modulation of the post-Romantic thesis that the workings of creativity are inseparable from an impulse to destroy. On the street,
cruder versions prevail. In a recent issue of *Elle*, for instance, the
novelist Jackie Collins confesses (but actually boasts), 'I've been
trashed by certain journalists, and I've taken revenge in my
books,' the pop singer Richard Jobson announces that 'Writing
has always been my way of avenging myself on those who have
done me wrong,' and the journalist Joanna Briscoe asks, 'isn't the
very *raison d'être* of achievement revenge?'[12] The currency of such
views would alone suggest that it is time to reassess revenge tragedy.
Vengeance is at the root of what many people now think they are
doing when they write, or sing, or just strive for 'achievement'.

*   *   *

Most tragic protagonists are responsible for how they suffer. More
than rats in traps, tennis-balls bandied by the stars, they help create
the circumstances in which events unfold. Recognition of their role
in the making of what afflicts them is a large part of what makes
their catastrophes tragic. A revenger's position is different. His
predicament is imposed on him, and to know this is part of his
plight. Injured by another, or urged towards vengeance by a raped
mistress or murdered father, he is forced to adopt a role. His
qualities colour the drama of which he is part; tragedy can mourn
the waste which follows from the narrowing down of his personality
to the bare demands of action; but for as long as he remains a
revenger the proportions of the acts he engages in are determined
by an injury he never gave or a request he did not make. The story
of Prince Hamlet would be tragic even if he had no character.

   That claim has a familiar ring. 'A work could not be a tragedy if
there were no action', Aristotle says in the *Poetics*, 'But there could
be a tragedy without *mimēsis* of character' (1450a). Once again, the
philosopher's arguments are peculiarly relevant to revenge drama.
He concedes that 'character', *ēthos*, is realized in choice or decision
(*proairesis*), and that choice gives shape to action. Without *ēthos* there

---

[12] *Elle*, June 1993, 63–9.

would not be the misjudgement, the *hamartia*, which turns the *muthos* towards disaster. Yet *ēthos* is not primary. It follows, as it were, from action. Different conceptions of Orestes can inhabit the same tragic *muthos*, as surely as Hamlet's character is incidental to his tragedy. Start with plot-design, Aristotle urges the dramatist, and only then add *ēthos*, for the art of tragedy resembles that of painting, and 'the most beautiful colours, if smeared on at random, would give less pleasure than an uncoloured outline that was a picture of something' (1450b). In this regard, Hegel's meditations on the 'unified character' of Greek protagonists still exercise undue influence. When, in the closing section of the *Philosophy of Fine Art*, he argues for the 'plasticity' of Greek consciousness, for its refusal in tragedy to distinguish between 'self-conscious life . . . and the objective significance of the fact accomplished',[13] his categories owe more to idealist epistemology than the practice of classical theatre. Those who read the *Poetics* under the shadow of Hegel can, like John Jones, in his exhilarating study *On Aristotle and Greek Tragedy*,[14] invoke the primacy of *muthos* to illuminate the unreflective grandeur of tragic agents in Aeschylus, but they cannot, by the same lights, value the equally fifth-century readiness of Euripidean figures to impute misjudgement and sophisticate blame. What is needed is a grasp of how the theory of choice and responsibility implicit in the *Poetics* is consistent with both Aristotle's relationship to fifth-century notions of volition and the secondary role which he allots to *ēthos*.

Certainly, the legal records which survive from Athens show that, while modern ideas of inwardness may be hard to find, terms bearing on inclination (*hekon*), deliberation (*boulēsis*), choice (*hairesis*), and necessity (*anankē*) were discriminated. Revenge was instrumental in promulgating and maintaining this terminology because, as Jean-Pierre Vernant notes, 'the law. . . followed criteria designed to regulate, in the name of the State, the exercise of private vengeance, by drawing distinctions . . . between the various forms of murder calling for different legal sentences.'[15] Depending on the degree of 'voluntariness' imputed, homicide was not only subject to different sanctions but to judgment by different courts. As we know from his ethical writings, the author of the *Poetics* was eager to

---

[13] G. W. F. Hegel, *Hegel on Tragedy*, ed. Anne and Henry Paolucci (1962; Westport, Conn., 1978), 69.   [14] *On Aristotle and Greek Tragedy* (London, 1962).
[15] 'Intimations of the Will in Greek Tragedy', in Jean-Pierre Vernant and Pierre Vidal-Naquet, *Myth and Tragedy in Ancient Greece*, tr. Janet Lloyd (New York, 1988), 49–84, pp. 60–1.

establish that bad men are responsible for what they do; but this does not mean that he thought they willed their badness in the manner of Milton's Satan. Aristotle recognizes that it is possible to do something voluntarily without consciously making a choice, and that a choice can be made which does not match all your intentions. What happens in the story of your life might only be glancingly related to decisions which spring from your ethical character.[16]

Returning, with this in mind, to *ēthos*, it becomes plainer why so many since Hegel should have found in Greek revenge plays a massive, almost sculptural, violence. When a protagonist such as Aeschylus' Orestes inherits through blood, status, and long nurture the task of destroying his father's killers, his inclinations, deliberations, and choices are consistent with the necessity of the *muthos* which the playwright inherits and plots. There are moments of painful decision-making, as when Clytemnestra exposes her breast to him, but the formula 'he would not be Orestes if he did not take revenge' sums up the situation. The very strength of Orestes' motivation, however, is an index of the compound pressure which makes him act simultaneously as himself (to cut a long story short) and as Agamemnon's agent, the dead man who kills the living. It follows, indeed, though paradoxically, that, precisely because of this doubleness, the most glaring instance of dramatic reflexivity in extant Greek tragedy comes in a revenge play. In a sequence often labelled parodic, Euripides' Electra resists recognizing her brother by rejecting those tokens of identity which had satisfied her predecessor in *The Libation Bearers*.[17] The Old Man urges her to compare her locks with those left on her father's tomb, and suggests that she set her feet in the prints scattered around the site, but she scorns the notion that a rugged young man's hair could resemble hers, a male foot be shaped like her own. While Euripides highlights the implausibility of Aeschylus' plotting, Electra stands obliquely towards the *muthos*, resisting the role which it would force upon her, until, seeing on Orestes' brow a childhood scar, she capitulates.

Euripides is, characteristically, testing the limits of tragic decorum here. Yet Electra and the audience react against Aeschylus'

---

[16] For guidance see e.g. Albrecht Dihle, *The Theory of Will in Classical Antiquity* (Berkeley, 1982), esp. 56–60, Bernard Williams, *Shame and Necessity* (Berkeley, 1993), chs. 2–3.   [17] *Libation Bearers*, 165–245, *Electra*, 487–584.

tokens on different planes. In Renaissance drama, by contrast, the boundary is not observed. Such protagonists as Vindice and Antonio make much of the fact that, as revengers in an imposed scenario, they resemble actors in a play. The theatrical topos was, of course, ubiquitous, and Shakespeare, for one, did not need revenge tragedy to make him think 'men and women merely players', all with 'their exits' and 'their entrances'.[18] But it is striking that he should explore that motif most urgently, not in *Love's Labour's Lost* or *Twelfth Night*, but in his greatest play of vengeance. As he tries to come to terms with the task which his father has imposed, Hamlet imagines himself as a stage murderer. He is 'the rugged Pyrrhus' killing Old Priam, the lethal Lucianus, 'nephew to the king' in *The Murder of Gonzago*, or a Senecan villain of the 1590s, crying, from *The True Tragedy of Richard III*, 'Come, the croaking raven doth bellow for revenge.'[19] The melancholy humour of such moments has an improvised air, a sense of provisionality in being. These tonalities begin and end in an awareness, which the Prince in some part shares, that this particular Hamlet might belong to other actions. Such a notion is compatible with the Aristotelian perception that different versions of the prince could all be tragic in *Hamlet*, but its dramatic effects are more complex even than those registered in Euripides' *Electra*. According to Aristotle, the best plays draw their *muthoi* from a common stock based on the histories of a few families (for how else could the pleasures of knowledge-as-recognition be guaranteed to an audience?). *Ēthos* is then applied, painted into the plot. In *Hamlet*, by contrast, even Polonius recognizes that drama has multifarious tragical-comical-historical-pastoral possibilities. Why, the Prince wonders, should obedience to revenge make his life conform to the shape of some old pot-boiler (the audience will be thinking of the *Ur-Hamlet*)?[20] Why is he in *this* play?

If revenge worked only towards the subordination of the revenger, the consequences would be claustrophobic. Hamlet would be like the protagonists of *Rosencrantz and Guildenstern are Dead*, caught up in an action which oppressed him but from which he felt detached. In fact, the motive cuts two ways at once, subordinating

---

[18] *As You Like It*, II. vii. 140–1.　　　　[19] II. i. 452; III. ii. 244, 253–4.
[20] This tragedy, recorded from 1589 and 1594, and probably written in the late 1580s, is regarded by most scholars as a major lost source for Shakespeare's play.

the agent to a situation but, at the same time, prompting him to shape events towards that action's end. This generates a theatricality which registers even in non-dramatic literature. Homer's Odysseus, for example, returns to his palace disguised; he plays a beggar's part, and only the old nurse and faithful dog recognize him. Once admitted, he traps his victims, throws off his rags, and uses the bow which proves his identity to take revenge upon his enemies. Move slightly up the scale of intrigue, and you find a work like *King Horn*, the first romance to emerge from what survives of Early Middle English. Again a hero is avenged upon usurpers, rescuing his sweetheart Rymenhild from the strong-arm rival Fikenhild and her too pliant father, King Aylmar. This time, however, because revenge is more pronounced, and not secondary to a motif of return, exile counts for less, and lethal play is heightened. Horn comes for Rymenhild dressed not as a beggar but a minstrel. He and his accomplices form a troupe of harpers and fiddlers, and it is this disguise (rather as in *The Revenger's Tragedy*) which gains them admission to Fikenhild's fortress. Once inside, they play and sing, weaving a device about Fikenhild and his followers, before slaughtering everyone in sight. Roland Barthes's observation comes to mind: 'violence always organize[s] itself into a *scene*: the most transitive of behaviour (to eliminate, to kill, to wound, to humble) [is] also the most theatrical'.[21]

Because drama is by nature, as Aristotle and his contemporaries recognized,[22] a peculiarly 'mimetic' medium, it tends to sophisticate the histrionic, in plays about revenge, by displaying an imitative element within the '*scene*'. It is not surprising that René Girard— who is even more obsessed than Aristotle with man's imitative instincts—should have been drawn to the study of antagonistic interaction, dramatic doubling, and vengeance.[23] 'Revenge', as Byron's Faliero says, is 'not an impulse of mere anger', it is 'a virtue by reflection'.[24] The avenger reflects upon what has been done in order to reflect what has been done. His killings are

---

[21] *Roland Barthes*, tr. Richard Howard (London, 1977), 160.

[22] Aryeh Kosman, 'Acting: *Drama* as the *Mimēsis* of *Praxis*', in Amélie Oksenberg Rorty (ed.), *Essays on Aristotle's 'Poetics'* (Princeton, 1992), 51–72, p. 55.

[23] For Aristotle see e.g. *Poetics*, 1448b; Réné Girard, *Violence and the Sacred*, tr. Patrick Gregory (Baltimore, 1977), chs. 1–2.

[24] IV. ii. 103–4, in *Lord Byron: The Complete Poetical Works*, ed. Jerome J. McGann, 7 vols. (Oxford, 1980–93), iv.

distinguished from common murder by the sign, the evidence, of their fittingness. Hence the impulse to display, where the murderer's urge is to conceal. Symptomatically, *deik-*, the Indo-European root of 'revenge', 'vendetta', and 'vindicate' also gives rise to Greek *deiknunai*, 'to show', Latin *dicere*, 'to say' and *dicare*, 'to proclaim', Old English *tacen*, 'sign, token', *tacnian*, 'to signify', and Old French, *tache*, 'mark, stain'.[25] When B takes an eye for an eye, he emulates Aristotle's dramatist by imitating A's action, and shows the justice of his act. Thus, in Kyd's *Spanish Tragedy*, Hieronimo stages before the royal court a multi-lingual playlet of his own composition, on the subject of Soliman and Perseda. This entertainment chimes with the circumstances of his son's murder, and Hieronimo has those involved in that initial scene of violence replay their parts in its action—except, that is, for Lorenzo, the leading villain, who is stabbed (for real) by the father who acts the part which Lorenzo once played. If revenge attracts the dramatist because, by submitting characters to a scenario, it does as a matter of course what his own writing does perforce, it also attracts him because the revenger is a surrogate artist. (Kyd himself wrote a play called *Soliman and Perseda*, published at about the same time as *The Spanish Tragedy*.) In pursuit of retribution, the avenger must manipulate a fluid and contingent world with a dramatist's inventiveness and authority. He must be, in the play, an image of its author, transmuting creative ambition into narrative and stage action.

This helps explain the familiar posture of the Elizabethan revenger, standing slightly outside his role, examining his actions like a playwright at work. 'Come Lorrique', says Hoffman, after his first act of murder and the first act of Chettle's tragedy,

> This, but the prologue to th'ensuing play,
> The first step to revenge, this scene is done.
> Father, I offer thee thy murderer's son. . . .
> He was the prologue to a Tragedy
> That, if my destinies deny me not,
> Shall pass those of Thyestes, Tereus,
> Jocasta or Duke Jason's jealous wife.
> So shut our stage up, there is one act done

[25] See e.g. Calvert Watkins (rev. and ed.), *The American Heritage Dictionary of Indo-European Roots* (Boston, 1985).

> Ended in Otho's death; 'twas somewhat single;
> I'll fill the other fuller . . .[26]

As Hoffman closes the discovery-space curtain, he might be Chettle, musing and making promises—to himself or to his audience. This kind of imagery arises so readily that, in weak Renaissance revenge plays, it is obvious and unearned. More often, the motif is associated with so much vindictive ingenuity—poisoned helmets and pictures, trick chairs, man-traps—that its aestheticism forms part of something larger. It becomes involved with the perverted creativity which De Quincey analysed in his essay 'On Murder Considered as One of the Fine Arts'.

Painting, the fine art which Aristotle turns to when making comparisons with tragedy, offers a particularly rewarding means of exploring such creativity. In Calderón's *El Pintor de su deshonra*, for instance, the gentleman artist, Don Juan Roca, is married to a younger woman. Seraphine accepted him believing that her lover, Alvaro, was dead. When Alvaro returns, alive, she is tempted to elope, but resists; and when she is snatched away by him, she remains faithful to her husband. Thinking himself betrayed, however, Roca longs for revenge. Disguised as an impoverished painter, he sets off in pursuit. At the residence of the Prince of Orsino, who has become an admirer of Seraphine, Roca paints a mythological subject (Nessus carrying off Deianira) which anticipates his vengeance (for Hercules is 'placed at the edge of the composition').[27] His creativity becomes still more ominous when Orsino asks him to paint the portrait of an unnamed beauty and he instructs his servant to pack a brace of pistols along with his colours and brushes. Discovering that the beauty whom he is required to paint, from a place of concealment, is the sleeping Seraphine, Roca contains his fury long enough to set to work. But when she awakens from a dream of her own death, screaming, and Roca sees Alvaro rush in to embrace her, the husband imagines the worst and shoots them both dead. 'Here you have a painting', he tells the prince, 'sketched in blood by the hand | of one, the painter of his dishonour' (3102–4). Like Calderón's *El Médico de su honra*, this tragedy is interested in how far a jealous revenger imagines the offences he acts against.

---

[26] Lines 239, 407–13 (modernized).
[27] Calderón, *The Painter of his Dishonour: El Pintor de su deshonra*, ed. and tr. A. K. G. Paterson (Warminster, 1991), 2694.

Here, though, art itself precipitates violence. The mimesis of painting goes into reverse; life imitates art, in that the play ends with the innocent Deianira being destroyed along with Nessus. Writers of De Quincey's generation—some of them, like Shelley, admirers of Calderón—take this principle further. In Byron's *The Two Foscari*, for example, Loredano's at least half-imagined grievances against the Foscari license a vengefulness which renders reality plastic, turns it into an aesthetic phenomenon. 'You are ingenious, Loredano, in | Your modes of vengeance,' declares Barbarigo, 'nay, poetical, | A very Ovid in the art of *hating*'.[28] De Quincey has been credited with making explicit the thought that homicide may 'be treated *aesthetically*', because his use of that adverb, in 'On Murder Considered . . .', is the first recorded instance in English.[29] As Chettle and Calderón demonstrate, however, revenge tragedy has long been familiar with murder's artful sublimities. It is founded on the principle that violence can provide satisfactions which are, at least in prospect, bound up with form and signification, and so with the aesthetic as well as with the ethical. By driving a wedge between the former and the latter, De Quincey disrupted some of the most tenacious Kantian assumptions of his age. But his provocative insights were anticipated by the distinction which emerges in revenge tragedy between the uneasy moral neutrality characteristic of many denouements and the vivid apprehension of structure. When B 'gets even' with A, and inherits or cancels A's guilt, the resulting moral vacancy—however quickly colonized by a sense that there are differences between assault and response, that two wrongs cannot make a right—throws into sharp relief the lucidity of the completed arch. De Quincey's aestheticizing of violence anticipates Nietzsche, surrealism, the Theatre of Cruelty. Yet the aesthetic which Genet (for instance) advocates transferring wholesale into life seems less surprising if one remembers Aristotle stressing unity of action in tragedy, and acknowledging that savage deeds can be the stuff of shapeliness: 'Acts', Genet writes, 'must be carried through to their completion. Whatever their point of departure, the end will be beautiful. It is because an action has not been completed that it is vile.'[30]

---

[28] V. i. 134–6, in *Byron: Complete Poetical Works*, ed. McGann, vi (with Barry Weller).

[29] Cf. Joel Black, *The Aesthetics of Murder: A Study in Romantic Literature and Contemporary Culture* (Baltimore, 1991), 3.

[30] Jean Genet, *The Thief's Journal*, tr. Bernard Frechtman (1965; Harmondsworth, 1967), 178; cf. Black, *Aesthetics of Murder*, 73.

How far does this reflexivity figure in the drama available to
Aristotle? Compared with Calderón, Byron, and De Quincey,
Greek revenge tragedy is reticent. When Orestes, for instance,
near the end of *The Libation Bearers*, brings out on the displaying-
machine called the *ekkuklēma* the corpses of Aegisthus and Clytemnestra, his declarations register but do not theatricalize what has
been done. With an imperative 'idesthe', he urges the audience to
'Behold' (973), but then draws attention to the scene's impersonal
demonstration that, having sworn to kill Agamemnon together and
die as lovers together, his enemies kept their covenant and have
been, by their killing, destroyed. Repeating his imperative, Orestes
draws into the tableau the net or robe in which his victims
murdered his father. This is not, like Hoffman's curtain, a material
sign of the avenger's control of the aesthetic framing of action, but a
piece of the past's actuality that sets its seal on the present. It was
not through his own virtuosity, Orestes says, but with the help of
'right', *dikē*, that he punished his mother (988). Nor can this
revenger, after many lines of declarative apologia, 'shut our stage
up' and declare 'one act done'. In the closing lines of the play, the
Erinyes (invisible to all but Orestes) begin to harry him for his
mother's death. Aeschylus is misunderstood if this is thought a
coup de théâtre. In Greek aesthetic theory, the maker finds in matter
the form of what he imitates.[31] Rather similarly the tragic hero with
mimetic powers—i.e., the revenger—works within a flow of action
to realize the retributive form of his *muthos*. How he does this
amounts to *ēthos*. When he makes the form of *dikē* articulate,
Orestes educes the Furies; they are another facet of the action of
which he is an agent, not the less ineluctable (as Aristotle would put
it) for being unexpected. The agent's choice brings out consequences which were not part of his intention. He joins the audience
in acquiring knowledge which is something like recognition.

*   *   *

Orestes deals in *dikē* and its cognates, words which cannot be
accurately translated by using 'right' (as above) or 'retribution',
'la justice', 'das Recht', or any of the other terms which strive, in
modern European vocabularies, to define the sphere of just-dealing.

[31] See e.g. Jean-Pierre Vernant, *Myth and Thought Among the Greeks*, tr. Janet Lloyd
(Boston, 1983), 274–5.

His defence turns on a word of such wide-ranging significance in Athenian culture that it appears, where we might speak of 'order' or 'vengeance' or 'coherence' or 'stability', in a variety of contexts from the political to the scientific. Is Orestes even a 'revenger'? Ancient Greek has no equivalent, but speaks of 'the man who deals *dikē*', or of *poinē* ('recompense') and *timōros*, 'he who restores honour or status or respect', or, through the verb *tinusthai* and substantive *tisis*, of 'the person who exacts a price, reciprocates, enforces an exchange'. Rather than talk of Orestes 'revenging' his father's death, it might be better to use an obsolete word and say that he 'venges', not least because that highlights the extent to which our own language of violent reciprocity has, since the fourteenth century—when 'revenge' entered English as a verb (it is not recorded as a noun until 1547)—come to take for granted, and to inscribe in miniature through the Latin prefix 're-',[32] what Hieronimo's playlet and Hoffman's crowning display more largely: a mimetic againness (re-venge, re-tribution, even re-cognition). On the other hand, while *dikē*'s lack of coincidence with, say, 'right' is a problem for translators, it is problematic in another way from—and not necessarily *more* problematic than—the difficulties which face native speakers when they attempt to cope with the instabilities which afflict such words as 'justice'. Both sorts of uncertainty keep revenge tragedy open to argument. When work is produced in this genre it is written around complex keywords, and even in translation (perhaps especially in translation) their semantic intricacy provides fuel for debate. From this comes much of the power of *The Oresteia*, *Hamlet*, and *El Pintor de su deshonra* to reach beyond the ages which formed them.

While retributive violence can be inflicted under many names, the principle itself has proved remarkably stable and persistent. Some would trace this to our genetic legacy, arguing on sociobiological grounds that the 'reciprocal altruism' which helps the survival of particular groups carries with it the sanction 'revenge injuries'.[33] Others invoke the game theorists who show that 'TIT FOR TAT, the strategy which cooperates on the first move and then does whatever the other player did on the previous move' is the most

---

[32] 'Back, again, anew', passing (as the *Oxford English Dictionary* notes) 'into cases where the action itself is done a second time'.

[33] e.g. Peter Singer, *The Expanding Circle: Ethics and Sociobiology* (Oxford, 1981), 16–22, 37–53.

'successful' sort of 'decision rule' when strategies are put into conflict and left to establish themselves.[34] For whatever reason, or array of factors, *lex talionis* has been foundational in Western thought and social practice. Though the phrase itself is Latin (meaning 'law of repayment in kind'), the doctrine is immemorial.[35] Plato derives the teaching 'from ancient priests'.[36] It was almost universally held in classical Athens that the evildoer should suffer evil. Reflecting these assumptions, Aristotle says that 'To take vengeance on one's enemies is nobler than to come to terms with them; for to retaliate is just (*dikaion*), and that which is just is noble'.[37] The obvious question—does the evil which repays an evil become a good, and, if so, does that mean that it can no longer repay?—was asked, but, perhaps inevitably, left unresolved. Such difficulties did not prevent the notion of doing harm to enemies becoming a bridge between the vengeance of individuals and the operations of law. 'Not only are enmity and revenge accepted as natural motives for a lawsuit' writes Mary Whitlock Blundell, in her study of Sophocles and Greek ethics, 'but language of revenge came to be used for legal punishment, while litigation is often treated as legalised revenge.'[38]

We are also the beneficiaries of Judaeo-Christian tradition. *Lex talionis* is notoriously part of that heritage. The injunction, 'life for life, Eye for eye, tooth for tooth, hand for hand, foot for foot, Burning for burning, wound for wound, stripe for stripe' (Exodus 21: 23–5) was designed to set *limits* to violence.[39] But Hitler was not the first to view it as positively inciting vindictiveness,[40] and Scripture can be found declaring that 'The revenger of blood himself shall slay the murderer: when he meeteth him, he shall slay him' (Numbers 35: 19). When Jesus urged his followers to 'turn the other cheek', tempering the injunctions of Exodus with an appeal 'That ye resist not evil',[41] he was pointing towards an ideal which, even in

[34] Robert Axelrod, *The Evolution of Cooperation* (New York, 1984), 20, cited by e.g. Lawrence C. Becker, *Reciprocity* (London, 1986), 347–9.
[35] See Albrecht Dihle, *Die goldene Regel* (Göttingen, 1962), 13–40.
[36] *Laws*, 872c, ed. and tr. R. G. Bury, 2 vols. (London, 1926).
[37] *Rhetoric*, 1367a, in *The 'Art' of Rhetoric*, ed. and tr. John Henry Freese (London, 1926).
[38] *Helping Friends and Harming Enemies: A Study in Sophocles and Greek Ethics* (Cambridge, 1989), 55.
[39] For contexts see Isidore Singer (gen. ed.), *The Jewish Encyclopedia*, 12 vols. (New York, 1901–6), under 'Retaliation, or Lex Talionis', and Anthony Phillips, *God B.C.* (Oxford, 1977), 11 n.   [40] See below, p. 304.
[41] See Matthew 5: 38–9, Luke 6: 29.

the New Testament, is heavily qualified. As I shall show in Chapters 5–10, arguments in favour of retributive justice were for long supported by the evidence, in Deuteronomy 32: 35 and Romans 12: 19 ('Vengeance is mine; I will repay'), that God's own mode of punishment is vengeful. Theories of full retribution and the practice of private revenge went together in Christian Europe, at odds but hand in hand, until the eighteenth century. Influentially modified by Kant, the retributive tradition continues in secularized forms. Thinkers as different as Agnes Heller (pupil of Lukács) and the libertarian Robert Nozick have recently offered their modifications—Heller in evidently Kantian vein, Nozick interpreting retribution as message-bearing and as capable of connecting the criminal with 'correct values' in a social grammar.[42] Over the last two or three decades, indeed, there has been a retributivist revival. Arguments based on deterrence and prevention have lost a great deal of ground in criminology and legal studies as well as in moral philosophy;[43] and, at a popular level, as newspapers, opinion-polls, and party conferences show, 'The doctrine of retribution—the infliction of pain to ease pain—is shambling back.'[44] There is now a sharper division than there has been for generations between those with broadly utilitarian views about punishment and those drawn to full retribution, and more dividedness of mind for those who remain unsure. That is another reason for thinking a study of revenge tragedy timely.

For revenge and retributive justice are hard to disentangle. Once an action is referred to the legal realm, responsibility for exacting an eye for an eye shifts from the victim or his agent to a judge, but A still loses an eye to a power that acts on behalf of a group—however socially extended—which feels responsibility for what has happened to B. Punishments may be reduced from the strict severity of *lex talionis*, with a range of scaled-down penalties inflicted for the loss of lives, eyes, or teeth, yet, for as long as sanctions remain proportionate, the retributive structure remains. But then,

---

[42] Agnes Heller, *Beyond Justice* (Oxford, 1987), esp. 156–79, Robert Nozick, *Philosophical Explanations* (Oxford, 1981), s. 4. iii. On retributive punishment and the widely admired Kantianism of John Rawls, *A Theory of Justice* (Oxford, 1972), see Michael J. Sandel's invigorating *Liberalism and the Limits of Justice* (Cambridge, 1982), esp. 82–95.

[43] For a survey see e.g. John Braithwaite and Philip Pettit, *Not Just Deserts: A Republican Theory of Criminal Justice* (Oxford, 1990), 2–5.

[44] Neal Ascherson, 'When Punishment Becomes Revenge We're on the Road to Barbarism', *The Independent on Sunday*, 30 Jan. 1994.

to reject retribution entirely, and rely on deterrence and prevention, is to uncouple justice from the principle that punishment should follow an offence and to head towards the conclusion that it would reduce the sum of misery to impose penalties on those *likely* to offend. It would plainly reduce crime if all men aged between 16 and 21, living in inner cities, were detained at Her Majesty's pleasure. Few would think it right. Philosophers often try to manage the tensions created by these problems by seeking a 'middle way. . . between a purely forward-looking scheme of social hygiene and theories which treat retribution as a general justifying aim'; but, as H. L. A. Hart has ruefully observed, these questers rarely find a way through 'the serpent-windings of Utilitarianism'.[45]

In what is, by general consent, the most interesting recent attempt to marry utilitarian and retributive theories, Joel Feinberg manages to avoid the more obvious pitfalls of the 'middle way' by contending that, since punishments can be distinguished from mere penalties by their '*symbolic significance*', morally coherent punishments are those which graft demonstrations of punitive aptness into roughly proportionate penalties.[46] 'The pain-fitting-wickedness version of the retributive theory does erect its edifice of moral super-stition on a foundation in moral common sense,' he writes, 'for justice *does* require that in some (other) sense "the punishment fit the crime."' What justice demands is that the *condemnatory aspect* of the punishment suit the crime' (p. 118). In practice, Feinberg wants to make the criminal an actor in a revenge play. '*Symbolic*' punishments would be imposed to express collective disapproval of a crime. Actual suffering would be minimal. Regretting the wastefulness (by utilitarian standards) of 'penal servitude', Feinberg imagines replacing it with 'an elaborate public ritual, exploiting the most trustworthy devices of religion and mystery, music and drama, to express in the most solemn way the community's condemnation of a criminal for his dastardly deed' (pp. 115–16). This might be a description of Greek tragedy, or—if it were not for Marston's vivacity—of *Antonio's Revenge*, performed (as it first was) by the choristers of St Paul's in their theatre in the cathedral precincts.

Feinberg's arguments are suggestive for some of the same reasons

[45] H. L. A. Hart, *Punishment and Responsibility: Essays on the Philosophy of Law*, rev. edn. (Oxford, 1970), 232–3.
[46] Joel Feinberg, 'The Expressive Function of Punishment', in his *Doing and Deserving: Essays in the Theory of Responsibility* (Princeton, 1970), 95–118, p. 98.

as currently make revenge tragedy interesting. A genre which foregrounds displays of imitative violence can expect to reward attention at a time when retributivism is (as it were) expressively persuasive yet vulnerable enough from other philosophical angles to be worth contesting. An explanation along these lines for the success of the genre in such thoughtfully violent films as Clint Eastwood's *Unforgiven* would supplement John Carey's bloodthirsty, but ponderable, diagnosis: 'we need to feel the sweetness of revenge so constantly that life cannot satisfy our requirements. We have to keep inventing villains, and inventing stories in which vengeance catches up with them, because otherwise we should be starved of a vital part of our moral diet.'[47] It would also leave room for the reflection that recent revivals of Jacobean tragedy in England, like the proliferation of vigilante movies in America, owe something to a feeling that the modern state is taking too much of the initiative in punishing criminals away from individuals, a process which encourages the dramatisation, and sometimes the glamourisation, of those who exact full retribution independently.

Screen vigilantes usually have retributive motives of their own (a wife murdered, a daughter gang-raped)[48] for going about the streets and shooting criminals as a public service. But they also routinely complain that, these days, justice is not law, that there are, in the title-words of one thought-provoking treatise, *Conflicts of Law and Morality*[49] which let criminals off the hook. Understood more largely, conflicts of this sort explain why revenge tragedy so often carries events into the court-room. A transposition from action to argument allows the genre to explore the differences between what social institutions offer and what full retribution urges. It is part of Orestes' tragedy to be judged. That is why he explains himself to the Argives over the *ekkuklēma*, at the end of *The Libation Bearers*, and why he is caught up in the dispute between the Erinyes and Apollo which concludes the *Eumenides*. These scenes of argument, of persuasion, are not codas loosely tacked on but the continuation of the action by other means. Hence their frequent modulation from verbal to gestural expression. This happens most spectacularly in medieval epic and romance, where, as I shall show in Chapter 6,

---

[47] 'Revenge', *The Independent* magazine, 20 Mar. 1993, 20–1, p. 21.
[48] See e.g. the Charles Bronson character in *Death Wish* and *Death Wish II*, discussed by Susan Jacoby, *Wild Justice: The Evolution of Revenge* (London, 1985), 174–5.
[49] By Kent Greenawalt (New York, 1987).

scenes of judgment can turn as much on agonistic combat as on witnessing and deliberation; but stage drama can also explore the relations between legal rhetoric and action. Viewed from this perspective, indeed, Hieronimo's playlet makes a deposition. A Knight Marshal, and so a magistrate, by office, Hieronimo presents the King and his court with a literal version of the vivid picture of events (or *evidentia*) which such rhetoricians as Quintilian urged the lawyers of antiquity to summon up before the eyes of judges. His taking retribution is part of the case which he brings.

Once again, Aristotle helps. In the *Poetics* he discusses three kinds of *mimēsis*: of action, of character, and of intellect. The first two sections of this chapter have touched on *praxis* and *ēthos*. By imitation of intellect or *dianoia* is meant representations of rhetorical activity. This indispensable element of tragedy is often overlooked in accounts of the *Poetics*, because Aristotle does not discuss it at length, noting (at 1456a) that it is covered by his *Rhetoric*. Persuasion, *peithō*, is an iceberg phenomenon in the *Poetics*, and one which those who read Aristotle and Greek tragedy in the shadow of Hegel neglect, either by suggesting that events precipitated by rhetoric somehow just happen, or (in more structuralist vein) by representing 'language' as a social force quite as permeating as the Hegelian 'ethical substance'. Both approaches diminish the significance of the individual speech acts, the relentlessly angled and interested attempts at persuasion, which are the stuff of ancient drama. When John Jones, for example, discusses the finale of *The Oresteia*, he is alert to the agonistic symmetry which—reflecting the paired and doubled exchanges between prosecution and defence in actual homicide trials—sets the Erinyes against Orestes and his advocates. But for Jones, as for many others, opposed positions in tragedy enshrine and give voice to natural or cultural forces rather than being shaped by *mimēsis* of intellect. As a result, the culmination of the scene, if not the entire trilogy, prompted by Athene's turn to the goddess *Peithō* (885ff.)—that great sequence of stichomythia in which the Furies become 'kindly ones'—goes without analysis, and is imaged as an interim to be slept through: 'A transformation of curse into blessing crowns the *Oresteia*,' Jones declares, 'natural and prodigious, like a snowfall in the night to the morrow's wakers.'[50] One wonders why Athene bothers to thank 'Persuasion' for this metamorphosis (970–2).

[50] *On Aristotle and Greek Tragedy*, 136.

At the moment there is controversy in America about the televising of court cases (a practice just started in Britain). Transmitting pictures of grief-deranged widows, sharp-tongued advocates, and defendants acting up to the judge, the democratic eye of television makes soap-opera out of people as real as people can be under the pressure of the law. Greek legal process had for centuries before *The Oresteia* more closely resembled TV drama than did, for instance, the assize courts known to Kyd (who was by training a legal scrivener). A famous passage of the *Iliad* runs: 'The men had gathered in the market-place . . . two men quarrelling over the blood money (*poinēs*) for a man who had been killed . . . The people were taking sides, and shouting their support for either man . . . And the elders sat on the polished stone seats in the sacred circle.'[51] In this dramatic setting, a branch of B insists on exacting retribution from A, while both appeal to an audience more or less excitably involved. The use of mass juries during the fifth century institutionalized this kind of scene: speeches in court resembled those of actors on stage; theatre audiences were full of potential, or active, jurors. Homicide cases were especially dramatic, and not just because of the persistence (from the old Draconian code) of the death penalty for those found guilty. To reduce the risk of moral contagion from a blood-polluted killer, actions for murder were presented (as in theatres) in the open air. Written charges and evidence were used in ordinary cases, but witnesses to homicide seem to have offered their views orally. Theatrically immediate in speech, murder trials also included a quasi-dramatic spread of participants. Women, children, and slaves (not usually admitted as witnesses) seem to have been heard in murder trials. Moreover, the session in which judgment was passed was the fourth in a sequence of hearings. Three preliminary *prodikasiai* were held, a month apart, with speeches for the prosecution and defence, so that the action could be rehearsed (the verb seems right) and the persuasive force of arguments tested.[52]

Sartre hits the nail on the head, though rather bluntly:

---

[51] Tr. Martin Hammond (Harmondsworth, 1987), based on *Homeri Ilias*, ed. Thomas W. Allen, 3 vols. (Oxford, 1931), XVIII. 497–504.

[52] For an account of the practices interpreted here see e.g. Douglas M. MacDowell, *The Law in Classical Athens* (London, 1978), ch. 7, and Sally Humphreys, 'Social Relations on Stage: Witnesses in Classical Athens', *History and Anthropology*, 1 (1985), 313–69, S. C. Todd, *The Shape of Athenian Law* (Oxford, 1993).

The law *is* theater. For at the roots of theater there is not merely a religious ceremony, there is also eloquence. Consider the characters of Sophocles, of Euripides, even of Aeschylus—they are all lawyers. . . . They come forward with a cause to defend. Others take the opposite side and plead against them. At the end, there is a catastrophe in which everyone is judged, and matters return to normal. The stage is the courtroom in which the case is tried.[53]

Tragedy, especially revenge tragedy, does spring from these 'roots'. The 'eloquence' of its characters is part of the action which it imitates, the way it tells its story. Quintilian was being a Roman Sartre when he compared the law court with the stage and argued that both legal speech-making and tragedy depend on *prosopopoeia*, on a verbally active performance in which the participants assume the identities of those whom they represent.[54] But Aristotle lies behind both writers. As Kathy Eden notes, he helps us see that

The tragic poet and the forensic orator . . . both face the task of transform-ing . . . past action—the outline of a plot or the facts of a case—from a random and inexplicable series of isolated events into a logical sequence of cause and effect. Insofar as the spectators at a theatrical performance or the jury at a legal trial witness, as if with their own eyes, an action that has been skillfully represented according to these requirements, they will—in Aristotle's view—learn from that representation not only *what* happened but *why*. And they will be moved in both cases to fear and to pity and to reach the kinds of judgements that accompany those responses.[55]

There was another strain of thinking. Plato mistrusted the affinity between law courts and the theatre, and it was the role of persua-sion which most troubled him. His notorious hostility to tragedy is inseparable from his attack on rhetoric. In the dialogue named after him, the sophist Gorgias is prompted by Socrates to admit that 'rhetoric . . . is a producer of persuasion for belief, not for instruc-tion in the matter of right and wrong'.[56] Defenders of the new *technē* held that it facilitated justice; the Platonic anxiety was that, with the help of forensic tricks, a prosecutor left defendants subject to the excitable reactions of an audience rather than to the justice of their

[53] 'Interview with Kenneth Tynan' (1961), repr. in *Sartre on Theater*, ed. Michel Contat and Michel Rybalka, tr. Frank Jellinek (London, 1976), 121–34, pp. 126–7.
[54] *Institutio Oratoria*, 6. 1. 25–6.
[55] *Poetic and Legal Fiction in the Aristotelian Tradition* (Princeton, 1986), 5.
[56] '. . . peri to dikaion te kai adikon' (455a), in '*Lysias*', '*Symposium*', '*Gorgias*', ed. and tr. W. R. M. Lamb (London, 1925).

case. What matters here about this famous quarrel is the continued vitality of both points of view. Revenge tragedies last beyond the epoch of their production because retributive attitudes are ingrained and because such works can renewably show how actions are modified when they enter the realm of law. But they are also machines for producing ethical deadlock: moments of trial within and beyond character in which rhetoric is, in the liveliest sense, an agent of action. They can thus explore the intractable question of whether rhetoric disentangles problems or is, in the worst sort of way, a moral solvent. For all the violence of its action, a revenge drama like *The Spanish Tragedy* has a dialectically fraught verbalness: Hieronimo moves between crises of judgement which generate passionate but highly formal utterances. There is no inconsistency in thinking of revenge tragedy as being, to a unique degree, founded in the energies of action and in associating it with some of the most copious, patterned writing of the classical and Renaissance periods. The antagonism of A and B generates not only a structured *muthos* and anguished *ēthos*: it facilitates the production of those varieties of stichomythic speech, of sophistical dialectic and inwardly divided monologue which remain staple in European tragedy through and beyond the lifetimes of Shakespeare, Calderón, and Byron.

Part II

EXCHANGES WITH ANTIQUITY

2. Aeschylus and Dracula

THE actions of life no more end in death than they begin at birth. Hair grows, nails lengthen; before and after they switch off the life-support, parts of me can be transplanted. Medicine increasingly blurs that moment of unlife which, until recently, was equated in most Western countries with the escape of the soul; in doing so, it is recovering a gradualist notion of death familiar from traditional societies. Ever since Robert Hertz published his formidable essay on collective representations of death,[1] anthropologists have been interested in the shadowy phase which falls between inhumation and 'secondary disposal'. Across a range of cultures, from Malaysia to rural Greece, it is held that, during the period of buried decay, before the bones are scattered or placed in an ossuary, an individual, caught in a transitional state, remains open to social intercourse. Anyone who has enjoyed or endured the experience of feeling a recently dead person to be as alive as a friend just out of the room will sense the psychological force of such beliefs. More difficult for us to grasp is how natural the dimming of life through death appears in societies which cannot abolish the body in the blaze of a crematorium. The gravedigger tells Hamlet that a corpse lasts eight years in the earth—nine, if it is a tanner's (v. i.163–8). What he does not need to mention, as he throws skulls up from under, is the way the dead return. Chemical changes shift corpses underground and thrust hands above the sod. Scavengers reveal bodies, landslips display them. Most cadavers plump and flush ruddily after burial; gore trickles from the mouth. Connoisseurs of revenge tragedy will be glad to learn that killing a hale person produces a corpse particularly slow to decay. Take a hawthorn stake in one hand and a mallet in the other. Is it any wonder that suicides and murder victims can seem not so much unliving as 'undead'?

None of this would matter if the buried were incapable of hatred. Visit a graveyard after dark and you quickly feel their malice. This atavistic dread can be rationalized as a fear of death linked with

[1] 'Contribution à une étude sur la représentation collective de la mort', *Année socio-logique*, 10 (1907), 48–137.

those who most embody it, those most likely to spread its contagion—a chain of association the more binding for its utter circu-
larity. When the dead are those we love, fear is compounded by
guilt at not accompanying them into the grave. The mourning
which adapts us to their loss placates them for losing us. Pallid
and in black, mourners try to resemble corpses. As the dead dissolve
in the earth, this apotropaic disguise is shed because resentment
from the buried recedes. The pathology of mourning is full of
examples of those who starve, immure, and wound themselves
out of anguished empathy with the dead. Some cultures require
such behaviour, judging it a duty of relatives to keep the departed at
bay. Richard Huntington and Peter Metcalf describe the rites of the
Berawan in Borneo, where a widow will be 'cooped up for as many
as eleven days in a tiny cell made of mats, next to the corpse'. No
wonder Old Hamlet felt neglected. 'She may not bathe, and must
. . . eat only the poorest of foods, which she "shares" with the
deceased. . . . She suffers', they note, 'because of the *vengeful soul*
of the deceased. Its envy of the living, caused by its own miserable
state, is softened by the spectacle of the hardship visited on those it
formerly loved.'[2]

At the beginnings of European theatre, in fifth-century Greece,
'sharing' took the more palatable form of feasts at the place of
burial. Relatives at least symbolically joined the dead in consuming
a ritual meal, burned upon the grave. As the ceremonies at the start
of *The Libation Bearers* suggest, the site of burial or cremation was
highly charged. The buried were thought to sense the approach of
friend and foe.[3] From about the eighth century, heroes like Agamemnon became the subject of cults centred on their graves.[4]
During the age of Aeschylus and Sophocles, the dead and the
chthonic powers were stirred into malevolent action by leaden
tablets, inscribed with names, grudges, and curses, deposited underground with the dead. Those who had died violently were favoured
recipients of these *katadesmoi*. Such victims were thought likely to act
punitively for others because hostile towards a world which har-
boured those who had killed them. The murdered have a special

[2] *Celebrations of Death: The Anthropology of Mortuary Ritual*, 2nd edn. (Cambridge, 1991), 93.
[3] Robert Garland, *The Greek Way of Death* (London, 1985), 4.
[4] Walter Burkert, *Greek Religion: Archaic and Classical*, tr. John Raffan (Oxford, 1985), 203.

pathos and, in many cultures, by the same token, form a uniquely dangerous class of spirits. According to an 'ancient tale' recorded with respect by Plato in the *Laws*, a murdered man 'is wroth with his slayer when newly slain, and being . . . disquieted himself . . . with all his might disquiets his slayer' (865d–e). Revenge could give ethical point to a malevolence which was plausibly but amorally imputed to those innocently done to death. Meanwhile Athenians appeased the departed by making animal sacrifice, offering honey-cake and, most often, pouring draughts of wine into the grave.

Many have detected in these practices the remains of ancient bloodthirsty rites. That the pyre of Patroclus consumes twelve Trojans in the *Iliad* (XXIII. 166–76), and that the tomb of Achilles drinks wine and the gore of Polyxena in Euripides' *Hecuba* (518 ff.), need not mean that offerings at fifth-century graves had the same baleful aura. But there is some evidence that ritual slaughter survived into classical times,[5] and the cravings of the lost were known to be intense. Homer's Odysseus, instructed by Circe, digs a pit and cuts the throats of a ram and black ewe over it, and a host of *psuchai*—brides, unmarried youths . . . and a great throng of warriors killed in battle'—throng towards the gore.[6] Without blood, these shades drift listlessly through Erebus. Drinking it, they gain substance, and are encouraged to speak. Relations between *psuchai* and chthonic forces in the fifth century are controversial. But when Aeschylus' Erinyes, acting for Clytemnestra, say that her 'blood spilled on the ground . . . soaked and drained into the ground' should be repaid by Orestes, they sound (even more than Homer's spirits) like visitors from Transylvania:

> You must give back for her blood from the living man
> red blood of your body to suck, and from your own
> I could feed, with bitter-swallowed drench,
> turn your strength limp while yet you live and drag you down
> where you must pay for the pain of the murdered mother . . . [7]

Not for the first time in *The Oresteia*, the mortal claims of *dikē* and *poinē*—'blood stroke for the stroke of blood . . . paid', as the Chorus of libation bearers puts it[8]—are violently linked to images of blood

---

[5] Garland, *Greek Way of Death*, 35; cf. Walter Burkert, *Homo Necans: The Anthropology of Ancient Greek Sacrificial Ritual and Myth*, tr. Peter Bing (Berkeley, 1983), esp. chs. 1–2.

[6] *The Odyssey*, tr. E. V. Rieu, rev. D. C. H. Rieu (Harmondsworth, 1991), XI. 34–50.

[7] *Eumenides*, 264–8.   [8] *Libation Bearers*, 312–13.

cast upon the earth. But here the recollection, ultimately, of Iphigenia's sacrifice by Agamemnon[9] merges with the idea of blood appeasing the agents of the departed through vampirism. In ways which seem suggestive for tragedy at large, the envy and hostility of the dead world towards the living finds scope in revenge drama, where blood calling for blood is more than a metaphor of retribution.

At this point, large gestures could be made about sacrifice and tragedy. Because the major dramatic festival of Athens was called the 'Great Dionysia', nineteenth-century scholars looked for the origins of tragedy in rites of blood and (its ritual substitute) wine associated with the tearing and crushing of Dionysus. *The Bacchae* was revalued, and the vengeance of Dionysus on Pentheus—subjecting him to that *sparagmos* or scattering dismemberment which the god himself mythically endures—was said to reveal deep sources of energy in the genre. Images of sacrifice are so abundant in Greek tragedy[10] that the persistence of theories of origin which involve ritual killing and the expulsion of scapegoats (*pharmakoi, katharsia*) is understandable. More interestingly, in this context, these theories are so compatible with revenge action that their survival is a sign of how far vengeance permeates Greek drama. Revenge victims are often killed with an elaboration and display of piety which revive the sacrificial verb *sphazein*. Sacrifice impinges the more because the pollution attached to a murderer, *agos*, was believed (perhaps rightly) to stem from *hag-*, root of *hagnos, hagios* 'sacred'.[11] Murder of a malefactor purges the tragic world, and inwardly, it may be, the audience's realm of feeling. As the *katharsion* is cast away, pity and fear are roused, and what Aristotle calls *katharsis* occurs. It is no accident that the Aegisthus of Euripides' *Electra* should be killed while sacrificing a bull—a compounding of death which the messenger makes us visualize as a lavish offering to Zeus. In the same way, Orestes' escape from being a human sacrifice in *Iphigenia at Tauris* shows Euripides resolving revenge action by transcending a principle of sacrifice which had fostered the chain of killings from Agamemnon's rites at Aulis through Orestes' murder of his mother.

Of all the scholars drawn to sacrificial interpretation, Pater strikes

[9] *Agamemnon*, 231–47.
[10] See e.g. J. -P Guépin, *The Tragic Paradox: Myth and Ritual in Greek Tragedy* (Amsterdam, 1968), ch. 1.   [11] For contexts see Burkert, *Greek Religion*, 269–71.

the most suggestive note when, in his 'Study of Dionysus', he imagines the 'rural Dionysia'. 'Then the goat was killed, and its blood poured out at the root of the vines', he writes—recalling that 'tragedy' means 'goat song'—'and Dionysus literally drank the blood of goats; and, being Greeks, with quick and mobile sympathies . . . some among them, remembering those departed since last year, add yet a little more, and a little wine and water for the dead also; brooding how the sense of these things might pass below the roots, to spirits hungry and thirsty, perhaps, in their shadowy homes.'[12] At the source of tragedy, in this view, is an act of solidarity reaching the dead through repayment of the god's wine in blood. And there clearly *is* a sense in which tragedy gives blood to the ghosts. Where the plots of Greek Old comedy are fantastic, shot through with contemporary references but not claiming to represent the world, those of tragedy give the dead substance by recovering an heroic past. In some plays—such as *The Persians*, where the ghost of Darius appears—*eidōla* are conjured up on stage. More largely, as Jacqueline de Romilly notes, the verb used of raising spirits—including Darius—*psuchagōgein*, is employed by Aristotle, Plato, and Isocrates to describe the way poetry, the art of rhetoric, and, above all, tragedy, beguiles.[13] Whether or not ritual origins can be traced back to bloody repayment cast on the ground, vengeance again claims centrality. For revenge plays have dead pasts which impinge so urgently on the present that figments of what has been return as *eidōla*. Yet, if this is so, why, in the magnificent first scene of *The Libation Bearers*, should the dead Agamemnon not be seen to respond to Electra's and Orestes' grief-stricken summons, their *goos*? Libations, and the young man's lock of hair on the grave, stir no clear response. What tends to be forgotten is that the king has been mutilated before burial. Aegisthus and Clytemnestra must have heard the same 'ancient tale' as Plato, and taken steps to disable the corpse.[14] Lopped of his extremities in an archaic rite called *maschalismos*, Agamemnon has been subjected to the fifth-century equivalent of being staked and wreathed with garlic.

The vampire cult in modern literature seems to stem from Enlightenment Europe's discovery of superstitions on its eastern

---

[12] 'A Study of Dionysus: The Spiritual Form of Fire and Dew' (1876), repr. in *Greek Studies: A Series of Essays* (1895; London, 1928), 1–41, pp. 12–13.

[13] *Magic and Rhetoric in Ancient Greece* (Cambridge, Mass., 1975), 15.

[14] See *Libation Bearers*, 439–43.

and Mediterranean margins which reach back many centuries.[15] Polidori's story, *The Vampyre* (1819), which did so much to launch Draculan fiction, is partly set, indeed, in Greece: that is where Aubrey learns about the living dead, and where the blood-sucking Lord Ruthven strikes. Putative links between Aeschylus and early nineteenth-century Hellas are less to the point, however, than the way Dracula highlights in revenge tragedy horrors of a kind which rationalistic analysis plays down. For a start, vampires epitomize the vengefulness of the 'undead': 'I saw the Count lying within the box upon the earth', writes one of Bram Stoker's narrators, 'and the red eyes glared with the horrible vindictive look which I knew too well.'[16] The idea is so commonplace that Peter Tremayne, acclaimed author of *Zombie!*, risked tautology when he called his 1978 shocker *The Revenge of Dracula*. Relatedly, vampire fictions recover a charged sense of grave sites, carnally accessible to life, which the neat lines of tombstones in modern cemeteries attempt to repress. Dracula's boxes of earth go with him because, like the Erinyes, he needs a chthonic base. As Christianity loses faith in devil-worship and witches, the Satanism of vampire fiction satisfies our need to feel that life is hedged about by forces that demand sacrificial propitiation. Vampires latch on to the blood which retributivism demands from the law. In what other myth, with such extremity, does the bitten become a biter, and lost blood cry out for blood? Above all, vampires are not just ominous to those who hurt them in life: favoured victims are friends and relatives, those who want the 'undead' back and let them in when they scratch at the shutters. If too much attention is given to antagonism in revenge drama—A and B on the open stage—the destructive implications of loyalty will be missed. Old Hamlet is, in the end, his son's as well as Claudius' nemesis; it is the avengers, as well as their victims, who display a drained pallor, and behave like 'the living dead', in, for instance, Euripides' *Orestes* (200–7).

Even more than classical tragedy, drama of the Renaissance makes the 'undead' come to life. In Spain, both Jeronimo Bermúdez and Luis Vélez de Guevara dramatized—like the author of *The Second Maiden's Tragedy*—the story of Inés de Castro, murdered by order of King Alfonso IV, then disinterred and crowned, while her

[15] See e.g. Paul Barber, *Vampires, Burial, and Death: Folklore and Reality* (New Haven, 1988), chs. 1–4.   [16] *Dracula*, ed. A. N. Wilson (Oxford, 1983), 376.

assassins were executed, when Alfonso's son inherited the throne. Her humblest English equivalent—Gloriana in *The Revenger's Tragedy*—is so galvanized by 'Revenge' (which is what 'Vindice' means) that, though no more than a skeleton, she can kiss the wicked Duke to death. On the scaffold of execution, where his enemy is about to die, the villainous D'Amville of *The Atheist's Tragedy* quaffs a blood-red goblet of wine. In the gory tale of Albovine, dramatized by Davenant (but there are Spanish analogues), the still more vampirish practice of drinking wine from a conquered man's skull is the mainspring of revenge. Webster is an addict of blood myths and werewolves, Marston even more lurid. Brooding on his father's murder among the 'Graves, vaults, and tombs' of St Mark's Church, the protagonist of his *Antonio's Revenge* promises to 'suck red vengeance | Out of Piero's wounds'.[7] When Piero's son unwisely arrives, Antonio cries 'Thy father's blood that flows within thy veins . . . is that revenge must suck', and stabs the plaintive child (III. iii. 35–6). Ranting in Bram Stokerish vein about 'the wolf' and 'the full-cheeked moon', he sprinkles gore on his father's tomb, in a parody of Mosaic rites, and '*From under the stage a groan*' is heard (43–50). 'Ghost of my poisoned sire,' Antonio cries:

> suck this fume
> To sweet revenge, perfume thy circling air
> With smoke of blood. I sprinkle round his gore
> And dew thy hearse with these fresh-reeking drops.
> Lo, thus I heave my blood-dyed hands to heaven,
> Even like insatiate hell, still crying; 'More!
> My heart hath thirsting dropsies after gore.'
> Sound peace and rest to church, night-ghosts and graves;
> Blood cries for blood, and murder murder craves. (63–71)

Because Marston's unnerving kitsch predates the Enlightenment 'discovery' of vampires, it draws on a volatile mixture of classical and popular sources. Later authors of revenge tragedy could take for granted a more stable set of stereotypes and on that basis use vampirism to support some spine-tingling effects. Zola, for example, writes *Thérèse Raquin* with the economy of a thriller. In this sensational narrative, where the heroine and Laurent her lover murder her feeble husband, but are then destroyed by guilt, blood chiefly

[7] John Marston, *Antonio's Revenge*, ed. W. Reavley Gair (Manchester, 1978), III. i. 9, III. ii. 78–9.

figures as a sign of biological destiny. 'I have chosen people', writes
Zola, 'completely dominated by their nerves and blood, without
free will.'[8] Thérèse, born of an African mother, is said to have
passion in her blood. Camille, her cousin and companion of childhood—the husband wished upon her by Mme Raquin—shows the
pale and listless petulance of many a spoiled child of civilization in
fiction. Significantly, however, Laurent experiences the guilt of
killing Camille as the inflamed, continual itching of a scar upon
his neck, inflicted by a bite from his victim as Camille was hurled
into the Seine. Vampirish dreams overwhelm him—'The corpse
held out its arms . . . uttering a hideous cackle and poking out a bit
of black tongue between its white teeth' (p. 131)—and, as these
evidences accumulate, dead metaphors become 'undead'. Recalling
that Thérèse, 'taking her revenge' in adultery, cried, 'They have so
smothered me in their middle-class refinement that I don't know
how there can be any blood left in my veins. . . . I was just as dead-
and-alive as they were' (p. 66), the reader starts to wonder whether
the novel shocked Zola's contemporaries because, behind its scandalous sexuality, they sensed the greater scandal of his diagnosing
Draculan voracity in bourgeois prudence. The Raquin household is
a nest of vampires where a cosseting mother sucks life from her
children to secure their support in her declining years.

In what remains the most remarkable part of the novel, Zola has
the lovers marry, settles them in Mme Raquin's home, and decisively moves the old lady into the realm between life and death.
Crippled by a stroke, but fiercely alive within, the conscious corpse
of Mme Raquin preserves the memory of Camille. Thérèse and
Laurent, full of acrimony, betray each other to the widow and
prompt an unflinching determination in her to survive until they
are ruined. Plato said in the *Laws* that, when the murdered man
'with all his might disquiets his slayer', he 'takes conscience as his
ally' and uses memories to haunt the murderer (865e). As Greek
tragedy developed, the Erinyes apparently mutated from being
blood-snuffling chthonic forces, or embodiments of the curses of
the dead,[9] to projections of guilt which in *Orestes* pursue the
revenger yet are seen by no one else. Nothing in ancient drama,

---

[8] *Thérèse Raquin*, tr. Leonard Tancock (Harmondsworth, 1962), 22.
[9] See e.g. Lewis Richard Farnell, *The Cults of the Greek States*, 5 vols. (Oxford, 1896–
1909), v. 437–9.

however, and little but *Macbeth* at the Renaissance, traces in such detail that gnawing of guilty memory—'the bite', in Nietzsche's formulation, 'of conscience'[20]—which devours the will to live in Laurent and Thérèse. Equally, the statue of Mitys, which falls (in Aristotle's example of tragedy)[21] to crush his killer, has a crude explicit *praxis* compared with the stony Mme Raquin, whose only movements consist of changes within the eyes perceived or imagined by Thérèse or Laurent. It is those eyes, vindictive as Dracula's, which blaze out from her 'undead' body at the climax of the novel, to survey the final integration of vampire myth with revenge tragedy. As the despairing Thérèse and Laurent share poison and collapse in a tangle, the retributive bite of Camille and the incestuous vampirism of the Raquins fuse together in a tableau as eloquent as anything in Aeschylus or Kyd: 'Her mouth hit her husband's neck on the scar left by Camille's teeth. . . . And for nearly twelve hours, until about noon next day, Madame Raquin, stiff and silent, contemplated them at her feet, unable to feast her eyes enough, eyes that crushed them with brooding hate' (p. 256).

* * *

The rural Dionysia described by Pater became a more elaborate phenomenon when it took the form of that urban festival which Athenians called 'Anthesteria'.[22] On the first day, cartloads of new wine came in from the country and the vintage was deposited in a sanctuary devoted to Dionysus. At nightfall the vessels were opened, and libations poured to the god. After a day of merriment, revellers carried their garlands and jugs to the marshes near the city, where, in conditions of extreme secrecy, the wife of the *archōn* seems to have been mystically wedded to Dionysus as part of a fertility rite. The festival ended on 'the day of the Pots' when Athenians, like survivors after Deucalion's flood, ate a simple meal of grains boiled with honey and made sacrifices to chthonic Hermes. At the core of the festival lay that second day of revels, 'Choes', 'the day of the

---

[20] 'Der Gewissensbiss', *Götzen-Dämmerung oder Wie man mit dem Hammer philosophirt*, I. 10, in *Friedrich Nietzsche: Sämtliche Werke*, ed. Georgio Colli and Mazzino Montinari, 15 vols. (Berlin, 1988) vi. 10; tr. as *Twilight of the Idols*, in *The Portable Nietzsche*, ed. and tr. Walter Kaufmann, rev. edn. (New York, 1968), 467.   [21] See above, p. 6.

[22] Cf. e.g. Sir Arthur Pickard-Cambridge, *The Dramatic Festivals of Athens*, 2nd edn., rev. John Gould and D. M. Lewis (Oxford, 1968), 1–25, Burkert, *Greek Religion*, 238–42, and *Homo Necans*, ch. 4.

Wine Jugs', when 'delight and dole', ghosts and theatricality, pollution and competitive drinking were mixed in a wild confusion which
makes the modern reader think of *Hamlet*.[23] For on this day the souls
of the dead were said to be at large in the city. To keep destructive
spirits away, doors were painted with pitch and apotropaic buck-
thorn was chewed. Because it was a time of *miasma*, 'defilement',
temple doors were closed. Identities were in flux as mummers
paraded through the city, and heavy drinking took the form of
competitive, oddly unconvivial, bouts. Revellers would sit at separate tables, in silence, each with a measure of wine. When the word
was given by the festive king, a trumpet was sounded and the
participants downed their rouses.

   Though Athenians were not familiar with *Hamlet*, they did think
of revenge when explaining these obscure customs. Euripides
follows the usual aetiology when, in *Iphigenia at Tauris*, he has
Orestes relate that, fleeing from the Erinyes after the murder of
his mother, he arrived in Athens to find his friends avoiding him 'as
one unclean'. Then they took pity on him, sat him at a separate
table,

sent me a cup

When their love-bowl was passed, but then would turn
Away and would not look at me nor speak
To me—because I was a killer. . . .

This, Orestes says, is what the Choes commemorates, 'Everyone
drinking with his own cup in silence' (949–60). At the risk of
seeming as speculative as Pater, one could say that 'the day of the
Wine Jugs' is a time of pollution as well as revels because to be alive
is to accept a measure of guilt at countenancing the death of others.
That malevolence which radiates from the grave is again associated
sharply with revenge, and the city-invading hostility of the dead is
felt as guilt which afflicts those bitten with conscience while enjoy-
ing the crushed fruits (so like blood itself) of festivity. 'The day of the
Pots' would then follow the Choes as an image of survival; revellers
ate their meal of pottage to celebrate their not having been lost in
that calamity which has swept so many into the world of the dead.
The Anthesteria reminded participants that all men are in some
degree Orestes, and threaten others with pollution.

---

[23] I. ii. 13.

Underlying this, on the one hand, is a notion which some cultures make explicit: that every death, entailing guilt, carries blame. Among the Piaroa of Venezuela, for instance, it is held that, when people die, the member of another tribe must have directed magic against them. In ways which, by now, will not surprise, death is described as a gnawing and eating away, and revenge involves action in which pieces of the corpse are used. The right index finger, the sole of the right foot, and other parts of the dead person are taken to a shaman and combined with violent poisons. Relatives hold the package by a length of rope, while charms are recited by the shaman. Knives, axes, machetes, and the like are placed on the ground nearby. This magical practice is supposed to dispose of the lost man's enemy.[24] There is all the kin-solidarity and equipage of revenge, without risk: the dead are placated and enabled to punish, while guilt, turned into blame, is expelled from the community. And here that other aspect of the Anthesteria comes into focus: its spreading defilement through images of blood-guilt. This miasmal stuff clung and could not be removed without rites of purification. The stain was tangible, yet such writings as the *Third Tetralogy* of Antiphon also characterize it metaphysically, as the pollution of avenging spirits. 'Appease the wrath of the spirits of vengeance by putting the defendant to death', a jury is urged, 'and thereby cleanse the whole city of its defilement.'[25] Athens filled with ghosts and demons during the Anthesteria as an expression of the *miasma* which drew them. The alienness of Greek blood-guilt partly lies in this refusal to distinguish between defilement and its supernatural concomitant. Its accessibility depends not least on the idea that, though *miasma* affects killers most of all, it smirches anyone associated with death. Mourners do not just wear black to propitiate the departed; their community with the dead requires them to be marked out as, for that liminal period, not socialized.

It is hardly to be imagined that a fifth-century Athenian, on hearing that a relative had been murdered, would retreat into mourning and leave the killer to the ire of spirits. Belief in ghosts and furies encouraged the use of legal process. Kin were said to be

[24] Joanna Overing, 'Images of Cannibalism, Death and Domination in a "Non-Violent" Society', in David Riches (ed.), *The Anthropology of Violence* (Oxford, 1986), 86–102, esp. pp. 86–9.

[25] 3. 7, in *Antiphon, Andocides*, ed. and tr. K. J. Maidment, Loeb Classical Library Minor Attic Orators, 1 (London, 1941).

at risk from the displeasure of the dead if they did not prosecute
killers; speeches in court threatened juries with similar pollution
and vengeance if they slighted a murdered man's interests.[26]
Changes in law between Homeric and classical times meant that
kin-violence and *poinē* as blood-money were replaced by state-
supervised retribution. What sounds like a weakening in the economy of vengeance in fact empowered the dead, since settlement was
no longer possible between the living. It is true that the logic of
pollution did not coincide with that of the law. If you killed and
were acquitted, purification was still usual. One of Orestes' problems in Aeschylus is that, although he has been cleansed by Apollo,
some kind of legal solution is required to persuade the Furies to call
off their pursuit. That a dramatic example comes to mind is,
however, significant. In Homer, Orestes is untroubled by the
Erinyes, and Oedipus continues to govern Thebes even after the
discovery of his incest. Tragedy presents a different picture; and it is
hotly debated by classicists whether the evidence of pollution-
anxiety in the fifth century found by E. R. Dodds and others
indicates a social shift (away from 'shame culture', perhaps, to
'guilt'),[27] or is a function of the prominence in research of quotations from tragic literature.[28] Certainly *miasma* offers the dramatist,
as against the epic poet, opportunities. Like the mark of Cain it can
separate and alienate, yet also (as in *Oedipus Tyrannus*) merge a
protagonist's sufferings into those of the choric community.
Because guilt and defilement do not always coincide, pollution
can leave such characters as Orestes both victimized and at fault.
Attracting the hostility of gods and furies, and stirring revulsion in
other people, the polluted man sends out shock waves of action:
there is a peculiarly dramatic dynamic of tormented fixity and
turbulence. Above all, in revenge plots, *agos* makes the links
between A and B, on the open stage, at once more elemental and
perplexed than Aristotelian analysis concedes. Individuals bound in
violence do not stand as clear of each other in blood-space as they
do in the field of action. As Robert Parker points out, 'The same

---

[26] Antiphon, *First Tetralogy*, 1. 2–3, 3. 9, 11, *Second Tetralogy*, 3. 11–12, *Third Tetralogy*, 1. 3–4.
[27] E. R. Dodds, *The Greeks and the Irrational* (Berkeley, 1951), ch. 2, but see e.g. Margaret
Visser, 'Vengeance and Pollution: Orestes' Trail of Blood', *Journal of the History of Ideas*, 45
(1984), 193–206.
[28] Cf. Robert Parker, *Miasma: Pollution and Purification in Early Greek Religion* (Oxford,
1983), 16.

word (*prostropaios*) can be used of the polluted killer himself, of the victim's polluting blood, and of the victim himself in his anger, or his avenging spirits; *palamnaios* is applied to the killer, the demons that attack him, and the (demonic) pollution that radiates from him; words like *miastōr*, *alastōr*, and *alitērios* work in very similar ways.'[29]

Exile weakened pollution. The soil of foreign ground did not absorb a killer's blood-taint so retentively as that of home.[30] From a functionalist perspective, departure to another land avoided aggravating kin and prevented the flare-up of blood feuds. Not surprisingly, according to Plato (in that 'ancient tale' cited in the *Laws*), the dead man in his grave was soothed by the removal of the killer from his own old haunts. But radical cure was more spectacular: purification from blood required the use of blood. A piglet would have its throat slashed and be held over the killer, so that its gore spouted on to the hands which had been stained by murder. Orestes, in the *Eumenides*, explains:

> The stain of blood dulls now and fades upon my hand.
> My blot of matricide is being washed away.
> When it was fresh still, at the hearth of the god, Phoebus,
> This was [expelled through cleansing] by sacrifice
> of swine . . . (280–4)

The rationale of this remains uncertain. Some claim, rather blandly, that, because blood was used in other rites of purification, it is here simply employed for its powerful detergent effect. In his magisterial *Greek Religion*, Walter Burkert offers an explanation which might be more substantial, but sounds too psychotherapeutic to be true: 'The ritual', he writes, 'is a demonstrative and therefore harmless repetition of the shedding of blood in which the result, the visible defilement, can equally demonstratively be set aside; in this way the deed is not suppressed but overcome' (p. 81). Analysis can go further by recalling that belief in homeopathy—applying like to cure like—ran deep in Greek culture. When Aristotle, for instance, describes the effect of tragedy, the method of purification (one meaning of that complex word *katharsis*) is of this kind. Pity and fear purge pity and fear, clarifying reason in the audience. As it happens, this example is more than random: splashing blood on bloody hands cancels blood for the same reason that, in ancient

---

[29] Ibid. 108–9.   [30] Ibid. 118.

drama, blood demands blood and the action of *poinē* is cathartic. In classical Greece, Parker notes, 'The language of "wiping out blood with blood" is sometimes found not in relation to the purification ceremony, but to actual vengeance killing.'[31] A great deal of revenge theatre dramatizes a desire to shed blood on the polluted spot, to wipe the stain out of Desdemona's sheets by murdering her in the adulterous bed. Vengeance is formative of ancient tragedy not least because Aristotle's theory of *katharsis* responds to a dynamic of expurgation generally felt to matter in plays, as in ritual.

But plays are not ritual, and it would be wrong to imply that Greek drama induces bouts of *katharsis* merely by rehearsing situations in which blood expunges blood. The sources of pity and fear lie in part beyond that economy, in obscure and threatening excess. Consider the revenge-killing of Clytemnestra in Sophocles' *Electra*. 'The courses are being fulfilled', says the Chorus, as Orestes and Pylades set to work within the house:

> those under the earth are alive;
> men long dead draw from their killers
> blood [in recompense].
>
> And here they come. The red hand reeks
> with War God's sacrifice. I cannot blame them.   (1417–22)

Even here, accepting that there is no blame depends on taking 'The red hand' as an emblem of war rather than murder (no *agos* is incurred in battle), an instrument of sacrifice to Ares. It is easy to want to disinfect the deed, as the Chicago translator does when he renders 'blood in recompense' 'blood to answer blood'—a phrase which imposes a self-cancelling and purifying order only possible in an uninflected language. The Greek lines turn on 'palirruton', a verb of draining which attributes to the 'undead' Agamemnon what J. H. Kells (in his sober Cambridge edition) calls 'vampire-like activity'.[32] The symmetry of Orestes' hostility towards his murderous mother is complicated by obscure blood-slurping from another antagonist underground. The very insistence of the Chorus' 'I cannot blame them' suggests that, for some auditors, Orestes' 'red hand' coming out of the *skēnē* would have appeared as shocking as those held up by Shakespeare's conspirators after bathing them in the blood of Caesar, 'sacrificed' under Pompey's vengeful

---

[31] Ibid. 373.   [32] *Electra* (Cambridge, 1973), 220.

statue as a 'dish fit for the gods'.[33] Given the socio-religious links already established, it is a measure of such resistance that Heraclitus should have written, 'They are purified in vain with blood, those polluted with blood, as if someone who stepped in mud should try to wash himself with mud.'[34] On a larger field than the human body—though continually referring back to wounds, stains, violent signs on that miniature—Greek drama is aware that cancelling bloodshed with blood can compound it.

The clearest evidence of this lies, of course, in those references to blood spilled on the ground which run through *The Oresteia*. Iphigenia was made a blood sacrifice so that the Greek fleet could sail for Troy. When the tapestries stained purple by the murex are strewn before Agamemnon's feet, their 'crimson path' recalls this, evoking the 'Pouring . . . to the ground' of the sacrificed girl's 'saffron mantle'.[35] After the king's entry into the *skēnē*, the Chorus asks, 'But when the black and mortal blood of man | has fallen to the ground before his feet, who then | can sing spells to call it back again?'[36] Clotted with earth, fallen blood (*phonos*) hinders those who would placate the shades, like the libation bearers who lament that 'Through too much glut of blood (*haima*) drunk by our fostering ground | the vengeful gore (*phonos*) is caked and hard, will not drain through.'[37] In Aeschylus, 'both *haima* and *phonos* are the point of the Erinyes' existence. Blood soaks down to earth and calls them up. They are angered by it, avenge it, lap it, call for more.'[38] As the Chorus of libation bearers says,

> It is but law that when the red drops have been spilled
> upon the ground they cry aloud for fresh
> blood. For the death act calls out on Fury
> to bring out of those who were slain before
> new ruin on ruin accomplished. (400–4)

Similar allusions recur as far as the Erinyes' unrelenting words at Orestes' trial, 'He has spilled his mother's blood upon the ground,'[39] and they hammer home links in a chain of violence

---

[33] *Julius Caesar*, II. i. 173, III. i. 105–16.
[34] CXVII (D. 5, M. 89), in *The Art and Thought of Heraclitus: An Edition of the Fragments with Translation and Commentary*, ed. and tr. Charles H. Kahn (Cambridge, 1979).
[35] *Agamemnon*, 908–11, 239. [36] Ibid. 1019–21.
[37] *Libation Bearers*, 66–7.
[38] Ruth Padel, *In and Out of the Mind: Greek Images of the Tragic Self* (Princeton, 1992), 172.
[39] *Eumenides*, 653.

rather than double in cancelling purgation. The ground is saturated with gore, but the dead and their Furies are unsatisfied. To extend Heraclitus: blood cast upon blood on the ground creates a mire rather than *katharsis*.

So familiar yet potent an emblem did this become that, when Euripides wanted to resolve a revenge plot as one among several, in the *Ion*, he chose the same motif. What makes this example remarkable is that, in the first extant revenge tragicomedy in Western literature, bloody libation precipitates a benign solution without losing its power to threaten. When the Old Man, directed by Creusa, hands the protagonist wine poisoned with Gorgon's blood, Ion, warned by a word of ill-omen, orders that first draughts should be offered to Apollo, his patron. A flock of thirsty doves descends, and the bird that drinks the 'libation of Dionysian grapes | Mingled for murder with blood drops' (1232–3) falls dead. This is the pivotal moment of an action which culminates in Creusa discovering that Ion is her long-lost son by Apollo. The vital, condensed beauty of the play owes much to its complexly affirmative conclusion being neither superimposed on tragedy nor a product of that cathartic paradigm claimed by the Chorus of Sophocles' *Electra*. Blood and the juice of Dionysus constitute the very means of vengeance, and the futile destructiveness of the ethos is revealed through the action of casting to the ground.

*　　*　　*

These ideas of pollution and sacrifice might sound so archaic and alien as to be like nothing in post-classical tragedy. Yet recall the words of Beatrice-Joanna to her father, after De Flores has stabbed her in *The Changeling*:

> Oh come not near me, sir, I shall defile you:
> I am that of your blood was taken from you
> For your better health; look no more upon't,
> But cast it to the ground regardlessly:
> Let the common sewer take it from distinction.[40]

Jacobean drama has an accessibility which disguises its strangeness; but occasionally, as in this speech, it discloses premises as distant as

---

[40] Thomas Middleton and William Rowley, *The Changeling*, ed. N. W. Bawcutt (London, 1958), v. iii. 149–53.

anything written in ancient Greek. '*I* am that of your blood . . . look no more upon'*t* | But cast *it* to the ground': the shifting pronouns indicate an unselfconscious immersion in paternal blood that is closer to Iphigenia's relations with Agamemnon, as branches of the Atreidae, than to anything in modern literature. Significantly, when T. S. Eliot cited this speech in the essay which established Middleton's modern reputation, he wrote not 'I am *that* of your blood' but 'I that *am* of your blood'.[41] The transposition revitalized the line by translating it into the metaphors which govern our own idiom. There was nothing abstract or figurative, though, about the 'tie of blood' for Middleton and Rowley. Innocent of William Harvey and his theory of circulation—not to mention ideas of the blood-group, cutting across lines of kin—their essentially Galenic beliefs had genuine continuities with Aeschylus. Untroubled by new science, Middleton and Rowley were able to show Beatrice's polluted self waning in a flow of gore cast to the ground before her father.

This is not to deny that early audiences would have understood Eliot's version of the speech. Jacobeans did use 'blood' in a genealogical way. When Beatrice is trying to resist De Flores's sexual blackmail, she appeals to the status of her family, saying: 'Think but upon the distance that creation | Set 'twixt thy blood and mine' (III. iv. 130-1). Historically speaking, however, comprehension does not flow the other way. The atavistic, almost bestial sense of blood which De Flores displays when, seeing Tomazo, he guiltily mutters, 'I smell his brother's blood when I come near him' (IV. ii. 41), is closer to Greek tragedy—Aeschylus' Erinyes snuffling at Orestes' trail—than it is to us. The spoor of Harry, in Eliot's Oresteian *Family Reunion*, has no scent, just as, after various experiments in production, the Furies of that play had to be cut[42] leaving Harry racked only inwardly by what he had done. 'I smell his . . . blood' stirs us, but only obscurely. We talk too much of 'guilt', while Jacobean gore, though an 'it', has (as Macbeth acknowledges) a life of 'its' own:

---

[41] 'Thomas Middleton', in his *Selected Essays*, 3rd edn. (London, 1951), 161-70, p. 169; my italics. The reading presumably derives from *The Changeling* in *Thomas Middleton*, ed. Havelock Ellis, 2 vols. (London, 1887-90), i.

[42] See T. S. Eliot, 'Poetry and Drama', in his *On Poetry and Poets* (London, 1957), 72-88, p. 84.

It will have blood, they say; blood will have blood:
Stones have been known to move and trees to speak;
Auguries and understood relations have
By maggot-pies and choughs and rooks brought forth
The secret'st man of blood.   (III. iv. 121–5)

Similarly, when Lady Macbeth wrings her hands, crying 'Out, damned spot' and 'Here's the smell of the blood still' (v. i. 5, 50), a modern audience is encouraged by the presence of the Doctor to view the scene from the same psychotherapeutic angle as Burkert explaining purification with pig's blood. Like the compulsive hand-washers in Freud, Lady Macbeth becomes a neurotic expressing her symptoms in code. Her actions are transparent, however, to both the Doctor and her gentlewoman; the dreadful interest of the scene lies not in an oblique revelation of 'guilt' but in the awesome clinging of blood-stuff. 'A little water clears us of this deed', Lady Macbeth had said (II. ii. 64). Even after the visible marks have gone, the pollution left by Duncan's blood lingers—like that of Aeschylus' Clytemnestra, after the sacrifice of Apollo's swine.[43]

Yet there is no doubt that, the closer one comes to discussing defilement in moral terms, the greater appears the difference between ancient and Renaissance tragedy. In gauging that unlikeness, Book II of *The Faerie Queene* could be our guide. For the story of Guyon, Knight of Temperance, begins in a classical milieu but develops, through misplaced revenge plots, intimations of a world in which Divine grace overrules human vindication. Hardly has the Book started than Guyon is provoked, by a false appeal from Archimago, to 'reuenge' the rape of Duessa upon the Redcrosse Knight. Only the sight of the cross upon his shield, 'The sacred badge of my Redeemers death', prompts second, better thoughts in Guyon (II. i. 27). Unchastened, the knight then broaches the major adventure of his Book. He encounters the woeful Amavia, who has stabbed herself out of grief for the death of Mortdant, contrived by Acrasia. In the hope of exculpating her suicide, Amavia has arranged for her child's 'litle hands' to be 'embrewed' in her own blood, as 'pledges' that 'cleare she dide from blemish criminal' (i. 37). Overlooking her sinfulness, Guyon joins the Palmer in giving both Mortdant and his wife a Greek Tragedy burial:

[43] Cf. e.g. *Macbeth*, II. ii. 57–60, and *Libation Bearers*, 73–5.

The dead knights sword out of his sheath he drew,
  With which he cut a locke of all their heare,
  Which medling with their bloud and earth, he threw
  Into the graue, and gan deuoutly sweare;
  Such and such euill God on *Guyon* reare,
  And worse and worse young Orphane be thy paine,
  If I or thou dew vengeance doe forbeare,
Till guiltie bloud her guerdon doe obtaine:
So shedding many teares, they closd the earth againe.   (II. i. 61)

'Such and such' shows a characteristic recoil by Spenser from blasphemous mumbo-jumbo. Guyon's rite satisfies anger and a desire for unity in the face of suffering; but it overlooks the moral allegory of Mortdant's death from intemperance, and the evil of Amavia's suicide. Significantly, when Guyon turns his attention to the child, 'His guiltie hands from bloudie gore to cleene. | He washt them oft and oft, yet nought they beene | For all his washing cleaner' (II. ii. 3).

Spenser has shaped this situation in such a way that a reader could still think that blood sticks to the child's hands as a 'pledge' that Amavia's suicide was justified, or (as Guyon later rationalizes) that 'The bloudy-handed babe' is reddened and should be 'called *Ruddymane* . . . T'auenge his Parents death on them, that had it wrought' (II. iii. 2). Many scholars, neglecting the larger allegory of Book II, maintain the latter, and in effect see the red hands as a bodily, ingrained version of the robe or net preserved by Aeschylus' Orestes: a token of wrong to be retributed. That they ignore Spenser's longer perspective can be gathered from their consequent failure to recognize that Guyon's intemperate punishment of Acrasia's intemperance, in his savaging of the Bower of Bliss, is not some undisciplined reflex of authorial 'puritanism' but a sign that Guyon remains reactive, that retributive energies direct his career. One problem for the classical knight is that, while the *Nicomachean Ethics* say that the magnanimous man 'does not bear a grudge, for it is not a mark of greatness of soul to recall things against people, especially the wrongs they have done you', Aristotle still accepts proportionate reciprocation: 'for men demand that they shall be able to requite evil with evil—if they cannot, they feel they are in the position of slaves'.[44] Guyon's fumbling attempts to

---

[44] 1125a and 1133a, in *Nicomachean Ethics*, ed. and tr. H. Rackham (London, 1936).

explain his failed purification of the child—saying that God marked him as a sign of His horror of bloodshed, or impurity (II. ii. 4)—imposes a retributive logic which our Redeemer died to resolve. The knight has yet to realize that, as the poet announces at the start of canto viii, there 'is . . . care in heauen . . . th'exceeding grace | Of highest God'.[45] What he cannot cleanse from Ruddymane, because it requires 'exceeding grace', is the stain of original sin. Hence, in the Cave of Mammon, Guyon does not recognise the 'wretch' immersed in water, whose 'hands' were held 'on high extent, | And faynd to wash themselves incessantly; | Yet nothing cleaner were for such intent' (II. vii. 61). Because he is baffled, Pontius Pilate must introduce himself. That Guyon does not register the archetypal futile handwasher of Scripture means that, in the allegory of Book II, he, as much as Pilate, is excluded from the purification available to the elect in what Revelation calls the blood of the Lamb: 'For if the blood of bulls and of goats . . . sanctifieth to the purifying of the flesh', says Hebrews 9, 'How much more shall the blood of Christ . . . purge your conscience from dead works to serve the living God' (13–14).

In the secular late twentieth century, thoughts of blood pollution might seem as arcane as Spenserian views of election. Given access to biological washing-powder, would a murderer now be thrown by Alsemero's sudden question:

> What's this blood upon your band, De Flores?
> DE FLORES Blood? No, sure, 'twas wash'd since.
> ALSEMERO   Since when, man?
> (V. iii. 95–6)

The answer is surely yes, because fear of death continues to associate with flows of that stuff which science, as much as superstition, says is the juice of life. A high yield of misogynistic dread can still be activated by menstrual flux, and anxieties about blood pollution have been heightened by AIDS. If guilt and dread are triggered by stains on a murderer's hand, a splash of HIV-infected plasma stirs fear, and, in some, hatred. No great art has yet been produced to articulate the emotions surrounding AIDS. When it appears, it will have to deal with blood anxieties as they relate to

[45] II. viii. 1; cf. Hugh MacLachlan, 'The "Careless Heauens": A Study of Revenge and Atonement in *The Faerie Queene*', *Spenser Studies*, 1 (1980), 135–61, esp. pp. 151, 157.

revenge—not just because of the argument that 'AIDS is God's judgment on a society that does not live by His rules'[46] but because HIV is circulated by exchanges.

At this point a familiar figure returns, with sharp teeth and a sweeping cape. For Dracula's links with blood defilement and moral contagion make him peculiarly expressive both of AIDS paranoia and of the more intriguing—because medically unfounded—anxiety which attaches to menstruation. His role as the King of HIV is plain in films such as Coppola's *Dracula* (1992), which makes much of the scenes of transfusion in Bram Stoker's novel, and which was publicized by trailers showing pools of blood slowly infecting one another. One reason why this aspect of the movie is relatively faithful to its source is that Stoker's novel is itself energized by late-Victorian fears of a syphilis pandemic, spread by female promiscuity. Lucy Westenra, who begins the novel as a type of naïve virtue, becomes corrupted by profligate blood-sucking and ends up displaying the 'voluptuous' properties of the three 'thrilling and repulsive' female vampires who threaten Jonathan Harker in Dracula's castle (pp. 37–9). The novel's other infected woman, Mina Harker, never becomes a voluptuary. But where Lucy is 'drained' by vampirism, Mina is infected by a 'horrid poison', 'a poison in my blood, in my soul, which may destroy me' (pp. 320, 330). Carrying Dracula's contagion, she is marked by a fierce scar, resembling a syphilitic sore, on her forehead, until the source of her contagion is extirpated by a closely bonded male group (rather like a scientific research team) led by their professor, Van Helsing.

The AIDS analogy[47] can only be strengthened by the suggestion—strong in Bram Stoker, and developed in various camped-up movies—that Dracula's desires are homosexual. Although he infects the women, what he really wants are the men—especially Jonathan Harker, whom he keeps from the trio of vampettes with the cry, 'This man belongs to me!' (p. 39).[48] Viewed from that perspective, the undead are victims of the 'gay plague', their flesh

---

[46] Jerry Falwell (founder of the Moral Majority), quoted by Elaine Showalter, *Sexual Anarchy: Gender and Culture at the Fin de Siècle* (London, 1991), 190.

[47] See e.g. Patrick McGrath, 'Suckers for Punishment', *The Sunday Times*, 6 Sept. 1992; Elaine Showalter, 'Blood Sell: Vampire Fever and Anxieties for the Fin de Siècle', *Times Literary Supplement*, 8 Jan. 1993.

[48] See Christopher Craft, ' "Kiss me With Those Red Lips": Gender and Inversion in Bram Stoker's *Dracula*', in Elaine Showalter (ed.), *Speaking of Gender* (New York, 1989), 216–42.

corrupting, living apart from the fully alive, secretly longing to be released into true death. Like the (largely imaginary) AIDS sufferer most demonized in the media—the one who infects others in revenge for his or her being ill—the undead spread their pollution to sustain a *vindictive* cycle. 'And you, their best beloved one,' Dracula tells Mina, 'are now to me flesh of my flesh; blood of my blood; kin of my kin; my bountiful wine-press for a while . . . You shall be avenged in turn; for not one of them but shall minister to your needs. But as yet you are to be punished' (p. 288). To his male pursuers, he cries: 'My revenge is just begun! . . . Your girls that you all love are mine already; and through them you and others shall yet be mine . . . ' (p. 306).

In certain societies, menstrual flux is thought as deadly as HIV-infected plasma. The Mae Enga, for instance, believe that 'menstrual blood introduced into a man's food . . . quickly kills him, and young women crossed in love sometimes seek their revenge in this way'.[49] Of course, entire cultures view 'the flowers' as positive (a sign of continuing fertility). In some of them, it is at the point of her first bleeding, the menarche, that a female shaman discovers her powers, is peculiarly receptive and prophetic, and these gifts recur with each lunar cycle.[50] Feminist writers tend to sympathize with these positive accounts. When the poet Grace Nichols writes an 'Ode to My Bleed',[51] she is trying to change attitudes. Western perceptions of 'the curse', however, are still affected by the notion that it represents a dangerous flow of inner stuff outside the order of the body: a classic case of 'matter out of place' (in Mary Douglas's phrase) judged a pollutant.[52] Generally, in patriarchal Europe, menses have not been regarded with warmth. The behaviour-swings associated with periods have been interpreted less as symptoms of magical sensitivity than as 'complaints' to be medicated

---

[49] Mervyn J. Meggitt, 'Male–Female Relationships in the Highlands of Australian New Guinea', *American Anthropologist*, 66 (1964), 204–24, p. 207, quoted in Thomas Buckley and Alma Gottlieb, 'A Critical Appraisal of Theories of Menstrual Symbolism', in Buckley and Gottlieb (eds.), *Blood Magic: The Anthropology of Menstruation* (Berkeley, 1988), 3–53, p. 34.

[50] Penelope Shuttle and Peter Redgrove, *The Wise Wound: Menstruation and Everywoman* (London, 1978), 65.

[51] In her *Lazy Thoughts of a Lazy Woman and Other Poems* (London, 1989), 24.

[52] Mary Douglas, *Purity and Danger: An Analysis of the Concepts of Pollution and Taboo* (London, 1966). But see her 'Self-Evidence' (1972), repr. in her *Implicit Meanings* (London, 1975), 276–318.

away, or as visitations of demonic unreason (as though the Furies harried menstrual bleeders)—the kind of violence which Strindberg dramatized with misogynistic enthusiasm in *Miss Julie*.

The threatening, toothed vagina which is a cliché of masculine fantasy finds a ready link with vampirism when, during menstruation, it becomes a polluted orifice trickling blood. The menstruater is defiled and defiling because, as she bleeds, she strays beyond the socialized towards the realm of death. Since the female body is Draculan (once a month, at least), it must crave what it has lost. And indeed, as Elaine Showalter notes, gynaecologists contemporary with Stoker 'held that woman's blood lust came from her need to replace lost menstrual blood'.[53] Some such train of buried associations leads the poets Penelope Shuttle and Peter Redgrove to end their study of menstruation, *The Wise Wound*, with a chapter called 'The Mirror of Dracula'. In the course of this they produce a list of film titles which certainly includes some gems: *Countess Dracula*, *The Vengeance of She*, and the psychoanalytically piquant *Blood from the Mummy's Tomb*. But they are strangely quick to regard horror movies as liberating fantasies, as when they say, of Christopher Lee's 'ladies', in Dracula films of thirty years ago:

Before they were bitten, they were chlorotic weak creatures with vapours . . . After their blood had been shed for the vampire, though (and it is always from the *neck*, as we say neck or cervix of the womb) . . . why, what creatures they became! The corsets were replaced by practical white unhampering shrouds . . . and their smiles, full of bright teeth with handsome canines, like neat panthers, were flashing and free . . . Dracula opened the permissive sixties with his chorus of happily-bleeding women, with broad hints about sexual menstruation. (pp. 267–8)

In fact, modern myths of menstruation can be violent, oppressive, and compact with the darker elements of revenge tragedy. Film, video, and pulp-fiction show the residual power of blood mythology, removed from the artistic sphere occupied by *The Oresteia* and *Macbeth* but retaining a capacity to disturb. Stephen King's bestselling *Carrie*, for instance—the film version of which Shuttle and Redgrove mention in passing—begins with its teenage heroine in the school showers, enduring her first period against a chorus of girlish mockery. The child of a fundamentalist, repressive mother

---

[53] *Sexual Anarchy*, 180.

who fears witch-like powers in her daughter, and who obsessively connects sexuality with pollution, Carrie has not been told what menstruation is. Along with shock, however, her menarche brings an access of power, a Draculan glare, a telekinetic force (in the pompous jargon of horror fiction) which can, and eventually does, destroy over four hundred people and most of a town. For all his sympathy with the heroine, King heightens menstrual dread and makes it drive his narrative.

Carrie's mother might be warped when she says: 'Boys. Yes, boys come next. After the blood the boys come. Like sniffing dogs, grinning and slobbering, trying to find out where that smell is. *That . . . smell!*'[54] But it is equally clear that King, not Mrs White, has read *The Oresteia*, and sees an opportunity in Carrie's menstruation to put his novel in buskins by echoing it. Shakespeare appears to similar effect. The novel climaxes with Carrie flexing her telekinesis against a hall full of teenagers. In a ritual reinforcement of her initial shame, she is chosen as Queen of the High School Prom, doused with pig's blood by a girl with a grudge against her, laughed at, and goaded into revenge. She becomes, like Beatrice-Joanna, 'A woman dipp'd in blood' (III. iv. 126). As she staggers away from the hall, a witness reports her '*grinning* . . . like a death's head. And she kept looking at her hands and rubbing them on her dress, trying to get the blood off and thinking she'd never get it off' (p. 165). King, more earnest to be clear than subtle, adds, 'She was unaware that she was scrubbing her bloodied hands against her dress like Lady Macbeth' (p. 174). This kind of ambiguity, which pities Carrie but uses her bleeding, amplified through the bucket of blood, to smear her with guilt, with sinful pollution, even affects King's use of the Bible. After striking her daughter for agreeing to go to the ball, Mrs White sees on her cheek a 'blood red' patch—what she grandly calls 'The mark', the Mark of the Beast in Revelation (p. 90). Yet what compels Carrie to go to the dance clad in scarlet, like Babylon, the great whore? Does the pig's blood not merely manifest what that dress, chosen by King, implies? Or is blood applied to blood meant to be a purgation? If so, from stain of what? Is it only Mrs White who recalls the blood of the Lamb, and thinks menstruation a sin: 'Blood, fresh blood. Blood was always at the root of it, and only blood could expiate it. . . . The only way to kill sin, true black sin, was to drown it in the blood of (she must be sacrificed) . . . ' (p. 137)?

In an interesting essay on 'Menstrual Politics: Women and Pigs in Rural Portugal', the anthropologist Denise L. Lawrence examines a village called Vila Branca, where menstruous women are kept from pork-curing. The taboo exists not because of antipathy between women and pigs but for a like-affects-like logic of the kind found in ancient purification. With an anatomical structure similar (it is said) to that of pigs, menstruating women are 'able to contaminate the pig with their own "illness"'.[55] We should not find this strange: research by Patricia Crawford has shown that, as late as the 1870s, menstruous women in various parts of Britain did not pickle pork (they may also have avoided making bacon);[56] Shuttle and Redgrove give 'swinish' and 'sowish' as current terms for menstruation (p. 54). There is a deep, offensive structure of analogy behind the retributive jibe, as Carrie's bucket is swung into place, 'Pig blood for a pig' (p. 108). As it happens, several features of the Vila Branca taboo could be correlated with what has been found in tragedy. For example, its strength is shown in the fact that the only male saint carried in effigy at the annual *festa* is São Bras (St Blas), whose hand was permanently stained red by God because, once in his hot youth, he went so far as to put his hand up the skirts of a menstruating woman.[57] What is most remarkable, however, and likely to make one concede the ingenuity, if not the savour, of King's novel, is the way Carrie's telekinesis works through sight.

When she gazes shut the doors of the hall, starts up the fire sprinklers and causes massive electrical flashes, Stephen King knowingly recalls some of the great, claustrophobic scenes of revenge tragedy: Odysseus' allies in Homer, locking the doors to trap the suitors, the thunder and lightning which orchestrate such set-pieces as the denouement of *The Revenger's Tragedy*. Her violence thrills the reader because it offers the ultimate fantasy of the body turned into a lethal weapon, 'killing with a look'. In this it recalls such vampires as Lucy Westenra, who, from under brows wrinkled like 'the coils of Medusa's snakes', threatens Van Helsing's party with her master's 'basilisk' stare: 'If ever a face meant death—if

[55] 'Menstrual Politics: Women and Pigs in Rural Portugal', in Buckley and Gottlieb (eds.), *Blood Magic*, 117–36, p. 124.

[56] Patricia Crawford, 'Attitudes to Menstruation in Seventeenth-Century England', *Past and Present*, 91 (1981), 47–73, p. 61.   [57] Lawrence, 'Menstrual Politics', 123–4.

looks could kill—we saw it at that moment' (p. 212). Strong, occult feelings link the evil eye with blood pollution[58] because those who kill in revenge are so often, in their pale and worn desperation, 'More dead than living',[59] bearers of death if not 'undead'. Their affinity with the realm beyond unbleeding life is what brings ghosts, revengers, and (if only monthly) menstruaters together, and what gives the latter their baleful look. No doubt the Gorgon's blood, given to Ion, was menstrual. 'A menstruating woman is believed to be able to cause the pork to spoil simply by looking at it', writes Lawrence.[60] 'A fiend so violent is that fiend of menstruation', says ancient Persian scripture, 'that, where another fiend does not smite anything with a look, it smites with a look.'[61] The superstition runs deep, and it leaves a mark on more than Mina Harker's forehead. *Carrie* might not be a major work; it is certainly a dubious one. But it shows that nerves can still be jangled by fear of gory defilement, that glaring, red-eyed Dracula was by no means laid to rest in Agamemnon's tomb.

---

[58] See e.g. *Dracula*, 10, 348.   [59] Euripides, *Orestes*, 386.
[60] 'Menstrual Politics', 125.   [61] Shuttle and Redgrove, *Wise Wound*, 229.

3. Sophocles in Baker Street

WHEN John H. Watson, MD, is introduced to the young Sherlock Holmes, in a chemical laboratory at Bart's Hospital, he is stunned to be told, with nonchalant clairvoyance, 'You have been in Afghanistan, I perceive.'[1] A few days later, in their new digs at 221B Baker Street, Holmes again astonishes Watson by identifying a passing messenger as a 'retired sergeant of Marines' (p. 25). Both feats are technically similar, but whereas Conan Doyle shapes the initial encounter in such a way that neither Watson nor the reader can grasp how Holmes achieves his *coup*, the 'retired sergeant' is a testing-ground for those 'rules of deduction' which Holmes expounds in his article, 'The Book of Life'. There it is claimed that minds can be read from 'a momentary expression, a twitch of a muscle or a glance of an eye', and that 'By a man's finger-nails, by his coat-sleeve, by his boots . . . [his] calling is plainly revealed' (p. 23). From clusters of such evidence, Holmes explains, he could infer Watson's service in the Afghan wars and decode the passing messenger. Mystery gives way to method, to a demonstration of the essentially simple—though practically complex—way in which analysis can unlock the world.

This movement from obscurity to elucidation, in the opening pages of *A Study in Scarlet*, the first Sherlock Holmes adventure, is typical of the dynamics of detective fiction in the classic phase which reached maturity, during the 1930s, in the work of Agatha Christie, Michael Innes, and Dorothy L. Sayers. It would be a less convincing effect without the sense of insecurity registered beyond Baker Street. Wounded at a crumbling imperial frontier, Watson returns with broken health to a disturbingly indifferent London. In 'that great cesspool into which all the loungers and idlers of the Empire are irresistibly drained', he himself becomes social flotsam, 'leading a comfortless, meaningless existence' (p. 16). The city breeds fraud and violence, and a *fin-de-siècle* decadence which infects even the

---

[1] *A Study in Scarlet*, in Sir Arthur Conan Doyle, pref. Charles Morley, *The Penguin Complete Sherlock Holmes* (Harmondsworth, 1981), 15–86, p. 18. All stories quoted from this edn.

great detective. Holmes passes the time by injecting cocaine, scraping his violin, and indulging in the kind of 'art jargon' which gives *A Study in Scarlet* its Whistlerian title. Watson, meanwhile, quotes Carlyle. A profoundly conservative figure, his trust in the world has been damaged by anomie. He is gripped by the kind of existential lassitude which manifests itself in the consumption of late breakfasts. In his autobiography Conan Doyle recalled the collapse of his own beliefs—he had been brought up a Roman Catholic—during 'the years when Huxley, Tyndall, Darwin, Herbert Spencer and John Stuart Mill were our chief philosophers, and . . . even the man in the street felt the strong sweeping current of their thought'.[2] Though published in 1887, *A Study in Scarlet* is set almost a decade earlier, during just those years of crisis. Young men in the late 1870s found an old vision of the world collapsing and set off in search of a new. That is why Watson redeems himself by meeting Holmes in a laboratory.

For what most strikes us now, in the writings of Tyndall or Huxley, is their reassuring confidence in the regularity of natural phenomena. In place of biblical narrative, popular post-Darwinian science substituted a coherent, connected story legible in the rocks. Truth need not rely, it said, on that doctrine of 'papal infallibility' which (according to Conan Doyle) led men of 'intellectual self-respect' to leave the Church.[3] There were empirical routes to certainty. Thus, when Watson first meets Holmes, the latter is fizzing with excitement at having found an 'infallible' test for bloodstains. As others have pointed out,[4] Holmes's practice of 'reasoning backwards' from fingernails and coat-sleeves resembles the mode of 'retrospective prophecy' which Huxley celebrates in 'On the Method of Zadig'. In that lecture of 1880, the scientist is compared to the character in Voltaire who learned so much about the queen's missing spaniel and the king's missing horse from traces they left behind that he was accused of stealing them. 'Zadig's great principle', says Huxley, is 'that like effects imply like causes, and that the process of reasoning from a shell, or a tooth, or a bone, to the nature of the animal to which it belonged, rests absolutely' on that point.[5] Holmes's philosophy is identical. In 'The Five Orange

---

[2] *Memories and Adventures*, 2nd edn. (London, 1930), 39–40.   [3] Ibid. 26.
[4] Following Régis Messac, *La 'Détective Novel' et l'influence de la pensée scientifique* (Paris, 1929).
[5] 'On the Method of Zadig: Retrospective Prophecy as a Function of Science', in Thomas H. Huxley, *Collected Essays*, 9 vols. (London, 1894–1908), iv. 1–23, p. 13.

Pips', he compares Cuvier's ability to 'describe a whole animal by the contemplation of a single bone' to the skill of that 'ideal reasoner' who 'would, when he had once been shown a single fact in all its bearings, deduce from it not only all the chain of events which led up to it but also all the results which would follow from it' (pp. 224–5). Armed with similar confidence, Huxley felt able to overrule those Humean doubts about causality which had dogged the empiricist tradition,[6] and, in his lecture 'On a Piece of Chalk' (1868), to crush biblical literalism with paleontology. Reading the chalk deposits of East Anglia, he accumulates 'Internal evidence . . . collateral proofs . . . positive testimony' and 'negative justification' until the 'writing upon the wall of cliffs at Cromer' is said to have 'an authority which cannot be impeached'.[7]

Chalk embedded with fossils, however, cannot verify hypotheses by muttering, 'it's a fair cop'. The struggles of that murderous avenger, Jefferson Hope, as he is handcuffed in *A Study in Scarlet*, more decisively endorse Zadig than anything to be found at Cromer. A confession of guilt in Baker Street confirms the 'infallibility' of science and coherence of the world. It is a measure of the metaphysical comfort which this gave early readers that so many of them chose to believe in Holmes's actual existence, sending him offers of marriage, employment, and the like. Even the gaping holes in his logic[8] seem to have enhanced his aura by making his 'deductions' seem intuitive. In practice, Holmes's method is abductive, based on inferences which proceed from general rules through particular instances to likely conclusions.[9] He insists, however, that his logic is 'deductive', and boasts that his 'conclusions [are] as infallible as so many propositions of Euclid' (p. 23). Rather like those ancient Greek scientists who provide a context for reading Sophocles—medical writers, especially, who lay claim to logical 'necessity' but provide 'generally quite informal' proofs[10]—

---

[6] Cf. David Hume, *A Treatise of Human Nature*, ed. L. A. Selby-Bigges, 2nd edn., rev. P. H. Nidditch (Oxford, 1978), 651–4, and Huxley's *Hume: With Helps to the Study of Berkeley* (1878), repr. as *Collected Essays*, vi. 143–4.   [7] *Collected Essays*, viii. 1–36, pp. 18, 27.

[8] See e.g. Marcello Truzzi, 'Sherlock Holmes: Applied Social Psychologist', in Umberto Eco and Thomas A. Sebeok (eds.), *The Sign of Three: Dupin, Holmes, Peirce* (Bloomington, Ind., 1983), 55–80, p. 70.

[9] See e.g. Thomas A. Sebeok and Jean Umiker-Sebeok, '"You Know My Method": A Juxtaposition of Charles S. Peirce and Sherlock Holmes' and Massimo A. Bonfantini and Giamaolo Proni, 'To Guess or Not To Guess', in Eco and Sebeok (eds.), *The Sign of Three*, 11–54, 119–34.

[10] G. E. R. Lloyd, *Magic, Reason and Experience: Studies in the Origins and Development of Greek Science* (Cambridge, 1979), 103; cf. 122.

Holmes, when thinking about his cases, was obsessed by mathematical demonstration. The 'chain of reasoning', the 'long chain of deductions', the 'chain of logical sequences' which led him through London to the disguised Jefferson Hope,[11] had to be ineluctable if it was to match the causal 'chains' of nature.

Not all chains shackle, but late nineteenth-century ideas of causation tended to exact determinism as the price of coherence. Such views composed a tragic world. Indeed, Jacques Barzun has called detective fiction, as the characteristic product of the age, 'pure tragedy, in which the protagonist himself prepares his downfall. The fatal flaw in him is the error he makes while committing the crime, an error which comes to light because of inescapable necessity in the workings of physical nature.'[12] This perception is acute but too inward, in that it imagines events from a point of view—that of the criminal—which, if it were actually available before the detective's final résumé, would destroy narrative suspense and make every story in the genre labour to be *Crime and Punishment*. If we trust the drift of reading, and place the detective at the centre of things, the tragic features of the kind come more clearly into focus. As he hunts down Jefferson Hope, like Nemesis in a deerstalker, Holmes is a 'scourge and minister'.[13] Dr Watson, the confidant of this Hamlet, is a Pylades or Horatio: sober foil of retribution and chronicler of the hero's deeds. Ambivalent in his relations with the 'powers that be',[14] the detective either supplements the efforts of Scotland Yard or, more interestingly, like wild Hieronimo, goes outside the law for the sake of justice. Detection stirs in his 'prophetic soul',[15] and is partly introspective. This is a phase, at least for Holmes, of reverie and low-voiced chatter (his mode of soliloquy). But there is also active sleuthing under the cover of an 'antic disposition'. Some detectives, like Lord Peter Wimsey and Hercule Poirot, exploit the guise of folly which goes with upper-class eccentricity or alien status. Holmes, a man almost passionless, without a past or clear social niche, capitalizes on his blankness to become protean: a master of false beards and eye-patches, he enjoys passing himself off as 'a drunken-looking groom' or 'Nonconformist clergyman' (pp. 167, 170).

[11] *Penguin Complete Sherlock Holmes*, 49, 85.

[12] 'From *Phèdre* to Sherlock Holmes', in *The Energies of Art: Studies of Authors Classic and Modern* (New York, 1956), 303–23, p. 308.   [13] *Hamlet*, III. iv. 175.

[14] Romans 13: 1; see below, p. 155.   [15] *Hamlet*, I. v. 40.

Holmes's histrionic brio helped earn Conan Doyle's stories a place on the Victorian stage.[16] Within the narratives themselves, however, theatrical tropes register in a more localized way: at just those points, in fact, where such tragedies as *Hamlet* become reflexive. Much detective fiction starts *in mediis rebus*, in the manner of the ancients, with the company scarcely assembled for their country-house weekend before a corpse is discovered in the library. The hero who reconstructs the scene of violence, must, like the Prince of Denmark, do so by back-reaching the action through something like 'The Mousetrap'. Recalling the murder of Hope's first victim, poisoned in an empty house off the Brixton Road, Holmes tells Watson: 'Patent-leathers stood still while Square-toes walked up and down. I could read all that in the dust; and I could read that as he walked he grew more and more excited. That is shown by the increased length of his strides. He was talking all the while, and working himself up, no doubt, into a fury. Then the tragedy occurred' (p. 34). As Holmes warms to his reconstruction, the coherence of his hypothesis (matching the development of the crime) carries us from an idea of narrative, constructed through reading, to the dramatic immediacy of 'the tragedy'. Still more formidable is the intellectual violence of the Holmesian denouement, where verification of a theory, achieved in a masque-like scene, takes on vindicative theatricality. 'Watson insists that I am the dramatist in real life,' says Holmes in *The Valley of Fear*:

Some touch of the artist wells up within me, and calls insistently for a well staged performance. Surely our profession, Mr. Mac, would be a drab and sordid one if we did not sometimes set the scene so as to glorify our results. The blunt accusation, the brutal tap upon the shoulder—what can one make of such a *dénouement*? But the quick inference, the subtle trap, the clever forecast of coming events, the triumphant vindication of bold theories—are these not the pride and the justification of our life's work? (p. 809)

The Valley of Fear was written almost three decades after *A Study in Scarlet*. Yet not much has changed in Baker Street. Hansom cabs trot by, Mycroft dozes in his club, Watson stands ready with his blunt wit and service revolver. If the scenery and props remain constant, so does the narrative pressure out from intellectual 'vindication' to

[16] See e.g. *The Annotated Sherlock Holmes*, ed. William S. Baring-Gould, 2 vols. (London, 1968), i. 27–32.

vengeance. Blackmail, treasure-hunting, espionage, murder by snake-bite: Conan Doyle has many subjects. Yet his plots typically gravitate towards violent patterns of behaviour which are extended and fiercely consistent. Both *A Study in Scarlet* and its successor, like 'The Resident Patient' and others, thus chronicle the impact of revenges generated at frontiers by outgroups. These sects are bound by criminal vows (as in *The Sign of Four*), by the weird rituals of the Ku-Klux-Klan ('The Five Orange Pips'), or by a lurid form of trade-unionism (as in *The Valley of Fear*). Jefferson Hope pursues Stangerson and Drebber because they are Mormons who, claiming the hand of his fiancée, Lucy Ferrier, against the wishes of her father (a Mormon by chance rather than conviction), have, together with a posse of 'Avenging Angels', caused the death of both. Watson makes much of Hope's 'power of sustained vindictiveness' (p. 73), and the murderer himself, when not invoking the Gothic aid of the ghosts of Lucy and John Ferrier (p. 80), claims that he was driven by the mathematical principle that Drebber and Stangerson, 'guilty of the death of two human beings . . . had, therefore, forfeited their own lives' (p. 78). With its calculating mode of connective atrocity, its impulse to symmetrical violence, Hope's revenge plot shares a world-picture with Joule's work on the Conservation of Energy.

Yet Holmesian proof can only be secured by a huge narrative dislocation. Having started *in mediis rebus*, the tale of Jefferson Hope loops back at its centre to an absolute beginning. Once the hand-cuffs click around Hope's wrists, the story returns to zero, to the germ of the whole adventure, with John and Lucy Ferrier stranded 'On the Great Alkali Plain' before their rescue by the Mormons (p. 52). This gigantic detour (like the equivalent one in *The Valley of Fear*) often annoys commentators, because it moves away from the gaslit metropolitan milieu which Conan Doyle depicts so well. In some respects, however, it is the decisive moment of the story, its own 'triumphant vindication', showing the connectedness of all. The writer's leap of Huxleyan faith, his commitment to a belief in chains of causation, opens narrative vistas which firmly demon-strate closure. In other words his leap is the opposite of a reader's skip. Readers of detective fiction dare not jump over humdrum passages (except to look at the end of the book) in case they miss crucial clues. The material typically regarded as optional by rapid novel readers—accounts of the layout of rooms, descriptions of paper-knives and pokers—are precisely what cannot be scanted. To skip them would be like a hunter taking his eyes off the trail.

It follows that, though this genre is 'realist' in appearance, it is covertly a form of tragic romance. Reader and sleuth are questers through a region precharged with human significance. When forced to register the actual, disconnected otherness of objects, as in Alain Robbe-Grillet's *The Erasers* (1953), the mode flattens, becomes inconsequential. Paper-knives and pokers are no longer answerable, as they are in Conan Doyle, where every 'coat-sleeve' has something to divulge, and where hypotheses are constructed and (it may be) 'vindicated' in the process of our reading. When G. K. Chesterton says that the fictional detective 'crosses London with something of the loneliness and liberty of a prince in the tale of elfland', and that, in Holmes's city, 'there is no stone in the street and no brick in the wall that is not actually a deliberate symbol— a message from some man', he catches the romance debt.[17] For Chesterton, 'Anything which tends, even under the fantastic form of the minutiæ of Sherlock Holmes, to assert this romance of detail in civilisation . . . is a good thing' (pp. 159–60). Holmes himself was more ambivalent. In the opening chapter of *The Sign of Four*, 'The Science of Deduction', he rebukes Watson for seeking 'to tinge' the events of *A Study in Scarlet* 'with romanticism'. Against the repeated claim that the case resembled 'the fifth proposition of Euclid', Watson insists that 'the romance was there'. By this he partly means that passions of the heart were involved. Hope's narrative shows how much anguish has been suffered by a hero who remains, for Holmes, drily 'reasoning from effects to causes', mere data. But Watson also, more ponderably, notices the deflection of romance questing through Holmes's 'genius for minutiæ' (pp. 90–1).

Indeed, *A Study in Scarlet* traces a double pursuit. Holmes's quest for a murderer tracks Hope's for Drebber and Stangerson. As a 'hunter' from the Rocky Mountains (p. 61) becomes the hunted, ironies emerge. 'A human bloodhound' driven by 'vengeance' (p. 76), Hope meets his match in that 'amateur bloodhound' (p. 36) who reminds Watson, at the scene of Drebber's murder, where 'vindication' is sought, 'of a pure-blooded, well-trained foxhound, as it dashes backward and forward through the covert, whining in

[17] 'A Defence of Detective Stories', in *The Defendant* (London, 1901), 157–62, pp. 158–9.

its eagerness, until it comes across the lost scent' (p. 31). At times, as in 'The Boscombe Valley Mystery', Holmes, 'hot upon . . . a scent', becomes positively atavistic: 'His face flushed and darkened. . . . His nostrils seemed to dilate with a purely animal lust for the chase' (p. 211). Such descriptions point to a phenomenon far more ethically unsettling than that described by Agatha Christie: 'The detective story was the story of the chase . . . the hunting down of Evil and the triumph of Good.'[18] It reaches back through evolutionary time, in the manner of Holmes's favourite book, *The Martyrdom of Man*, to that instinctive 'Curiosity', that urge to examine, observe, and interpret symptoms, which was said by post-Darwinians to animate the higher animals.[19] As interestingly, though less consciously, it goes back to William Godwin's *Caleb Williams*, a work of tragic intensity as well as the earliest detective novel in English, in which the protagonist admits that 'The spring of action which . . . characterised the whole train of my life, was curiosity. . . . I was desirous of tracing the variety of effects which might be produced from given causes.' This, Caleb says, 'made me a sort of natural philosopher' and 'produced in me an invincible attachment to books of narrative and romance'.[20]

In *Caleb Williams*, a revenge plot is continuously grounded on hunting. When the initial detector, Caleb, discovers a vengeful wrong in Falkland's life—a murder rashly committed—he is pursued and harried by his master, trapped in 'the snares of [his] vengeance' (p. 144), yet is himself possessed of knowledge which ravages the hunter. Within this double pursuit, a series of passages elaborates the narrator's desire for 'vindication', his longing to free at least himself by proving and publicizing Falkland's fault. It has been noted by Ian Ousby that Caleb shares certain characteristics with Jacobethan revengers: the scholarly detachment of Hamlet and Vindice, a fascination with the crimes he deplores.[21] Of more fundamental interest, though, is the concinnity of detection and vengeance which led Godwin to draw inspiration from John Reynolds's massive compilation (and source for *The Changeling*),

[18] Quoted by Dennis Porter, *The Pursuit of Crime: Art and Ideology in Detective Fiction* (New Haven, 1981), 160–1.

[19] Winwood Reade, *The Martyrdom of Man* (London, 1872), 437.

[20] William Godwin, *Caleb Williams*, ed. David McCracken (Oxford, 1970), 4.

[21] *Bloodhounds of Heaven: The Detective in English Fiction from Godwin to Doyle* (Cambridge, Mass., 1976), 22–5.

The Triumph of God's Revenge against the Crying and Execrable Sin of Murder.[22] The claustrophobic providentialism of Reynolds becomes Falkland's all-seeing intelligence, remorselessly tracking his tracker. As in the work of Conan Doyle, the detective, following clues, does more than establish guilt. When a case is sufficiently complex for fear to grow from pursuit, the development and 'vindication' of hypotheses make the hunt itself punitive. By this means, detective fiction explores the ancient, ultimately tragic relations between tracking, analysis, and violence.

*   *   *

At the start of Tony Harrison's recent, and most brilliant, play, *The Trackers of Oxyrhynchus*, Bernard Pyne Grenfell and Arthur Surridge Hunt—'*the Holmes and Watson*', as the playwright calls them, '*of British papyrology*'[23]—are scrutinizing bits of papyrus under a hot Egyptian sun. A pair of quintessential late-Victorian Englishmen, clad in '*baggy khaki shorts*' and '*solar topis*', they stand in scholarly contrast to the chorus of Fellaheen diggers: locals who would, if given half a chance, pilfer the papyrus they unearth and use it as compost for vegetable-growing. 'We're trackers (Ἰχνευτες)', Grenfell explains: 'First we dig, then we decipher, then we must | deduce all the letters that have mouldered into dust.'[24] Like Holmes, at the start of *The Valley of Fear*, decoding a message in digits by the use of Whitaker's Almanac, they bring semiotic guile to bear on refractory texts. But they are also driven men. Grenfell is haunted by Apollo, who urges him to retrieve a work itself called *Ichneutae*—the satyr play by Sophocles, lost since antiquity, which deals with the theft of the sun-god's cattle, with their tracking down by the satyrs, and (after the text breaks off) with the seizure of the power of music by Apollo, taking from the infant rustler, Hermes, a lyre strung with thongs from his beasts. 'I'll pursue you until you track down my play', Apollo warns Grenfell. 'Just keep on the track | And remember Apollo's right at your back' (pp. 18–19). As for his companion,

---

[22] 1621–35; Godwin indicates his debt to the altered 1770 edn., *God's Revenge against Murder and Adultery*, in the 1832 preface. See *Caleb Williams*, ed. McCracken, 335–41, p. 340.

[23] *The Trackers of Oxyrhynchus*, rev. edn. (London, 1991), 9, cf. p. xv.

[24] *Trackers*, 9, echoing the Fellaheen chant, 'Ichneutae (*Ixneytés*) Ichneutae (*Ixneytés*) Ichneutae (*Ixneytés*)'.

Hunt, 'Hunt!' is what the god cratylicly commands: 'Hunt out more fragments and find me the rest. | Hunt!' (p. 25).

In Harrison's drama, as historically, Grenfell and Hunt do find the *Ichneutae*. That, in a sense, is when the real tracking begins. The Holmes and Watson of scholarship must pick their way through mouldering papyri in search of a play about searching. What they find is not only demandingly Sophoclean but comically robust and earthy: a work which, in its broken way, is a 'clue' to the forgotten 'wholeness' of ancient theatre,[25] to a fifth-century cohesion between high and low which breaks down and polarizes, in Harrison's extension of Sophocles, into Apollo's South Bank élitism versus the destructive, vital energy of satyrs turned into football fans. What mobilizes these ironies is the process of tracking itself. As Harrison's frame opens into a performance of Sophocles' frag-ments, Grenfell and Hunt are seen to participate in the same quest as the satyrs. 'After two thousand years, lads, look,' says Silenus, 'there's your text. | It's up to you, to track what comes next. | And once you've tracked down each missing Greek word | then sniff out the trail of Apollo's lost herd' (p. 30). It is not just that, when the actor playing Hunt doubles as Silenus, the leading tracker, he finds in himself, like the snarling Holmes, a mythic or phylogenetic basis for running and noting and pursuing. Sophocles' satyrs have a *technē* and *tropos*;[26] they claim expertise in 'art' and 'method'. There is thus a wry elision between philological tracking and the problems met by the satyrs when the redolent, shit-mired cattle-prints get reversed before Cyllene's cave: 'Hey, look here at this! It's stupid, daft. | Their backlegs are forrad, their front legs aft.' For Hermes, of course, like Cacus stealing the oxen of Hercules, has blurred the trail of Apollo's cattle to avoid detection. An early exponent of that 'cunning intelligence', *mētis*, celebrated by Detienne and Vernant,[27] he produces tracks even more confusing than those of the racehorse, Silver Blaze, tracked by Holmes across Dartmoor until his prints begin to go backwards (p. 344).

As they follow these '*maze-like tracks*', Tony Harrison's satyrs '*become*' (as a stage direction says) '*a parody of the Furies in the National*

[25] *Trackers*, p. xi.

[26] *The Searchers*, 90–2, in the Loeb Classical Library Select Papyri, 3, ed. and tr. D. L. Page (London, 1941).

[27] Marcel Detienne and Jean-Pierre Vernant, *Cunning Intelligence in Greek Culture and Society*, tr. Janet Lloyd (Hassocks, 1978), 41, 301–3.

Theatre Oresteia, *sniffing for the blood of Orestes*' (p. 31). This is a useful reminder of the occult links between tracking and tragic revenge. Not least because Harrison wrote the text on which the National Theatre *Oresteia* was based, it also signals 'the unity of tragedy and satyr play'—a 'unity' which, as Harrison understands it, did not just find expression in the ancient practice of staging satyr plays after every group of three tragedies. It went deep into the conception of how catastrophe was to be lived through, what tragic tonalities meant. In a 'proto-satyric' drama like Euripides' *Alcestis*, the inclusion, in a tragic milieu, of a 'satyr' figure (the gluttonous Heracles) achieves a Shakespearean compounding of low with high.[28] Sophocles has traditionally been thought the most austere of tragic dramatists. Consider, though, the opening of *Ajax*. 'Odysseus', says Athena:

> I have always seen and marked you
> Stalking to pounce upon your enemies;
> And now by the tent of Ajax, where he keeps
> Last place upon the shore, I find you busy
> Tracing and scanning these fresh tracks of his,
> New-printed on the sand, to guess if he's inside.
> You've coursed him like a keen Laconian hound.   (1–8)

The commanding verse of the goddess, bitter foe of Ajax, has a kind of ominous buoyancy. Knowing what has happened, she derives an icy pleasure from seeing Odysseus hunt down like an animal that hero who, the night before, had pursued and ravaged cattle under the illusion that they were Greek generals. Denied the armour of Achilles, Ajax had resolved to take revenge on Odysseus and the sons of Atreus, but, deceived by Athena, he had become a common butcher and, like something from the *Ichneutae*, driven his chief enemies, mooing and bleating, back to his tent, for torture. Within a few lines of this opening, Athena invites Odysseus to 'laugh' at Ajax's plight (78–9). It is laughter which dies behind our eyes, as the *skēnē* is opened up, or an on-stage tent is pulled aside, and we see the warrior, still half-mad, squatting in his shambles.

It has been said that the *Ichneutae* parodies the *Ajax*. In practice the plays seem connected in a more disturbingly mutual way. That is why Harrison's inclusion, in the National Theatre text of *Trackers*,

---

[28] *Trackers*, pp. xi–xii.

of the '*terrifying scream of Marsyas*' (p. 123)—the cry of a satyr flayed
alive by Apollo for presuming to compete with his musicianship—is
apt. At the moment of cultural separation, when high and low
divide, tragedy and satyr play are seen to merge and part, as the
audience is reminded of that point in the *Ajax* where the hero boasts
of flaying Odysseus (107–10). Certainly, from our own now split
perspective, the *Ajax*, as tragedy, sets up more philosophical reso-
nances in the idea of detection than the *Ichneutae*. Nor are these
undertones generated only by the choric passages and set speeches,
such as Ajax's on mutability: 'Strangely the long and countless drift
of time | Brings all things forth from darkness into light, | Then
covers them once more' (644ff.). The very shape of the action, its
recursive rerunning of the hunt, pursues Ajax, strips him of dignity,
and makes him, after his lonely, anachronistic suicide on the open
sea-shore, again an object of tracking. Here, as in the *Oedipus
Tyrannus*, questions of hiding and being seen, of human shame
and exposure, engage the audience across many levels from the
use of the *skēnē* for discovery into details of imagery. In both
tragedies, physical gestures—as slight as the lifting of a mantle—
are felt to draw significance from a trail which ends in something
like proof.

Thus, when the semi-choruses go in search of Ajax, after his exit
to suicide, they recall the start of the play with their talk of scanning,
traces, and signs (871–7). Tecmessa, more lovingly intuitive, discovers the corpse before them, impaled on the sword of Hector.
But even she deduces suicide like an ancient Sherlock Holmes: 'This
blade, packed in the ground, | On which he fell, declares it' (908–
9). Her main verb is *katēgorein* ('prove, indicate'), and her production
of *atechnic* evidence (the sword), might have come straight from
Aristotle's discussion of proof in the *Rhetoric*.[29] Then, as Teucer
arrives, to open the play's long last phase, with the debate about
burial, he says that, when he heard of his brother's 'disaster', he was
'In haste to seek the truth and trace it home' (996–7). Now he
literally follows traces[30] to the *moros* (at once 'fate', 'death', 'corpse')
of his brother, using words which link the chase to legal prosecution
('diōkōn') and intellectual enquiry, 'kaxichnoskopoumenos'. Indeed,

---

[29] 1355b–56a, 1375a–77b.
[30] On the echo of Athene's opening lines, here, see W. B. Stanford, in Sophocles, *Ajax*,
ed. Stanford, corr. repr. (1963; London, 1981), 187.

when he finds the corpse and raises the cloth from Ajax's face, he says 'ith', ekkalupson, hōs idō to pan kakon' (1003). Seeking to catch the high tragedy of this, the Chicago translation offers Lear-like starkness: 'Come and uncover; let me see the worst.' Yet 'ekkalupson' has a further timbre. A word frequently used of argued disclosure, de-tection, it will modulate in Hellenistic Greek into the fully philosophical verb, *ekkaluptein*, meaning that illumination of the mind which comes in Stoic proof. As Jonathan Barnes explains: 'a demonstration is an argument (*logos*) which . . . has a non-evident (*adēlon*) conclusion, and which reveals (*ekkaluptein*) that conclusion'.[31]

It should by now be more than clear that Sophocles was interested in how a tracker's pursuit of signs to a quarry resembles higher-order modes of enquiry as they tend towards proof. What makes him a deeper tragedian, however, than Conan Doyle, is his doubt in the capacity of *technē* to arrive at just results. Repeatedly his plays wonder whether the violent clarification, the intellectually driven recognition, towards which his actions tend, might satisfy a desire for coherence at the expense of complex circumstance. Hence the sense of perversity and ethical narrowing, as well as of elated despair, when, at the climax of *The Women of Trachis*, a long array of consequences, from Heracles' killing of Nessus with a venomed arrow, through the recovery of the centaur's blood as a love-potion, and its administration to the hero by Deianira, returns Heracles' violence upon himself. Ezra Pound's version of the moment of *anagnōrisis*—'Come at it that way, my boy, what | SPLENDOUR, | IT ALL COHERES'[32]—finely registers and amplifies that sense of 'triumphant vindication' with which the Sophoclean victim/detective draws strength from his own defeat. What its upper-case fervour drowns out, though, is the play's sense that the consolation derived by Heracles from this particular pattern of evidence reduces, at a critical moment, his tragic awareness. The information which the hero needs, to make his death cohere with his life, is gathered in a series of questions, shaped by legal *technē*, directed at Hyllus, his son (1120ff.). As the cross-examination proceeds, and Heracles finds a logic in Nessus' revenge, the pathos (above all) of Deianira's suicide, reported—not for the first time—

[31] 'Proof Destroyed', in Malcolm Schofield, Myles Burnyeat, and Jonathan Barnes (eds.), *Doubt and Dogmatism: Studies in Hellenistic Epistemology* (Oxford, 1980), 161–81, pp. 164–5.   [32] *Sophocles: 'Women of Trachis'* (1956; London, 1969), 66.

in the same stichomythic passage, is taken askew and disvalued. Commentators used to blame Sophocles for neglecting Deianira in the final scenes,[33] for excluding her physically from the action. The dramaturgy maintains a separation of husband and wife, however, starkly to set before its audience a hero who confuses the coherent with the complete, where coherence is a sign of partiality.

When *Oedipus Tyrannus* is approached from this angle, it becomes clear that its pre-eminence among the plays of Sophocles owes less to sombre fatality or psychoanalytic resonance than to its educing, with peculiar resourcefulness, the problematic relations which hold between vengeance, evidential coherence, and proof. Certainly a language of detection is apparent throughout the work. Take that point in the prologue where Creon returns from the oracle with news that the murderer of Laius must be punished if the plague at Thebes is to end. 'The God commanded clearly', he reports: 'let some one | punish with force this dead man's murderers.' Oedipus then replies:

> Where are they in the world? Where would a trace
> of this old crime be found? It would be hard
> to guess where.   (106–10)

The quest should begin from spoor (the word for 'trace' is 'ichnos') but the language of hunting is compounded with up-to-date technical diction. The Chicago verb, 'guess', is thus inadequate for 'dustekmarton', grounded in the verb *tekmairesthai*, meaning 'enquire into, divine, judge from signs'. According to Bernard Knox this word 'sums up, in its fifth-century meaning—"to form a judgment from evidence"—the new scientific spirit' of fifth-century Athens.[34] Without doubt its analytical overtones will have been strengthened, for early audiences, by Oedipus' stress on tracking causes. For the translator's phrase 'to guess where' conceals 'aitias', from *aitia*, root of 'aetiology' and those cognates which descend through Western science from Aristotle's account of causality in the *Posterior Analytics*.[35] Trace, analysis, cause: here, it might be thought, are the materials of Holmesian deduction. And the framework of demonstration has a decidedly Baker Street structure: expiation in blood

---

[33] Cf. *Trachiniae*, ed. P. E. Easterling (Cambridge, 1982), 1–2.
[34] *Oedipus at Thebes* (New Haven, 1957), 122–3. On relations between science and law see Lloyd, *Magic, Reason and Experience*, 129, 252–3.
[35] Esp. 94a–95b; cf. *Physics*, 194b–95b, *Metaphysics*, 1013a–1014a.

closes an action begun by murder. The hunt for a murderer is a quest for proof which leads towards his mutilation by proceeding detectively back towards the death which he inflicted. At lines 100–1 Creon speaks, with grammatically clotted insistence, of 'ε̄ phonō phonon palin | luontas' (payment of blood by blood), and at 107 his verb for 'punish', 'timōrein', is often translated 'avenge'.

The notion that *Oedipus* is some sort of detective story has been creeping up on the play ever since the period when Grenfell and Hunt unearthed their papyri. For a time the idea was most honoured by intelligent resistance. E. R. Dodds, for example, explaining why we should never look beyond what a Sophocles text actually says, declared: 'There is only one branch of literature where we *are* entitled to ask such questions about *ta ektos tou dramatos*, namely the modern detective story.'[36] This is, of course, quite wrong, partly because the reader would feel cheated if Agatha Christie palpably held back information which might clinch the identity of the villain, but more largely because the quality of Oedipus' questions—an index, for Dodds, of his greatness (pp. 187–8)—cannot be judged without reference to what he might have asked but did not. Recently, critics influenced by post-structuralism have focused on just such gaps and silences, noticing, in particular, that, having single-handedly murdered, at a crossroads, a man old enough to be his father, Oedipus is comforted to hear that Laius was killed by plural bandits, yet, when faced with a shepherd who was at the scene of the fight, and could definitively tell him how many persons were involved, he is deflected by the matter of incest away from the problem of his father's end.[37] To ask 'Whodunit?' of the tragedy, and conclude that Oedipus either did not commit the crime or might not have done so, only applies to Laius' death and cannot affect the marriage with Jocasta. However, when Voltaire, the author of Zadig's adventure—significantly enough—anticipates deconstructive accounts by inferring from Oedipus' interrogation of the herdsman that 'Sophocles forgets that vengeance for the death of Laius is the subject of his play',[38]

---

[36] 'On Misunderstanding the *Oedipus Rex*', *Greece and Rome*, NS 13 (1966), 37–49, repr. in Segal (ed.), *Oxford Readings in Greek Tragedy*, 177–88, pp. 180–1.

[37] See esp. Sandor Goodhart, 'Ληστὰς Ἔφασκε: Oedipus and Laius' Many Murderers', *Diacritics*, 8/1 (1978), 55–71, Frederick Ahl, *Sophocles' Oedipus: Evidence and Self-Conviction* (Ithaca, NY, 1991).

[38] Voltaire, *Lettres sur Oedipe*, III; tr. and quoted by Goodhart, 'Ληστὰς Ἔφασκε', 63.

he raises a radical objection. As in the case of the *The Women of Trachis*, though, the difficulty has less to do with Sophoclean incompetence than with his play's drawing attention to a set of mind, a pathology of detection, which insists on finding coherence.

My theme is what Caleb Williams calls 'curiosity'—*philomatheia* and the like—not an eagerness in Oedipus to take guilt upon himself and become a sacrificial victim for his people. Judaeo-Christian influence makes the latter interpretation of the protagonist's self-incrimination seem plausible[39] until the debts of *Oedipus Tyrannus* to particular fifth-century disciplines are recalled. Sherlock Holmes's skill with coat-sleeves and trouser-knees was modelled on the nosological prowess of a medical professor, Dr Joseph Bell.[40] Various words used of signs and clues in *Oedipus* recur in the diagnostic language of Athenian medicine, an art which exhibited, at this date, 'an empirical spirit and an optimistic confidence . . . not to be seen again in Western Europe until the nineteenth century'.[41] Another influence, at least as profound, came from mathematics. Without this skill, it was felt, nothing could be understood: 'Everything that can be known has number,' said Philoloas, 'for it is impossible to grasp anything with the mind or recognize it without this.'[42] Euclidean demonstration, to the sureness of which Holmes aspires, was the paradigm of reliable discovery.[43] Yet when Bernard Knox notices the array of numbers in *Oedipus*—centred in that perplexity of the one and many bandits—and offers an interpretation in which two versions of the protagonist (admirable *turannos* and incestuous parricide) are brought together in a 'final equation', where Oedipus is 'equated to himself',[44] his quasi-demonstrative confidence should make the Dr Watson in us protest. Like Oedipus, Knox is lured towards the necessary in a field of probability. Even Aristotle, celebrating the coherence of *Oedipus Tyrannus*, was careful to describe its *peripeteia* and recognition as *either* 'necessary (*ex anankēs*) or probable (*eikos*)'.[45] Few concepts

---

[39] See e.g. Girard, *Violence and the Sacred*, ch. 3.

[40] See e.g. *Annotated Sherlock Holmes*, ed. Baring-Gould, i. 7–8. Cf. Lawrence Rothfield, *Vital Signs: Medical Realism in Nineteenth-Century Fiction* (Princeton, 1992), 142–4.

[41] Knox, *Oedipus at Thebes*, 139–47, p. 139.

[42] Quoted by Knox, *Oedipus at Thebes*, 148.

[43] See e.g. Lloyd, *Magic, Reason and Experience*, 117–22.

[44] Knox, *Oedipus at Thebes*, 149.

[45] *Poetics* 1452a; the Greek source is *Aristotle: 'Poetics'*, ed. D. W. Lucas (Oxford, 1968).

have a more complex history than the latter, varied, as it was, through Ciceronian theories of 'verisimilitude' and the 'probable signs' of post-Renaissance classicism;[46] but, in the course of this philosophical and semantic development—eventually suspending 'probability' between proof, likelihood, and chance—not everything in *eikos* was misrepresented. To say that *Oedipus* is concerned with probability is to mean that it deals with signs as potential proofs of things, each of which may indicate but cannot produce what is represented.

If Christian ideas of guilt and sacrifice are hard to expunge from thoughts about Sophoclean detection, it is still more difficult to compensate for the influence of the Peripatetics. Though Aristotle 'thinks of cause in terms of explanation',[47] he sometimes analyses phenomena with a necessitarian rigour which seems closer to the views of Victorian scientists following Laplace[48] than to Greek tragedy. It is true that, for him, an event (or object) can be marked by what precedes it without the consequent following necessarily, and that signs (*sēmeia*) are often merely probable; they are the stuff of persuasive proof (*pistis*) as well as demonstration (*apodeixis*).[49] As a result, he does not promote the index—the sign as an effect of a cause—into the only clue worth having. On the other hand, when a sign is necessary (*ex anankēs*), like the fever which shows a man to be sick, Aristotle uses that *Oedipus* word for enquiry by tokens and calls it a *tekmērion*. In the *Rhetoric* (1357b) he adds that *tekmar*, in the old language, meant the same as *peras* ('end, limit, boundary'). This suggests how a necessary sign could be thought teleologically as well as logically conclusive.

It clarifies our sense of tragedy, as well as of detective writing, to compare Sophocles' probabilistic use of 'sign', 'proof', and 'cause' with the more Holmesian tenets developed from Aristotle by the Stoics.[50] For in them we find the doctrine that everything has a

---

[46] See e.g. Eden, *Poetic and Legal Fiction*, 115–24, Douglas Lane Patey, *Probability and Literary Form: Philosophic Theory and Literary Practice in the Augustan Age* (Cambridge, 1984), chs. 1–5.
[47] Richard Sorabji, *Necessity, Cause and Blame: Perspectives on Aristotle's Theory* (London, 1980), 69. [48] e.g. *Essai philosophique sur les probabilités* (Paris, 1814), ch. 2.
[49] For contexts see M. F. Burnyeat, 'Enthymeme: Aristotle on the Logic of Persuasion', in David J. Furley and Alexander Nehamas (eds.), *Aristotle's Rhetoric: Philosophical Essays* (Princeton, 1994), 3–55, esp. pp. 31–9.
[50] See esp. M. F. Burnyeat, 'The Origins of Non-Deductive Inference', in Jonathan Barnes *et al.* (eds.), *Science and Speculation: Studies in Hellenistic Theory and Practice* (Cambridge, 1982), 193–238, pp. 206–24.

cause, and that events follow exceptionless regularity,[51] being associated with the idea that 'proof, as serving to reveal a conclusion,
belongs to the genus sign'.[52] The latter has a corollary. As Jonathan
Barnes explains,

> What a sign signifies must be non-evident; but the sign itself must be pre-
> evident . . . But if that is right, then the Stoics cannot allow *sequences* of
> proofs, in which the conclusion of one argument is used as a premiss for the
> next; for any proved proposition will be non-evident, and therefore
> ineligible to appear as a premiss. Stoic proofs, unlike Aristotelian proofs,
> are strongly individualistic: they do not club together to form system-
> atically concatenated demonstrative sciences.[53]

It has been said that tragedy, for Aristotle, 'is a preeminently
rational construct . . . with the syllogism as model'.[54] With hardly
more exaggeration it could be argued that the tragedies of Seneca
exemplify causal necessity through abrupt, revelatory actions which
resemble Stoic proof. These plays are turbid yet fatalistic, punctu-
ated by choruses which spiral away from the tragic foreground to
the wild and elemental, to the living *pneuma* in which the protagonist
is causally meshed. Unable to argue his way out of the inevitable, he
generates a rhetoric of 'menacing fervor',[55] sprawling into lists, cries
of grief, wishful subjunctives, and unanswered appeals.

It follows that Seneca's Oedipus is less a hunter than an object of
pursuit (e.g. 642–6), less a tragic detective than a locus of demonstration. The play begins with *anagnōrisis*, not enquiry. Seneca
replaces the ambiguous communications of the Delphic oracle—
an unreliable source for many in Sophocles' audience, because of its
pro-Spartan pronouncements—with the relentlessly detailed
speeches of Manto (302ff.), describing the inward marks (*signa*) of
ill omen found in a sacrificed heifer. Every hidden part of this beast,
withered, spotted, and monstrous, signifies disaster. Exemplary
rather than diagnostic, the signs show chains of causation working
obscurely through the body of nature. They offer forceful, but
foreshortened, proof. Any lingering doubt about the murder is

---

[51] See e.g. Sorabji, *Necessity, Cause and Blame*, 64, S. Sambursky, *Physics of the Stoics*
(London, 1959), 49–57, and, for sources, Anthony A. Long and David N. Sedley (eds.),
The Hellenistic Philosophers, 2 vols. (Cambridge, 1987), i. 333–43.
[52] The view is reported by Sextus Empiricus, *Outlines of Pyrrhonism*, ed. and tr. R. G.
Bury (London, 1933), ii. 131.   [53] 'Proof Destroyed', 180.
[54] Eden, *Poetic and Legal Fiction*, 53–4.
[55] Thomas G. Rosenmeyer, *Senecan Drama and Stoic Cosmology* (Berkeley, 1989), 190.

removed by a passage in which the spirit of Laius reports his death and desire for vengeance. Here, in other words, is an *Oedipus* to satisfy Voltaire. Individuals are not led to seek coherence by tragic curiosity: the whole weight of the play, its fatalism (e.g. 980–2) and linguistic frustration, stands behind Jocasta when she takes up Oedipus' sword—that sword with which (as she says) her second husband killed her first, his father—and thrusts it into her womb, to expiate, at source, the action of murder and incest. If Sophocles' Oedipus is a detective destroyed by uncertain proofs, and Holmes a figure whose demonstrations establish the form of other people's tragedies, the characters of Seneca are crushed by the necessary burden of tragic 'effects'. Hence, in part, the weight remarked by Polonius, when he says, of the travelling players, '*Sceneca* cannot be too heauy, nor *Plautus* too light[;] for the lawe of writ, and the liberty: these are the only men.' What needs detecting now, is why, in the second quarto of *Hamlet* (F3ʳ), '*Sceneca*' should have that extra 'c'.

*   *   *

During the last few months of the Great War, the Holmes and Watson of Shakespeare scholarship met in the pages of *The Modern Language Review.* In 1917, W. W. Greg published 'Hamlet's Hallucination'. This 'subversive article'[56] deduces, from Claudius' non-reaction to the dumb-show which starts 'The Mousetrap', that the king did not pour poison into Old Hamlet's ear, that the ghost's story was concocted from Hamlet's knowledge of *The Murder of Gonzago*, and that the spirit must be a figment of the prince's imagination.[57] The cunning of Greg's paper lies in its Baker Street coherence. His is the language of positivistic science, setting out to 're-establish the play-scene upon a new and logical basis' (p. 402) and to move from detail to detail until 'Our chain of evidence is complete' (p. 416). Stirred to 'a sort of insanity' by Greg's analysis,[58] John Dover Wilson set about a refutation which, beginning with a reply-article in April 1918, would lead him through Elizabethan ghost-lore into the intricacies of textual bibliography. If Coleridge found himself in Hamlet's melancholy inwardness, Dover Wilson was drawn to his

---

[56] W. W. Greg, *Biographical Notes 1877–1947* (Oxford, 1960), 12.
[57] *Modern Language Review*, 12 (1917), 393–421.
[58] *What Happens in 'Hamlet'* (Cambridge, 1935), 4.

detective intellectualism, his pursuit of the signs of crime. Years later, in dedicating *What Happens in 'Hamlet'* to Greg (1935), he was still identifying with the prince's quest, using imagery of 'the chase' to explain how 'as one clue led on to another, the scent grew stronger and the huntsman more confident that he was on the right trail, until in the end he had run to earth—Shakespeare's own *Hamlet*, as he believes it to be! To the sleuth', he points out, 'important clues are often provided by the most trivial or insignificant details. . . . I started off with the clue you gave me, a little puzzle about . . . the dumb-show' (p. 19).

Critics interested in proof still gravitate to *Hamlet*, and find their way to 'The Mousetrap'. However, the most searching recent discussion—'Hamlet's Burden of Proof' by Stanley Cavell[59]—is representatively marred by a reluctance to establish what 'proof' might have meant to a Renaissance prince. Cavell's thesis is 'that the advent of skepticism as manifested in Descartes' *Meditations* is already in full existence in Shakespeare'.[60] In practice he posits a groundlessness which owes more to philosophical pragmatism than Pyrrhonism. To put it another way: his account of *Hamlet* is vitiated by a failure to mention 'probability'. For Descartes's commitment to quasi-mathematical demonstration makes him unrepresentative of the age. Along with Newton, he stands at odds with that probabilistic revolution which, during the sixteenth and seventeenth centuries, eroded the boundary between late-Aristotelian *scientia* and opinion, substituting degrees of likelihood where the syllogism had reigned supreme, and creating a field of enquiry in which discoveries were made and hypotheses tested by means of repeated experiment.[61] If one were looking for a neglected analogue of 'The Mousetrap', it would be in the experimental practices of probabilistic science. Eager to test the ghost's word and to catch the conscience of the king, Hamlet puts on the kind of 'show' which Boyle and Hooke mounted in their 'houses of experiment' and set up for royalty to watch.[62]

---

[59] In his *Disowning Knowledge in Six Plays of Shakespeare* (Cambridge, 1987), 179–91.

[60] *Disowning Knowledge*, 3.

[61] See e.g. Ian Hacking, *The Emergence of Probability: A Philosophical Study of Early Ideas about Probability, Induction and Statistical Inference* (Cambridge, 1975), Barbara Shapiro, *Probability and Certainty in Seventeenth-Century England: A Study of the Relationships between Natural Science, Religion, History, Law, and Literature* (Princeton, 1983), esp. ch. 2.

[62] See Steven Shapin, 'The House of Experiment in Seventeenth-Century England', *Isis*, 79 (1988), 373–404, p. 402, and the letter by Christopher Wren quoted in Shapin and Simon Schaffer, *Leviathan and the Air-Pump: Hobbes, Boyle, and the Experimental Life* (Princeton, 1985), 31.

Simon Schaffer has already noted the links between vivid rhetorical proof, *evidentia*, and the theatricality of experiment.[63] Whereas Hieronimo stages 'Soliman and Perseda' to reveal to the Spanish court what is known to him and the theatre audience, bringing legal rhetoric to life in a display of evidence which is demonstrative not investigative, Hamlet (matching Kuhn's distinction between early and later patterns of Renaissance experiment)[64] supervises repeated 'trials'—the dumb show followed by Act I of *The Murder of Gonzago*—for the sake of a degree of proof.[65] He stages the inset play, as the Dramaturg in *The Messingkauf Dialogues* (invoking Bacon and Galileo) says that Shakespeare and his company staged *Hamlet* itself, 'in a spirit of experiment'.[66] The effects of the playlet are tested on Claudius, and Hamlet declares himself satisfied—though, as Horatio implies,[67] the experimental findings are ambiguous, and, to the end of the play, it can only be a rational probability for the prince (whatever the absolutes of his heart) that the king killed Old Hamlet. 'Within empiricist schemes of knowledge', writes Steven Shapin, 'the ultimate warrant for a claim to knowledge is an act of witnessing'.[68] Where should a judicious witness stand in Elsinore? Like a seventeenth-century scientist the prince is both inside his experiment (as unofficial chorus, or Lucianus, nephew to the king) and its observer. And the Dr Watson of the piece, the studious and respected Horatio, takes up the role of gentlemanly validator, called upon to authenticate and testify what happens before this audience of 'the Curious'.[69]

Dover Wilson's 'curiosity' was whetted by Hamlet's riddles. No doubt recalling the use in detective fiction of textual scraps, enigmatic maps, and code, he compares such quibbling lines as 'A little more than kin, and less than kind' with 'the problems with which writers of detective stories pose their readers'.[70] Parallels of this sort

[63] 'Self Evidence', *Critical Inquiry*, 18 (1992), 327–62, pp. 328–30.
[64] 'Mathematical versus Experimental Traditions in the Development of Physical Science', in Thomas Kuhn, *The Essential Tension: Selected Studies in Scientific Tradition and Change* (Chicago, 1977), 31–65, p. 43.
[65] On the legal reach of probabilism see Barbara J. Shapiro, *'Beyond Reasonable Doubt' and 'Probable Cause': Historical Perspectives on the Anglo-American Law of Evidence* (Berkeley, 1991).
[66] Bertolt Brecht, *The Messingkauf Dialogues*, tr. John Willett (London, 1965), 60. Cf. Brecht's *Life of Galileo* (1938/43) and, on Bacon, the short story 'Das Experiment', in *Kalendergeschichten* (1948).   [67] II. ii. 290.
[68] 'House of Experiment', 375.   [69] Ibid. 390, 395; 386.
[70] I. ii. 65; *Hamlet*, ed. John Dover Wilson (Cambridge, 1934), p. xl.

were bound to strike a scholar who had tracked through early editions in the manner of Grenfell and Hunt. Dover Wilson's sleuthing among substantives and accidentals enabled him to establish—while admitting that 'Probability is not proof'[71]—that the second quarto of *Hamlet* was set from autograph copy, and to 'vindicate' (as he put it)[72] numbers of its stranger readings. In *The Manuscript of Shakespeare's 'Hamlet'* (1934), he said of his research, 'we are still discoverers and detectives, . . . our quarry is . . . Shakespeare himself' (ii. 176). It was a manhunt considerably eased by observing that Hand D, in *The Book of Sir Thomas More*, had a number of orthographic peculiarities. This hand (patently Shakespeare's) wrote, for instance, 'Scilens' for 'silence'.[73] 'To the sleuth'—Dover Wilson had told Greg—'important clues are often provided by the most trivial or insignificant details.' What, then, could be more telling than the superfluous 'c' in Polonius' '*Sceneca*'?[74] For it is a measure of Holmes's acumen that, at the scene of Jefferson Hope's first murder, where 'RACHE' is written on the wall, he does not just read for the signified but traces effects within the signifier. Inspector Lestrade imagines that the murderer was interrupted while writing 'RACHEL' (pp. 31–2). Holmes knows the German for 'revenge' too well to credit this: so much better in fact, that, from inside the sign, he can distinguish between true and false 'revenge'. As he later points out to Watson (and to any reader not helped by illustrators), the inscription has a capital 'A' deformed to lend a Gothic air and so point to a feud among German political exiles: 'a real German invariably prints in the Latin character' (p. 33). The idea of political murder is a blind, a false trail, what Aristotle calls a paralogism; by discriminating effects, Holmes identifies causes through 'the writing on the wall' (p. 46) as surely as Huxley interpreted 'the writing upon the wall of cliffs at Cromer'.[75]

Oddly enough, Dorothy L. Sayers opts for the same image when she says, of *paralogismos*, 'That word should be written up in letters of gold on the walls of every mystery-monger's study.'[76] What she

---

[71] *The Manuscript of Shakespeare's 'Hamlet' and the Problems of its Transmission*, 2 vols. (Cambridge, 1934), i. 92.   [72] Ibid. 104.

[73] See Alfred W. Pollard *et al.*, *Shakespeare's Hand in the Play of Sir Thomas More* (Cambridge, 1923), 129, 169.   [74] *Manuscript of Shakespeare's 'Hamlet'*, i. 115.

[75] See above, p. 61.

[76] 'Aristotle on Detective Fiction', in her *Unpopular Opinions* (London, 1946), 178–90, p. 185.

values in Aristotle's term is the way it identifies the detective writer's 'art of *framing lies in the right way*': leading the reader, that is, to behave like Lestrade and draw false inferences from sound data. Sayers's lecture, 'Aristotle on Detective Fiction', coincides more than chronologically with Dover Wilson's books on *Hamlet*. The mid-1930s mark the apogee of detective writing because Holmesian science, already threatened in the universities by the quantum mechanics glanced at in Sayers's *Gaudy Night* (1935), was sufficiently established as the 'common sense' of a reading community to frame assumptions about reality within which other generic conventions—the country-house setting, obscure poisons, maids in crisp linen—could take shape. With generic maturity came critical reflection, evident not only in the large claims of Sayers's lecture, but in the tendency of up-market crime-writers to be aware of their Jacobethan precursors, and, far more elaborately than, say, Godwin (who makes tactical use of *Hamlet* and *Macbeth*), to develop a literary reflexivity about murder which makes knowledge of earlier tragedies integral to what is detected and how.

Thus, one of the most successful crime novels of the 1930s, Michael Innes's *Hamlet, Revenge!*, centres on a country-house production of Shakespeare's play which tries out all the latest theories—those of Dover Wilson, Granville-Barker, *et al.*—about Elizabethan inner stages, verse speaking, and acting style. Innes is the pseudonym of the Shakespeare scholar J. I. M. Stewart, and his handling of these matters is, within the limits of what was known, impeccable. Murderous suspense is built up, for instance, by a series of threatening quotations from *Hamlet*, but also, for the sake of bafflement, from *The True Tragedy of Richard III* (that work spouted, in the play-scene, by the prince) and, in the phrase which gives the book its title, the lost Ur-play. This element could become inert, as it does when P. D. James lards *The Skull Beneath the Skin* (1982) with scraps of Webster. But Innes handles his citations so adroitly that it is not surprising to be told that W. W. Greg read *Hamlet, Revenge!* 'again and again' with 'the same kind of scrutiny he gave to the variants in the first quarto of *King Lear*'.[77] More ambitiously, through the figure of the psychologist, Sir Richard Nave, Innes draws on *Hamlet* to meditate on delay and exhibitionism. At his best, Innes fuses Shakespearean ingenuity with the bizarrerie of crime fiction, as

---

[77] J. I. M. Stewart, *Myself and Michael Innes: A Memoir* (London, 1987), 119.

when it is shown that—rather as the action of 'The Mousetrap' opens out into the play of which it is part—Lord Auldearn was shot, in the role of Polonius, just as he was calling for help in the bedchamber scene, ensuring that his cry would be interpreted as the scripted '*Help, help!*',[78] to gratify, and give a margin of safety to, the killer. Yet the cleverest device of all is the book's paralogistic use of *Hamlet*. Inspector Appleby can only resolve the plot when it is realised that, so far from Auldearn's murder being '"long-delayed revenge"' (p. 232), a consummated 'pursuit of vengeance' (p. 295) by the rival of his youth, Professor Malloch, it draws on another strain in Shakespeare: the Polonian theme of spying. After being Lestraded by too narrow a recall of *Hamlet*—by a tendency to reduce it (for the sake of coherence) to a play simply about revenge—the reader learns that the motive for murder lay in a foreign power's desire to seize a document which the statesman carried with him.

This kind of manipulative awareness is most brilliantly exemplified by Cecil Day-Lewis, in the detective novels he published under the pseudonym Nicholas Blake. In *Thou Shell of Death* (1936), for instance, clues are sown for the reader in the use and misappropriation of lines from *The Revenger's Tragedy*. 'Did you ever read any of the post-Elizabethan dramatists?' asks Fergus O'Brien, early in the book: 'Grand stuff. Shakespeare slew his thousands, but Webster slew his tens of thousands. I must say I like the stage littered with corpses at the final curtain. And what poetry! "Doth the silkworm expend her yellow labours."'[79] In a work of domestic realism, a minor slip such as this—ascribing a play attributed to Tourneur[80] to the wrong dramatist, Webster—would no more matter than the exact position of the aspidistra in the drawing-room. Detective fiction of the 1930s, however, is sophisticated enough to sow clues in the field of signs in which it is, itself, written. Much will hang on this Freudian reflex of a character who knows *The Revenger's Tragedy* well—quoting from it more than once—to suggest that he knows it badly. For O'Brien, the glamorous war hero, the natural good-guy of the novel, is covering his plot. Like Vindice, he plans revenge for a long-dead mistress. The title of Day-Lewis's novel not only alludes to the poisoned 'shell' of a nut which carries off one of

---

[78] *Hamlet, Revenge! A Story in Four Parts* (London, 1937), 90.

[79] Nicholas Blake, *Thou Shell of Death* (London, 1936), 58, cf. 190.

[80] The play is now usually given to Middleton, but Blake, like his characters (see 190), follows 1930s wisdom.

the cast but to a memorable speech addressed by Vindice to Gloriana's skull. The denouement of the novel largely consists of the detective, Nigel Strangeways, giving his uncle a tutorial on *The Revenger's Tragedy*, pointing out, by means of quotation and summary, how O'Brien set out to frame his enemy, Edward Cavendish, into seeming his murderer, in order to punish Cavendish for the death, years before, of a young girl destroyed between them for love. In his deft, ingenious way, Blake sustains, throughout the book, this pattern of inference through literary texts to hypotheses which can be solidly 'vindicated'. It may be said, for instance, that the crime was 'solved by a professor of Greek' as well as 'a seventeenth century dramatist' (p. 187) because a crucial trail of footprints— leading towards the scene of the crime, across a freshly snowed-on field, but not back—reminds the professorial intelligence of the tale of Cacus and the oxen (p. 107). Evidently, the suspected murderer emulated the *Ichneutae* and walked away from the place of violence with his shoes on back-to-front.

In Nicholas Blake's finest work, *The Beast Must Die* (1938), the mysteries of *Hamlet* are deployed not only to paralogistic ends but to generate tragic pathos. Prompted by an actual incident in which Day-Lewis's son was almost run over,[81] the novel explores the rage, self-blame, and tenacious sleuthing of a father determined to avenge a child mown down by a hit-and-run driver. In keeping with the work's reflexivity, Frank Cairnes is a successful author of detective fiction who, during his cat-and-mouse game with the guilty driver, George Rattery, claims to be 'working out a very pretty murder—quite my masterpiece, I think'.[82] In fact, such writing as Day-Lewis provides is the journal which makes up the first half of the novel, a document which sufficiently refracts events to baffle the reader, Nigel Strangeways, George Rattery, and, in Hamlet mode, Frank himself, who uses its pages for perplexed soliloquy. Detective fiction often has a parasitic relationship with *Hamlet*. It can hardly be said that Agatha Christie's *Sparkling Cyanide* (1945), for instance, or, indeed, her *Mousetrap* (1954) develop the play they draw on. The journal of Frank Cairnes, however, written through his authorial persona, Felix Lane, perceives, in Shakespear-ean vein, the conflicts which harrow a would-be killer, sees how

[81] Sean Day-Lewis, *C. Day-Lewis: An English Literary Life* (London, 1980), 109.
[82] *The Beast Must Die* (1938; London, 1989), 73.

'slips of the tongue' are likely to betray him (p. 9), and recognizes the power of remembrance—the memory of something so simple as a child's hand clutching a paper bag—to provide an 'importuning ghost' (p. 11). How can the prince's despondency find redemption in revenge? 'A month ago', Felix writes—a little month, no doubt—'when first the idea of killing Martie's murderer began to insinuate itself into my mind, I had no wish to go on living. But my will to live somehow grew strong, as my will to kill flourished' (p. 30).

The most Hamlet-like feature of the diary, however, is the way its moral self-deceptions modulate into paralogism. Rationalizing his motives, Felix not only puzzles his will but interprets his situation through texts in the same way as the Prince of Denmark sifting the Trojan play and *The Murder of Gonzago*. Such precursors can mislead. When he finds himself delaying, Felix writes in his journal: 'just as the lover often procrastinates, not through timidity but to prolong the sweet anticipation of love's fulfilment, so the man who hates wishes to savour his hatred . . . Doesn't it explain, too, the long "indecision" of Hamlet? . . . It would be an agreeable piece of irony for me to write an essay on Hamlet, proposing this theory, when I've finished with George' (p. 66). This is just the clue which Strangeways needs, for the writing on this particular wall cannot for long deceive him. 'Your entry of August the 12th', he tells Felix/Frank at the denouement,

struck me as slightly out of key, you know. You develop a theory about Hamlet's procrastination. You protested too much: it was somehow a little false and literary: it suggested that you wanted to conceal from the imaginary reader the real reason for your own procrastination—that you couldn't bring yourself to kill a man till you were certain of his guilt. That, of course, was the real reason for Hamlet's indecision, too.   (p. 196)

This is beautifully managed, not only in the way 'protested too much'—Gertrude's phrase in the play-scene (III. ii. 230)—marks the detective's inference with the sign of 'literary' authority needed to make the judgement contained by the phrase, but in the way the reading proceeds from just the kind of partiality (*Hamlet*, for Strangeways, is merely a tale from Baker Street) which a detective would be likely to hold—though, as it happens, in this case, with good cause and to consequent effect.

By using a revenger's diary, laden with paternal grief, to convey large stretches of the plot, *The Beast Must Die* catches something of the open-ended pain of loss. Even so, it prefers to concentrate on the directed pleasures of proof. Kafka developed this distinction when he said, of the whole detective genre:

Every second, without noticing we pass by thousands of corpses and crimes. That's the routine of our lives. But if, in spite of habit, something does succeed in surprising us, we have a marvellous sedative in the detective story, which presents every mystery of life as a legally punishable exception. It is—in Ibsen's words—a pillar of society, a starched shirt covering the heartless immorality which nevertheless claims to be bourgeois civilisation.[83]

These words cannot be idle when, every night, on TV, pictures of the starved and murdered enter our living-rooms, and we switch over to Inspector Morse. Detective fiction seems an agent of tragedy—in a century said to lack tragedy through some combination of philosophy and mass atrocity—because of its special corpses, its making each death unique. But the particularity of each death is a 'technical' feat, a matter of signs. What interests us about the corpse in the library is not what it has in common with us, or with general human suffering, but what makes it at least as ingeniously puzzling as all the other corpses in Ngaio Marsh and Ruth Rendell. The body is only a simulacrum of the dead prince of traditional tragedy. Value is drained from death by its belonging to a narrative which claims that deaths can be, somehow, cleared up.

Revenge also implies, in various ways, that deaths can be cleared up. Expiation offers to cancel, to free, even (as blood for the ghosts) to bring the dead back to life. Somewhere in this matrix, where expiation is declared, lies the deepest link between revenge tragedy and detective fiction. The gravitation of Conan Doyle to the sustained effectedness of vengeance helps explain, at the level of plotting, attraction between the genres. So does the retributive role of the detective, given the punitive force of his quest. It is in the heightened attention which both kinds bring to signs, however, that the most vital congruence can be found. I have already noted that the root of revenge is *deik-*, 'indication'. A revenger who (like Hamlet) kills with a goblet and unbaited, venomed rapier, is

[83] Gustav Janouch, *Conversations with Kafka*, tr. Goronwy Rees, 2nd edn. (London, 1971), 133.

exacting punishment precisely by making his violence indicate a message. The marks which he leaves upon Claudius, even that inward trace of poison, are a record of the wrongs—not necessarily those identified by critics[84]—for which the king is punished. Compare the way in which the poisoned first victim of Jefferson Hope, like many another Baker Street corpse, is read by Sherlock Holmes, and then decoded for Watson and his readers. Like a body on the pathologist's table (to recall the medical origins of Holmes's *technē*), the corpse has wounds and odours which, as motivated, caused effects, are perspicuous to diagnosis. Yet the body itself is strangely absent. The awesome yet banal, slumped presence of a corpse, to say nothing of its gore and gristle, resolves into a set of traces. What matters in detective fiction is the length of the razor marks, that smell of almonds about the mouth. Often enough the victim, dead by page 30, has not been previously introduced to the reader, preventing emotional involvement. And we are rarely forced to recognize, as tragedy often makes us recognize, that death works to destroy rather than create physical difference.

Can significance of this sort—imposed on the victims of violent crisis—be considered tragic? If this question probes the generic status of *Hamlet*, it cuts much more deeply against works which, like *Titus Andronicus*, cultivate exacting vengeance (below, pp. 195–200). The impulse to reciprocal signification (A marking B as A was marked) impels rigorous revenge plots towards, and perhaps beyond, the limits of tragedy. Certainly this is the case if one thinks of tragedy as educing complexes of value and meaning from a protagonist's life at a moment of immense loss (usually loss of that life). By comparison with these recognitions, the process of marking and decoding plot-resolving traces from a scene of violence, or a corpse, is a lesser, even a degrading, activity. It is true that, at least in *Hamlet*, a modified tragedy of meaning could be found in the conflict between Claudius' life seeking completeness (rather tenaciously) in its own terms and Hamlet's coherence-seeking desire to make it function as part of the afterlife of his father. But it would then be a virtue of the play that it shows how even a damaged life like Claudius' has enough validity in its incoherence for us not to be able confidently to conclude that to die by violence, and be revenged, or to be murdered for the sake of

---

[84] See below, p. 187.

revenge, is better—from some general perspective—than just to die. It sounds absurd to suggest that it could be. In reduced and 'bourgeois' terms, though, this is what Agatha Christie makes us think: that dying in a library signifies, and that, if human beings are not immortal, they at least belong to a chain which runs unbrokenly before and after. Plots which lead from, and back to, such ends offer satisfactions which tragedy is bound to be drawn to, but which work against it. As Sophocles memorably shows, in his visits to Baker Street, to find much meaning in death is to set about cheapening life.

4. Medea Studies: Euripides to

Pasolini

IN Delacroix's magnificent painting of 1838 (Fig. 1), Medea strides into darkness. Her powerful figure, bare to the waist, is clad in scarlet and black. Sprawling under her arms, protected yet threatened by a dagger, are the two sons she bore to Jason. These are the children she will sacrifice to vengeance, now that Jason has abandoned her. Medea's face is turned in profile. As though in fear of pursuit, she looks back towards a patch of sky which is the only light source on a canvas mostly sunk in the chiaroscuro of a grotto. Thick and firm brush-strokes shape the moulding of her body. But the robe across the back of one child is traced in feathery sweeps, and on the face of the other is the detailed gleam of a tear. Delacroix's technique is eclectic here, from the Rubensesque crown which glints on Medea's forehead to the impressionistic, scumbled brushwork around her feet.

As it happens, the composition is defective. Yet how much does it matter that Medea's stride is askew? Delacroix later insisted that 'the imperfect leg in the *Medea*' shows how 'men of talent are struck by an idea to which everything must be subordinated. Hence the weak parts, which of necessity are sacrificed. It is good luck', he added, 'if the idea is clearly defined at birth, and if it develops itself.'[1] Given the nature of his subject-matter, it is remarkable that Delacroix should characterize creative ruthlessness by talk of birth and sacrifice. Certainly the oil sketch on which the canvas is based—a blaze and whorl of colour—shows a fierce involvement with the 'idea' of this heroine, with the energy of her emergence as much as with the figure itself. Delacroix was 'preoccupied' with Medea 'throughout his working life',[2] and the painting of 1838

---

[1] *The Journal of Eugene Delacroix*, tr. Walter Pach (New York, 1937), 623; entry for 26 Feb. 1858.
[2] Humphrey Wine *et al.*, *Tradition and Revolution in French Art 1700–1880: Paintings and Drawings from Lille*, Catalogue of a National Gallery Exhibition (London, 1993), 116.

points to an intimate identification between the rage of the passionate mother and the artist's experience of his art. In this, Delacroix is not unique. Towards the end of this book, I shall look at what modern feminists have made of the figure of Medea. More immediately, I want to show how, time and again, since Greek antiquity, she has stood for the natural, the magical, and the barbaric in ways which have served to define, by opposition or excited alliance, the operations of (usually male) creativity across a range of media: from drama, through opera, to film.

Not that there is only one story. In the version which reached Delacroix—a devoted classicist—from Euripides, Medea is the Colchian princess who, after helping Jason steal the Golden Fleece, flees the land of her birth and lives with him for ten years. Learning that he will marry the Princess of Corinth (called Glauce by the scholiasts), and that she must go into exile, Medea sends a poisoned robe and crown to her rival—gifts which destroy King Creon as well as his daughter—and then murders both her children, before flying off in the sun god's chariot to continue her career in Athens. Yet in one early account, given by Eumelus (8th c. BC), Medea kills the children in error while trying to give them immortal life. Still more interestingly, Creophylus declares that Medea did not kill her offspring at all. They were murdered, in revenge for Creon's death, by relatives of the king. It was even rumoured in antiquity that Euripides had been paid five talents by citizens of Corinth (enemies of Athens at the time) to pin the crime on Medea.[3] Hence the acerbity of the Down Stage Woman in Tony Harrison's *Medea: A Sex-War Opera* (1985), when she denounces the 'male version' of the myth. The 'true story', she insists, tells of fourteen children, not two, all stoned to death by Corinthians. 'Euripides blackened the woman in his play | because these murderers bribed him. He was in their pay.'[4]

Harrison's opera challenges the bogeywoman image of Medea. Even in Euripides, however, the pressure of alternatives is felt. Early in the play, the Nurse urges the children indoors, away from their mother, because 'I've seen her already blazing her eyes at them | As though she meant some mischief' (92–3). These forebodings can

[3] See *Medea*, ed. Denys L. Page, corr. edn. (Oxford, 1952), pp. xxi–xxv and, more largely, Emily A. McDermott, *Euripides' 'Medea': The Incarnation of Disorder* (University Park, Pa., 1989), 5 ff.
[4] Tony Harrison, *Theatre Works 1973–1985* (1985; Harmondsworth, 1986), 431.

only be reinforced by Medea's cry, on their exit, 'I hate you, | Children of a hateful mother. I curse you | And your father. Let the whole house crash' (112–14). Yet in her emotionally tangled monologue, where vengeful *thumos* debates with solicitude,[5] she leaps beyond confusion and cries, 'No . . . This shall never be, that I should suffer my children | To be the prey of my enemy's insolence' (1059–61). In what sounds like a gesture towards Creophylus' account, Medea persuades herself that fear for her children's safety, after the murder of the princess, forces her to take their lives. Delacroix may not be so explicit, but his ambiguously poised design, which combines the iconography of Charity and her children with the violence of Raphael's *Massacre of the Innocents*,[6] is artfully unbalanced by Medea's backward glance. Pencil sketches survive which show one or more figures in pursuit, coming down towards Medea from the direction of the light. Is it the angry Jason, or a group of Creon's men? Either way, Medea has not simply chosen to take the path into darkness. Drawing her children about her, she flees from male revenge.

If juxtaposing Euripides and Delacroix reveals continuities in the representation of Medea, it also suggests a contrast. One early viewer, Delécluze, praised the 'carnality' of Delacroix's figure, and she reminded Gautier of the actress Rachel, a specialist in passionate roles.[7] For deep cultural, as well as immediately theatrical, reasons, the masked, male performer who played Euripides' heroine in 431 BC will have created a different impression. The point is not that Athens knew nothing of sexual resentment in marriage. Though it is sometimes claimed that relations between husbands and wives were affectively cool in classical Greece, and that jealousy developed only between male partners or between men and courtesans,[8] there is plenty of evidence in poetry, philosophy, and the visual arts to show that those who lived together and

[5] For analysis see Helene Foley, 'Medea's Divided Self', *Classical Antiquity*, 8 (1989), 61–85; on the larger dilemmas of infanticide, distinguishing this Medea from what she (influentially) became in Seneca, see P. E. Easterling, 'The Infanticide in Euripides' *Medea*', *Yale Classical Studies*, 25 (1977), 177–91.

[6] René Huyghe, *Delacroix, ou le combat solitaire* (Paris, 1964), 348–9, Jack J. Spector, 'Delacroix's "Fatal Mother": "Medea Killing Her Children"', *Arts Magazine*, 55 (1981), 156–60, pp. 157–8, Lee Johnson, *The Paintings of Eugène Delacroix: A Critical Catalogue*, 6 vols. (Oxford, 1981–9), iii. 80.   [7] Johnson, *Paintings of Eugène Delacroix*, iii. 80.

[8] e.g. Elaine Fantham, 'ΖΗΛΟΤΥΠΙΑ: A Brief Excursion into Sex, Violence, and Literary History', *Phoenix*, 40 (1986), 45–57.

had children, like Jason and Medea, were capable of passionate attachment and savage alienation.[9] The author of *Andromache* and *Electra* knew about female jealousy.[10] In *Medea*, however, he explores the question, 'Is [loss of the marriage bed] so small a pain, do you think, for a woman?' (1368; cf. 263–6, 1354–5) through a rage which owes more to Ajax, denied the armour of Achilles, than to the abandoned sexuality of Delacroix's heroine.

Alert to what Medea shares with the warriors of Homer and Sophocles, Elizabeth Bryson Bongie points out that, when she is betrayed, she complains of an 'insult . . . to her honour, not to her heart. She does not call on the gods to witness that Jason has broken her heart, but rather that he has broken his oaths. She wants him and his new bride utterly destroyed because they have treated her unjustly.'[11] Euripides' use of *timē*, *dikē*, and their cognates is indeed pointed enough to ensure that 'honour' and 'retribution' leave their mark on translations of this play. What Bongie fails to notice, though, is how those terms relate. For *timē* already contains an impulse towards reciprocity. As well as 'honour', it means 'worth, price', leading to 'value, estimation' and 'compensation, reward'. In legal use, *timē* can be an '*estimate of damages* done: hence, *penalty, punishment*'.[12] Ancient Greek makes no sharp distinction between revenge and the honour retributed. This colours *Medea* not least by shadowing crucial passages with a sense that language is dishonoured by broken reciprocity. When the Oxford editor calls the vocabulary of Jason's vengeful prayer against Medea 'dignified and uncommon',[13] he is responding only to the surface of a request that *Dikē*, 'justice, Requitor of blood', punish the child-killer. As Medea scathingly replies, 'What heavenly power lends an ear | To a breaker of oaths, a deceiver?' (1390–2).

Bongie discounts the notion that Medea is 'a jealous wife seeking revenge'. As she reads Euripides' play, the honour-fixated heroine does not conduct herself as we should expect 'a jealous wife' to

---

[9] Cf. David Cohen, *Law, Sexuality, and Society: The Enforcement of Morals in Classical Athens* (Cambridge, 1991), esp. 167–8.

[10] See e.g. *Andromache*, 181–2, 465–70, and *Electra*, 1030–40.

[11] 'Heroic Elements in the *Medea* of Euripides', *Transactions of the American Philological Association*, 107 (1977), 27–56, p. 35; cf. Bernard Knox, 'The *Medea* of Euripides', repr. in *Word and Action: Essays on Ancient Theater* (Baltimore, 1979), 295–322.

[12] Henry George Liddell and Robert Scott, *Greek-English Lexicon*, 9th edn., rev. Sir Henry Stuart Jones, with a supplement by E. A. Barber *et al.* (Oxford, 1968).

[13] *Medea*, ed. Page, 179.

behave, and 'Jealousy and lust, of course, are universal and timeless emotions'.[14] This is rash in several ways. Semantically it is so because, even in our own tongue, 'envy' and 'jealousy' are intuitively different yet hard to separate, and between them they seem overlappingly to divide the range of feelings depicted in *Medea*. The resentments of this heroine cannot be placed in a single modern category. Historically, indeed, as philology helps us see, emotions are construed variously through time, and the Greek words most often translated as 'jealousy', *phthonos* and *zēlotupia*, shift during the classical period (as they do, again, in Christian usage, where *zēlos* takes on positive connotations of 'zeal'). Aristotle, for instance, formalizes a distinction between *phthonos* as negative envy and *zēlos* as emulation. So influential was his account of those passions (*Rhetoric*, 1387b-1388b) that the operation of jealousy tended to be differently understood after the fourth century BC.

Moreover, a key assertion in his text—'the ambitious are more envious (*phthoneroteroi*) than the unambitious' (1387b)—shows the history of *phthonos* to be entwined with that of *timē*. Aristotle's word for 'the ambitious', 'hoi philotimoi', 'those who love *timē*', can mean 'those who are jealous', and, as Peter Walcot observes, in the best book on the topic, this is more than a semantic quirk, in that 'envy is related to the concept of honour and so an integral part of the Greek value system'.[15] You did not need to be a Sophoclean hero to be jealous (in this sense) of your honour. The status of ancient Athenians, like that of many people in present-day Mediterranean peasant societies,[16] was bound up with their *timē*, and injury (or *hubris*) involved damage to reputation.[17] Near the start of *Works and Days*, in a passage often echoed in antiquity, Hesiod says, 'neighbour vies with (*zēloi*) his neighbour as he hurries after wealth. . . . And potter is angry with potter, and craftsman with craftsman, and beggar is jealous (*phthoneei*) of beggar, and minstrel of minstrel.'[18] Strife of this sort was perceived as ubiqui-

---

[14] 'Heroic Elements in the *Medea* of Euripides', 46.

[15] *Envy and the Greeks: A Study of Human Behaviour* (Warminster, 1978), 21.

[16] See e.g. J. G. Peristiany (ed.), *Honour and Shame* (London, 1965), Anton Blok, 'Rams and Billy-Goats: A Key to the Mediterranean Code of Honour', *Man*, NS 16 (1981), 427–40, David D. Gilmore (ed.), *Honor and Shame and the Unity of the Mediterranean* (Washington, DC, 1987).

[17] See e.g. Nick Fisher, 'The Law of *Hubris* in Athens', and Oswyn Murray, 'The Solonian Law of *Hubris*', in Paul Cartledge, Paul Millett, and Stephen Todd (eds.), *Nomos: Essays in Athenian Law, Politics and Society* (Cambridge, 1990), 123–38, 139–45.

[18] Lines 23–6, in *The Homeric Hymns and Homerica*, ed. and tr. Hugh G. Evelyn-White, rev. edn. (London, 1936).

and, though potentially fractious, desirable:[19] a principle spurring individuals to achievement.

Even the *Medea*, as a drama, was caught up in emulation. Like almost all the tragedies which survive from the fifth century, it was presented in competition at the Great Dionysia, and poet was jealous of poet when it came to the award of prizes. It was thus a nice irony of Aristophanes to give Euripides the opening line of this play about 'hoi philotimoi' to quote as his proud, first example in the contest staged in *The Frogs* (1382). Against Aeschylus's verse from the lost *Philoctetes*, he sets the Nurse's exclamation of regret that the Argo flew through the waves to Colchis. Certainly his tragedy as a whole, in detail as well as largely, is interested in *phthonos* and *zēlos*. Given what has been established about *timē*, it must be so concerned, as inevitably as with *dikē*. When the Nurse, shortly after the passage quoted by Aristophanes, seeks information from the Tutor, she says 'me phthonei phrasai'—literally, 'don't envy me a reply' (63). This is as integral to the play's texture[20] as Medea's deceitfully telling Creon, 'Nor do I grudge it you (*phthonō*) that your affairs go well' (312). What spurs the heroine to revenge is the *phthonos* endured by *philotimoi* when they lose status by rejection. This pain is the more acute for her being forced to recognize that Jason's marriage to the princess may well—as he almost double-bluffingly claims (551–65)—have less to do with appetite than with acquiring honour and status. Nor is jealousy of this sort simply radiated out to others. The fact that Medea no longer attracts envy, is no longer honoured as Jason's wife (e.g. 1144), is partly what makes her malicious. At lines 241–3 she says that, if women organize their lives 'carefully, | And the husband lives with us and lightly bears his yoke, | Then life is enviable (*zēlōtos*)'. And at 1032–5 she reflects that, if she kills her children, they will not be there to lay her out, and she will not enjoy the satisfaction (even though dead) of having people envy ('zēlōton') her those sons.

Delacroix wanted to be the envy of the art-world, and his involvement with Medea and her tragedy might well have been driven by a reverence for, and despair at, the kinds of 'sacrifice' which such eminence required. Yet his determination to be counted among 'men of talent' did not entail the view that envy was essential

---

[19] 'This Strife (*Eris*) is wholesome for men'; *Works and Days*, 24.
[20] *Pace* Walcot, *Envy and the Greeks*, 3.

to human life. According to the ancient attitude shared by Medea, by contrast, unless one is both jealous of honour and the object of envy one lacks human worth and credit. The consequence of this attitude is risk. As various scholars—most astutely, Bernard Williams[21]—have pointed out, much Greek thought recognizes more willingly than post-Kantian morality that a successful life is likely to be vulnerable to factors beyond individual control. I shall explore the general implications of this for revenge tragedy in Chapter 14. For now it is enough to notice that a paradigmatic example of such a life going wrong would be Medea's, if we concede that Euripides—with typical provocativeness—has founded her glamorous marriage on betrayal (of her father), theft (of the Golden Fleece), and, in a crime which the dramatist circumstantially worsened, murder (of her brother). The tragedy of Medea flows from the zeal with which she embraced risk in order to achieve status and happiness (since, in helping Jason, she left herself without protective family and homeland), and, more immediately, from her life's heightened openness—by virtue of its being an eminent life—to the jealousy which is a measure of its success.

To throw this into relief, Euripides registers a contrary view. This philosophy advocates diminishing risk. It is maintained by the Nurse, when, after Medea's cry, 'Let the whole house crash' (114), she broods on the irascibility of the great, and says:

> How much better to have been accustomed
> To live on equal terms with one's neighbours.
> *I* would like to be safe and grow old in a
> Humble way. What is moderate sounds best,
> Also in practice *is* best for everyone.
> Greatness brings no profit to people.
> God indeed, when in anger, brings
> Greater ruin to great men's houses.   (122–30)

Virtuous moderation is mixed, here, with ignoble praise of obscurity, and the whole, slightly unpalatable recipe is underwritten by talk of divine envy. Unlike Aeschylus, Euripides rarely (and only with irony) builds this concept into the fabric of his plays, and at this point there is a distinct impression that fear of human malice towards the successful is being projected into a supernatural

---

[21] See esp. *Ethics and the Limits of Philosophy* (London, 1985), chs. 1 and 10.

realm. Medea identifies the same resentment when, in a spirit of manipulative bitterness, she protests that she should not be prevented from staying a little longer in Corinth just because she has the reputation of being intelligent. 'A person of sense ought never to have his children | Brought up to be more clever than the average', she tells Creon, 'For. . . It will make them objects of envy (*phthonon*)' (294–7). Jealousy of this sort might be what one wants, but it brings the risk of exile:

> And if you are thought superior to those who have
> Some reputation for learning, you will become hated.
> I have some knowledge myself of how this happens;
> For being clever, I find that some will envy (*epiphthonos*) me,
> Others object to me. (300–4)

How does this relate to revenge? One innovative account of envy in contemporary Mediterranean societies is entitled *Gifts and Poison*.[22] There is an involving analysis of prestation in North India called *The Poison in the Gift*.[23] Behind both lies Marcel Mauss's perception[24] that the doubleness of *Gift* in Germanic languages (at once 'donation' and 'poison')—a volatility shared by the benign/destructive implications of Greek *pharmakon, philtron*, and Latin *venenum*—indicates a universal ambivalence. It is possible to indulge vindictiveness by acts of generosity[25] because the obligations imposed by a gift can be as disabling as a dose of arsenic. In a society dominated by *timē*, the 'honour-bound' are likely to be oppressed by what they receive. Hence the nature and the vehicle of Medea's vengeance. 'Such poison will I lay', she says, 'upon the gifts I send' (using one of those two-sided words for poison): 'toioisde chrisō pharmakois dorēmata' (789). It is true that the robe and crown are emblems of wicked ingenuity. When an audience sees them placed in the hands of Medea's children, for delivery to court, it will recall the cunning feared by Creon which is enshrined in the heroine's name (*medomai*, 'devise').[26] Then it might

---

[22] F. G. Bailey (ed.), *Gifts and Poison: The Politics of Reputation* (Oxford, 1971).

[23] Gloria Goodwin Raheja, *The Poison in the Gift: Ritual, Prestation, and the Dominant Caste in a North Indian Village* (Chicago, 1988).

[24] Marcel Mauss, *The Gift*, tr. Ian Cunnison, corr. edn. (London, 1969), 127 n. 101.

[25] On the psychological piquancy of 'benevolent vengeance'—at a revealing cultural remove from Greek tragedy—see George Eliot, *The Mill on the Floss*, ed. Gordon S. Haight (Oxford, 1980), 251–3.

[26] Cf. Mary R. Lefkowitz, *Women in Greek Myth* (London, 1986), 124.

moralize and wonder whether Medea snares the princess through her vanity, as the Messenger later hints (1156–66). Developing this strain in the story, in Charpentier's opera of 1694, Créuse[27] explicitly envies Medea's robe and Jason is persuaded to acquire it (I. ii). She has a musically and visually splendid entry in Medea's garment (IV. ii) before the poison takes effect. Recalling those nineteenth-century French novels in which women throw vitriol at their rivals,[28] a modern audience might even interpret the gift as a way of making literal an envious desire to destroy 'the setting of [the princess's] eyes . . . the shapeliness of her face' (1197–8). All of these frames of reference are relevant, but none is particularly helpful if *timē* is neglected.

This is so because *philotimos* meant more than 'honour-loving' and 'enviable': it signified 'munificent, generous' and, as a neuter plural, 'gifts'. When this is borne in mind, *Medea* emerges as a tragedy built on deeply held ancient values realized in celebratory and vindictive gift-giving. For Creon to refuse the offerings would be for him to break a social grammar; it would humiliate Medea by denying her the one manifestation of honourable munificence (i.e. *philotimia*) which, in her envy-reduced state, remains open to her; and it would damage Creon's status by suggesting that he and his daughter are too weak to sustain (and thus to deserve) the honour of this tribute. By inflicting an injury through a benefit, Medea raises a principle with large consequences for revenge tragedy (as Chapter 5 will show). She also exploits the economy which makes the agents of vengeance, A and B, resemble one other. Clad in Medea's gown, the rival who ousts Medea is physically ravaged by poison as the heroine is torn by *phthonos*. In the most ambitious modern version of the myth, Pasolini makes visible use of this motif by having the princess, in Medea's robes, look, in cinematic long shot, just like Medea. He has the avenger dream of the newly gowned princess literally bursting into flames, while we see her, not much less painfully, leaping to her death, inwardly aflame with guilt at having taken Jason. Later in this chapter, I shall examine Pasolini's film more closely, because it represents, in various ways, a bold and

[27] Creusa, rather than Glauce, is the princess's name in versions which follow Seneca's *Medea*.
[28] See Ruth Harris, *Murders and Madness: Medicine, Law, and Society in the Fin de Siècle* (Oxford, 1989), ch. 6, and cf. Joëlle Guillais, *Crimes of Passion: Dramas of Private Life in Nineteenth-Century France*, tr. Jane Dunnett (Cambridge, 1990), esp. 148–9.

insightful development of the ancient tragedy. Before going to the movies, however, it is necessary to think harder about the attire of Euripides' heroine.

*　　*　　*

The earliest surviving picture of Medea's Corinthian adventures is very different from Delacroix's. On a vase decorated by the Policoro Painter (c. 400 BC), Medea stands in the snake-drawn chariot of her grandfather, the sun-god Helios, with flaring robes and an oriental cap (Figs. 2–3). Below lie the bodies of her children, mourned by a kneeling Tutor. Jason rushes in from the right, a hastily snatched gown in one hand, in the other an ineffectual sword. The tomb in which this vase was found contained others with dramatic subjects, and it may have been the burial-place of a poet or an actor.[29] Whatever the profession of the dead man, the Painter seems to have drawn on his own theatrical knowledge. For in Euripides' play there is no mention of serpents pulling the chariot of Helios, and no indication that Medea wears a Colchian cap. Stage practice, it would seem, suggested those features of the vase, just as Medea's robe owes much to the garb of tragic actors. Certainly the Painter has chosen to depict a memorable *coup de théâtre*: the point at which Euripides'[30] theme places such a strain on tragedy that the limits of his medium are tested. At first a type of abused womanhood, sided with by the Chorus, Medea rises through violence to claim the divinity of her lineage, taking command of the flying stage machine, the *mēchanē*, reserved for gods. The tables of sympathy are not turned, exactly, in the final tableau, but Jason's shabby ordinariness will always strike audiences as less threatening than the fierce phenomenon in the sky.

This denouement is an affront to those who want to believe that the heavens punish murder, and many attempts have been made to defuse the problem which Euripides, so characteristically,[31] bequeathed. Corneille, for instance, in an epistle prefacing his *Médée*, admitted that 'here you will find crime in its triumphal

---

[29] A. D. Trendall and T. B. L. Webster, *Illustrations of Greek Drama* (London, 1971), 96.

[30] For convincing argument in favour of Euripides as source (against e.g. Neophron), see Oliver Taplin, *Comic Angels and Other Approaches to Greek Drama through Vase-Paintings* (Oxford, 1993), 22–3.

[31] For similarly provocative uses of the *mēchanē* in his revenge drama see the judgments of Apollo in the *Orestes* (1625 ff.) and Dionysus near the end of the *Bacchae*.

chariot' but tried to placate didacticism by comparing poetry to painting. Just as the latter can produce beautiful portraits of an ugly woman, so the former may confront audiences with attractive imitations of an action which should not be emulated. It is not witnessing the punishment of wickedness which deters us from evil deeds but seeing its ugliness finely displayed. As though to demonstrate the weakness of this defence, later writers and artists (including Delacroix) found Corneille's Médée alluring. During the Romantic period, the serpentine heroine acquired that cruel, corrupted beauty which can be found in Coleridge's snake-like Geraldine and Swinburne's Cleopatra.[32] When Gautier compared Delacroix's Medea to Rachel, he relished her 'expression vipérine'.[33] This ambivalence has persisted into our own time. In Samuel Barber's ballet suite, *The Serpent Heart*, for example, Medea is associated with chromatic slithers which are seductive as well as chilling. For all that, however, and despite sympathetic feminist retellings of the myth (see Chapter 13), most Greek scholars now read Euripides' play in an oddly neoclassical spirit. There is a moralistic desire to find Medea repellent, and *punished*. The trick is either to invoke a version of the story with an ending which seems retributive—such as Anouilh's, in which Medea kills herself—and imply that it realizes what is latent in the Greek,[34] or to argue that even in Euripides, 'The granddaughter of Helios may stand in triumph on her dragon chariot, but Medea the woman is dead.'[35]

As well as placating the moralist, a suicidal Medea has expressive possibilities. She allows Euripides' harsh ending to be appropriated by remorse. A succession of pathetical Medeas runs from Ovid's *Heroides* to Chaucer's *Legend of Good Women*; but her distresses were hugely elaborated by Romantic dramatists such as Grillparzer,[36] and a suicidal heroine achieved full scope in Cherubini's *opéra tragique* of 1797. His *Medea* is a work of extraordinary energy and grace. Its third act, in particular, is full of musical and dramatic brilliancies—as when the motif of serpentine motherhood is varied and Medea, suppressing her tenderness (lullingly sustained by

---

[32] On the type, see Mario Praz, *The Romantic Agony*, tr. Angus Davidson, 2nd edn. (Oxford, 1951), ch. 4.   [33] Johnson, *Paintings of Eugène Delacroix*, iii. 80.
[34] Jennifer March, 'Euripides the Misogynist?', in Anton Powell (ed.), *Euripides, Women, and Sexuality* (London, 1990), 32–75, p. 43.
[35] Eilhard Schlesinger, 'On Euripides' *Medea*', in Segal (ed.), *Euripides: A Collection of Critical Essays*, 70–89, p. 89.   [36] See e.g. the close of Act III of his *Medea*.

strings), cries to the children, 'Snakes, leave me alone! | Do not embrace me, you strangle me!'[37] In Cherubini the principles of Corneillean honour, already far-removed from *timē*, achieve fresh poignancy. Medea's self-destruction comes from anger against the world, but also from that ultimately reflexive dynamic of jealous despair which Stendhal (writing of feminine passion) characterizes in *De l'amour*: 'You kill yourself to avenge your honour.'[38] Before she shuts herself in the blazing temple, promising to meet Jason on the banks of the Styx, this Medea soars between plangency and imprecation in a thrilling display of virtuosity, while her husband and the citizens of Corinth howl for blood. Part of us is bound to be with them, because music urges such a crescendo that death is the only way forward left by the score. Here suicide defies a call for vengeance, yet surreptitiously fulfils a desire for it.

Other versions of the act are possible. When Virgil's Dido, for example, abandoned by her lover, utters a copious final prayer before stabbing herself on the funeral pyre,[39] the rhetorical abundance is symptomatic of a typically feminine predicament: grievance, thwarted by powerlessness, displaced into heightened language.[40] But the reader's sympathy must be modified by an awareness that her hatred is given wings and barbs by her death. It was an ancient belief that the curses of the dying were potent,[41] and the animosity which Dido predicts between Carthage and Rome does indeed come about. Classicists have long recognized that Dido's curse is shaped by Ariadne's imprecations against Theseus in Catullus 64, and that both are influenced by Medea's outcry against Jason, in Apollonius Rhodius' *Argonautica*: 'may my avenging Furies (*Erinues*) forthwith drive thee from thy country, for all that I have suffered through thy cruelty!'[42] As Richard C. Monti points out, however, 'Medea and Ariadne wish to requite their lovers eye for eye and tooth for tooth, no more no less. . . . The same sense of strict justice prevails in Dido's curse of Aeneas.'[43] In

---

[37] Libretto by F. B. Hoffman, tr. Mária Steiner, accompanying Lamberto Gardelli's recording with Sass, Luchetti, Kováts, etc., the Hungarian Radio and TV Chorus, and the Budapest Symphony Orchestra (1978).

[38] *Love*, tr. Gilbert and Suzanne Sale (London, 1957), 118n.

[39] *Aeneid* IV. 607–29, 651–62.

[40] 'Woman's poor revenge . . . dwells but in the tongue,' as Webster's Vittoria puts it; *The White Devil*, ed. John Russell Brown, 2nd edn. (London, 1966), III. ii. 283–4.

[41] See e.g. Lindsay Watson, *Arae: The Curse Poetry of Antiquity* (Leeds, 1991), 27.

[42] *The Argonautica*, ed. and tr. R. C. Seaton (London, 1912), IV. 385–7.

[43] Richard C. Monti, *The Dido Episode and 'The Aeneid': Roman Social and Political Values in the Epic* (Leiden, 1981), 59–60.

effect, Dido contrives a *revenge* suicide. There is a less than inverse
relation between her end and that of Euripides' Medea: a chariot-
borne imprecator,[44] transformed, as Gilbert Murray once put it,
'into a sort of living Curse'.[45]

Quoting Dido, Hélène Cixous places her—along with Medea
(and Ariadne)—in a line of moping women. 'All history is thus
troubled with her incessant moanings,' she writes,

> which insist, die down, come up again, always unheard. For it is a question
> of life or death for her.
> An endless choir swollen by sobs and silences, breathless gasps, hysterics'
> coughs.
> That is the origin of opera. And I say that only men capable of that
> emission, those tormented ones who give in to their femininity, can love
> opera.[46]

Cixous is vague about where the female might be concealed when
male images of feminine grief compose the 'gasps' and 'coughs'
(thinking of *La Traviata*) from which opera, apparently, originates.
This particular account, or myth, of musical creativity does not
pause to wonder how much torment is likely for men—not much,
we might assume—who identify with a femininity which is largely
of their own fabrication. A less charitable view of 'the origin of
opera' would stress, instead, its tendency to push vindictive (or just
fiercely faithful) female characters into self-destruction. As the
Down Stage Woman in Harrison sings, shedding light on Cherubini's reworking of Euripides,

> Remember when you hear her cries
> and the MEDEA you see before you fries
> a man's the cause,
> though women in their last death-throes
> have always drawn male fans' bravos
> and fags' applause! . . .
>
> Tosca, Carmen, Butterfly,
> it seems all women do is die
> in music drama. (p. 369)

This might be an extract from Catherine Clément's *Opera, or the*

[44] See e.g. lines 112–14, 607–8, 976–88, 1333.
[45] *Medea*, tr. Gilbert Murray (Oxford, 1910), p. xi.
[46] From 'Sorties', in Hélène Cixous and Catherine Clément, *The Newly Born Woman*, tr.
Betsy Wing (Minneapolis, 1986), 63–132, p. 107.

Undoing of Women, where it is argued that, in opera, women 'suffer, they cry, they die. Singing and wasting your breath can be the same thing.'[47] The diva who receives her accolade may not be in voice for long, but for now she is vulnerably set apart because identified (through her roles) with death. Her alterity is not just marked by such names as 'Tosca' and 'Butterfly'. As Clément notes: 'Malibran, Callas, Caballé, Sontag. . . . Strange, foreign names. The prima donna comes from somewhere else, as if exile were necessary for her to become famous' (p. 30).

This recalls the Policoro vase. For Medea's Colchian cap, though less visually striking than the dragon-chariot, is of immense significance. Euripides' predecessor, Eumelus, seeking (it would seem) to support Corinthian claims to Black Sea territory,[48] had represented Aeëtes, Medea's father, as a Corinthian who emigrated to the East. Eumelus' Medea returned to govern Corinth and remained essentially Greek. Euripides, by contrast, stressed his heroine's Colchian background, and, if the vase-painting can be trusted, had her dressed, at least in the finale, as a foreigner. His tragedy may not centre on cultural conflict with the same firmness as, say, Henri René Lenormand's *Asie* (1932), where Jason is a French colonialist returning home with an Indo-Chinese princess, or Elisabeth Bouchaud's *Médée* (1993), in which the racism facing North Africans in Paris is imaged in the hostility of Jason's mother, who denies Greek citizenship to her son's partner and thus (without the existence of a rival) precipitates infanticide. But Euripides is partly responsible for such works as Lenormand's and Bouchaud's because he was interested in the combination of weakness and threatening strangeness which Medea's barbarian identity brings. Jason may smugly inform his wife that he has enabled her to 'inhabit a Greek land and understand our ways, | How to live by law instead of the sweet will of force' (537–8). Medea's exotic drugs, however, and the 'overbearing nature' with which she sweeps aside civic rationality,[49] show her scarcely to have internalized Greek values.

* * *

[47] Catherine Clément, *Opera, or the Undoing of Women*, tr. Betsy Wing (London, 1989), 11.
[48] See Robert Drews, 'The Earliest Greek Settlements on the Black Sea', *Journal of Hellenic Studies*, 96 (1976), 18–31, esp. p. 19.
[49] Edith Hall, *Inventing the Barbarian: Greek Self-Definition Through Tragedy* (Oxford, 1989), 203.

Among the singers listed by Clément, the great Medea was, of course, Maria Callas. It was her command of *bel canto* which brought Cherubini's opera back into the repertoire. She sang the role repeatedly, and, even after years of vocal decline, Medea remained important to her. One of Callas's final undertakings was to act the part of Euripides' tragic heroine in Pasolini's film. The strength and persistence of this connection has led many admirers to regard her as, in some way, embodying Medea. Clément protests that Callas is 'figured and disfigured, eternally confused with her heroines' by men (p. 28). Neither sex, however, has enjoyed a monopoly on the tangling of life and art which has helped make Callas seem Medea. The singer's friend, Margherita Wallmann, for instance, pointing to her life as a wanderer, an exile, and her capacity 'to cut long-held ties' and go on, says that 'Medea inspired Maria very deeply. She identified with the role.'[50] More racily, opportunistically, even absurdly, Arianna Stassinopoulos's *Maria* constructs Callas's life as revenge tragedy.[51] The reader is told that the young Maria learned how 'to exchange blow for metaphorical blow' (p. 17), that 'Resentment and anger . . . became a reservoir, almost a quality of her being, lurking in her eyes, circulating in her blood' (p. 24), and that, performing Cherubini shortly after she had been fired by the Met, 'That night Maria *was* Medèa, singing out much of the fury' (p. 164). It is even hinted that the abortion which Aristotle Onassis talked Callas into, not long before he took up with that American princess, Jackie Kennedy (p. 239), must have seemed like infanticide. Having produced the paradigm, Stassinopoulos can announce that, when Callas was offered the lead in Pasolini's film, 'Maria recognized the parallels, and through Medea she could relive her own story' (p. 256).

Callas resisted being equated with Medea in her own person,[52] but her technique as an artist did involve a greater degree of identification with roles than had been true of earlier singers. The savage dieting which ultimately reduced her vocal power began as an attempt to fit her body to the shape of Medea. She found her face 'too fat' for the part, unable to convey 'certain very hard phrases, cruel phrases or tense phrases'.[53] And she was willing

---

[50] John Ardoin, *Callas: The Art and the Life* (London, 1974), 64–5.

[51] *Maria: Beyond the Callas Legend* (London, 1980).

[52] See e.g. the interview with Kenneth Harris, *The Observer*, 8 and 15 Feb. 1970, repr. in David A. Lowe (ed.), *Callas As They Saw Her* (London, 1987), 55–64, p. 57.

[53] Quoted by Stassinopoulos, *Maria*, 96.

to invoke the ethos of Medea when explaining how to perform Cherubini. Teaching 'Dei tuoi figli' from Act I, she told students: 'This aria is a killer. . . . Before you try to sing it, plan it out carefully, cold-bloodedly. . . . If you sing the whole aria as big as its climaxes, you are dead.'[54] You would be dead, musically speaking, two hours before the moment came. Callas invested so much in Medea's scheming and violence that it became natural for her to express through the role her often antagonistic relations with the public. On her return to La Scala in 1961, for instance, when hissing broke out in the auditorium, she paused between the first and second cry of 'Crudel!' which Medea throws at Jason in Act I, turned directly to the audience, and delivered the rebuke at them.[55] Again, in the last *Medea* she sang in Milan, 'At the moment of the famous phrase "Ho dato tutto a te," Maria moved directly forward on the stage and sang that avowal, her eyes fixed on the audience, instead of addressing herself to Jason.'[56]

Clément exempts Pasolini from her attack on Callas's male admirers (p. 28). In some ways this is just. His response to the singer's being 'a stranger . . . a wanderer', was even more sympathetic than Euripides' to Medea because he felt able to associate Callas with those peasant societies which he saw being desecrated by capitalism. Pasolini's *Medea* (1970) begins with a disquisition on the anti-naturalistic mind-set of archaic cultures, delivered by the Centaur who is bringing up young Jason. 'All is sacred' he says (in the subtitles), 'There is nothing natural in nature; remember that. When nature seems natural to you, all will be finished and something else will begin.' Explaining how, 'in the ancient world, myths and rituals are living reality', the Centaur tells the growing, more rationalistic Jason that he will find that world in Colchis. Then the film cuts sharply to the sunbaked landscape of Goreme, in Turkey. Medea's people drive goats and tend patches of intensely green crops among domes, spires, and walls of rock, pocked-marked with scooped-out dwellings. This is a world, it seems, still close to the origins of tragedy. When Colchians fertilize the fields, it is by means of blood sacrifice and in the guise of a masked, tragic chorus (Fig. 4). We first see Callas in close up, contemplating a young man about to

[54] John Ardoin, *Callas at Julliard: The Master Classes* (London, 1988), 39.

[55] Stassinopoulos, *Maria*, 205–6.

[56] Sergio Segalini, 'Singing Rediscovered', in Lowe (ed.), *Callas As They Saw Her*, 115–22, p. 122.

be ritually slaughtered. Crowned with shoots of grain, he is publicly decapitated and dismembered to the accompaniment of eery ululations and sporadic clapping. Pasolini retrieves from behind Euripides' tragedy the Medea visible in Eumelus: the sorceress reputedly able to 'bring about rebirth and rejuvenation by killing and cutting in pieces'.[57]

It is more than usually difficult to say whether Pasolini's 'ancient world' signifies a lost and valuable part of our own past, because his idea of Colchis is shaped by Mircea Eliade's *The Myth of the Eternal Return*, and a culture devoted to Eliadean rituals of recurrence has no concept of time linear enough for it to belong to history. 'The barbarians that I depict are always outside history, they are never *historical*', Pasolini explained: 'In my films, barbarism is always symbolic: it represents the ideal moment of mankind.'[58] Medea represents 'barbarism' in that sense, and her tragedy, in this film, lies in the confusion which follows her fall into history, with its secular reasoning, after her liaison with Jason. The difference between their worlds is caught by another rapid cut, from the Colchian royal family grouped in a rock-carved room to a loose line of Argonauts extended across an open plain. Jason and his followers represent logicality and relaxed purposefulness. The silence and calm of Colchis contrast with his humour and mischief (he laughs, he whistles, his men are brigands). The Argonauts have no fear of the gods, and they accept the Golden Fleece from Medea without qualms. When they reach land after fleeing Colchis they casually make camp; but Medea (who has been reading Eliade) cries: 'This place will sink, because it has no foundation. You do not call God's blessing on your tents. You speak not to God, you do not seek the centre, you do not mark the centre. Look for a tree, a post, a stone.'[59] That the place does not in fact sink is only her first taste of how ancient belief can be flouted. She experiences what the Centaur calls 'spiritual catastrophe'.

Almost from the outset—in Aeschylus' *Oresteia*—revenge tragedy has celebrated and questioned 'the ancient concept of progress'.[60]

[57] Carl Kerényi, *The Heroes of the Greeks*, tr. H. J. Rose (London, 1959), 273.

[58] 'Interview with Michel Maingois', *Zoom* (Oct. 1974), 24; quoted in Naomi Greene, *Pier Paolo Pasolini: Cinema as Heresy* (Princeton, 1990), 129.

[59] Cf. 'The Symbolism of the Center' and 'Repetition of the Cosmogony', in Mircea Eliade, *The Myth of the Eternal Return*, tr. Willard R. Trask (London, 1955), 12–21.

[60] See the title-essay in E. R. Dodds, *The Ancient Concept of Progress and Other Essays on Greek Literature and Belief* (Oxford, 1973).

Hamlet moves from the high feudalism of the old king's combats with the Polacks to the mercenary, gunpowder-and-diplomacy ethos of Claudius and young Fortinbras. When, in Faulkner's *The Unvanquished*, Bayard Sartoris faces down the attorney, B. J. Redmond, without firing a shot, he signals not only the end of one feud but a transition from the values of the Old South. This makes it the less surprising that, as a romantic Marxist, nostalgic for an 'ancient world' of peasant solidarity, Pasolini should have been attracted to the genre. Indeed, the film which he shot just before *Medea*—the *Appunti per una Orestiade africana*—examines, with help from Aeschylus, a clash between traditional African culture and the Western-style bureaucratic society which threatened its existence. It was heresy on the Left, at the time, to be so critical of post-colonial Black Africa; but the distress at the quashing of archaic values which animates Pasolini's revenge films squares with his repeated charge that the Italian Communist Party had become complicit with consumerism. The casting of Callas as Medea helped enforce his critique because she already signified for audiences both barbaric strangeness *and* cultural prestige.

That raises the question, however, of whether Clément is right to clear Pasolini of confusion between woman and opera-image. 'In my films', he said,

I do not use representation. If I want to show a tree, I show a real tree. The actor is no different. He is himself. With Maria Callas, her personal qualities fascinated me. I see Callas as a modern woman in whom dwells an ancient woman—strange, magical, with terrible inner conflicts. These I tried to capture in *Medea*.[61]

This shows Pasolini attempting, with limited success, to out-argue the structuralists on film theory.[62] In defence of his own aesthetic, he instantiates (like Delacroix) an image of Medea—in this case, one whose vengeful, ancient strangeness is not represented, arbitrarily, by an actress, but embodied in a Callas who replicates the part she plays. '*Medea*', the posters announced: 'It's a movie about a woman who beheads her brother, stabs her children and sends her

[61] Quoted in Ardoin, *Callas: The Art and the Life*, 257; cf. Pasolini's remarks in Jack Buckley, 'An Ancient Woman', *Opera News*, 13 Dec. 1969, 8–13, p. 11.
[62] Cf. e.g. 'The End of the Avant-Garde', in his *Heretical Empiricism*, ed. Louise K. Barnett, tr. Ben Lawton and Louise K. Barnett (Bloomington, Ind., 1988), 121–41, pp. 133–4.

lover's wife up in flames. For Maria Callas, it's a natural.'[63] Clément has overlooked the extent to which Pasolini's empathy with the singer went along with an extreme version of that appropriation which she complains of in others.

Pasolini's view of film history resembles, in telescoped form, his idea of cultural development. After a brief phase of early twentieth-century experimentation, he says, cinema

underwent a rather foreseeable and inevitable desecration. In other words, all its irrational, oneiric, elemental, and barbarous elements were forced below the level of consciousness; that is, they were exploited as unconscious elements of shock and persuasion. A whole narrative convention—which fueled useless and pseudo-critical comparisons with the theater and the novel—was rapidly built upon this hypnotic '*monstrum*' which always constitutes a film.[64]

Medea tries to roll back the tide, to recover the foundation, present-ing (especially in the Colchian scenes) an almost pre-talkies movie, orchestrated with reeds and horns. As in Euripides, and Greek tragedy generally, the barbaric is defined against rationality and language.[65] Pasolini's historical thesis explains his double-layered characters. When the Centaur visits Jason in Corinth, for instance, he is at first a four-legged creature—a 'monstrous' *monstrum* as well as a 'portent'—and then, to all appearances, human. The latter, though, contains the former. Jason, he explains, has 'known two' centaurs: 'A sacred one, when you were a boy. A desecrated one, when you were a man. But the sacred is preserved within the desecrated.'

If this makes the Centaur sound suspiciously like a personification of modern cinema, the same holds, more forcefully, for Medea. The revival of her barbarous identity through violence, after the lapse into Corinthian rationalism, figures out in a myth of revenge what Pasolini hoped his own creativity would bring to cinema, as surely as the passion of Delacroix's Medea images *his* beliefs about the importance of the 'idea' in art. Thus, the film opens with an atmospheric shot of the sun spilling light across an undesecrated

---

[63] Ardoin, *Callas: The Art and the Life*, 257.

[64] 'Il cinema di poesia', tr. as 'The "Cinema of Poetry"', in *Heretical Empiricism*, ed. Barnett, 167–86, p. 172, though I prefer to follow, here, the translation given by Greene, *Pier Paolo Pasolini*, 112–13.

[65] Hall, *Inventing the Barbarian*, 199–200.

MEDEA STUDIES: EURIPIDES TO PASOLINI 107

landscape. This is a vision of primitive reality but also of the grounds of film itself, for, as Pasolini once said, 'In essence cinema is a question of the sun.'[66] Medea's descent from Helios is a sign of her privileged relationship with the medium which presents her. Moreover, it is revenge tragedy that, by reviving 'barbaric' violence, reasserts this reflexive relationship after she has gone to Corinth. When urged to act against Jason, Medea initially resists. 'I have become someone else', she tells her women: 'What was reality is no longer reality.' But she then retreats to her chamber, slumps into sleep or trance, and dreams that vision of the sun over which the film's titles had rolled. This repetition awakens her. She is roused to the sight and sound of the sun, her grandfather, shining through her window. Helios prompts her to put on Colchian attire, to gather her women and chant, 'O Light of the Sun! . . . I shall have a just revenge.' Interestingly, this sequence begins with a breach of filmic convention. Pasolini has turned his camera directly towards the sun, and the spread of honeyed, reddened light is partly produced by distortion in the lens. The moment of exposure to the source is simultaneously a disclosure, a revelation, of the cinematic machine. It is a distant but suggestive equivalent of that moment in Euripides when the rules are frighteningly broken by the vengeful Medea's elevation to the *mēchanē*, the chariot of the sun.

Pasolini believed that the 'hypnotic "*monstrum*"' could be communicated through 'free indirect discourse'.[67] Just as the camera should avoid taking up the stance of an omniscient narrator (a technique which creates the effect of naturalism), so it should shun the perspective of characters (implying the presence of guiding consciousnesses). The lens should observe things seen by agents without quoting their point of view. This quasi-dramatic procedure—we might think, again, of Euripides—is a feature of many of his films, but the effect in *Medea* is remarkable because at odds with what cinema usually does with jealous sight. Jealousy has from earliest times been associated with seeing. The Greek verb, *baskainein*, for instance, can mean 'to be jealous' but also, more sinisterly, 'to bewitch by the evil eye'. 'Envy' is from Latin *invidere*, which contains *videre*, 'to see'. Cinema provides the technology for collectivizing fascination,[68] and, in stories of tragic jealousy, the

---

[66] Quoted by Greene, *Pier Paolo Pasolini*, 21.

[67] 'The "Cinema of Poetry"', 175–8; for discussion see Greene, *Pier Paolo Pasolini*, 113 ff.

[68] Cf. *fascinare*, 'to bewitch or control with a look'.

camera typically quotes the possessive agent's line of sight. In *Medea* this effect is modified because so many of Pasolini's close-ups convey an impersonal, barbaric attention to and faith in objects. Medea's regard of Jason can be vigilant (she looks even while he sleeps), but because her point of view is not the lens's it does not register as acquisitive. While filming *Medea* Pasolini became obsessed with Callas's face,[69] yet his camera-work acknowledges the impervious, mask-like qualities of her visage, the estranged, more operatic than cinematically manipulable cast of her bearing in barbaric costume (Figs. 5–6).

Jealousy, as modernity understands it, is a narrative passion. The manic eye finds plots involving the desired object on every side, conspiracies against itself. It is symptomatic that Alain Robbe-Grillet, wanting to analyse the indifference of the material world to human emotion, found his way to the theme. In his novel *La Jalousie* (1957), the protagonist, who behaves like a camera, is notated through what he sees, and so narratively connects, in a closed (almost Racinian) set of windows, chairs, a veranda. There is a hugely repetitive yet fluctuating account of visual minutiae (curls of hair, a lizard on the hand-rail), all recorded in ways which deprive them of significance by foregrounding how the observer processes them into plots. In shots communicating Pasolini's 'hypnotic "*monstrum*"', by contrast, the camera resists narrative. The film is no more driven by the diegetic mania of sexual jealousy than is Euripides' drama. Exchanges are broken by counter-subjective cuts and shifts of angle. At what should be the height of plot excitement, as Glauce puts on the enchanted robe, the camera stops to gaze at water-melons on a pavement, whole and segmented. The audience is not invited to translate this into a symbol of the princess, or of anything else. The objects are simply there, part of the same world as Glauce; their substantiality is poetic. 'My fetishistic love for the "things" of the world keeps me from considering them as natural,' Pasolini said: 'It does not link them in a proper flow, it doesn't accept this flow. But it isolates and idolizes them, more or less intensely, one by one.'[70]

What is usually called revenge was a perfect subject for Pasolini because the repetitiveness which makes it narratively potent can

---

[69] Cf. the sketches he drew of her face, in wine, oil, vinegar, and coffee grounds; Enzo Siciliano, *Pasolini*, tr. John Shepley (London, 1987), 333.   [70] Ibid. 302.

also obstruct 'flow'. The two almost identical versions of Glauce's death, for instance (above, p. 96), initially puzzle the viewer: they thwart a narrative advance. In the same way, when that opening shot of the sun returns, or when the viewer recognizes in Medea's decapitation and dismemberment of her brother, as she helps the Argonauts flee, a recapitulation of the human sacrifice at Colchis, there is a barbarous absence of 'flow' which exalts events towards that state of recurrence which, according to Eliade, is found by primitive peoples in the circulation of heavenly bodies. In this sense, Pasolini did not think of Medea's story as belonging to revenge tragedy at all, because the genre distinguishes its equivalent acts of violence by time as much as by agency (B's striking A after A struck B makes it vengeance). He thought of the myth as transcending that rationalistic teleology—and, implicitly, as establishing a congruence between violent recurrence and the energies of primitive-Marxist revolution. 'What makes Medea kill is not born from a spasm of vengeance or hate or passion,' he says: 'Rather, her crazed and criminal actions assume the significance of a flight from a world that is not hers and in which she can no longer live. For Medea and her race, death is not an end, but only a prelude to rebirth in another world. So her faith spurs her on to killing her children so that they all may return in regeneration.'[71]

The thought is quietly frightening: it challenges deep assumptions about the sanctity of children's lives and the pathos of their deaths. As I show in Chapter 13, recent versions of the Medea story tend to regard infanticide as a taboo which should not be broken but may have to be. Feminist writers bring out the cost to the mother of killing children, *and* of raising them; they can even (as in Toni Morrison's *Beloved*) make us see how mothers might think of children as being better off dead; but they do not present infanticide as atavistically redemptive. It is true that, in Euripides, Medea speaks lines which have a Pasoliniesque timbre: 'I wish you happiness,' she tells her children, 'but not here in this world. | What is here your father took' (1073–4). These sentiments are placed, however, by a tragedy which, out of its concern with munificence and gift-giving, can think of children as gifts from heaven, and of killing them as a huge affront to how gods interact with the world. The exchange between Aegeus and Medea does more than estab-

---

[71] Quoted by Ardoin, *Callas: The Art and the Life*, 362.

lish a safe haven for her in Athens, and thus encourage murder. Aegeus has gone to consult Apollo's oracle because he is childless, in need of heirs. Vellacott's translation of what Medea says when she promises him help with drugs (the benign side of her skill with *pharmaka*), 'So may the gods *grant* you fertility,' is less accurate than Chicago's 'So may your love, with God's help, lead to the bearing | Of children' (714–15), but it responds to something in the play, much as, later, when translating the Chorus's lines about children as blessings or burdens, or as dying young by the will of the gods, he renders 'glukeron blastēma', 'The sweet *gift* of children' (1099).[72]

Medea's sons are gifts from the gods not least because they descend from Helios. That is why her violently perverse escape on the sun-divinity's chariot made such a strong impression on the Policoro Painter. It continues to appal today because Christian thinking about children—formed by the birth of Samuel (1 Sam. 1: 11), by Psalm 127, and the mystery of the incarnation—encourages us, still, to think of them as gifts sent down from heaven. Modern rewritings of Medea may discount the blasphemy of infanticide, but they think of child-murder as challenging an order of things so deeply rooted in our culture as to seem God-given. In Pasolini, by contrast, rage and horror climax in Medea's burning of the palace and her last exchange with Jason. What might have been the crisis of the film—the infanticide—is worked into a calm domestic ritual of bathing and putting the children to bed. Only a close-up of a blood-stained knife on stone shows that Medea's children do not lie asleep. The slow yet unsuspenseful style of shooting, here as throughout, forces the audience to witness events through 'barbaric' eyes, and to understand how, as Eliade puts it, 'Like the mystic, like the religious man in general, the primitive lives in a continual present.'[73] In Pasolini's *Medea*, Euripides' drama of *timē* becomes a drama of time. A revenge plot undoes modernity, establishing a 'regeneration of time' (Eliade's phrase)[74] in the space before history starts.

---

[72] '*Medea*' *and Other Plays* (Harmondsworth, 1963), 39, 51; my italics.
[73] *Myth of the Eternal Return*, 86.   [74] Ibid.

5. Of Anger:

Seneca, Milton, Shakespeare

JASPER HEYWOOD was not satisfied with Seneca's *Thyestes*. Translating the play in 1560, he reproduced its action and sought to catch in fourteeners the point and flow of its Latin. But he added some remarkable material. In Seneca, Atreus lures his brother, Thyestes, to Argos with promises of joint rule, only to eviscerate, dismember, and cook Thyestes' children and feed them to their father in revenge for his seduction of Atreus's queen. The tragedy ends abruptly, in a knot of triumph and guilt. Heywood disentangled this denouement by adding a final scene in which Thyestes denounces himself as a criminal and demands that he be punished. 'Let torments all of hell', he cries, 'Now fall upon this hateful head that hath deserv'd them well!'[1] The privations which afflict Tantalus in the underworld should be imposed on Thyestes, his grandson. The vultures which tear the guts of Tityus should come and rend his stomach. When 'foulest fiends' fail to arrive, Thyestes invokes divine anger. He will hasten round the globe, he says, in pursuit of the 'skies' which flee him, 'And on your wrath for right reward to due deserts will call. | Ye scape not fro me so, ye gods: still after you I go | And vengeance ask on wicked wight your thunderbolt to throw!' (60–2).

These appeals are not without precedent. When Seneca's Atreus reveals what his brother has eaten, Thyestes calls on Jupiter to ravage the blighted world, or at least destroy his child-consuming body, with thunderbolts. He then curses Atreus. 'The gods will be present to avenge', he cries: 'to them for punishment prayers deliver thee.'[2] There is a significant difference, however, between this terse outburst against pollution and the Elizabethan Thyestes' call for

---

[1] *Thyestes*, tr. Jasper Heywood, ed. Joost Daalder (London, 1982), v. iv. 23–4.
[2] 'Vindices aderunt dei; | his puniendum vota te tradunt mea'; *Thyestes*, 1110–11, in *Seneca: Tragedies*, ed. and tr. Frank Justus Miller, 2 vols., rev. edn. (London, 1929).

punitive 'wrath'. Encouraged by the Stoic doctrine of *sumpatheia*, which holds that different parts of the universe interact harmoniously, Senecan tragedy presents a natural order which convulses with horror at human perversion.[3] That is why, when Thyestes devours his children, the stars and planets go awry and darkness covers the day (784 ff.). Such an outlook does not, however, mean that nature is governed by divine anger. In Stoic thought the Godhead is not passionate and cannot be swayed by curses. Seneca's philosophical work, indeed, tends to subsume the divine into nature and subjects both to causal fatalism.[4] The Heywood who translated *Thyestes* was, by contrast, so ardent a Christian that, within months of completing his version, he had joined the Society of Jesus. This is what motivates his ending. Christian eschatology makes him vary Seneca. He respects just prayer, and shares the same impulse as his protagonist to submit horrible actions to divine wrath.

Heywood's approval of anger in the heavens is replicated, more uneasily, at the human level. In the closing lines of his prologue, he describes how he urged the Fury of Seneca's first scene to 'Inspire' his 'pen', only to find himself possessed:

> My hair stood up, I waxed wood, my sinews all did shake,
> And as the Fury had me vex'd my teeth began to ache.
> And thus enflam'd with force of her, I said it should be done,
> And down I sat with pen in hand, and thus my verse begun.
>
> (339–42)

History does not record the state of Heywood's dental health in 1560, but it does appear that, after a wild and unstable youth, he was troubled by visits from fiends.[5] There may, in other words, be personal experiences behind the encounter with *furor poeticus*. Autobiography can hardly rationalize, however, the clash between this prologue and what the Fury represents in the translation proper: a destructive spirit of ire which drives Thyestes and Atreus to disaster. These conceptual awkwardnesses are not restricted to *Thyestes*. When Heywood translated Seneca's *Troades*, for instance, he added an entry for the spirit of Achilles (the first vengeful ghost of Tudor

---

[3] See e.g. Rosenmeyer, *Senecan Drama and Stoic Cosmology*, ch. 4.
[4] See e.g. *De providentia*, 5. 7–8, and cf. above, pp. 75–6.
[5] See John J. O'Keefe, 'An Analysis of Jasper Heywood's Translation of Seneca's *Troas, Thyestes*, and *Hercules Furens*', Loyola University of Chicago, Ph.D. (1974), 12, 14, 42.

FIG. 1. Eugène Delacroix, *Medea* (1838). Reproduced by permission of the Musée des Beaux-Arts de Lille.

FIGS. 2–3. Policoro Painter, *Medea* (*c.*400 BC). Reproduced by permission of the Museo Nazionale della Siritide.

Fig. 4. Pasolini, *Medea* (1970). Reproduced by permission of Pandora distribution, Paris.

FIG. 5. Pasolini, *Medea* (1970). Reproduced by permission of Pandora distribution, Paris.

FIG. 6. Pasolini, *Medea* (1970). Reproduced by permission of Pandora distribution, Paris.

FIG. 7. 'Two Years for Fan Who Bit Off Police Dog's Ear', *The Sun*, 27 October 1987. Reproduced by permission of *The Sun*.

FIG. 8. Henry Peacham (?), drawing of *Titus Andronicus* (c.1595), Longleat Portland Papers, 1, fo. 159ᵛ. Reproduced by permission of the Marquis of Bath.

The Lamentable and Tragical History of *Titus Andronicus*.

With the fall of his five and twenty Sons in the Wars of *Goths*, with the manner of his Daughter *Lavinia* by the Empresses two Sons, through the means of a bloody Moor; taken by the Sword of *Titus*, in the War; his revenge upon their cruel and inhuman Act.

To the Tune of, *Fortune my Foe*.

Fɪɢ. 9. From *The Lamentable and Tragical History of Titus Andronicus* (broadside ballad, printed *c.*1655–65). Reproduced by permission of the British Library (Huth 50 (69)).

revenge tragedy). Where Seneca's Achilles is briefly irate, Heywood's expansively threatens 'the furies wrath' against the Greeks, and warns of 'iust vengeance' on what the translator (in a betrayingly Christian turn of phrase) calls 'the yrefull day'.[6] Heywood wants to develop in his characters a human version of divine ire. Believing that the gods are above anger, Seneca thinks that men should be so too.

Such clashes and failures of accommodation derive from a divergence, in late antiquity, between classical thinking about anger and the views of the Christian church. In the *Rhetoric*, Aristotle defined anger (*orgē*) as 'a longing, accompanied by pain, for a real or apparent revenge (*timōria*) for a real or apparent slight . . . when such a slight is undeserved' (1378a). Seneca acknowledged the link between anger and revenge, but challenged the morality of both. Approving divine wrath and, by extension, just rage in man, the Fathers of the Church (notably Aquinas) proved sympathetic to Aristotle. Scriptural sources and Aristotelian arguments came to dominate European thinking about ire. But Senecan arguments revived during the age of Shakespeare and Milton, and a certain amount of turbulence—as Heywood amply demonstrates—was caused by the elision of Christian and Stoic views.[7] In this chapter I shall explore these divergent traditions, and suggest that some of our own uncertainties about anger go back to their confluence at the Renaissance. Since broad changes are more in question than shifts of argument in the schools, literary works will loom as large as philosophical and religious texts. I shall look at plays and at poems, but also, finally, at cursing. This follows aptly from Heywood's *Thyestes*, given that, when he added the final scene, he adapted a series of maledictions from another Senecan tragedy—the *Hippolytus*—in order to associate anger with something like passionate prayer.

Though Seneca, in the *De ira*, broadly accepts Aristotle's association of anger with vengeance (I. iii. 3), he denies that rage can be useful (I. ix. 1–2). Far from being 'a spur to virtue', as the Peripa-

---

[6] Quoting the text in *Jasper Heywood and his Translations of Seneca's 'Troas', 'Thyestes' and 'Hercules Furens'*, ed. H. de Vocht (Louvain, 1913), II. 1.

[7] For contexts see e.g. Leontine Zanta, *La Renaissance du stoicisme au xvie siècle* (Paris, 1914), Jason Lewis Saunders, *Justus Lipsius: The Philosophy of Renaissance Stoicism* (New York, 1955), Günter Abel, *Stoizismus und frühe Neuzeit* (Berlin, 1978).

tetics maintain, anger reduces a man to 'an utter monster'. Think of such a person

when he is enraged against a fellow-man, with what fury he rushes on working destruction—destructive of himself as well and wrecking what cannot be sunk unless he sinks with it. Tell me, then, will any one call the man sane who, just as if seized by a hurricane, does not walk but is driven along, and is at the mercy of a raging demon, who entrusts not his revenge (*ultio*) to another, but himself exacts it, and thus, bloodthirsty alike in purpose and in deed, becomes the murderer of those persons who are dearest and the destroyer of those things for which, when lost, he is destined ere long to weep?[8]

Seneca is often terse, but here his mobile syntax—dramatically delaying 'destroyer', 'carnifex', in the Latin, as though to a moment of horrible recognition[9]—is driven by what it describes. As the prose sweeps along, the man whose passion destroys others himself becomes its victim—rather as, in *Thyestes*, Atreus is spurred to revenge by 'a raging demon' (i.e. the Fury) and left with the empty glory of wishing his crime had been worse (1056–7). The thrusting energy of the passage dramatizes the Senecan belief that *furor* is both anger and insanity.

Seneca's reaction against Aristotle does not make him picture the mind as entirely at the mercy of anger. He regards *ira* as consequent on the experience of registering an injury and therefore the action 'of a mind proceeding to revenge by choice and determination' (II. iii. 5). A dualistic urge, partly derived from Posidonius, to speak of the enslavement of reason by passion (e.g. I. vii. 3–4) is thus modified by the early Stoic belief that 'passion and reason are only the transformation of the mind toward the better or worse' (I. viii. 3). This makes for a supple model of psychology, one which preserves Aristotle's insistence on the cognitive dimension of the emotions while identifying internal oscillations between reason and impulsive rage. Equally significant, however, is Seneca's account of the relations between revenge (*ultio*) and punishment (*poena*). Though the former is in the foreground of his analysis, he recognizes its affinity with *talio*[10] and repeatedly writes of *poena*. The socio-political reach

---

[8] III. iii. 1–3, in *Moral Essays*, ed. and tr. John W. Basore, 3 vols. (London, 1928–35).

[9] 'Quid ergo? Sanum hunc aliquis vocat, qui velut tempestate correptus non it sed agitur et furenti malo servit, nec mandat ultionem suam, sed ipse eius exactor animo simul ac manu saevit carissimorum eorumque quae mox amissa fleturus est carnifex?'

[10] e.g. II. xxxii. 1. On *talio* as repayment in kind, full retribution, under the law, see above, p. 22.

of *poena*—extending from 'revenge' through 'quit-money' to legal
sentencing—allows him to develop what is, in effect, the most
comprehensive attack on retributive punishment to be found
before the Enlightenment.

The attack has several prongs. Making a Stoic appeal to nature,
Seneca denies that it is natural for anger to incite punishment, for
'human life is founded on kindness and concord' (I. iv. 3). Since
'Man's nature . . . does not crave vengeance', ire cannot 'accord
with man's nature, because anger craves vengeance (*poena*)' (I. vi. 5).
Morever, according to Plato, '"The good man . . . does no injury."
Punishment injures; therefore punishment is not consistent with
good' (I. vi. 5). In practice Seneca admits retribution in his eagerness to resist anger. If a good man sees his father murdered and
mother raped, 'he will not be angry, but he will avenge them (*sed
vindicabit*)' (I. xii. 1). He even concedes that revenge might be worth
taking if it were expedient, but points out (with the acumen of a
Roman politician) that it usually involves pointless risk. In any case,
'the really great mind, the mind that has taken the true measure of
itself, fails to revenge injury . . . because it fails to perceive it' (III. v.
7–8). Early Christians equated this philosophical detachment with
moral sloth. Seneca's persuasiveness comes, however, from his
counsel of invulnerability being grounded in a keen awareness of
man's exposure to the pains of life. When Emily Dickinson writes,
'Mine Enemy is growing old— | I have at last Revenge',[11] she
strikes a Senecan note. To be ill, to age, to die: these are not
blessings. 'Can you wish for the victim of your wrath a greater ill
than death?' Seneca asks, 'Even though you do not move a finger,
he will die' (III. xliii. 3).

Above all, Seneca identifies a link between vengeance and excess.
Much revenge tragedy is structured by grim equivalence. As I noted
in Chapter 1, when a character such as Chettle's Hoffman is
murdered under a red-hot crown for having murdered someone
under a red-hot crown, there is a morally piquant reversal and a
strongly closed ending. Yet how plausible is the psychology on which
that sort of scheme is based? Reprisals are not automatically
limited, given that many people find it easier to return injuries
than to receive them, and given that, despite the principle of
equivalence, there is a residual asymmetry between A's blow and

---

[11] *The Complete Poems of Emily Dickinson*, ed. Thomas H. Johnson (London, 1970), 634.

B's retaliation (in that the former is unprovoked and asks for several blows in return).[12] Even if an angry person were inclined only to reciprocate, would his or her response be measured against how what had been inflicted struck a contemporary or how it struck the revenger? The latter brings into play all sorts of variables—partly because of body chemistry, whether one is thinking of Galen on choler or Albert F. Ax arguing that anger is produced by secretions of epinephrine plus norepinephrine,[13] but partly, too, because people do different things and have memories, so that, in the most obvious way, a revenger's reaction will chain up with all sorts of characteristic hurts and deprivations. Wrathful revenge must be compound, no matter how simplifying it may feel to be infuriated. When Jimmy Porter (for instance) looks back in anger, the vengeance given scope in his marriage to Alison ('Oh yes. Some people do actually marry for revenge. People like Jimmy, anyway'),[14] cannot be traced to distinct sources. The experience of nursing his father, wounded in the Spanish Civil War, blurs into the death of Hugh's Mum and the fact that English Sundays are boring. If there were an answer to what motivates his rage, he would not be so thoroughly irate, so evidently looking to be vindictive in the hope that his revenges might show him what he is angry about.

The oblique and abrupt ending of *Thyestes* is right for a tragedy of anger which does without grim equivalence. True, Seneca is not averse to some gnomic signalling of aptness. Thyestes is punished through his children, for instance, so that his brother can force him to recognize that, since adultery left Atreus unsure of his heirs' paternity, the very fact of Thyestes' children being Thyestes' made them peculiarly killable. That is the gist of the elliptical exchange,

THYESTES What was my children's sin?
ATREUS That they were thine.
THYESTES Sons to the father—
ATREUS Yea, and what gives me joy, surely thy sons.[15]

---

[12] On the antiquity of this see e.g. Hesiod, *Works and Days*, 709–11.
[13] See e.g. Carol Tavris, *Anger: The Misunderstood Emotion*, rev. edn. (New York, 1989), 86–7.   [14] John Osborne, *Look Back in Anger* (1957; London, 1960), 67.
[15] THYESTES Quid liberi meruere?
    ATREVS Quod fuerant tui.
    THYESTES Natos parenti——
    ATREVS Fateor et, quot me iuvat,
    certos. (1100–2).

But Atreus's answer feels so impressively loaded because it is inadequate. Instead of a defining equivalence, there is excess. Aristotle regards 'Gentleness' (i.e. moderate anger) as a mean between irascibility and want of spirit.[16] Seneca responds by saying that, if something is unnatural and bad for you, then to have a modest amount of it cannot be ideal: it is simply better than having a lot of it (I. xiii. 1–2). His stronger, recurrent reply, though, is that anger, as a passion, knows no mean. Control has to come from something that is not anger. Because a Fury governs *Thyestes*, the motif of abandoned moderation, of unfixed limits, ubiquitous in Senecan drama, is enormously prominent. Her injunction, 'and mean of ire procure there may be none' (I. 26 in Heywood's translation), determines the shape of the action. From Atreus's self-urging boast, 'Crimes thou dost not avenge (*non ulcisceris*), save as thou dost surpass them' (195–6), to his late rebuke to his brother, 'Crimes should have limit, when the crime is wrought, not when repaid (*non ubi reponas*)' (1052–3), the play is true to *De ira* by subjecting characters not to God's wrath but to passionate urges beyond moderation which leave them in 'frantic tumult . . . hurried I know not whither, but . . . hurried on' (260–2).

*   *   *

Arguments against *De ira* were advanced in pagan antiquity, but the first extensive criticism came from the Christian convert, Lactantius (b. AD 250/60). In general, late Stoicism proved attractive to early Christians. That embattled Father of the Church, Tertullian, calls Seneca 'often one of us'.[17] However, Lactantius saw the difficulty of reconciling Scripture with a Stoic resistance to anger. It was not that he accepted the Aristotelian alternative systematically approved by Aquinas. He granted that there was in human nature a desire to repay pain with pain, but he regarded this *furor* or *iracundia* as an unjust form of anger which man should not indulge and which God (being above human aggravation) could not experience. What both God and man could and should experience was ire in the form of a punitive reaction against wrong. 'Anger', according

---

[16] *Nicomachean Ethics*, 1108a, on *praotēs*.
[17] Quoted by A. A. Long, *Hellenistic Philosophy: Stoics, Epicureans, Sceptics* (London, 1974), 236.

to Lactantius, 'is an emotion of the mind arousing itself for the restraining of faults.'[18]

Lactantius was keen to defend just ire because God is so often enraged in Scripture. Aquinas would later argue that references such as that in Psalm 106 ('Therefore was the wrath of the Lord kindled against his people' (v. 40)) are metaphorical. 'Anger and the like are ascribed to God by a metaphor drawn from their effects', he wrote: 'For it is characteristic of anger that it stimulates men to requite wrong. Divine retribution is therefore metaphorically termed anger.'[19] Modern scholarship is less inclined to generalize, finding different modes and stages of wrath operating in the Bible.[20] At times, in the earliest parts of the Old Testament, God's anger appears unaccountable; it just breaks out, and can be appeased by offerings (e.g. Num. 22: 22, 1 Sam. 26: 19). More often, as in Psalm 106, wrath is the response of a personal God to betrayal by the chosen people. Before the Babylonian exile wrath is rarely pro-claimed against the Gentiles, because God's dealings with the nations are not of the same close nature as those involving the children of Israel. But his actions against, for instance, Phar-aoh—bringing down the plagues of Egypt (Exodus 7–12)—can be seen as expressions of anger against a stubborn enemy. This pattern becomes standard in later books of the Old Testament. 'The Lord revengeth, and is furious; the Lord will take vengeance on his adversaries, and he reserveth wrath for his enemies.' These uncompromising assurances from Nahum against Nineveh (1: 2) introduce some of the most spectacular images of divine retribu-tion—'The mountains quake at him, and the hills melt' (1: 5)—in Scripture.

Biblical accounts of divine wrath have an affinity with revenge tragedy. They show wrongdoers being smitten by that heavenly punishment announced in Deuteronomy[21] which, in post-classical literature, avengers often claim to be exacting (on God's behalf) against individuals. Yet relations between an all-powerful Deity and

[18] *A Treatise on the Anger of God, Addressed to Donatus*, in *The Works of Lactantius*, tr. William Fletcher, 2 vols. (Edinburgh, 1871), ii. 1–48, p. 36.
[19] I q. 3 a. 2, in *Summa Theologiæ*, gen. ed. and tr. Thomas Gilby, 61 vols. (London, 1964–81); cf. I q. 59 a. 4 and I q. 19 a. 11.
[20] See e.g. Hermann Kleinknecht *et al.*, *Wrath*, tr. Dorothea M. Barton (London, 1964), Singer (gen. ed.), *Jewish Encyclopedia*, under 'Anger', Colin Brown, ed., *New International Dictionary of New Testament Theology*, 3 vols. (Exeter, 1975–8), under 'Anger, Wrath'.
[21] Cf. above, p. 23, below, p. 120.

an entire people make for structures of action and suffering quite different from those to be found in the agonistic writing which descends from classical Athens to Seneca. When they represent single omnipotence and multiple human frailty, A and B become incommensurable. Imagine what Greek tragedy would make of, for example, those Egyptian plagues. Moses would be the obvious protagonist, yet how could his encounter with the burning bush hope to persuade an Athenian audience? A chorus of Hebrews might seem desirable, but what then could be done with the race of blighted Egyptians? And how could the contribution of the plagues to a story of national salvation be dramatized without developing the action far beyond the spatio-temporal confines of classical tragedy? Such a Greek play about Exodus was, in fact, written by Ezekiel the dramatist, a Jew working in Alexandria (c. 2nd c. BC). His *Exagoge* survives only in fragments. Even so, it is clear that, like Seneca, he knew fifth-century tragedy well, and that one of his models was Aeschylus' drama of conflicting peoples, *The Persians*.[22] To compare the two is to be reminded, however, that ancient Greek historiography lacks the sense of divine guidance which is integral to Exodus. Ezekiel cannot be persuasive when he recasts the angry Yahweh as an irritable, Euripidean deity inflicting scourges of 'frogs and lice' and 'hail mixed | with fire' on the Egyptians.[23]

Old Testament writers are preoccupied with the role of Yahweh's anger in history. How does it relate to the mercy which, in Hosea and other prophets, is mingled with wrath? How far is wrath to be understood as the misery produced in the world by sin (as Jeremiah often seems to imply) rather than a venting of divine rage? After the Babylonian exile, and particularly in Daniel, 'wrath' is often presented impersonally. It becomes a force at work in human society which God's mercy stands over and against. That is also how wrath usually appears in those writings of St Paul which, together with the anonymous Epistle to the Hebrews, provide the richest discussions of this topic in the New Testament. The interpretation of Paul on anger can, however, be difficult. Take Romans 12: 19, a crucial passage for the central chapters of this book. 'Dearly beloved, avenge not yourselves (*mē heautous ekdikountes*), but rather give place

---

[22] See *The 'Exagoge' of Ezekiel*, [ed. and tr.] Howard Jacobson (Cambridge, 1983), 23–8.
[23] Lines 132–92, quoting 135 and 141–2, in Jacobson's text.

unto wrath (*tei orgē*): for it is written, Vengeance is mine; I will repay (*emoi ekdikēsis, egō antapodōsō*), saith the Lord.'[24] That this disapproves of human revenge seems plain, but is 'wrath' the same as 'Vengeance'? Commentators agree that the 'orgē' (Aristotle's word for anger) is finally God's, but that does not solve the problem. For if 'wrath' works itself out through sinfulness, in the sphere of law and punishment, then it might be different in nature and immediate provenance from the 'justice-giving' or 'avenging' ('emoi ekdikēsis' relates to the *dikē* of classical tragedy) which belongs to God. Against this, the allusion signalled by 'it is written' to His statement at Deuteronomy 32: 35, 'To me belongeth vengeance, and recompence', tends to elide 'Vengeance is mine' with 'wrath', bringing Paul's God closer to the wrath-dealing Jehovah of the Pentateuch.

Those who stress the former aspect of the verse reinforce 'Vengeance is mine; I will repay' as a limiting condition ('leave it to God to decide whether an injury affecting you should or should not be punished by Him') and prevent it seeming an aggressive promise. By contrast, those who insist that the allusion to Deuteronomy imports an Old Testament conception of God make it possible to restore some validity to human revenge, since retributing wrong becomes consistent with a divine promise to see 'Vengeance' exacted and an avenger can regard himself as God's agent. As I shall show in Chapter 6, Paul himself provides the basis for such a belief in Romans 13. In various ways, Romans 12–13 encouraged the efflorescence of English revenge tragedy after the Reformation.[25] But then, it is no accident that, during the same period, views of the atonement changed. A modern scholar has said that, 'If we once allow ourselves to be led into thinking that a reference to the wrath of God in the New Testament means that God is conceived of as angry, we cannot avoid some sort of theory of expiation. We cannot avoid maintaining that in some sense the Son endured the wrath of the Father, we cannot avoid thinking in forensic terms.'[26] The stress placed by reformers on the Deutero-

---

[24] Quoting the Greek from the Nestle-Aland Revised Standard *Greek–English New Testament*, 2nd edn., prepared by Kurt Aland *et al.* (Stuttgart, 1971).

[25] See e.g. Lily B. Campbell, 'Theories of Revenge in Renaissance England', *Modern Philology*, 38 (1931), 281–96, tempered by Fredson Bowers, *Elizabethan Revenge Tragedy 1587–1642* (Princeton, 1940), ch. 1, and Ronald Broude, 'Revenge and Revenge Tragedy in Renaissance England', *Renaissance Quarterly*, 28 (1975), 38–58.

[26] Anthony Tyrrell Hanson, *The Wrath of the Lamb* (London, 1957), 193.

nomic element in Romans 12 did encourage a convergence between God's 'wrath' and 'Vengeance' which had consequences for the crucifixion.

Early patristic accounts of the atonement describe Christ on Calvary as a second Adam, furnishing 'ransom' to Satan to free mankind from death. St Anselm modified this by arguing that Jesus died to 'satisfy' the Father for the 'dishonour' caused by man's disobedience in the Garden of Eden. Some theologians, such as Bernard of Clairvaux, resisted the negative effect which this had on perceptions of the Father's mercy, but the prevailing explanation of the atonement until the sixteenth century remained that of Anselm. What altered the picture was the emergence of a revised 'satisfaction' theory, associated with 'contract' theology. Protestant reformers were less concerned with divine honour than with what man owed in obedience. They argued that the fall and its legacy of sin had left a 'debt' due to an angry God, and that 'satisfaction' was rendered on the cross. Christ was man's substitute in paying for disobedience, since only his divine sacrifice could be large enough to meet the bill. As the young Milton put it, in 'Upon the Circumcision':

> he that dwelt above
> High-throned in secret bliss, for us frail dust
> Emptied his glory, even to nakedness;
> And that great covenant which we still transgress
> Entirely satisfied,
> And the full wrath beside
> Of vengeful justice bore for our excess . . .[27]

This was to remain his position. Familiar with Lactantius' *De ira Dei*,[28] Milton gives an account of 'full wrath' in *Paradise Lost* largely compatible with the treatise's distinction between a punitive resistance to wrong by God and irate revenging by Satan. The poet's attitude to the atonement, however, edged his version of the Christian story into troubling relations with revenge tragedy.

To marry the wrath of the Father with the *orgē* and *ira* of ancient

---

[27] 'Upon the Circumcision', 20–4; all quotations from *The Poems of John Milton*, ed. John Carey and Alastair Fowler (London, 1968). Cf. C.A. Patrides, *Milton and the Christian Tradition* (Oxford, 1966), 132–41.

[28] An extract, on why God permits there to be evil in the world (ch. 13), is the second item in his *Commonplace Book*.

epic presented, of course, its own difficulties. When, in the induction to Book IX, Milton says that his subject is God's 'Anger', he is careful not only to link his theme with but to distinguish it from 'the wrath | Of stern Achilles' and the 'rage | Of Turnus . . . Or Neptune's ire or Juno's' (IX. 10–18). It is a sign of creative awkwardness as well as of the poet's understanding of sin that, though virtuous figures sometimes speak of divine ire—as when Abdiel warns Lucifer's followers that they risk His 'wrath | Impendent' (V. 890–1) if they rebel—it is the fallen who are most aware of it. After their defeat, Satan, newly arrived in hell, calls God 'the potent victor in his rage', an 'angry victor' equipped with 'ministers of vengeance' (I. 95, 169–70), and Beelzebub and Moloc follow him in speaking of His 'vengeful ire'.[29] Wrath is plural, however, because these same speakers display an *iracundia* which descends from Achilles and Turnus.[30] This sort of anger was their undoing— 'impious rage' at the exaltation of the Son precipitated their fall (V. 845)—and it continues to blaze in hell. There the furious devils clash 'flaming swords' on their shields (I. 664–9), and, more playfully, tear up rocks and hills 'with vast Typhoean rage' as part of their Homeric games (II. 539).

Good angels can also be angry. Abdiel is 'fervent' (i.e. 'burning') when he warns the rebels against disobedience; those fighting Lucifer in heaven are variously roused to 'rage'.[31] But Satan is particularly furious, and once defeated his *iracundia* shows itself as 'desperate revenge' (III. 80–5). His 'guile | Stirred up with envy and revenge' is the first 'cause' cited by the poem of the events which it describes (I. 28, 34–5), and his opening speech in hell urges 'study of revenge' (I. 107).[32] If Milton's early plans to write *Paradise Lost* as a tragedy had been realized, Satan would have resembled the angry and tormented villain-revengers of Jacobethan drama,[33] punishing but also being punished by what he does to Adam and Eve (IX. 168– 73). Even in the poem as we have it, Satan has some of the rhetoric of a Stoic stage hero, and it is easy to imagine him acquiring the

---

[29] I. 148; cf. e.g. II. 155–9, 170–4.

[30] On anger and devils elsewhere in Renaissance epic, see Colin Burrow, *Epic Romance: Homer to Milton* (Oxford, 1993), esp. 251–2.   [31] V. 849; VI. 199, 217, 635.

[32] e.g. I. 604, II. 987, III. 160 (the Son on Satan), IV. 123, 385–7, VI. 905 (Raphael on Satan); also IV. 1–12 (Satan as the dragon of Revelation).

[33] Cf. Helen Gardner, 'Milton's "Satan" and the Theme of Damnation in Elizabethan Tragedy', *Essays and Studies*, I (1948), 46–66.

Senecan equipment described in Milton's 'Elegia Prima' ('when a fierce avenger of crime returns from the darkness of death, recrosses the Styx, and perturbs conscience-stricken souls with his dismal firebrand'),[34] to become a character less like Homer's Achilles than the Achilles of Heywood's *Troas*. Drama could not register, however, so readily as could epic—with its immense flashbacks—the relations of creation and fall in an eternity which has no extension in time for God, nor, with any naturalness, demonstrate (what the *Exagoge* of Ezekiel sought to realize, and what *Paradise Lost* XI–XII manages to communicate) the place of human disobedience and salvation in a long historical sequence involved with divine wrath and mercy.

Wrath, not mercy, though, lies at the heart of *Paradise Lost*. The formal centre of the poem, as Milton first published it in 1667, is occupied by a description of the Son's chariot, based on the vision of Ezekiel the prophet (VI. 746–800), flanked by two speeches each of twenty-three lines, '23 being a number that symbolized both divine vengeance upon sinners . . . and the consummation of the salvation of man'.[35] These passages do imply redemption for the just (735), but they emphasize, repeatedly, the hatred proper to God,[36] His anger, indignation, and revenge. Invoking Romans 12: 19—'Vengeance is his, or whose he sole appoints' (808)—the Son advances in his machine. With a 'countenance' 'full of wrath' (825–6), He rides over the enemy in 'ire' (843). This does not augur well for mankind. For the 'just avenging ire' which damns the bad angels (VII. 184–6) is also deserved by humanity. Anticipating Adam's disobedience, and wondering (as it were) how the sin can be expiated, the Father says in Book III, 'Die he or justice must' (210). The introduction, at just this point, of a statement about the atonement draws *Paradise Lost* towards revenge tragedy in ways more profound yet also more subtle than those involved in Satan's campaign against humanity. For the Son's offer to pay what God calls 'rigid satisfaction, death for death' (III. 212) works full retribution into the grounds of mercy by using a language of harsh equivalence to express gracious substitution. That one component or aspect of the divine is willing to pay for the wrong which has

---

[34] Lines 43–4, quoting Carey's tr.   [35] Fowler, n. to VI. 761.
[36] For contexts see Michael Lieb, '"Hate in Heav'n": Milton and the *Odium Dei*', *English Literary History*, 53 (1986), 519–39.

been done to God (as man himself could not) means that potentially infinite anger at human disobedience against the Infinite can be checked. The Son creates a symmetry which prevents endless *orgē* by embracing, by taking upon Himself, full retribution. Here, in part, is the answer to Adam's anxiety that divine wrath might take a leaf out of Seneca's book and 'draw out, | For anger's sake, finite to infinite | In punished man, to satisfy his rigour | Satisfied never' (x. 801–4). The pattern is equally clear when, in slightly more positive terms, the Son offers 'life for life' to satisfy God's 'vengeful ire': 'on me let thine anger fall . . . on me let Death wreak all his rage' (III. 236–41). He will return to heaven after achieving man's salvation and see, in the Father's visage, a 'face, wherein no cloud | Of anger shall remain . . . wrath shall be no more' (262–4).

Pleased with this, God calls his Son 'the only peace | Found out for mankind under wrath' (274–5) then goes on to develop the symmetries of full retribution into a complacent-sounding rhetorical escalation:

> So man, as is most just,
> Shall satisfy for man, be judged and die,
> And dying rise, and rising with him raise
> His brethren, ransomed with his own dear life.   (294–7)

Should we be equally gratified? In a lively comparison of Milton with Seneca, Gordon Braden objects that this version of the atonement makes God 'a Thyestes who acts not in horrid ignorance but who kills his "youngest son" (3. 151) in full consciousness and deliberation.'[37] It can equally be objected that God's plan ignores an elementary principle of justice. Penalties should be paid by offenders, and when God and the Son agree to the atonement (as time is expressed in the poem) the latter does not participate in human nature. The Protestant imagery of debt-paying (as in 'ransomed with his own dear life') may soften the impact of this, since it is less repugnant to justice for one man to pay a fee to save others from death than for him to die in their place; but the difficulty recurs whenever we are reminded that Christ suffered in blood. A lack of discrimination between objects of bloody retribution, so long as they can stand one for another, is characteristic not of just process but of vendettas. These value their

---

[37] 'Epic Anger', *Milton Quarterly*, 23 (1989), 28–34, p. 32.

overall economy above the individual properties of those fulfilling them. Michael, for one, brings out the awkwardness of sacrificing a sinless thing in place of a sinful when he explains to Adam, in Book XII, that Jews under the Law, discovering that purification can be but faintly achieved 'by those shadowy expiations weak, | The blood of bulls and goats', will (or may) 'conclude | Some blood more precious must be paid for man, | Just for unjust' (289–94).

At this point we return to curses, a powerful motif in epic since Dido's outburst against Aeneas and his descendants in Book IV of the *Aeneid*.[38] For Michael tells Adam that, to fulfil the terms of the atonement, Christ will die a 'cursed death . . . shameful and accurst . . . this is satisfaction' (404–19), and he is not talking about oaths flung at Jesus on the cross. At Galatians 3: 13 it says, 'Christ hath redeemed us from the curse of the law (*tēs kataras tou nomou*), being made a curse (*katara*) for us: for it is written, Cursed (*epikataratos*) is every one that hangeth on a tree.' The citation is (again) from Deuteronomy, this time a phrase in 21: 23: 'for he that is hanged is accursed of God'. The disagreement among interpreters of Galatians 3: 13 resembles that at Romans 12: 19. Some find Paul's omission of the words 'of God' ('hupo Theou') highly significant, while others, especially those writing in the wake of the Reformation, take him to be implying the whole phrase from which he quotes. The former approach leads to a Christ who died among criminals, participating fully in the fallen state of man. 'But', as Bishop Lightfoot asserts (unconsciously deleting the curse entirely), 'He was in no literal sense *kataratos hupo Theou* and St Paul instinctively omits those words.'[39] Admitting 'of God', by contrast, allows Galatians 3: 13 to be related to those other parts of Scripture in which an irate God pronounces or enforces curses. There are plenty of instances in the Old Testament. For, while the view that curses can take effect without being morally justified or divinely aided leaves its mark in the Bible (e.g. Psalm 109, esp. 17–20), imprecations are generally thought to resemble prayers—effective only when righteous.[40] A weapon in the mouths of the poor and downtrodden

---

[38] Above, pp. 99–100; on other Renaissance recastings see David Quint, *Epic and Empire: Politics and Generic Form from Virgil to Milton* (Princeton, 1993), ch. 3.

[39] *Saint Paul's Epistle to the Galatians*, ed. J. B. Lightfoot, 10th edn. (London, 1890), 140.

[40] See e.g. Singer (gen. ed.), *Jewish Encyclopedia*, under 'Cursing', Brown (ed.), *New International Dictionary of New Testament Theology*, under 'Curse, Insult, Fool', and Sheldon H. Blank, 'The Curse, Blasphemy, the Spell, and the Oath', *Hebrew Union College Annual*, 23 (1950–1), 73–95.

(e.g. Proverbs 11: 26, 30: 10), just curses are always fulfilled when uttered by those in authority or otherwise divinely favoured (e.g. 2 Kings 2: 24). They are associated with anger at wrongdoing, and the curse of God Himself is irresistible. His 'wrath' can be 'poured out' through the agency of human curses (e.g. Numbers 23: 8) or be unleashed when the Covenant is broken and its binding curses triggered (see Deuteronomy 27: 14–26, 28: 15–68). Most important for those who read in 'of God' at Galatians 3: 13, however, are the curses of Genesis 3. After cursing the serpent for tempting Eve (3: 14), God says to Adam, 'Because thou hast hearkened unto the voice of thy wife . . . cursed is the ground for thy sake' (3: 17). At both points the Septuagint (translating participles of Hebrew '*rr*, 'he cursed') uses the same word, 'epikataratos', as St Paul.[41] Protestant reformers emphasized that it was to free man from the curse of Genesis 3: 17 that Christ died on the cross.

Milton accepted these arguments, and he writes movingly in *De doctrina christiana* (a text which I take to be his) about the effect of God's anger on the crucified Christ: 'The curse also to which we were obnoxious, was transferred to him . . . accompanied with a dreadful consciousness of the pouring out of the divine wrath upon his head.'[42] But his recognition of how post-Reformation doctrine could develop, in Christian epic, the Virgilian motif of the curse was inseparable from his awareness of the epic potential of another curse-plot: one in which the crucified Christ became man's revenge against Satan. Before Michael explains the atonement, Adam is crushed by a sense that 'All that I eat or drink, or shall beget, | Is propagated curse. . . . what can I increase | Or multiply, but curses on my head?' (x. 728–32; cf. 817–22). The archangel's allusions to Galatians 3: 13 will eventually alleviate this distress. Yet Adam is already possessed of a comforting text, words which he recalls to Eve when the thought of bringing children into the 'cursed world' (x. 984) makes her contemplate suicide. For between his renditions of God's curses on the serpent and on the ground (x. 175–8, 198–208) Milton has placed an orthodox (though firmly Protestant)

[41] See e.g. *The Old Testament in Greek According to the Septuagint*, ed. Henry Barclay Swete, 2nd edn., 3 vols. (Cambridge, 1895).
[42] 'Et exsecratione nobis debita in se translata . . . iræque divinæ in se effusæ horribilu sensu', in *De Doctrina Christiana*, ed. James Holly Hanford and Waldo Hilary Dunn, tr. Charles R. Sumner, in *The Works of John Milton*, gen. ed. Frank Allen Patterson, 20 vols. (New York, 1931–40), xiv-xvii, at xv. 304–5; cf. xiv. 62–3, xv. 216–17, 342–3.

version of words known as the *protevangelium* (Genesis 3: 14):
'Between thee and the woman I will put | Enmity, and between
thine and her seed; | Her seed shall bruise thy head, thou bruise his
heel' (179–81). These words to the serpent are what Adam quotes to
Eve. Warning that God has no doubt 'wiselier armed his vengeful
ire than so | To be forestalled' (by suicide), he takes the 'serpent' to
mean 'Satan' and adds: 'to crush his head would be revenge indeed'
(1022–36). As yet he knows nothing of Jesus; but he recognizes that
he and Eve must stay alive so that their 'seed' can bring Satan 'his
punishment ordained' (1031, 1038–9). With dim foreknowledge
Adam recognizes that Christ's sacrifice on the cross, and his
harrowing of hell in death, constitute a 'revenge' action.

When Satan returns to hell with news of his success in Eden, he
also paraphrases the *protevangelium* (X. 494–501). As soon as he does
so, he brings down the full weight of God's curse at Genesis 3: 14
('upon thy belly shalt thou go, and dust shalt thou eat'). In a
grotesque display of revenge symmetry, the devils metamorphose
into the instrument of their vindictive plot against man. Satan first
becomes 'A monstrous serpent . . . punished in the shape he sinned,
| According to his doom' (514–17), but, very quickly, his followers
join him:

> hiss for hiss returned with forked tongue
> To forked tongue, for now were all transformed
> Alike . . .
> And the dire hiss renewed, and the dire form
> Catched by contagion, like in punishment,
> As in their crime.   (518–20, 543–5)

The whole passage is finely inventive about cursing as a vehicle of
vengeance. In a parody of the benign interchanges of social reciprocity, the devils transform each other by uttering evil (root sense
of 'malediction') at one other, an evil which sticks. Such, we are led
to see, is the binding effect of God's curse, as so often with His
punishments: it leaves the devils free to take His revenge upon
themselves. This, after all, is why Satan is allowed to rise from
hell's 'burning lake' in the first place, 'That with reiterated crimes
he might | Heap on himself damnation . . . Treble confusion,
wrath and vengeance' (I. 210–20). It is to the larger conjunctions
of wrath and revenge with malediction and exchange that I must
finally turn.

*   *   *

Though Seneca believed that a philosopher had no reason to fear curses,[43] he recognized that *maledicta* reveal a great deal about the workings of ire. In *Medea* and *Hippolytus*,[44] as well as *Thyestes*, he shows the miserable cursing because they cannot achieve, by other means, what their passionate words intend. Lack of physical power disinhibits and escalates the threat, making malediction a register of rage rather than a scheme of prudent retaliation. This conjunction of excess and incapacity can seem absurd. Perhaps that is one reason why, in Seneca, the proverbially eloquent and potent curse of Thyestes is left so uninsistent (above, p. 111): reticence makes it more credible. In the *Tusculan Disputations*, Cicero had mocked the dramatist Ennius for what he had done with this curse. Taking a Stoic view of death, he accuses Seneca's precursor of writing glorified nonsense when he has Thyestes pray for Atreus not just to die in a shipwreck but to be 'transfixed and burst asunder' on 'rugged rocks', and to 'have no tomb to hide in'. Cicero wonders why Atreus should care what happens to his body when it will be 'without sensation'.[45]

It is hardly surprising that in all three plays—*Medea, Hippolytus*, and *Thyestes*—Seneca links cursing with vengeance. When Lindsay Watson scrutinized the Greek *arae* and Latin *maledicta* which survive from antiquity, he found that 'The majority of curses proceed from a desire for revenge.'[46] Many explicitly appeal to *lex talionis*, and this principle shapes their structure. If anger cannot find relief in the infliction of violence, because of weakness or distance, it turns out imprecations which, in their statements of why and how, foreshadow the shape of achieved vengeance, lovingly detailing torments which gratify the speaker. Curses of this sort are revenge tragedies by anticipation. The Strasbourg Epode, for instance, one of the oldest, angriest, and shortest of revenge texts in European literature, wishes agony upon an unnamed enemy; it asks that he be shipwrecked (like Atreus in Ennius) and beached, naked, among the savage Thracians, then be enslaved and survive in hardship. The

---

[43] See e.g. *Ad Lucilium epistularum moralium*, 44. 53.
[44] *Medea*, 1–27, *Hippolytus*, 1201–43.
[45] 1. 44, in *Tusculan Disputations*, ed. and tr. J. E. King (London, 1927).
[46] Watson, *Arae*, 6; but see Simon Pulleyn's notice, in *The Classical Review*, NS 43 (1993), 72–3.

Greek poet shifts tenses and moods to convey the leaps of vindictive fantasy, swinging back to the shoreline as he remembers to ask for the enemy to be piled with seaweed when he is cast up by the waves, teeth chattering from exposure. Only at the end is it revealed why there should be this emphasis on exile, isolation, and denial of a shared language: the curse seeks revenge for a broken social bond, an intimate one: 'This I would like to see (happen to) him who wronged me, and trampled on his oaths—he who was formerly my friend.'[47]

In tone, ancient Greek *arae* vary from the self-righteous retributiveness of Theognis ('may I inflict mischief in return for mischief. For thus it is fitting') to tit-for-tat bitchiness in the epigrams of erotic disappointment collected in the *Palatine Anthology*.[48] Roman curse-poems are often frivolous, but persistent belief in the efficacy of malediction encouraged writers to continue producing texts in the style of the Strasbourg Epode. As a result there was a certain overlap in mythological machinery and verbal texture between non-dramatic *maledicta* and more dramatically oriented revenge tragedies. To read the best recent commentary on *Thyestes* is to find, as early as line 13, a phrase ('in quod malum transcribor?') being traced to Ovid's *Ibis*.[49] This imitation of a curse-poem of Callimachus, in which the Greek poet refuses to give his enemy the name of anything more considerable than a bird notorious for its filthy habits, artfully reverses the situation in the Strasbourg Epode. It is written from Thrace, that is, by an exiled poet to an enemy who is doing him down in Rome. The phrase apparently picked up by Seneca comes from a passage in which Ovid discusses the afterlife. Having said that Ibis will not be safe even if the poet dies in Thrace, for his ghost will rise from hell and snatch at Ibis's flesh, Ovid threatens his enemy with being made over (*transcribere*) to the ancient torments of Sisyphus, Tantalus (the speaker at *Thyestes* 13) and the rest of those Tartarean sufferers so familiar from Senecan drama, and, indeed, from Seneca's satirical judgement of, and posthumous revenge against, Claudius, the *Apocolocyntosis* (143–96). The current of transcription almost seems to flow back, or forwards, to Seneca when Ovid imagines Ibis being forced to eat flesh like Thyestes (431–4, cf. 543–4).

---

[47] Quoting Watson's tr., in *Arae*, 57. [48] Watson, *Arae*, 66–9, p. 67; 142–5.
[49] *Thyestes*, ed. R. J. Tarrant (Atlanta, 1985), 89.

Like some other classical curses, *Ibis* has patches of obscurity. Its lists of mythological *exempla*, often doubled, embedded, and oblique, strike the ear with undertones of dark hermetic incantation. Despite its harsh ellipses, though, the text is highly articulate—all six hundred and forty-two lines of it. Ovid compares *Ibis* to a spear (46), and its packed aggressive style does give it the force of a missile. Cursing is more than anticipated revenge here: it becomes a mode of action, making the derivation of *vindicare* ('to avenge') from *vim* (the accusative of 'force') plus *dicere* ('to say') meaningful. At one point Ovid reminds his enemy of the fate of Lycambes (51–4). Having promised the hand of his daughter to the poet Archilochus, this unfortunate nobleman changed his mind and married her to someone more advantageous. On hearing the news, Archilochus composed a volley of satirical iambics and recited them at the festival of Demeter. So humiliated were Lycambes and his daughter that they promptly hanged themselves. This, Ovid says, is what awaits Ibis if he continues to disparage him in Rome. He will be rhymed, ignominiously, to death. Such threats have deep roots. They are grounded in a widespread and not-so-primitive sense of what S. J. Tambiah, in a classic article, called 'The Magical Power of Words'.[50] Arab tribesmen, for instance, until recently regarded the poet as a warrior, adept at flinging maledictions. The poet composed 'satire (*hijá*) against the tribal enemy. The satire was like a curse', and it was thought of 'concretely, as a weapon which rival poets hurled at each other as they would hurl spears . . . indeed a man at whom the *hijá* was directed might dodge, just as he would try to dodge a spear, by ducking and twisting and dancing aside.'[51]

As it happens, Renaissance scholars related 'satire' to the Arabic word for spear. Thomas Drant's preface to his translation of Horace's satires (1566) forges this link, while adding the shaggy-thighed satyrs of classical mythology, the melancholy planet Saturn, and Latin *satur* (meaning 'full' or 'charged with a mixture').[52] John Weever improved on even that eccentric derivation by claiming, in *Faunus and Melliflora* (1600), that Diana brought the first satyr into the world when, in revenge for being neglected by two lovers, she

[50] *Man*, NS 3 (1968), 175–208.
[51] Robert C. Elliott, *The Power of Satire: Magic, Ritual, Art* (Princeton, 1960), 15.
[52] Thomas Drant, *A Medicinable Morall* (1566), A4ᵛ.

gave them a child (an enemy to love) who 'satisfide her ires'.[53] This wordplay is intended to join two things which, for Renaissance commentators, went together for psychological reasons: imprecation and rage. Satire, like the cursing bound up with it, was angry. It was written in what Thomas Underdowne's extensively annotated translation, *Ouid his Inuectiue against Ibis* (1577), calls 'armed verse' (A7ʳ). In his preface, Underdowne recommends *Ibis* as a revenger's encyclopaedia: 'For therein shal you see all manner of vices punished, al offences corrected, and all misdeedes reuenged' (A3ᵛ). Even when early modern writers admit that lively satire involves more than good citizenship (punishing vice, etc.), they stress the importance of 'Resentments', of being 'heated by Revenge'.[54]

Significantly, Drant's 1566 collection includes 'The Wailynges of Hieremie', a paraphrase of Jeremiah. Post-Reformation satirists drew the rhetoric of their grievances from biblical sources as well as from Juvenal, Horace, and (though this has been neglected) the author of *Ibis*. Milton invokes Solomon and Christ when describing the 'well heated fervencie' and 'grim laughter' needed to rebut truth's stubborn opponents.[55] His *Apology against a Pamphlet* adduces a series of Old Testament prophets, as well as Horace, to defend the Christian's right 'to turne religion into a Comedy, or Satir; *to rip up the wounds* of Idolatry and Superstition *with a laughing countenance*'.[56] Most striking of all is another passage in the *Apology* which says that, during periods when prelacy is recalcitrant and calm reason cannot make itself heard,

then (that I may have leave to soare a while as the Poets use) then Zeale whose substance is ethereal, arming in compleat diamond ascends his fiery Chariot drawn with two blazing Meteors figur'd like beasts, but of a higher breed then any the Zodiack yeilds, resembling two of those four which *Ezechiel* and S. *John* saw, the one visag'd like a Lion to express power, high autority and indignation, the other of count'nance like a man to cast derision and scorne upon perverse and fraudulent seducers; with these

[53] Cited by Alvin Kernan, *The Cankered Muse: Satire of the English Renaissance* (New Haven, 1959), 55.

[54] Quoting Rochester, reported (plausibly enough) by Gilbert Burnet, *Some Passages of the Life and Death of Rochester* (1680), in David Farley-Hills (ed.), *Rochester: The Critical Heritage* (London, 1972), 47–92, p. 54.

[55] *Animadversions upon the Remonstrants Defence Against Smectymnuus*, in *Complete Prose Works of John Milton*, gen. ed. Don M. Wolfe, 8 vols. (New Haven, 1953–82), i. Cf. Joel Morkan, 'Wrath and Laughter: Milton's Ideas on Satire', *Studies in Philology*, 69 (1972), 475–95, pp. 478–81.   [56] *Complete Prose of Milton*, i. 903.

the invincible warriour Zeale shaking loosely the slack reins drives over the heads of Scarlet Prelats, and such as are insolent to maintaine traditions, brusing their stiffe necks under his flaming wheels.[57]

Milton is usually accused of identifying with Satan, but what he writes here chimes with his image of the irate Son, at the heart of *Paradise Lost*. The sublime satirist should crush his enemies like that agent of the Father's vengeance, riding 'O'er shields and helms, and helmed heads' (VI. 840). Here is a reason why the most wrathful books of *Paradise Lost* are also the most mocking. When Lucifer's pretensions are at their height, and he directly assaults God's majesty, the powers of heaven, and those of the poet, crush him with anger and burlesque.

Milton thought that satirists should rise to epic, indeed tragic, heights. Accepting the common, though not uncontested, view that satire derived from Greek tragedy, through the medium of satyr plays, he maintains that 'a Satyr as it was borne out of a *Tragedy*, so ought to resemble his parentage, to strike high, and adventure dangerously at the most eminent vices among the greatest persons'.[58] The currency of such ideas incited the merger of the loftiest tragedy with satire's 'vengeful ire'. The importance of this for revenge drama can be indicated by turning, in conclusion, to the one writer of the period who, if Drant's etymological fantasy about spears can be believed, was chosen by name to deal in satire. Jonson made the obvious quibble when, in his prefatory verses to the 1623 Folio, he urged the stellified Shakespeare to radiate down his 'rage' to earth, saying that, in each of his lines, 'he seems to shake a Lance, | As brandish't at the eyes of Ignorance.'[59] Rage and the wielding of spears owe as much to Jonson's self-image ('Arm'd with Archilochus fury') as to what one might feel about Shakespeare himself.[60] Yet there is no doubting his gravitation in tragedy—and especially in *Timon of Athens* and *King Lear*—towards ire and malediction. The imprecating witches of *Macbeth* may owe a debt to Seneca's *Medea*,[61] but there is nothing in Holinshed or *The True*

---

[57] Ibid. 900.   [58] Ibid. 916.
[59] 'To the Memory of My Beloved, the Author, Mr. William Shakespeare: and What He Hath Left Vs'; facsimile of 1623 text in *Riverside Shakespeare*, 66.
[60] From the 'Apologetical Dialogue' attached to *Poetaster* (158–67), quoted and discussed by Ian Donaldson, 'Jonson and Anger', *Yearbook of English Studies*, 14 (1984), 56–71, pp. 56–7.
[61] See e.g. Inga-Stina Ewbank, 'The Fiend-like Queen: A Note on *Macbeth* and Seneca's *Medea*', *Shakespeare Survey*, 19 (1966), 82–94.

Chronicle Historie of King Leir to compare with the terrible curses uttered by Shakespeare's Lear. And with the exception of the curse on his tomb, those of Timon the misanthrope seem also to have been added by the dramatist.

Timon's career turns on dichotomies. He passes from sociability to solitude, from culture to nature, from luxury to simplicity. What links the latter terms is that setting which signified (for most classical and Renaissance observers) retreat, wildness, and nullity: the forest. As Anne Barton has shown,[62] Timon becomes an emblem of the place to which he flees by turning into a wild man, a wodwose. Precisely the same locale was associated with satyrs, however, and therefore (since even the spellings were interchangeable) with satire. In Jacobean England, wodwoses and satyrs were thought indigenous and classical versions of each other, as is shown by the title of Richard Brathwait's *Natures Embassie or The Wilde-Mans Measures: Danced Naked by Twelue Satyrs* (1621). In a well-known passage, George Puttenham declares: 'and the first and most bitter inuective against vice and vicious men, was the *Satyre*: which to th'intent their bitternesse should breede none ill will . . . they made wise as if the gods of the woods, whom they called *Satyres* or *Sylvanes*, should appear and recite those verses of rebuke'.[63] Timon is not exactly a god of the woods, but his fierce invective against Athens allows Shakespeare to express a hostility which at least part of him must have felt towards the extravagance, greed, and ingratitude current in Jacobean society, while also exploring the pathology of a certain kind of rage.

When that incessant imprecator, Ezra Pound, wrote in Canto LXIII, 'I | read Timon of Athens, the manhater | must be (IRA must be) aroused ere the mind be at its best',[64] he was registering an exhilaration which every theatre-goer feels when the mighty engines of Shakespearean imprecation roar into life in Act IV. But whether Timon's curses show his 'mind' to better advantage than his naïve largesse in Act I is debatable. That equally accomplished imprecator, Wyndham Lewis (whose illustrations for *Timon of Athens*

---

[62] 'The Wild Man in the Forest', first of her 1994 Northcliffe Lectures (7 Mar. 1994).
[63] *The Arte of English Poesie*, ed. Gladys Doidge Willcock and Alice Walker (Cambridge, 1936), 31.
[64] *The Cantos of Ezra Pound*, rev. edn. (London, 1975), 353. Pound is citing the diary of John Adams (June, 1760); see Carroll F. Terrell, *A Companion to the Cantos of Ezra Pound*, 2 vols. (Berkeley, 1980–4), i. 227.

stimulated the production of the early Cantos), argued that, out in the woods, 'the manhater' steals the thoughts of Apemantus, the cynic, to dress up in something like philosophy an essentially banal annoyance. Timon is 'a puppet of a certain sort', Lewis writes: '"I have been full of *hubris*. I have been cast down. I complain," he says; and there is the end of it. That is what "tragedy" is about.'[65] Whether or not Western tragedy is systemically guilty of assuming that anyone dropped from a great height must be interesting, it is true that Timon's IV. i tirade is so indiscriminate in its targets before it curses society in general (e.g. 21–3) that it lacks philosophical focus. Yet Pound was not entirely deluded when he found it intellectually considerable, for its vindictiveness is coloured by the language of social critique:

> Itches, blains,
> Sow all th'Athenian bosoms, and their crop
> Be general leprosy! Breath, infect breath,
> That their society (as their friendship) may
> Be merely poison!   (28–32)

Like a classical curse-poem, this anticipates revenge: let them be punished by negative sociability, as they have betrayed me. It also indicates, partly as a result, a general debt to Seneca on reciprocity.

The idea that exchanging injuries goes along with exchanging benefits was commonplace in antiquity.[66] Seneca qualifies this assumption, and his arguments against what Milton calls 'vengeful ire' are consistent with his views on generosity to the extent that he regards benevolence rather than reprisals as natural. In *De beneficiis*, as in *De ira* (I. iv. 3), he calls the exchange of boons 'the chief bond of human society'.[67] Yet the psychology of Senecan beneficence resembles that of *furor* to the extent that excess is integral to both. There are different degrees of willingness, but, much as B's injury of A will tend to be larger than A's of B if it is to seem equal (especially in B's eyes) to his own, so, according to Seneca, we need 'to set before us the high aim of striving, not merely to equal, but to surpass in deed and spirit those who have placed us under obligation, for he who has a debt of gratitude to pay never catches up with

---

[65] Wyndham Lewis, *The Lion and the Fox: The Rôle of the Hero in the Plays of Shakespeare* (London, 1927), 253.
[66] See e.g. Blundell, *Helping Friends and Harming Enemies*, ch. 2.
[67] I. iv. 2, in *Moral Essays*, ed. and tr. Basore.

the favour unless he outstrips it' (I. iv. 3). The hint of coercion here, at 'eos, quibus obligati sunt', recalls the oppressive aspect of generosity already noted in relation to Medea (above, p. 95), and there is plainly enough ambivalence in this passage for a sceptical reader (such as Shakespeare) to identify a streak of disruptive, Timonesque extravagance in Seneca. It is true that *De beneficiis* warns that over-giving has its dangers, but almost the first thing it emphasizes (and returns to at its conclusion) is that 'There is no reason . . . why the multitude of ingrates should make us more reluctant to be generous' (I. i. 9). Meanwhile, though Seneca exhorts us to overcome our resentment when others do not repay benefits, his insistence that ingratitude is nefarious—worse than homicide, tyranny, theft, adultery, and sacrilege (I. x. 4)—establishes a tragic potential within benign reciprocity, as dramatically viable, in its way, as the revenge of injuries. This is where his influence registers not only in *Timon of Athens* but in *King Lear*.

Timon's initial devotion to Senecan reciprocity is plain. 'We are born to do benefits', he announces, 'and what better or properer can we call our own, than the riches of our friends' (I. ii. 101–3). Experience teaches him otherwise, and he rounds on the language of benefits. Consider the grace which he speaks before uncovering the dishes of stones and water, laid before his faithless friends. 'You great benefactors,' he prays,

sprinkle our society with thankfulness. For your own gifts make yourselves prais'd; but reserve still to give, lest your deities be despis'd. . . . The rest of your fees, O gods—the senators of Athens, together with the common lag of people—what is amiss in them, you gods, make suitable for destruction. For these my present friends, as they are to me nothing, so in nothing bless them, and to nothing are they welcome. (III. vi. 70–84)

What begins as a pastiche of *De beneficiis* turns into bitter parody,[68] and then into a curse. Grace-cursing was common enough in the period—we hear of John Story, for instance, 'said to have cursed Queen Elizabeth I daily as part of his grace at meals'[69]—for audiences to have understood Timon's tactics. His prayer, in any case, blossoms into invective which sounds as Jacobean as it is

[68] For a rather different analysis, see John M. Wallace, '*Timon of Athens* and the Three Graces: Shakespeare's Senecan Study', *Modern Philology*, 83 (1985–6), 349–63, p. 357.

[69] Keith Thomas, *Religion and the Decline of Magic* (1971; Harmondsworth, 1973), 609.

ancient: 'You fools of fortune, trencher-friends, time's flies, | Cap-and-knee slaves, vapours, and minute-jacks! . . .' (96–7).

Keith Thomas has shown that, during the sixteenth and seventeenth centuries, 'the line dividing a curse from a prayer was extremely thin, and that imprecations could frequently have a religious flavour about them'.[70] Milton was being orthodox when he wrote, in *De doctrina christiana*, 'We are even commanded to call down curses publicly on the enemies of God and the church; as also on false brethren, and on such as are guilty of any grievous offence . . . The same may be lawfully done in private prayer, after the example of some of the holiest of men.'[71] This is the belief which spurred him to compose the sonnet-prayer, 'Avenge O Lord thy slaughtered saints', and which, against a background of Protestant interpretations of Romans 12: 19 ('Vengeance is mine; I will repay'), fostered, at a popular level, the idea that the exploited and the abused could use devout cursing to call down retribution.[72] The desire of early modern imprecators to awaken divine revenge recalls the drift of classical *arae* to calls for vengeance sponsored by the gods.[73] As in antiquity, curses could take the form of *defixiones*, inscribed and buried tablets of stone.[74] And, of course, there were curses on graves. Timon's couplet, taken from Plutarch, 'Here lies a wretched corse, of wretched soul bereft; | Seek not my name: a plague consume you, wicked caitiffs left!' (v. 4. 70–1) can be compared with certain lines on a slab in Holy Trinity Church, Stratford, said to have been written by Shakespeare: 'Blessed be the man that spares these stones, | And cursed be he that moves my bones.'[75]

As surely as *Timon of Athens*, *King Lear* has been influenced by Jacobean cursing. It has even been proposed that it makes much of malediction to take advantage of its topicality during the passage into law of an act against stage blasphemy (1604–6).[76] Yet what motivates Lear's oubursts, dramatically speaking, is what drives ancient curse-poems: infuriated by his daughters' ingratitude, the otherwise powerless king seeks retribution through language. That

[70] Ibid. 605.

[71] *De Doctrina Christiana*, in *Works of John Milton*, ed. Patterson, xvii. 99.

[72] Thomas, *Religion and the Decline of Magic*, 605–11.   [73] Watson, *Arae*; e.g. 1–4.

[74] Watson, *Arae*, ch. 4, Thomas, *Religion and the Decline of Magic*, 607.

[75] *William Shakespeare: The Complete Works*, ed. Stanley Wells and Gary Taylor (Oxford, 1986), 887.

[76] F. G. Butler, 'Blessing and Cursing in *King Lear*', *Unisa English Studies*, 24 (1986), 7–11, p. 10.

is why his prayer to 'Nature . . . dear goddess', anticipates revenge. If Goneril 'must teem', he says,

> Create her child of spleen, that it may live
> And be a thwart disnatur'd torment to her.
> Let it stamp wrinkles in her brow of youth,
> With cadent tears fret channels in her cheeks,
> Turn all her mother's pains and benefits
> To laughter and contempt, that she may feel
> How sharper than a serpent's tooth it is
> To have a thankless child!   (I. iv. 275, 281–9)

This has a terrible authority, not just because a Jacobean curse carries special weight when spoken by a father—status which Goneril cannot take away from Lear, though she has taken away so much—but because the structure of imprecation gives focus and direction to anger. Moreover, Lear urges a punishment which, since it could be inflicted by none but a goddess, admits no limit to his royal power. Yet the gravity and command of the curse is inextricable from Lear's vulnerability, for it wishes as revenges the worst things he can think of, those things which he will, only too soon, suffer on stage before us. As tears spring to his old, newly disillusioned eyes, the king, aware of his frailty, fears the humiliation of weeping before his daughter and projects his distress on to her. She must be scored, like him, with wrinkles, be tear-fretted and endure filial ingratitude.

When Lear curses Goneril for the second time, his position is markedly weaker. At Gloucester's castle, Regan advises him to seek forgiveness from her elder sister and to return and live with her. 'Never', the king answers: 'All the stor'd vengeances of heaven fall | On her ingrateful top! Strike her young bones, | You taking airs, with lameness!' (II. iv. 162–4). The audience recognizes that although Lear's hostility is sparked off by his daughter's ingratitude, it is scaled up in proportion to his weakness. Yet in so far as an audience discounts his wrenchingly unpaternal vindictiveness by remembering his impotence, it is driven into excruciated embarrassment. The awfulness of this bind is not lost on the king himself, aware of his onstage audience, and the scene ends with a cry to heaven in which—once again, to avoid the shame of tears—anger pushes beyond cursing, with its implicit admission of defeat, and looks to the psychological excesses associated with Senecan *furor*. 'You heavens', Lear prays,

> touch me with noble anger,
> And let not women's weapons, water-drops,
> Stain my man's cheeks! No, you unnatural hags,
> I will have such revenges on you both
> That all the world shall—I will do such things—
> What they are yet I know not, but they shall be
> The terrors of the earth! You think I'll weep:
> No, I'll not weep.
> I have full cause of weeping, but this heart
>
> *Storm and tempest.*
>
> Shall break into a hundred thousand flaws
> Or ere I'll weep. O Fool, I shall go mad.   (II. iv. 271, 276–86)

It is symptomatic that the cry, 'I will have such revenges' derives from *Thyestes*, 269–70, where Atreus plans the bloody banquet.[77] The streak of *furor* in Lear owes as much to Senecan revenge tragedy as it does to the—grossly neglected—influence of the philosopher's prose works on what the king calls 'pains and benefits'. *King Lear* is not usually thought of as belonging to the same genre as *Thyestes*. But as Robert S. Miola notes, in his study of Shakespeare and Seneca, 'though the revenge dynamic . . . is enormously complicated in *Lear* (and, finally, subverted), rhetoric and action bear continual witness to its presence'.[78] To register the importance of Senecan *furor* is to recognize that the king's madness is not primarily senile dementia. His derangement, fuelled by a wrath which can find no outlet in revenge, and which spirals through cursing to expostulation, resembles that of characters like Kyd's Hieronimo—much as Edgar's more cunningly assumed Bedlam behaviour can be seen as a Hamlet-like antic disposition sustained until he has vindicated himself against (and punished) Edmund. Yet one also needs to recognize that ire does not descend to Lear in single form. Lily B. Campbell is too programmatic in her account of Shakespearean psychology, but she is right to think of the king's anger as incorporating Aristotelian as well as Senecan elements.[79] His rage, in other words, combines a noble reaction to

---

[77] See e.g. Gordon Braden, *Renaissance Tragedy and the Senecan Tradition: Anger's Privilege* (New Haven, 1985), 216.

[78] *Shakespeare and Classical Tragedy: The Influence of Seneca* (Oxford, 1992), 144.

[79] *Shakespeare's Tragic Heroes: Slaves of Passion* (London, 1930), ch. 14.

dishonour with dangerous Senecan insanity. And both aspects of pagan ire are complicated by the Christian view—so relevant to Lear's curses—that just anger is defensible and that it is right to seek divine punishment through prayer.

This last consideration is important because students of Seneca and his influence often think of Christianity in *King Lear* as centring on patience, even virtuous suffering, and as providing a redemptive dynamic. Thus the best general book on Senecan drama announces that *King Lear* 'fits rather comfortably into the frame of traditional Christian beliefs in the dualism of God and the Fiend . . . the purgatorial effect of suffering, and the saving power of love', while the editor of Heywood's *Thyestes*, comparing Seneca and Shakespeare, endorses the idea that Lear learns 'by suffering'.[80] Of course the tragedy does include situations in which suffering makes people think, along with expressions of redemptive hope which are couched in Christian terms. When the Gentleman says to Lear, 'Thou hast one daughter | Who redeems nature from the general curse | Which twain have brought her to' (IV. vi. 205–7), the play's interest in tragic malediction joins up with Genesis 3: 17 and Galatians 3: 13: 'cursed is the ground for thy sake', 'Christ hath redeemed us from the curse of the law. . . for it is written, Cursed is every one that hangeth on a tree.' Cordelia is not just killed: she is, quite specifically, hanged. But it could only be argued that this death made her a Christ-figure, atoning for the disobedience of 'twain' (Goneril and Regan if not Adam and Eve), at the risk of producing an inchoate tragedy, for it is remarkable that her death has been felt to be uniquely cruel and purposeless by readers who, like Dr Johnson, were possessed of a Christian faith.

As it happens, John Casey has argued that *King Lear* is indeed inchoate, but that its 'confusion' intelligently reflects the 'confused system of values' which 'our culture' has inherited from the classical and Christian worlds.[81] While 'we subscribe to a "pagan" wish that [Lear] be revenged upon his daughters', he writes, and 'find the impotence of his anger distressing', we are also 'willing half to believe that there is a transcendent value in Cordelia's unselfish love' (p. 225). This gets closer to the experience of the play than Bradleyan redemptive readings. But it construes 'pagan' attitudes

---

[80] Norman T. Pratt, *Seneca's Drama* (Chapel Hill, NC, 1983), 9; *Thyestes*, ed. Daalder, p. xxxi.   [81] *Pagan Virtue* (Oxford, 1990), 225–6.

too narrowly (*De ira* is nowhere mentioned), and it obscures the fact that Christian tradition would approve the just wrath in Lear and defend his right to curse. When a commentator as well informed as Casey is satisfied with such a picture, there is plainly some danger of 'our culture' becoming confused less because of what it inherits than because of amnesia about its origins. For the value-systems which now dominate the West do not include anything so simple as a conflict between 'pagan' anger and Christian love. Anger itself is compound.

Thus, the average European or American would accept the definition of anger which Seneca derived from Aristotle. Surveying current attitudes, James Averill found that 57 per cent of subjects agreed that anger involved a desire 'To get back at, or gain revenge on, the instigator' of some incident.[82] Yet most of these people, and others, would recognize as a form of anger that 'rage against injustice' which Christian tradition has handed on to certain political movements, even if they would disagree about the proper objects of such rage. Averill himself typifies mainstream opinion among psychologists when he calls anger 'representative of the class of conflictive emotions' (p. 19), a symptom, that is, of frustration—a modification of Aristotle for which Aquinas should take some credit.[83] Such an approach is compatible with a Senecan account of ire to the extent that it regards wrath as a sign of something gone awry. But in its more developed, eventually psychoanalytic form,[84] this line of explanation produces a quite contrary outcome, with anger being regarded as so toxic a pathogen that not to 'get it out of your system' is to cause guilt, anxiety, and depression—emotions producible, in this view, by 'unconscious impulses of revenge'.[85] Hence the further paradox induced by pop psychology, which holds that outbursts of rage are benign, that bottling it up is bad for you. This carousel of attitudes is certainly very 'confused', but it is tractable to analysis. There are varieties and traditions of anger,

---

[82] James R. Averill, *Anger and Aggression: An Essay on Emotion* (New York, 1982), 176–8.
[83] See e.g. *Summa*, I-II q. 25 (comparing Aristotle, *Rhetoric*, 1379a).
[84] On links between Stoicism and psychoanalysis see e.g. Philip Rieff, *Freud: The Mind of the Moralist*, 3rd edn. (Chicago, 1979), 17.
[85] Quoting Karl Abraham's germinal paper, 'Notes on the Psycho-Analytical Investigation and Treatment of Manic-Depressive Insanity and Allied Conditions' (1911), in *Selected Papers of Karl Abraham, M.D.*, tr. Douglas Bryan and Alix Strachey (London, 1927), 137–56, p. 146.

and in this, as in so much else, we are products of that great confluence of classical and Christian ideas which gathered during the Renaissance. To understand our rages, we should read Shakespeare and Milton.

Part III

HISTORIES AND READINGS

6. Orestès and Medieval

Vengeance

IN the middle of the twelfth century, with Louis VII on the throne of France and the Second Crusade thwarted at Damascus, the troubled figure of Orestes returned to European literature. Benoît de Sainte-Maure, a cleric in minor orders, compiled, during the 1150s and 1160s, from the works of Dares Phrygius and Dictys Cretensis (4th–6th c. AD), a *roman antique* on the war at Troy and the adventures which followed its fall. It was Benoît who, inspired by the new interest in *fine amor*, elaborated from hints in Dares the story of Troilus and Cressida—with what results in Chaucer and Shakespeare everyone knows—and he who grasped for the first time since late antiquity the full dimensions of the Trojan disaster. Admittedly his grasp was not Homeric. As they joust on the plains near Ilium, the warriors of the *Iliad* are transformed into medieval barons. Magic rings and potions, faery lovers, and silken pavilions carry Benoît's narrative towards that world of Arthurian romance which would reach maturity, during the 1170s, in the hands of Chrétien de Troyes. For all its peculiarities, however, the *Roman de Troie* remains impressive. Though now the province of a few academic specialists,[1] the poem has a reach and energy which demand wider recognition. Indeed, I want to argue that its account of Orestes constitutes one of the most intelligent, as well as histori- cally significant, contributions to revenge tragedy in the West.

Though the Orestès of the *Roman de Troie* visits a pagan temple and takes advice from an oracle, most of what he does would fit a twelfth-century prince. He acts against Egistus and Clitemestra, for instance, by mustering troops and besieging Mycenae. The punish- ments inflicted on the adulterers smack of the retribution which awaits those found guilty of *traïsun* in *chansons de geste*. When the justice of Clitemestra's death is questioned, the challenge is not

[1] For a way into the scholarly literature see J. L. Levenson, 'The Narrative Format of Benoît's *Roman de Troie*', *Romania*, 100 (1979), 54–70.

posed by the Furies but by a Menelaus who, like other acquisitive rulers in medieval literature, seems to have his eye on his nephew's lands. Much of this material comes from Dictys' *Ephemeridos belli Troiani*, Benoît's source for this part of his poem. At a number of sensitive points, however, the *Roman* develops conflicts hidden beneath the surface of Dictys' narrative. This gift for identifying areas of difficulty and potential growth helps explain why Benoît's account of Orestès should have remained canonical for so long. 'ȝonge Horrestes, ful of hiȝe prowesse' (as Lydgate called him, in his *Troy Book*),[2] appears in Guido delle Colonne's thirteenth-century chronicle, *Historia destructionis Troiae*, in Gower's *Confessio Amantis* (1390–3) and Caxton's *Recuyell of the Historyes of Troye* (1502). A version of him can be found as late as John Pykeryng's *Horestes* (1567), the first revenge play to be written in Renaissance England. For his longevity as well as his tragic stature, Benoît's hero deserves attention. But to understand how he took shape, and what he meant to medieval audiences, it is important to know something about the ethos of twelfth- and thirteenth-century France. In what follows I shall therefore concentrate first on feuding as collective revenge, as it finds expression in such *chansons de geste* as *Raoul de Cambrai*. The second part of my chapter will move from *Raoul* to the *Queste del Saint Graal*, looking at changes in the treatment of vengeance between epic and romance. Only when these contexts have been provided will Orestès—in section three—move centre-stage.

Many of Benoît's contemporaries accepted the justice of revenge. The blood feud had been a part of Frankish life for centuries; vendettas would persist among the French and German nobility until the early modern period. As Marc Bloch summarily puts it: 'The Middle Ages, from beginning to end, and particularly the feudal era, lived under the sign of private vengeance.'[3] It is true that, during Benoît's lifetime, the monarchy in France (as in Norman England) increasingly asserted its right to administer justice in cases of blood. Yet this was neither an irresistible nor a necessary development. 'To legal historians feud dies a slow, inevitable death, yielding to the superior equity of royal justice', writes J.

---

[2] *Lydgate's Troy Book*, ed. Henry Bergen, 4 vols. (London, 1906–35), v. 1485.

[3] Marc Bloch, *Feudal Society*, tr. L. A. Manyon, 2nd edn., 2 vols. (London, 1962), 125. For intellectual contexts see Marie-Madeleine Davy, 'Le Theme de la vengeance au Moyen Âge', in Raymond Verdier and Jean-Pierre Poly (eds.), *La Vengeance: Études d'ethnologie, d'histoire et de philosophie*, 4 vols. (Paris, 1980–4), iv. 125–35.

M. Wallace-Hadrill, in 'The Bloodfeud of the Franks': 'chaos and bloodshed give place to good order because they must. But it is possible to see the matter otherwise.'[4] What he has in mind—with some help from the anthropologist, Max Gluckman—is that the feud has political functions, that it serves the society which it decimates, and that a paradoxical state of 'peace in the feud'[5] can be the rule rather than the exception. Feuding should not be regarded as an outbreak of mindless violence licensed by a social order too primitive to keep it in check, but as 'a form of active problem solving'[6] in societies without centralized justice.

Anthropologists keen to counter anti-feuding prejudice tend to exaggerate the rigidity of the conventions implicated in 'active problem solving' (the half-conscious analogy is with modern penal codes). This temptation is most sagaciously resisted by Pierre Bourdieu. Starting from an examination of the honour culture of Kabylia (Algeria), he develops a 'theory of practice' which stresses multiplicity of choice, the importance—highly relevant to revengers—of *timing* in reciprocity (since both to rush and to delay a riposte affects the meaning of an exchange), and the intuitiveness with which decisions are made by agents in traditional societies.[7] To think of revenge actions in the light of Bourdieu's work is to recognize, once again, how quickly the retributive paradigm of A vs. B, from which this book began, needs to be modified—especially when the actions belong to pre-modern or non-European contexts. This is so not least because of Bourdieu's demonstration that temporally contingent problem solving is radially and dialectically shaped by the 'socially constituted system of cognitive and motivating structures' which he calls 'the habitus' (p. 76), even when reciprocal acts are governed by a desire to achieve immediate ends. 'In the interaction between two agents or groups of agents endowed with the same habitus (say A and B),' he observes,

everything takes place as if the actions of each of them (say, a_1 for A) were organized in relation to the reactions they call forth from any agent

[4] Repr. in *The Long-Haired Kings and Other Studies in Frankish History* (London, 1962), 121–47, p. 146.

[5] See Gluckman's essay, of that title, repr. in his *Custom and Conflict in Africa* (London, 1955), 1–26, cited by Wallace-Hadrill, 'Bloodfeud of the Franks', 123.

[6] Christopher Boehm, *Blood Revenge: The Enactment and Management of Conflict in Montenegro and Other Tribal Societies*, 2nd edn. (Philadelphia, 1987), 227.

[7] Pierre Bourdieu, *Outline of a Theory of Practice*, tr. Richard Nice (Cambridge, 1977), esp. 11–15, 24 ff.

possessing the same habitus (say, b_1, B's reaction to a_1) so that they objectively imply anticipation of the reaction which these reactions in turn call forth (say a_2, the reaction to b_1). But the teleological description according to which each action has the purpose of making possible the reaction to the reactions it arouses . . . is quite as naive as the mechanistic description which presents the action and the riposte as moments in a sequence of programmed actions produced by a mechanical apparatus.

Instead of regarding the vendetta as a sequence of fixed reactions, each 'directly determined by the antecedent conditions and entirely reducible to the mechanical functioning of pre-established assemblies, "models" or "rôles"', we should recognize how it is activated (and brought to settlement) by 'strategic' choices which grow out of the habitus.[8]

These observations are helpful when we approach medieval revengers because they point up the extent to which the warriors of epic and romance make choices about using violence which can be traced to socially constituted motives without the anguish of their decision-making being alleviated by reference to rules. When Bernier, for instance, in *Raoul de Cambrai* (1180–1220?), sees his mother lying dead in a blazing church, a psalter alight on her breast, as a result of Raoul, his liege lord's attack on the hapless town of Origny, he cannot fall back on custom, never mind consult a *coutumier*, but must struggle with divided impulses in tragic perplexity. The poet makes much of Bernier's frenzy, his fainting, his anxious search for counsel in Raoul's camp, the surge of hatred which he experiences when faced with his lord's indifference, his being struck by Raoul (which breaks the feudal bond) and his publicly declared revenge.[9] The motivating principles of the feud which Bernier now begins go far back into what has made him what he is—his being brought up alongside Raoul since childhood, the duty which, in this habitus, a good knight owes to a mother as well as to his lord. The phases of fainting and rage, of seeking advice in the hope of compromise, show a strategy emerging and an action taking shape out of longer-standing and more widely dispersed causes than can be found in what Raoul has done.

Bernier's position is the more grievous because, as a member of the family of Herbert of Vermandois, he belongs to the very kin-group which Raoul and his men are attacking when Origny is

---

[8] Ibid. 73.   [9] *Raoul de Cambrai*, ed. and tr. Sarah Kay (Oxford, 1992), 1299–1549.

burned to the ground. He is not, however, so committed to the Herberts that his allegiance can be switched with ease. With the help, it seems, of chronicle as well as legendary sources (for the events of *Raoul* have some basis in ninth- and tenth-century history), the poet has calculated the double-binds with care: on the one hand, though Bernier is a Herbert by blood, his mother was taken by force into his father's bed, and he is illegitimate; on the other, though not strictly kin to Raoul, the childhood which Bernier shared with the lord he now opposes was so close that the word *frere* is used between them. As anthropologists like to point out,[10] complications of this sort are not incidental in feuding societies. It is rare to find vengeful groups so distinct that members of A have no links through marriage, economic interest, or feudal service with B. In medieval literature, those burdened with such connectedness are natural tragic subjects, partly because their double-binds can take violence more deeply, much more treacherously, into the heart of the kin-group than can attacks from without (think of Kriemhild in *The Nibelungenlied*, destroying her brothers in revenge for the death of Siegfried, her husband), but partly, too, because they are the most likely peacemakers in feuds which they may well start. This is the plight of Bernier, after he has killed Raoul, and when Gautier, Guerri the Red, and other members of Raoul's kin-group insist on keeping up the violence.

Anthropological evidence suggests that, even within bitter feuds, there is an impulse towards vindictive symmetry which allows violence to register a desire to move through equivalence to settlement. As William Ian Miller points out, however, in his fine account of saga Iceland, there are countervailing pressures:

The model of balanced exchange, at least as it is presented in *Njáls Saga*, contemplated both escalation and settlements that initiated periods of peace of varying duration. . . . Favouring interminability was the fact that few return blows ever precisely balanced the wrong they were matched against. The notion of balance itself was innately ambiguous

---

[10] The sources which I have found most helpful (in addition to Gluckman and Boehm) are Jacob Black-Michaud, *Cohesive Force: Feud in the Mediterranean and Middle East* (New York, 1975), C. R. Hallpike, *Bloodshed and Vengeance in the Papuan Mountains: The Generation of Conflict in Tauade Society* (Oxford, 1977), Keith F. Otterbein, 'An Eye for an Eye, a Tooth for a Tooth: A Cross-Cultural Study of Feuding', *American Anthropologist*, 67 (1965), 1470–82, and G. W. Trompf, *Payback: The Logic of Retribution in Melanesian Religion* (Cambridge, 1994), 1–153.

since it was not mathematical, but socially contingent on a host of shifting variables, some of which were subject to conscious manipulation by the parties. There were always new debts to pay or old ones that had not been completely discharged. There was also the problem that each new killing wronged a class of people constituted slightly differently than the one which originally gave offense, thereby creating the possibility of new conflicts with different groupings and providing a structural impulse for expansion of the dispute."

The habitus of medieval Iceland was very different from that of Raoul's Cambrai. Even so, these generalizations chime with much in early French epic. The rage of Gautier and Guerri escalates vendetta into warfare, and the feud survives periods of peace. The participants manipulate the 'variables' by making alliances and rewarding their followers. King Louis's position as both monarch and Raoul's uncle ensures that the pivotal event of the poem—Bernier's revenge on his lord—impinges on the loyalties of what is, in more than one sense, a different 'class of people' from that affected by his mother's death.

But then, in any feud, the imbalance of 'different groups' would seem guaranteed by the principle that an object of retribution need not be the cause of the revenge. When you kill my brother, I kill your nephew, having first of all killed your son. For the aggressor, the men struck down are more interchangeable than for those bereaved. This is the most obvious way in which the A vs. B paradigm needs qualification when the agents of action are collective and revenge is extended through time: the proper victims of violence do not have to be those who have caused injury. This principle was familiar to the authors of *Raoul* and the other *chansons*. High medieval France inherited from the Germanic *faide* the assumption that you could be punished for what a relative, or fellow-warrior (in the *comitatus*), had done. Marc Bloch cites the case of Thomas d'Ouzuer, who, in 1260, wounded a knight called Louis Defeux. When Defeux complained to the Parlement of Paris, d'Ouzeur did not deny the assault, but explained

that he had himself been attacked some time before by a nephew of his victim. What offence, then, had he committed? Had he not, in conformity with the royal ordinances, waited forty days before taking his revenge—

" *Bloodtaking and Peacemaking: Feud, Law, and Society in Saga Iceland* (Chicago, 1990), 186.

the time held to be necessary to warn one's kindred of the danger? Agreed, replied the knight; but what my nephew has done is no concern of mine.

Even at this late date, the court held that 'an individual involved all his kinsfolk'.[12] Respect for interchangeability, added to the symmetry in d'Ouzuer's violence, won over the judges, and Defeux lost his case.

When we read that, among the East African Gisu, the kin of a murdered man are expected to wait until the son of the murderer is *precisely* the age of that man, and then kill him,[13] the combination of interchangeability with symmetry sounds alien and odd. In *The Non-Existent Knight*, Italo Calvino affectionately finds comic potential in the similarly displaced vindictiveness of medieval epic and romance (his guide to the territory being Ariosto). Raimbaud, the Orestès of this novella, joins the army of Charlemagne in the hope of avenging his father, killed by the Moorish leader, Isohar. When he reports to the pavilion of the 'Superintendency of Duels, Vendettas and Besmirched Honour', however, he finds his ambitions thwarted:

'So you wish to avenge your father, the Marquis of Roussillon, by rank a general! Let's see, now! The best procedure to avenge a general is to kill off three majors. We can assign you three easy ones, then you're in the clear.'
'I don't think I've explained properly. It's Isohar the Argalif I must kill. It was he in person felled my glorious father!'
'Yes, yes, we realize that, but to fell an argalif is not so simple, believe me . . . What about four captains? We can guarantee you four infidel captains in a morning. Four captains, you know, are equal to an army commander, and your father only commanded a brigade!'
'I'll search out Isohar and gut him! Him and him alone!'[14]

The joke for Calvino's Cold War readers,[15] of course, is that, for all the oddness of displaced revenge, Raimbaud encounters attitudes in the Superintendency very much like those which motivate the rank-obsessed and resourcefully inert bureaucracies of the modern military state.

Calvino's non-existent knight is the kind of *chanson* hero who has never read Bourdieu. Doing everything by rule, he expects others to

[12] Bloch, *Feudal Society*, 126–7.
[13] Simon Roberts, *Order and Dispute: An Introduction to Legal Anthropology* (Harmondsworth, 1979), 57.
[14] Italo Calvino, *The Non-Existent Knight*, in *Our Ancestors*, tr. Archibald Colquhoun (London, 1980), 297.   [15] *Il Cavaliere inesistente* was published in 1959.

behave in the same way. The perfect military machine, Agilulf is literally an empty suit of armour, driven only by will-power. One of the attractions of the novella is the way in which his mechanistic approach to valour is offset by the chaos of battle. In Calvino, as in *Raoul de Cambrai*, trading insults and plundering spoils often have a higher priority than fighting for a cause. The poet of *Raoul* is fascinated by the disorder of 'close fighting . . . with countless lances shattered and shields pierced, countless hauberks torn and their mail ripped apart' (3710–12), and he likes to remark how opponents, such as Gautier or Guerri vs. Bernier, 'would have renewed acquaintance', or 'would have come to blows again, but there were so many mail-clad knights around them, their helmets pulled down over their faces, that they drive them apart' (3845–7, 4053–5). Attempting to wrest a purpose out of what *Raoul* would call 'une dure meslee' (4021), Calvino's Raimbaud tracks down Isohar. After a fierce struggle, he discovers that he has been fighting the wrong argalif. Pointed in the right direction, this typically *chanson* hero hacks away at another enemy, only to discover that he is 'the Argalif Isohar's spectacle bearer' (p. 312). At this point Calvino amuses himself with coincidence. When Raimbaud, in a fit of pique, smashes the glasses which the spectacle bearer is carrying, 'At the same instant, as if the sound of lenses in smithereens had been a sign of his end, Isohar was pierced by a Christian lance' (p. 313). It is characteristic of vendettas that things which happen by accident can be interpreted as acts of revenge, or not, as it suits the politics of the situation.[16] Calvino homes in on the indeterminacy of such chances, leaving Raimbaud in a muddle 'of triumph at being able finally to say his father's blood was avenged, of doubt whether he had actually himself killed the Argalif by fracturing his spectacles and so considered the vendetta truly consummated' (p. 313). More far-reachingly, though, Calvino also touches on the transcendent possibility, commonly raised in medieval epic and romance, that accidental or unlikely occurrences—unexpected deaths, victories, marvellous visions—are demonstrations of divine purpose, signs of His justice and immanence. It is to the role of God's judgement in medieval revenge plots that I now want to turn.

*   *   *

[16] Cf. e.g. Black-Michaud, *Cohesive Force*, 112.

Towards the end of the first part of *Raoul de Cambrai*, the leading revengers, Bernier and Gautier, meet in single combat. They do not now struggle to encounter each other in battle, nor fight as once they did before, in solitude, seconded only by Aliaume and Guerri (4193–402). This time they duel before King Louis and his barons, on a field blessed by 'Saintes reliqes' laid on a green silk cloth. Moreover, they take vows, Bernier swearing that, 'By all the saints that you see here, and the others by whom God is glorified . . . I acted within my rights in avenging myself on Raoul', and Gautier responding, in closely matched phrasing (the verbal equivalent of a retaliatory blow), that 'young Bernier has sworn falsely'.[17] Like so many duels in later European literature, this gives the complexities of collective vengeance the clarity and aggressive focus of an A vs. B revenge plot.[18] Each baron has resentments to avenge on the other, but Bernier, as the one who seeks peace, is offering Gautier what later duellists would call 'satisfaction': the chance, though not the certainty, of paying him back for Raoul's death. The combat is also, however, recognizably a *judicium dei*. The practice of fighting before God for judgement was common in the period covered by *Raoul*, though it was falling out of use—resisted by the Church—by the time of the poem's composition.[19] A Christianized version of an old Germanic custom, this sort of *judicium dei* brought Dark Age practice into harmony with an early medieval belief (which also encouraged trial by ordeal) in the immanence of the divine.[20] The relics on the silk were meant to work like lightning conductors, drawing down God's judgement. The feud was to be resolved by having Him decide whether Raoul was 'treasonably' killed.

In the event, the outcome is uncertain. Gautier and Bernier trade blows until both are close to death. Then Guerri flares up (as often) and swears 'by the saints that if he sees Gautier done to death, he'll cut Bernier limb from limb' (4921–2). Ybert responds by rallying Bernier's forces and threatening similar vengeance on Gautier. An

---

[17] Lines 4766, 4773–6, 4785 ff.

[18] For later French practice see François Billacois, *The Duel: Its Rise and Fall in Early Modern France*, tr. Trista Selous (New Haven, 1990)—a splendidly fertile account—and, for larger contexts, despite its Marxist oversimplifications, V. G. Kiernan, *The Duel in European History: Honour and the Reign of Aristocracy* (Oxford, 1988).

[19] See e.g. R. Howard Bloch, *Medieval French Literature and Law* (Berkeley, 1977), 119–21.

[20] For contexts see e.g. P. Rousset, 'La Croyance en la justice immanente à l'époque féodale', *Le Moyen Age*, 54 (1948), 225–48, and Robert Bartlett, *Trial by Fire and Water: The Medieval Judicial Ordeal* (Oxford, 1986).

A/B balance is maintained by these promises, but they discredit any show of trust in *judicium dei*. They also, more worryingly for King Louis, threaten to renew the feud and reduce his realm to disorder. So he takes steps to separate the combatants, and to reconcile them. When he fails to bring round Guerri and Gautier—who remind him that Raoul was his own nephew, and that he should want revenge upon Bernier—the Church becomes involved. A learned and well-born abbot urges Raoul's kin to accept Bernier's overtures of peace. Bernier, Ybert, and their fellows reinforce this by prostrating themselves before Gautier and Guerri. In a highly charged gesture, they surrender their swords, guarantors of their safety, their honour, their warrior identity, and their role as justice-seekers. The whole episode is a showcase of high medieval attitudes—the more so when, in an unexpected twist, Louis reacts with anger to Gautier's faction being reconciled. Calling Bernier a bastard, he tries to revive the feud. This prompts Guerri to remind the king that it was *his* depriving Raoul of his lands which provoked the sacking of Origny and led to Raoul's death in the first place (5272–80). Louis is now set against Gautier's faction, as well as that of Ybert and Bernier, and general conflict breaks out. A sequence which began with just two men at odds ends with followers of the new alliance sacking and burning Paris.

The ceremony with the swords, in front of the faulty king, is emblematic of key features of baronial revenge. The twelfth century saw a concerted effort to replace collective vengeance with systems of arbitration and compensation, encouraging judgement in the courts rather than combat in the field. 'Peace movements', sponsored by monarchs and the Church, sprang up.[21] The valour of the nobility was directed into campaigns to recapture the holy places in Palestine. Interestingly, Benoît's poem about a crusade of Ancient Greeks to Asia Minor was composed at about the same time as Louis VII (in the wake of the Second Crusade) declared a ten-year general truce among his barons. Orestès' attack on his father's killers, his campaign against Clitemestra and Egistus, needs to be judged against this irenic background. However, the motives of the dispossessed Mycenean lord would have attracted sympathy. For attempts to discourage vengeance quickly ran into the problem that

---

[21] See e.g. Thomas Head and Richard Landes (eds.), *The Peace of God: Social Violence and Religious Response in France Around the Year 1000* (Ithaca, NY, 1992).

the section of the New Testament which most plainly discouraged feuding also endorsed the right of barons to deal out justice with their swords. 'Dearly beloved, avenge not yourselves, but rather give place unto wrath: for it is written, Vengeance is mine; I will repay, saith the Lord.' All that was familiar from Romans 12, but so was what followed it:

Let every soul be subject unto the higher powers. For there is no power but of God: the powers that be are ordained of God. . . . if thou do that which is evil, be afraid; for he beareth not the sword in vain: for he is the minister of God, a revenger to execute wrath upon him that doeth evil. (13: 1, 4)

In the decentralized governing structure of high medieval France, each baron bore a sword for God; each noble house, resisting the encroachments of the crown, wrought upon its own enemies the retribution which—as the church so strenuously insisted—lay in wait for wrongdoers in this world as well as the next.

Judicial combat was not always represented as problematic. A thrilling depiction of its capacity to distinguish treachery from just revenge, and to reconcile a king's devotion to his nephew with responsibility to what might be called the state, is provided by *La Chanson de Roland*. In breadth of reference and poetic brilliance, this early twelfth-century work is, of course, in another league from *Raoul de Cambrai*. Like that lesser chanson, however, it centres, from the start, on vengeance. *Roland* is a crusading poem; it celebrates the might of Christian swords against the puissance of Islam. But these swords owe their potency to their executing Godly 'wrath' within the Frankish camp as well as beyond it: they are the weapons of divinely aided revengers. Thus, when Marsile, king of the Spanish muslims, sues Charlemagne for peace, Roland urges the Franks to renew the fight rather than end it, not for the sake of a crusade *per se*, but because, as he reminds the emperor, two ambassadors were executed by Marsile and they go *unavenged*. 'Wage war the way you set out to do', he cries, 'Lead the army you have summoned to Saragossa, | Lay siege to the city, put all your heart into it, | And avenge (*vengez*) those the villain had killed.'[22] Such overt vindictiveness could not be missed by a reader or auditor. As the action proceeds, however, revenge structures

---

[22] *The Song of Roland: An Analytical Edition*, ed. and tr. Gerald J. Brault, 2 vols. (University Park, Pa., 1978), lines 210–13.

language down to barely perceptible equivalences. When Charlemagne, for instance, asks the fatal question about who will lead the rearguard, Ganelon declares 'Roland, this stepson of mine' (743). His *laisse* has the same assonance as that initial stanza, following Roland's outcry against Marsile, in which the hero proposed his stepfather as emissary to the infidel (274–95). The two situations are equivalently performative—Roland leaps up at hearing himself named, as Ganelon had done earlier—and also poised in utterance, in that both declarations contain the same number of syllables. 'To the last detail,' as Eugene Vance puts it, 'revenge in this poem is symmetrical.'[23]

Ganelon is a Judas among the twelve peers of France. Having betrayed the rearguard to the pagans, he ensures that Roland commands it. Because of this, the poem cannot finish with Charlemagne's (divinely enabled) vengeance upon the armies of Marsile and his overlord, Baligant. Ganelon must be punished. Scholars remain divided over the extent to which Charles seeks retribution against Ganelon for disloyalty to himself and the Frankish cause and how far he pursues a blood-grudge as Roland's uncle. In practice, the two motives are entangled. The claim which is made by Ganelon at his trial, and which is tested in judicial combat— '"Venget m'en sui, mais n'i ad traïsun"' (3778)—can be taken as using 'treason' in something like its modern sense but also as marking a distinction between open, just revenge and covert, unworthy violence. The battle between Ganelon's champion, Pinabel, and Charlemagne's Thierry, is formidable, and witnessed by a hundred thousand men. Pinabel is so fearsome that it seems as though he will win and *judicium dei* be discredited. When, against the odds, Thierry strikes him dead, 'The Franks shout: "God performed a miracle!"' (3931). In the punishments which end the poem, it is, once again, hard to separate heroic feuding from the politics of monarchy. Ganelon is torn apart by four horses (a recognized penalty for treason against the state), but when the emperor appeals to the barons he is also encouraged to put to death no less than thirty of Ganelon's kin, held as hostages during the trial—an unheard of outcome, legally speaking, and earnest of the rage of revenge. The *chanson* ends with some emphasis not only

[23] Eugene Vance, *Reading 'The Song of Roland'* (Englewood Cliffs, NJ, 1970), 18.

on the *geste* as 'something done, events told of, performed' but on its secondary implication, 'kin, lineage'.

What replaced *judicium dei*, as Georges Duby and others have shown,[24] was the inquest. This procedure has its roots in the Carolingian *enquête par turbe* (a probable source of the Norman, and ultimately English, system of indictment and trial by jury), but its emergence into general use, during the twelfth century, depended on changes within the Church. Abelard's *Ethics* (*c*.1135)—with its Delphic *incipit*, *Know Thyself*[25]—helped define a shift away from judgement which discriminates between just and unjust acts in the *rei gestae* (as in the distinction between open revenge and *traïsun*) towards one which concentrates on intent. For Abelard, 'sin lay solely in the intention. A man could not be called a sinner because he did what was objectively wrong, nor because he felt a sinful desire; sin, purely and simply, lay in consent to sinful desire.'[26] In the practice of everyday piety, such thoughts were pressed upon the laity by the institution of confession. Before the twelfth century this practice was rare, but, by the beginning of the thirteenth, holding an inquest into the self and its sinful desires was considered the duty of every believer. The Fourth Lateran Council of 1215—which also, interestingly, forbade clerics to be associated with judicial combats—specifically emphasized its importance. In confession the Christian believer explored the recesses of his sinful nature, a quest which finds its ostensibly secular equivalent in the psychologized landscape of romance. When knights seeking the Saint Graal break off their travels to consult hermits and wise men in the woods, there is no sharp disjunction between their chivalric *aventures* and the confessional scenes which punctuate them. Both stages in the journey are spiritual: one allegorically motivated, the other instructively explicit.

Certainly, there is a correlation in revenge plots between the psychological problematizing of *judicium dei* and the late twelfth-century emergence of romance. R. Howard Bloch has shown how, in *La Mort le roi Artu* (1230–5?), the queen's involvement in the death of Gaheris de la Porte—when she passes on, from Avarlan, a piece of poisoned apple which Avarlan hoped would be given to

---

[24] 'The Evolution of Judicial Institutions: Burgundy in the Tenth and Eleventh Centuries', repr. in his *The Chivalrous Society*, tr. Cynthia Postan (London, 1977), 15–58.

[25] *Liberi Magistri Petri Abelardi Qui Dicutur. Scito Teipsum.*

[26] Colin Morris, *The Discovery of the Individual 1050–1200* (1972; New York, 1973), 75.

Gawain—is first judged without reference to intent, but is then tested, in judicial combat, through the subtler, more inward perspective introduced by Lancelot. According to Mador, Guinevere killed his brother 'desloiaument et en traïson'.[27] Bloch paraphrases this as 'knowingly and treacherously', and says that it 'opens the delicate question of intention'.[28] In fact, Lancelot opens this door when, confronted with the possibility of death in *judicium dei*, he counters Mador's accusation with the qualifying verb *pensa*: 'And I am ready,' said Lancelot, 'to defend [the position] that she never thought disloyalty or treason.' To this, significantly, Mador 'ne se prent garde'. He both 'paid no regard' and 'was not on guard'—as when Gautier confronts Bernier, combat begins in the vows—to Lancelot's distinction. In consequence, he goes into battle under a disadvantage. That Guinevere's champion triumphs in the duel maintains the piety that God approves the right yet subverts easy faith by permitting the stronger knight (simply) to win.

On such distinctions the future of Arthurian society depends. The problem of intention proves inextricable from older, tragic questions: must men cling to kindred loyalty, and pursue revenge to collective destruction? Eventually, this is what happens. While Arthur, aided by the kin of Gawain, is in France, avenging himself on Lancelot for sleeping with Guenevere and (unintentionally) killing Gawain's brother, his bastard son Modred sharks up an alliance of Saxon lords, eager 'vengier de maint grant anui que li rois Artus lor avoit aucune fois fet' (p. 230). Seeking revenge, that is, for the many wrongs the king has done them, they fight the immense last battle in the West, and the round table is shattered. Not that the *Mort* finishes there, with the passing of Arthur. Unlike, say, Tennyson's *Idylls of the King*, it messily plays out the logic of collective revenge, as, in yet another campaign, Lancelot leads the kindred of Ban against the sons of Mordred. Though all the great events are gone, vindictive loyalties survive; the web of tragic relationships cannot be circumscribed. All the author can offer by way of finality is modulation into another way of life. As the echoes of battle die away, he leads the glorious survivors, Lancelot, Hector, and Bors, after much wandering, to a monastery. In this the *Mort*

---

[27] *La Mort le roi Artu*, ed. Jean Frappier (Geneva, 1954), 104.
[28] *Mediæval French Literature and Law*, 30.

retraces a larger medieval transition. First the *geste*, then a quest, and finally confession, reading, and prayer.

Another literary idiom was needed for quest romance, and it was established by Chrétien de Troyes. Fluid, subtle, exploratory, the idiom which he created in the 1160s and 1170s was original and seen to be so. This was a written language, not the written record of a spoken one. The notion of performative telling, so important in the *geste*, was replaced in romance (most scholars believe) by the murmur of private reading. The body of a singer of tales is swayed by what is described: the voice rings with exchanged blows, while eyes, tongue, and arms register the violence of what is imitated. In romance, the tenebrous structures of forest pathway and hermit's cell melt through frames and windows of interlaced, quietly consumed narrative, marked out with saws and inscriptions that invite pauses for meditation. Here again affinities can be found between emergent romance and medieval piety. What so delighted Todorov about the *Queste del Saint Graal*—that the book makes much of itself as a book, offered for contemplation[29]—has less to do with modern, indeed Calvinoesque, notions of reflexivity (once *The Non-Existent Knight* turns into quest romance, it proves to be a text which is being written, in a nunnery, by one of the characters) than with the growing emphasis in twelfth-century monasteries on the virtues of private devotion. There is much to support the view that, for all its chivalric trappings, the *Queste* was composed in a Cistercian context.[30]

Without doubt its view of vengeance is very different from that which held, more than a century earlier, in *Roland*. Far from celebrating the glories of combat, its author stresses the danger of mistaken identity among jousters and questers—so that Gawain kills his best friend, Owein, by mistake—and the perils of anger between knightly brothers: Bors, for instance, attacked by Lionel. So interested is the *Queste* in relating knightly combat to sinful, internecine violence that, in its version of the Golden Legend, it frames the story of Cain and Abel as a fraternal revenge tragedy, with Cain brooding on God's favour towards Abel till it becomes the grounds of vengeance, and delaying for a long time with hatred

[29] 'The Quest of Narrative', in Tzvetan Todorov, *The Poetics of Prose*, tr. Richard Howard (Oxford, 1977), 120–42.

[30] See e.g. Étienne Gilson, 'La Mystique de la grâce dans *La Queste del Saint Graal*', repr. in his *Les Idées et les lettres* (Paris, 1932), 59–91.

in his heart before whipping out an unbiblical 'coutel corbe' or little
curved knife, and stabbing his brother in the breast.[31] Like so many
avengers in European literature, Cain delays, conceals his resentment, and composes a murderous tableau by making Abel sit, half-
throned, before killing him. 'The voice of thy brother's blood cries
unto me from the ground where thou didst spill it,'[32] God tells
Cain. These words can be found in Genesis 4, and they are
routinely cited in medieval denunciations of murder. Yet what
follows, in the *Queste*, is apocryphal. From Abel's blood a sprig of
the tree of paradise (planted out of Eden by Eve) takes on a ruddy
hue, and Solomon, generations later, directs his men to turn a piece
of its wood into a scabbard for his father, David's sword. This, we
are told, is the sword used by Varlan against Lambar; this is the
sword which brought punishment from heaven against Nascien and
Parlan; and this is the sword which Galahad claims in the middle of
his quest.

The swords of mighty warriors are often the subject of epic
ekphrasis. Like their bearers, they bring in train stories which speak
of a noble past. The sequence in which Roland attempts to destroy
Durendal, to prevent it falling into pagan hands, is a good example.
We hear of Charlemagne's being advised by an angel to give the
sword 'to a captain count', of his girding it upon Roland, and of his
nephew's conquering many lands with its help. 'Saint Peter's tooth,
some of Saint Basil's blood', and 'Some of Saint Mary's clothing'
are said to be encased in the hilt (2319ff.). Durendal is an index of
the hero's achievements, of his faith and lasting worth (it refuses to
be smashed on a rock). Twelfth-century changes in attitudes to
heroism are registered in images of the sword. In Konrad's *Rolandslied* (early 1130s), for instance, the ideology of crusading, of the
warrior as a holy pilgrim, is more prominent than in *La Chanson de
Roland*. As a result, Charlemagne does not choose to give Durndart
to his nephew; in a myth of origin which validates 'the *militia Dei*,
the holy war which God institutes as chivalric *officium*',[33] the angel
directs him to donate it. Later in the century, knighthood became

[31] *La Queste del Saint Graal: Roman du XIIIᵉ Siècle*, ed. Albert Pauphilet (Paris, 1923), 216–
17.
[32] *The Quest of the Holy Grail*, tr. P. M. Matarasso (Harmondsworth, 1969), 228.
[33] Jeffrey Ashcroft, '*Miles Dei—gottes ritter*: Konrad's *Rolandslied* and the Evolution of
the Concept of Christian Chivalry', in W. H. Jackson (ed.), *Knighthood in Medieval Literature*
(Woodbridge, 1981), 54–74, p. 59.

quasi-sacramental. Before he joined his 'order' (like an ordained priest), a young warrior would lay his sword on an altar for blessing. Dubbing involved him being girt with his weapon by an abbot or bishop. One thirteenth-century prayer summarizes the whole ethos: 'Almighty Father . . . thou who hast permitted on earth the use of the sword to repress the malice of the wicked and defend justice . . . cause thy servant here before thee, by disposing his heart to goodness, never to use this sword or another to injure anyone unjustly; but let him use it always to defend the Just and the Right.'[34]

This sheds light on Galahad's sword, a weapon even more remarkable than Durendal. It is 'called "the Sword of the Strange Belt"', he cries, 'and the name of the scabbard is Memory of Blood. For no man of understanding will be able to look at that part of the scabbard which was made from the Tree of Life without recalling to mind the blood of Abel.'[35] When Galahad bears this sword, he carries something symbolic of David's prowess and Solomon's justice, and a memento of the primal revenge which is also a piece of the true cross before it became the true cross. Christ's blood provides atonement, in this legend, for the blood spilled by Cain as much as for the apple plucked from the tree. Clearly it is difficult to tease out an exact allegory when the *Queste* encourages the sort of local contemplation which makes overall inconsistencies unimportant; but the drift is clear enough. As he wanders the fallen world, Galahad executes 'wrath' with a weapon derived from Romans 13. Whereas, in *La Chanson de Roland*, many barons bear the Pauline sword, in the *Queste* it would seem that only the purest knight can act for God. In the closing stages of his narrative, indeed, as though insisting on one final act of purification, a complete severance from violence, the author deprives Galahad himself of the power of revenge. At the gory castle, which Malory makes so much of, where Perceval's sister died from letting blood, God destroys the fortress before Galahad's weapon can avenge the murdered maidens. This onslaught is called 'espiritel venjance', and a voice from heaven assures Galahad that retribution has been exacted: 'Ce est la venjance dou sanc as bones puceles.'[36] Where Malory is coolly agnostic about this intervention,[37] the author of the *Queste* is

---

[34] Bloch, *Feudal Society*, 319.   [35] *Quest of the Holy Grail*, tr. Matarasso, 237.
[36] *Queste del Saint Graal*, ed. Pauphilet, 244–5.
[37] See *Malory: Works*, ed. Eugène Vinaver, 2nd edn. (Oxford, 1971), 593.

reverent. It represents, for him, a culmination of Galahad's progress that revenge should recede beyond him, leaving God in command of events.

*   *   *

With these contexts in mind, we can return to Benoît de Sainte-Maure with a clearer sense of how his *Roman de Troie* mediates between the elevated story-telling of the *chansons* and the more inward procedures of romance. Like Chrétien, Benoît uses octosyllabic couplets rather than *laisses*, yet his verse movement is far from limber, and his narratives, though sometimes episodic, are not elaborately interlaced. More surprisingly, he largely excludes from the *Roman* those signs of divine judgement which figure so prominently in such epics as *Roland* and, of course, in the *Queste*. Like the other great classical cycles composed in the mid-twelfth century— the *Roman de Thèbes* (*c*.1150) and *Roman d'Eneas* (*c*.1155–60)—Benoît's poem was written in a courtly rather than a monastic milieu. Multivoiced, undogmatic, tolerant of pagan beliefs, it is throughout more interested in *fortuna* than in divine, providential direction. Though far from morally agnostic, the *Roman* repeatedly gravitates to scenes of debate and uses 'the estrangements of ancient history' to unsettle the preconceptions of readers and facilitate fresh reflection on the nature of virtuous conduct.[38]

Many of these features would be passed on to later translators and adapters. Benoît's most influential follower, Guido delle Colonne, has his moralistic flights, but they are (as C. David Benson puts it) 'too rhetorical and contradictory to qualify as serious instruction'.[39] Guido's pessimistic view of human nature—encouraged by his experiences as a judge in thirteenth-century Sicily (even then a home of the blood feud)—leads him to stress violence, self-interest, and other raw promptings even more strongly than Benoît. Throughout his Trojan history, 'The most common motive for action . . . is revenge.'[40] Gower is more encyclopaedic, and complex, in his account of human passions. Like Benoît, however, he employs the Orestès story to generate uncertainty and dialogue, to probe the characteristics of ire and

---

[38] Barbara Nolan, *Chaucer and the Tradition of the 'Roman Antique'* (Cambridge, 1992), 9.

[39] *The History of Troy in Middle English Literature: Guido delle Colonne's 'Historia Destructionis Troiae' in Medieval England* (Woodbridge, 1980), 12.

[40] Ibid. 20.

limits of just violence, in Book III of the *Confessio Amantis*. Not until the fifteenth century would monkish attitudes come to dominate Benoît's matter. Lydgate, in his *Troy Book* is hostile to paganism, even more given than Benoît to reflecting on the fragility of worldly fortune, and determined to show that God will punish adultery and murder through providential vengeance.

Benoît is not indifferent to the fruits of sin. The tales of illicit love which he develops from Dares and Dictys are, for the most part, unhappy. He is interested in showing how Achilles, for instance, lured to a tryst with Polyxena, is killed in revenge for Hector. When his Ulysses reaches Ithaca, the joyful reunion with Penelope is shattered by an encounter with Telegonus, fruit of his adulterous liaison with Circe: the son unknowingly murders his father.[41] It should not surprise us to find Benoît presenting with such sardonic gravity the consequences of the *fine amor* which he is often credited—thanks to his account of Troilus and Cressida—with having helped to invent. Jean Frappier has shown that, as compared with the southern troubadours, the poets of Northern France were likely to tie *fine amor* into the complications of social circumstance and marriage.[42] Quite deliberately, the *Roman de Troie* refuses to romanticize Egistus and Clitemestra. Dealing with audiences sympathetic to Lancelot and Guinevere, Tristan and Iseult, Benoît outdoes Dictys by having the pair kill Agamennon so promptly and vilely—'en murtre e par traïson', during his first night back in his kingdom[43]—that they can hardly retain approval. Even at this early stage in the Orestès story, however, Benoît's instinct for ambiguity is felt. For he does not entirely degrade Egistus. The man is an *arriviste*, 'neither king nor count nor duke', but also a figure of substance and reputation: 'Un vassal riche e renomé' (28050-1). It is a measure of Benoît's tolerance that his translators and adapters should, in almost every case, play up Egistus' baseness, and thus extirpate all traces of feuding equality between the kin of Atreus and of Thyestes (for that conflict is, classically, a motive in Aegisthus' murder of his cousin). In Herbort von Fritzlâr's late twelfth-century *Liet von Troye*, for example, Egistus is a landless *ritter*,[44] a rank-and-file

[41] Cf. Nolan, *Chaucer and the Tradition of the 'Roman Antique'*, 102-4, 116.
[42] 'Vues sur les conceptions courtoises dans les littératures d'oc et d'oïl au XIIe siècle', *Cahiers de civilisation médiévale*, 2 (1959), 135-56.
[43] *Roman de Troie*, ed. Léopold Constans, 6 vols. (Paris, 1904-12), 28058-60.
[44] *Liet von Troye*, ed. Karl Frommann (Quedlinburg, 1837), 17256-83.

knight whose killing of the king is more loathsome because of his lowly status. The tradition of abusing Egistus as 'nouþer . . . of birþe nor of blood | Litel or nou3t of reputacioun' reaches its climax in Lydgate (v. 1102–3). He can deal with the obvious question—what, then, did Clemestra see in him?—only because he inherits from Guido a misogynistic obsession with female lust.

Revenge was changed in the early Middle Ages by a shift in kinship structure from extension to lineage, with an attendant privileging of the 'spear' (the paternal line) over the 'distaff'. The effective size of the kin-group had shrunk several-fold by the time Benoît wrote about Orestès, and, over the same period, wealth and status were increasingly transmitted from father to son. Evidence of this transition can be found in the family chronicles which began to be written in the Merovingian era. From Vuitgerius' genealogy of Arnoul le Grand (c.950) to Lambert d'Ardres's *Historia comitum Ghisnensium* (c.1190) these accounts grow in complexity and retrospective ambition.[45] Benoît was involved in this codification of noble patrilineage, and his authorship—it would seem—of *The Chronicle of the Dukes of Normandy* (c.1175) is relevant to his treatment of Orestès. It is as though he had intuited, through tensions in twelfth-century social structure, the Aeschylean quarrel between Apollo and the Erinyes, about the extent to which the mother has a blood relationship with her son, and wondered how far Orestès was, in effect, an orphan, given that his legitimacy (and patrimony) did not descend from Clitemestra. Like Huon of Bordeaux, Perceval, and various other twelfth-century, early romance figures just emerging from *chansons de geste*, Orestès is a fatherless quester in search of a 'heritage'. But this, of course, intriguingly, makes him resemble Egistus. The young, dispossessed Orestès is himself a landless *ritter*. Benoît does not describe his hero as, in high medieval terms, a prince. Emphasizing his initiation into knighthood, he brings out his likeness to those 'poor bachelors' and *juvenes* whose unstable, errant position in twelfth-century knighthood has been much explored by historians.[46] Whereas the Orestes of Dictys simply reaches maturity before setting out, in Benoît he is prepared for vengeance by being made a knight (28289). Twelfth-century

---

[45] See R. Howard Bloch, *Etymologies and Genealogies: A Literary Anthropology of the French Middle Ages* (Chicago, 1983), ch. 3.

[46] See e.g. Duby, 'Youth in Aristocratic Society: Northwestern France in the Twelfth Century', repr. in his *Chivalrous Society*, 112–21.

readers would imagine what Caxton, at leisure, spells out: 'Whan Horrestes the sone of kynge Agamenon that was/ had foure & twenty yere of age/ The kynge ydumeus that had nourysshid hym made hym knyghte and maad a grete feste of the newe chyualerye of horrestes.'[47]

In Benoît the killing of Agemennon is merciless, but mercifully abrupt. Later versions are less reticent: they put the king to bed, have Egistus cut his throat. By the fifteenth century, the murder has become an excuse for heavy-duty deploration. The *Troy Book* adds sixty lines of lament before it even gets to the killing. What Lydgate describes, moreover, is both an assault on God's justice and on the pieties associated with late-medieval kingship. Refusing, as far as possible, to bring twelfth-century judgements to bear on the ancient world, the *Roman de Troie* had been wary of monotheism, and avoided quoting Scripture. When Lydgate thinks about the murder, by contrast, he instinctively reaches for that text from Genesis 4 which the *Queste* had cited against Cain. The murder of a 'prince', he says, 'crieth wreche to hiȝe God alofte | And axeþ vengeaunce to be take as faste: | Þouȝ it abide it wil oute at þe laste!' (v. 1066–9). This is a motif which Lydgate repeats when he introduces Horrestes' revenge:

> Þe vois of blood doth so ay contune
> To crye wreche with clamoure importune
> On hem, in soth, þat it iniustly shede; . . .
> And for þe mordre of Agamenoun,
> Þe myȝti Lord, whiche is most souereyn God,
> Made his mynystre of þe same blood,
> ȝonge Horrestes, ful of hiȝe prowesse,
> Texecute his dome of riȝtwisnesse,
> And gaf to hym power, grace, & myȝt. (v. 1471–87)

Here the weight of Romans 13 is added to Genesis 4. By making Horrestes 'the minister of God, a revenger to execute wrath', Lydgate attempts to stamp out the ambiguities which reach from Benoît to Gower, and recur beyond them both.

Certainly, in *Le Roman de Troie*, Orestès' *aventure* is not simply endorsed. Benoît points up mixed motives, for instance, within the hero's faction by having him draw reinforcements from King

[47] Raoul Lefevre, *The Recuyell of the Historyes of Troye*, tr. William Caxton, ed. H. Oskar Sommer, 2 vols. (London, 1894), ii. 684.

Focensis of Trofion. This episode is in Dictys, as is the information that Trofion hates Egistus not only because he murdered Agamennon but because he jilted his daughter in favour of Clitemestra; but twelfth-century readers would have recognized in this alliance the kind of feuding warfare which is a front for rape and pillage. In an essay on the district around Benoît's birthplace—Sainte-Maure in the Touraine—Stephen D. White notes that 'the process of raiding and plundering an upper-class enemy's lands and subject peoples was so closely associated with efforts to take vengeance against that enemy as to make one wonder whether feuding or plundering was the more important activity.'[48] This kind of pragmatic violence, amply represented in the *chansons*,[49] make the more understandable Benoît's regret that a 'bone pais senz autre guerre' should be broken by Orestès' aggression (28286). Admittedly he takes Mycenae with ease. Not with the instantaneous success recorded by Dictys: that would have struck twelfth-century readers accustomed to the kind of long stalemate which holds between Gawain and Lancelot in the *Mort Artu* as incredible, or divinely enabled. But even a fifteen-day siege has its victims, losses which count for something in the context of Louis VII's ten-year *treve* (above, p. 154).

The chief victim, of course, is Clitemestra. According to the figure of Confessor, in Book III of Gower's *Confessio Amantis*, while the mother's behaviour is unforgivable, Horestes himself 'wroghte mochel schame | In vengance of his fader deth.'[50] What Gower has in mind is the method of Clitemestra's execution, added by Benoît to Dictys. Whereas in the *Ephemeridos* Clytemnestra 'was immediately slain, along with many others who dared to resist',[51] in the *Roman de Troie* Orestès ravages his mother's breasts, in front of the people: 'Veant les ieuz as citeains, | Li traist les mameles del cors' (28368-9). Psychoanalysis is, quite rightly, rarely allowed near twelfth-century literature; but this bizarre recrudescence of the turbulent material explored in Clytemnestra's dream in *The Liba-*

---

[48] 'Feuding and Peace-Making in the Touraine Around the Year 1100', *Traditio*, 42 (1986), 195–263, p. 202.

[49] e.g. when Raoul orders his barons to set fire to Origny, they are not swayed by feelings of vengeance, but because 'they came eager for looting' (1277); the sack of Paris, likewise, is undertaken by 'Franc chevalier' eager to carry off booty (5293–5306).

[50] *Confessio Amantis*, III. 1960–1, in *The English Works of John Gower*, ed. G. C. Macaulay, 2 vols. (London, 1900–1).

[51] *The Trojan War: The Chronicles of Dictys of Crete and Dares the Phrygian*, tr. R. M. Frazer, Jr. (Bloomington, Ind., 1966), 121.

tion Bearers would almost win converts to Klein (above, pp. 9–10). Morally, it is just as disturbing. 'Horrible fu trop la venjance' is Benoît's laconic judgement (28375). Whatever sympathy a twelfth-century reader might have towards Orestès would be qualified at this point. It is true that Benoît softens the blow by having the execution anticipated. Consulting an oracle, before the attack—the equivalent of going to Delphi in the classical story—Orestes is told in Dictys that he is 'destined to kill his mother and Aegisthus' (p. 121), but in Benoît he is instructed by the gods to do so, and told precisely how to slay his mother. It was left to Guido delle Colonne to harshen the tale still further by omitting the gods' detailed advice, so that the reader is unprepared for the intimacy of Orestes' violence. Guido also adds the information that Orestes cuts off his mother's breasts with a sword, and then hacks her to death with blows. Gower reverts to Benoît's shocking vagueness about how the act was done, but that sword—so troubling in this context, as an adjunct of a 'minister of wrath'—is retained by Lydgate, who also goes back over the head of Guido (his chief source) to ensure that Horrestes' atrocity is exculpatingly anticipated and detailed by 'þe goddes' (1556–77). There is a note of morally satisfied sadism in his account of how Horrestes assaults his mother 'with a swerde, sharpe and kene whet, | Liche as þe goddes chargid hym to-forn' (1640–1).

Gower was less resolute. Indeed, James Simpson has argued that the story of Horestes defines a 'critical moment' in the *Confessio Amantis*. 'The tale of Orestes brings to light', he says, 'inadequacies within the terms of natural law alone: there are certain cases where natural law cannot decide the issue, since both parties are guilty of being "unkynde." Here recourse to bodies of law (divine, and especially positive, or human law) which surround and constrain natural law is necessary.'[52] This is a persuasive claim, and it helps explain why Gower does not, like Lydgate, work allusions to Romans 13 into the body of his narrative but waits until the perplexities of the story have registered before insisting that a judge should not spare traitors and felons, and that—in Pauline terms—'a kinges swerd is bore | In signe that he schal defende | His trewe people' against murder and robbery (2226–8). The legal

[52] 'Genius's "Enformacioun" in Book III of the *Confessio Amantis*', *Mediaevalia*, 16 (1993), 159–95, pp. 182–3.

and moral crisis marked by Gower would still be felt in the mid-sixteenth century, when John Pykeryng (who was a lawyer) intro-duced into *Horestes* the figure of Nature herself, pleading for mercy towards Clytemnestra. However, the raw materials of Gower's crux can be found in the *Roman de Troie*. Showing his usual appetite for dialogue and disagreement, Benoît follows his description of the deaths of Clitemestra and Egistus—the latter captured, somewhat treacherously, in an ambush—with a summary account of divided feelings among the common people of Greece. Some said that Orestès dealt justly; others disagreed. This interest in debate at even the lowest levels of society diverges from Dictys' imputation of force and self-interest: 'Throughout Argo the people were forced to take sides and tried to choose where best their interest lay' (p. 121).

Such considerations return, however, in Benoît's handling of Menelaus. Like the irresponsible uncle of Raoul de Cambrai, King Louis, the uncle of Orestès is slow to avenge a kinsman (his brother) and, the reader might well think, rather too interested in his nephew's lands. Since the Trojan war was fought to punish adultery and murder, it is suspicious that he should not just—as in the elliptical Dictys—lay 'many plots against Orestes' (p. 121) but, from Benoît onwards, seek to persuade the Greek nobility that his nephew is unworthy to govern Agamennon's realm. Who, then, would control it? Agamennon's brother, no doubt. The handling of the trial in which Menelaus confronts Orestès shows to full effect Benoît's skill as a story-teller. Dictys, in Benoît's source, is colourless: 'Orestes, it was decided unanimously, should go to Athens, and there stand trial before the court of the Areopagus. Thus Orestes plead[ed] his case, and the Areopagus acquitted him' (pp. 121–2). There is nothing here of the deadlock in Aeschylus, broken by Athene's casting vote—nor of the peculiar status of the Areo-pagus, by tradition a socially privileged as well as a formidable court in fifth-century Athens. Benoît recreates at once the standing of the Areopagus and the uncertainty of its judgement by making Orestès appear before a court of chivalry with a champion on offer for judicial combat, like Ganelon in *Roland*. Whereas an opponent can finally be found for Pinabel, however, and the combat goes ahead, none of the Grecian kings and lords will challenge Orestès' champion, Menesteus.

At this point, Benoît's narratorial reticence stands him in excel-

lent stead. His readers are left uncertain whether the peers hold
back because they believe Orestès' case to be strong—as Gower
and Lydgate suggest—or whether they are daunted to be faced
with so notable a champion. The question of the avenger's worth
and guilt is not put to *judicium dei.* Exploiting a morally charged flaw
in the procedures of twelfth-century justice, rather in the spirit of
the *Mort Artu,* Benoît can be true at once to his society and to the
classical myth which he was, without realizing the fact, recreating.
In his hands Orestès' tragedy recovers much of its ancient force, and
all of its ambivalence. 'Horrible fu trop la venjance.' Even in that
declaration, there is movement. 'Trop' in twelfth-century French
meant both 'very' and, as in the modern language, 'excessively
much'. Revenge was either grisly or it was unacceptably so; the
court pardoned Orestès or the case was never answered: battle-
scarred barons might take it one way, members of a peace league
another. What remained were the ancient perplexities, which stayed
with '3onge Horrestes' right through the medieval period. Some of
them, indeed, would be inherited by that prince who duels with
Laertes in a quasi-providential *judicium dei* staged before King
Claudius. One function of my next chapter will be to think out
from Aeschylus', Benoît's, and John Pykeryng's Orestes to the
Hamlet who became, in the post-medieval period, the new icon
of revenge.

7.   'Remember Me!': Horestes,

Hieronimo, and Hamlet

AT the start of *The Libation Bearers*, Orestes stands beside his father's tomb, thinking about the past. Apparently sunk in passive grief, he offers Agamemnon a lock of hair and laments that he was not in Argos to mourn at his funeral. Then, however, retrospection modulates into a cry for revenge: 'Zeus, Zeus, grant me vengeance for my father's | murder. Stand and fight beside me, of your grace' (17–18). Exactly the same movement of feeling is experienced by Electra when she, in turn, comes to the tomb with the chorus of libation bearers. Recalling the circumstances of Agamemnon's murder, she shifts abruptly to revenge: 'father, I pray that your avenger come, that they | who killed you shall be killed in turn' (143–4). Electra's prayer is answered. She finds the hair, and it matches her own; her feet fit into the prints left by her brother; and then Orestes steps forward, persuaded by what she has said that she will not betray him. In the vibrant passage which follows, brother, sister, and Chorus unite in reminding each other, the dead king, and the audience of the bloody deed performed in the first part of the trilogy. Here, even more clearly, thoughts of the past stir revenge: '[Remember]¹ that bath, father, where you were stripped of life', urges Orestes. '[Remember] the casting net that they contrived for you', responds Electra (491–2). A clamour of stichomythia begins, and it is only contained when the Chorus says:

> None can find fault with the length of this discourse you drew
> out, to show honor to a grave and fate unwept
> before. The rest is action. Since your heart is set
> that way, now you must strike and prove your destiny.   (510–13)

---

¹ Lattimore's 'Think of', in the Chicago translation, is an inexplicable rendering of 'memnēso'.

At this point it becomes clear that temporal relations have changed. The Chorus hints at delay, and Orestes' evasive response—'So. But I am not wandering from my strict course | when I ask . . . ' (514–15)—does not refute it. Identifying a paradox which recurs in revenge tragedy, Aeschylus shows the past inciting violence but notices how retrospection can offer its own satisfactions and draw an avenger back from his task. In this chapter, I want to demonstrate how this ambiguity can operate to dramatic effect at high levels of structural and psychological *detail* by examining two major plays of the English Renaissance—*The Spanish Tragedy* and *Hamlet*—and by relating both to a late version of Benoît's story of Orestès, in John Pykeryng's Elizabethan morality drama, *Horestes*.

Greek retrospection: Elizabethan remembrance. Aeschylus' revengers, like the Orestes and Electra of Sophocles and Euripides, have no memory of their father. They know about his life and death only because it is public knowledge. In the opening lines of *The Libation Bearers* Orestes says that his youth was spent in exile (6–7). Electra was in the palace when Agamemnon returned from Troy, but she must ask the Chorus to 'tell of how my father was murdered' because she was locked away, like a dog (445–7). The Chorus is, in fact, chief mediator of the past in Argos, and its mode of recall is impersonal. In the glorious passage beginning 'Numberless, the earth breeds | dangers . . . ' (585 ff.) the chanting dancers place the murder of Agamemnon in the same long perspective as the legends of Althaea, Scylla, and the Lemnian women. Clytemnestra and her husband are not named in the strophe which describes them. Like the other killers and victims of a myth-filled past, they are recalled with that same awestruck detachment as we 'Remember. . . the storm and wrath of the whirlwind' (592–3). This choric speech is to *The Libation Bearers* what the catalogue of ships is to the *Iliad* (II. 494–877). An act of cultural celebration, an opening of the archive,[2] it ends with words which set Agamemnon's murder in the dark backward and abysm of time: 'Delayed in glory, pensive from | the murk, Vengeance brings home at last | a child, to wipe out the stain of blood shed long ago' (649–51). Tellingly, the 'child' here is not Orestes, but the murder which he, as the agent of collective memory, will effect.[3]

---

[2] On the Homeric passage see Vernant, *Myth and Thought among the Greeks*, 77–8.

[3] Cf. *The Choephoroe* ('The Libation Bearers'), tr. Hugh Lloyd-Jones, rev. edn. (London, 1979), line 648 n.

Other views of the past were available. In Sophocles' *Electra*, for instance, even the dead 'remember' (e.g. 482–3). A witness to and sign of atrocity (*marturion* and *sēma*), the murdered corpse is an object which, by virtue of what has marked it, leaves those traces in the mind-stuff which characterize, in antiquity, memories.[4] By virtue of such thinking, Sophocles' Chorus can impute remembrance to the axe which struck down Agamemnon as well as to the dead king's body (482–7). As Michèle Simondon remarks, 'The memory of the axe is . . . an objective memory merging itself with the material trace, *marturion* of the crime.'[5] Euripides is interested in signs at once more personal and less determinate. The Old Man in his *Electra* brings brother and sister together by pointing to the *charactēr* formed by the scar on Orestes' brow, the *sumbolon* stamped above his eye when 'he slipped and drew | blood as he helped you chase a fawn' (572–4). Revealingly, however, though Electra says 'I see the mark (*tekmērion*)', and accepts her brother's identity, she does not say that she remembers the fall, or even that she remembers *him*. This is in keeping with a tragedy where revenge is motivated by *ressentiment*. Only residual reference is made, here, to Orestes' recall (through the collective memory) of his father. And when, in the *Orestes*, he prays to Agamemnon, it is not for assistance in killing Aegisthus. He hopes— both selfishly and vainly (since the dead appear to have forgotten him)—to prevent the Argolid assembly from condemning him to death, then looks for help in murdering Helen.[6]

Elizabethan revenge tragedy deals in renown and *ressentiment*, but it replaces Aeschylean exteriority with recollections which fluctuate between fame and inward memory. When Thomas Heywood's Orestes kills Egistus and cries 'oh *Agamemnon*, | How sacred is thy name and memory!',[7] he is not saying that he only remembers the dead king through public knowledge. Far from being a stranger to his father, he was among those who welcomed him to the palace on his return from Troy.[8] While Aeschylus helps us see that 'What the Greeks hoped to achieve for the dead was perpetual remembrance, by strangers as well as kin,'[9] revengers like Vindice and Chapman's

[4] See e.g. Plato's *Theatetus*, 191d–e, *Phaedrus*, 275d.
[5] *La Mémoire et l'oubli dans la pensée grecque jusqu'à la fin de V* siècle avant J. C. (Paris, 1982), 219.   [6] Lines 796–7, 1225–39. Cf. Simondon, *La Mémoire et l'oubli*, 219.
[7] *The Second Part of the Iron Age* (1612–13), in *The Dramatic Works of Thomas Heywood*, ed. R. H. Shepherd, 6 vols. (1874; New York, 1964), iii. 421–2.   [8] Ibid. 405.
[9] S. C. Humphreys, *The Family, Women and Death: Comparative Studies*, 2nd edn. (Ann Arbor, 1993), 157.

Clermont D'Ambois are possessed of piercingly individual memories of lost mistresses, brothers, and fathers. These intimate recollections are often, as in *The Spanish Tragedy*, shared with the theatre audience. In Kyd, objects held as mementos combine with a sweepingly explicit rhetoric to publish Hieronimo's bond with Horatio. But the memories disclosed by Hamlet imply others, lying deeper, unspoken. Receding into remembrance (and the equally obscure processes of forgetting), the prince excludes his audience, and, in the process, wins a depth and secrecy unlike anything to be found in Greek drama.

This would be of less interest if there were no link between Shakespeare and Aeschylus. Evidence is growing, however, that Elizabethan playwrights knew more ancient tragedy than Seneca. Emrys Jones's ponderable claim that the Roman revenge plays, *Titus Andronicus* and *Julius Caesar*, were influenced by Latin versions of Euripides' *Hecuba* and *Iphigenia in Aulis*,[10] has been extended by Louise Schleiner. She proposes that *Hamlet* is indebted to one of the Latin translations of the *Orestes* available during the sixteenth century, and that the play is partly based on Jean de Saint-Ravy's Latin rendering of the two-part redaction of *The Oresteia* which was standard in the sixteenth century.[11] The latter presumably lies behind Chettle and Dekker's lost tragedies on *Agamemnon* and *Orestes' Furies*, produced in 1599 (the year before *Hamlet*), for the medieval version of the story, as it runs from Benoît to Pykeryng, gives no account of Orestès' madness. Certainly it is difficult, when we see Barnardo and Francisco scanning the battlements in the first scene of *Hamlet*, not to think of the apprehensive Herald on the roof of the palace in Argos at the beginning of *The Oresteia*. And the sequence this chapter began from has similarities with *Hamlet* V. i. As Schleiner observes, 'When Hamlet and Horatio meditate on death, hear an approaching party of mourners, then "couch" behind cover to eavesdrop on the rituals at the tomb of an unquiet soul . . . the scene breathes the very air of the opening scene of the *Choephori* (in effect the third scene in the Saint-Ravy Latin *Agamemnon*), where Orestes and Pylades, having meditated upon the dead king, hear a procession approaching and duck behind cover to eavesdrop on the

---

[10] Emrys Jones, *The Origins of Shakespeare* (Oxford, 1977), 85–110.
[11] Louise Schleiner, 'Latinized Greek Drama in Shakespeare's Writing of *Hamlet*', *Shakespeare Quarterly*, 41 (1990), 29–48.

mourners trying to give rest to the troubled dead."[12] This chapter
will bring out differences between Aeschylus' scene and its Christianized equivalent in Shakespeare, and, more largely, between
ancient and Renaissance principles of tragic representation. It will
also take the view, however, that, without an awareness of the long
history of revenge tragedy, and, in particular, of the part played in it
by classical drama, something must be lost from our readings of *The
Spanish Tragedy* and *Hamlet.*

*   *   *

When Kyd's Hieronimo finds his son in the arbour, hanged and run
through with swords, he thinks of more than revenge. Dipping
Horatio's 'handkercher' or 'napkin' into his wounds, he declares:

> Seest thou this handkercher besmear'd with blood?
> It shall not from me till I take revenge:
> Seest thou those wounds that yet are bleeding fresh?
> I'll not entomb them till I have reveng'd:
> Then will I joy amidst my discontent,
> Till then my sorrow never shall be spent.[13]   (II. v. 51-6)

Hieronimo sets out to secure retribution by equipping himself with
objects charged with remembrance: the corpse, a surrogate ghost to
whet his purpose should it ever blunt, and the gory napkin, a
memento to be carried near his heart. In the previous, first act of
the play, after describing the death of Don Andrea in the war
between Spain and Portugal, Horatio told Bel-imperia: 'This scarf
I pluck'd from off his liveless arm, | And wear it in remembrance of
my friend' (I. iv. 42-3). This scarf, as Bel-imperia explains, had been
given by her to Andrea as a love token—a token which she in turn
grants Horatio. Kyd introduced the handkercher to extend this
chain of remembrances. His play has often been criticized for
dividing between two centres of interest—Andrea's revenge and
Horatio's—and thus for making redundant, by the end of Act II,
those framing figures whose comments punctuate and ultimately
direct the action: the ghost of Don Andrea and the spirit of
Revenge.[14] But the scarf and handkercher, complementary
emblems of remembrance, tie one plot into the other, and focus

---

[12] Ibid. 39.
[13] Thomas Kyd, *The Spanish Tragedy*, ed. Philip Edwards (London, 1959), II. v. 51-6.
[14] e.g. Bowers, *Elizabethan Revenge Tragedy*, 68.

The Spanish Tragedy around the relationship between memory and revenge.

In the first scene of the play, Andrea had risen from the underworld, like the Fury in Seneca's *Thyestes*, and told us that, after his body was buried by Horatio, his spirit crossed 'the flowing stream of Acheron', pleased Cerberus 'with honey'd speech' and presented itself to three judges. Aeacus deemed that the proper place for Andrea was among lovers on the 'fields of love', but Rhadamanth objected that 'martial fields' better suited the soldier. It was left to Minos, the third judge, 'to end the difference', by sending the spirit further into Hades to consult a higher authority. The dialectical nature of Minos's judgment[15] is echoed in the structure of the underworld: Andrea must take 'the middle path' of three if he is to reach Pluto's court. Interestingly, Virgil, Kyd's authority for most of the speech, reports in Book VI of the *Aeneid* that there are two paths, not three. Kyd clearly had some special purpose in establishing that, in the underworld, the road to justice leads through and beyond alternatives—and that it leads, in the end, to the Revenge which personifies (in Pluto's court) Proserpine's 'doom'. What the play shows is this journey becoming a pattern for Hieronimo's vengeance: though the Knight Marshal inhabits a more or less contemporary Spain, he explores the same moral landscape as the spirit of Andrea. In one way, indeed, he is compelled to travel towards Revenge, for the goddess of his play, Proserpine, has granted Andrea a providential as well as a judgemental 'doom', and Hieronimo is the instrument of her will. But in another sense— one readily available to audiences schooled in the paradoxes of predestinarian Calvinism—he actively chooses to make the journey; and he does so because of remembrance.

The Knight Marshal is contemplating a hellish pilgrimage as early as III. ii. 1–52. 'The ugly fiends do sally forth of hell,' he says, 'And frame my steps to unfrequented paths.' Dreams of remembrance ('direful visions' in which he sees the 'wounds' of his son) have made him susceptible to such temptation. At this stage, however, memory can provoke nothing but frustration, for Hieronimo does not yet know who murdered Horatio. He is caught between desire for action and an intolerable, tormenting patience,

---

[15] Cf. the 'doom' of the King of Spain at I. ii. 173–97, judging between Lorenzo and Horatio.

and the strain tells on his sanity. He thinks that everything must be caught up in his anguished dilemma. As Empson says in his poem 'Let it Go', at the borders of madness, 'The contradictions cover such a range':

> Eyes, life, world, heavens, hell, night, and day,
> See, search, shew, send, some man, some mean, that may—
>
> *A letter falleth.*

Seeking a 'mean' (both 'opportunity' and 'middle course'), Hieronimo hunts the kind of path along which Minos sent Andrea to Revenge. He finds it when Bel-imperia's letter falls from the stage balcony, telling him how to break the deadlock and advance into action: 'Me hath my hapless brother hid from thee', it says: 'Revenge thyself on Balthazar and him, | For these were they that murdered thy son.' '*Red ink*' reads the practical note in the Quarto margin, and the letter tells Hieronimo that it has been written in blood for want of ink. So the paper flutters to the stage looking very like Hieronimo's bloody handkercher: another memento inciting revenge.

By the end of the act, his desire for retribution unsatisfied, kept from the king by his son's chief murderer, Lorenzo, Hieronimo has once more become desperate, and he turns back to 'unfrequented paths'. Standing between the traditional tools of suicide, '*a poniard in one hand, and a rope in the other*', he tries to decide which offers the better route to justice:

> Hieronimo, 'tis time for thee to trudge:
> Down by the dale that flows with purple gore,
> Standeth a fiery tower: there sits a judge
> Upon a seat of steel and molten brass . . .
> Away, Hieronimo, to him be gone:
> He'll do thee justice for Horatio's death.   (III. xii. 6–9, 12–13)

Alone on the empty stage, the character is caught in a crux. Dagger and halter become parts of the scene: 'Turn down this path, thou shalt be with him straight, | Or this, and then thou need'st not take thy breath: | This way, or that way?' Again, it is remembrance of his loss that breaks the deadlock: 'if I hang or kill myself, let's know | Who will revenge Horatio's murder then?' The weapons are thrown down, both paths rejected, and what stands between, the man remembering, goes forward to revenge, along 'the middle path' of three.

The same dialectic operates at the third and most formidable point of deadlocked uncertainty, found in the soliloquy '*Vindicta mihi!* . . . ' (III. xiii. 1–44). The first five lines of this, in which Hieronimo considers the possibility of leaving God to revenge his son, are made the more moving by his choice of Romans 12–13. As Knight Marshal, a legal official, the kind of 'civil magistrate' that the marginal glosses of the Geneva Bible equate with Paul's 'minister of God',[16] Hieronimo is entitled to exact blood for the murder of his son. Yet because he would be acting in his own case—as a hating father not dispassionate judge—he cannot take the blood which in another sense he should.[17] Destabilized by this, Hieronimo is denied that vengeance which, for Elizabethan audiences, was the most essential adjunct of his office. It is hardly surprising, therefore, that he should go on from Romans to consider contrary advice, taken from Seneca's *Agamemnon*: '*Per scelus semper tutum est sceleribus iter.*'[18] Although it is not clear whether Hieronimo applies this paraphrase of Clytemnestra's decision to kill her husband to himself (who, like her, has a child to revenge) or to Lorenzo (who has a better claim to '*scelus*'), either way the line dictates action: vengeance or a pre-emptive strike. If he dithers, Hieronimo reflects, he will simply lose his life: 'For he that thinks with patience to contend | To quiet life, his life shall easily end.' Yet here the argument starts to recoil, for the ambiguity of 'easily' allows 'patience' and 'quiet life' to register as attractive positives even while they are being rejected as cowardly and dangerous. Hieronimo touches on a vein of soothing Senecanism indulged elsewhere by Balthazar's father, the King of Portugal:[19] the patient man lives and dies in ease. His will, in other words, is puzzled, and he consoles himself with classical commonplaces. If destiny allows one to be happy, one will be; and if not, then one has the comfort of a tomb. Moreover (thinking now of a famous line from *Pharsalia*), if

---

[16] For other applications of the phrase see Mary Mroz, *Divine Vengeance* (Washington, DC, 1941), 32–9.

[17] On this conflict see e.g. William Ames, *Conscience with the Power and Cases Thereof* (1639), III. iii. 4–7.

[18] 'Per scelera semper sceleribus tutum est iter' ('through crime ever is the safe way for crime'), line 115, in *Seneca: 'Tragedies'*, ed. and tr. Miller.

[19] e.g. I. iii. 5–42, III. xiv. 31–4.

destiny denies even that, 'Heaven covereth him that hath no burial.' Suddenly his memory sparks into life: Horatio lies unburied because of his father's delay. 'And to conclude',' he says (though logically it is no conclusion), 'I will revenge his death!' The tangle of impulse and argument is broken through, and nothing more is heard of patience.

With Horatio's memory uppermost in his mind, the magistrate is offered ' "The humble supplication | Of Don Bazulto for his murder'd son" ' (78–9). At first denying that anyone could claim such a bloody loss but himself, he then recognizes in Bazulto his 'portrait', his uncanny double, and offers to wipe the old man's tearful cheeks. As he draws out the handkercher, however, he is once again overwhelmed by remembrance, and, through that, by desire for revenge:

> O no, not this: Horatio, this was thine,
> And when I dy'd it in thy dearest blood,
> This was a token 'twixt thy soul and me
> That of thy death revenged I should be.   (86–9)

Hieronimo begins to rave about the journey he must make, down to 'the dismal gates of Pluto's court', within the walls of which 'Proserpine may grant | Revenge on them that murdered my son' (108–21). Why does he end this account (so reminiscent of Andrea's in the first scene) by tearing up the legal papers of Bazulto and his fellow petitioners? Because of his obsession with remembrance and revenge. Claiming that he has not damaged the documents, he says: 'Shew me one drop of blood fall from the same.' The papers are no concern of his: they are not the corpses of 'Don Lorenzo and the rest'; he cannot therefore have touched them. Moreover, the sheets of paper written with ink, unlike Bel-imperia's letter inscribed with gore, offer no purchase to the memory: yielding no blood, they cannot resemble the hand-kercher; Hieronimo cannot therefore have consulted them. Not until the performance of that play of his own devising, 'Soliman and Perseda', in the fourth and final act, are the two impulses so crazily at work here fully resolved.

Even in Act III, however, there are signs that 'doom' will satisfy remembrance. When Hieronimo sits in judgement over Pedringano for shooting Serberine, he does not know that Bel-imperia's servant was complicit in the death of Horatio, and that the murder for which he is being tried is part of an intrigue planned by Lorenzo to wipe out witnesses to the earlier crime. Faithful to full retribution—'blood with blood shall, while I sit as judge, | Be satisfied' (III. vi. 35–6)—the Knight Marshal condemns Pedringano to death. Like an over-confident Calvinist, believing himself elect, Pedringano expects a 'pardon' for his crimes, a 'remedy', 'good for the soul' which will show that his master 'hath remember'd' him (51, 77, 21–2). This feint towards remembrance sheds ironic light on his end. Horatio, after all, was not simply run through with swords. He was ignominiously strung up, hanged like a common criminal. This is what happens to Pedringano when the stage's tragic scaffold imitates an executioner's platform and the hangman '*turns him off*' (104). Hieronimo says more than he knows when he reflects, just before the hanging: 'This makes me to remember thee, my son' (98). And the retributive shape of memory is further invoked by the Deputy's insistence that Pedringano's body, like that of Horatio, lie 'unburied' (106). In Act III, Revenge directs a playlet without his hand being perceived by the characters. In the last act of the tragedy we witness a more conscious manipulation, by Hieronimo, of memory's vindictive dramaturgy.

Near the end of *The Libation Bearers*, Orestes displays the bodies of Aegisthus and Clytemnestra and the robe or net in which his father was murdered and summons up the past to justify his revenge to the Chorus: 'Did she do it or did she not? My witness is | this great robe. It was thus she stained Aegisthus' sword. | Dip it and dip it again, the smear of blood conspires | with time to spoil the beauty of this precious thing' (1010–13). The obvious Elizabethan parallel is Antony's speech to the mob in *Julius Caesar*, where Caesar's blood-stained robe is used to justify the revenge which the orator provokes in the people:

> If you have tears, prepare to shed them now.
> You all do know this mantle. I remember
> The first time ever Caesar put it on;
> 'Twas on a summer's evening, in his tent,
> That day he overcame the Nervii.
> Look, in this place ran Cassius' dagger through;
> See what a rent the envious Casca made;
> Through this the well-beloved Brutus stabb'd,
> And as he pluck'd his cursed steel away,
> Mark how the blood of Caesar followed it.   (III. ii. 169–78)

Yet the interplay between public and private here—between 'You all do know this mantle' and 'I remember' (that move which, for early audiences, authenticates Antony as a revenger)—is utterly different from the vivid openness of the Aeschylean tableau. And when Hieronimo, standing among the corpses of his enemies, produces the bloody 'napkin' to justify his climactic violence, the object of remembrance is even more private in its associations than the 'mantle'. How can the Spanish court—apparently confused to the end of the tragedy—make sense of what they are shown? How can they share the Knight Marshal's remembrance?

In chapter 3 of *Le Temps retrouvé*, Marcel's memory is prompted by the texture of a 'napkin':

the napkin which I had used to wipe my mouth had precisely the same degree of stiffness and starchedness as the towel with which I had found it so awkward to dry my face as I stood in front of the window on the first day of my arrival at Balbec, and this napkin now, in the library of the Prince de Guermantes's house, unfolded for me—concealed within its smooth surfaces and its folds—the plumage of an ocean green and blue like the tail of a peacock.[20]

Again there is an enormous shift in sensibility: for Hieronimo the past is sustained by the continuity of an object; it survives within Marcel experientially, as sensation, association, irridescence. But the link with Kyd, and even, though distantly, with Aeschylus, is there in the thought which the reverie evokes in Marcel: 'je remarquais qu'il y aurait là, dans l'œuvre d'art que je me sentais prêt déjà . . . à entreprendre, de grandes difficultés.'[21] Through the work of art which he, by undertaking, becomes, Proust's narrator can make his audience live through what has gone, but which, given the imperiousness of memory, seeks to command the present. Art can publish the past, even when it is private. Orestes creates a self-justificatory tableau out of the robe-net and the bodies, Antony performs a little play of passion over Caesar's corpse and mantle, and drama labours to communicate the significance of the hand-kercher which Hieronimo shows the court.

After the execution of Pedringano, a letter had been found in his pocket confirming the identity of Horatio's killers. When this

---

[20] Marcel Proust, *Time Regained*, tr. Andreas Mayor, rev. edn. (London, 1970), 226.
[21] *À la recherche du temps perdu*, ed. Pierre Clarac and André Ferré, 3 vols. (Paris, 1954), iii. 870–1.

missive was brought to Hieronimo, the outraged Knight Marshal had cried: 'Holp he to murder mine Horatio? | And actors in th'accursed tragedy | Wast thou, Lorenzo, Balthazar and thou . . . ?' (III. vii. 40–2). That drama returns when the 'tragedy' written by Hieronimo in his student days is performed before the court, the equivalent of Orestes' Chorus and Antony's mob. A reprisal effects a reprise. Once more a gentle knight is murdered so that his faithful mistress can be won by a royal lover. Balthazar plays what is (by this reckoning) his own part, that of Soliman, and Bel-imperia hers, that of the 'Italian dame, | Whose beauty ravish'd all that her beheld' (IV. i. 111–12). Horatio, however, cannot take the role of the knight Erasto, so Lorenzo does that, leaving Hieronimo to 'play the murderer' (133), the bashaw, the character who in the playlet is the equivalent of Lorenzo in 'th'accursed tragedy'. When Soliman agrees to Erasto's death, reluctantly, as Balthazar does to Horatio's, Hieronimo stabs Lorenzo, the arbour scene returns, the court is invited to grasp those memories which cluster around the handkercher, and, in the death of Lorenzo in Horatio's role, revenge is clinched in remembrance.

*   *   *

From the outset, the impulse to violence is more problematic in Elsinore. When the ghost exhorts Hamlet to 'Revenge his foul and most unnatural murther', the prince's response is only superficially 'apt'. 'Haste me to know't,' he says: 'that I with wings as swift | As meditation, or the thoughts of love, | May sweep to my revenge' (I. v. 25, 29–31). 'May' is not 'will', and the overtones of 'meditation' and 'thoughts of love' are at odds with what seems in prospect. Left with the valediction 'Adieu, adieu, adieu: remember me!', however, Hamlet takes his task to heart with all the passion which he can muster:

> Remember thee!
> Ay, thou poor ghost, whiles memory holds a seat
> In this distracted globe. Remember thee!
> Yea, from the table of my memory
> I'll wipe away all trivial fond records,
> All saws of books, all forms, all pressures past
> That youth and observation copied there,
> And thy commandement all alone shall live
> Within the book and volume of my brain,
> Unmix'd with baser matter. (95–104)

An Orestes-figure so devoted to the past will find it hard to avenge. Symptomatically, the Jacobean hero of Thomas Goffe's *Orestes* borrows Hamlet's speech-rhythms but substitutes thoughts of action for memory: 'Think on [thee], and revenge: yes, those two words | Shall serve as burden unto all my acts, | I will revenge, and then I'll think on thee . . .'[22] No doubt the Prince of Denmark said something equally conventional in the *Ur-Hamlet*. But in Shakespeare he firmly concludes: 'Now to my word: | It is "Adieu, adieu: remember me!" | I have sworn't'.[23] The contrast with Hieronimo is striking: Hamlet never promises to revenge, only to remember.

The language of this play is full of 'memory' and its cognates.[24] Hardly has it begun than it pauses to celebrate Old Hamlet as a representative of that lost and epic age in which political issues were decided by fierce, single combat, an age unlike that in which kings take power by poison and combat is a courtly exercise played with bated foils. After the nunnery scene, Ophelia recalls a lover whom we have never really known ('O, what a noble mind is here o'erthrown!' (III. ii. 150–61)), while the ballads which she sings in madness, remembering Polonius ('His beard was as white as snow, | All flaxen was his pole, | He is gone, he is gone . . . ' (IV. v. 195–7)), are equally loyal to the past. Such memories divert and slow the play, giving it an eddying, onward inclusiveness which contrasts with the movement of Shakespeare's other tragedies and which significantly departs from the remembrance-driven dialectic of *The Spanish Tragedy*. Set against these recollective impulses, others appear more selfish. Though he admits that 'The memory' of his brother is 'green', Claudius insists on 'remembrance of ourselves' (I. ii. 1–2, 7). Rosencrantz and Guildenstern accept from him 'such thanks | As fits a king's remembrance' (II. ii. 25–6). And Fortinbras winds up the tragedy by saying: 'I have some rights, of memory in this kingdom, | Which now to claim my vantage doth invite me' (V. ii. 389–90).

Such true, false, and cynical remembrances all reflect on the play's chief link with the past. Even before he sees the ghost, the prince remembers his father. When he first meets Horatio, for

---

[22] *The Tragedy of Orestes* (1633), G3ʳ, modernized.

[23] Lines 110–12. Cf. the parting of Laertes from Polonius, where a father again imposes precepts upon a son's remembrance (I. iii. 68–81).

[24] The word occurs more than twice as often in *Hamlet* as in any other play by Shakespeare; 'remember' is also more plentiful here than elsewhere in the canon.

example, he almost sees the apparition which his friend has come
to announce:

> My father—methinks I see my father.
> HORATIO   Where, my lord?
> HAMLET   In my mind's eye, Horatio.
> HORATIO   I saw him once, 'a was a goodly king.
> HAMLET   'A was a man, take him for all in all,
> I shall not look upon his like again.   (I. ii. 184–8)

Hamlet fends off his friend's recollection of the public man—the
shared, 'goodly king'. His words advertise a privacy which remains
his throughout the play. We can show that remembrance haunts
him, even to the point of madness, and call this the heart of his
mystery. But that heart can never, as he assures Guildenstern, be
plucked out. In memory, Hamlet eludes us. Plainly, however, his
words to Horatio are consistent with a degree of suffering. Even
when comfort is found in the past, that only makes the present more
desolate, 'an unweeded garden | That grows to seed' (I. ii. 135–6).
In bereavement, as the psychologist John Bowlby observes, 'because
of the persistent and insatiable nature of the yearning for the lost
figure, pain is inevitable'.[25] It is a measure of the prince's anguish
that loss produces an exaggerated estimate of 'the lost figure'. Old
Hamlet becomes 'So excellent a king, that was to this | Hyperion to
a satyr; . . . Heaven and earth, | Must I remember?' (I. ii. 139–43).
Claudius calls his nephew's dejection 'unmanly', accusing him of
'obstinate condolement' (93–4). But he is not two months bereaved
of a noble father, buried and replaced in the queen's bed with
scandalous despatch. In any case, we know that Hamlet, healthily
enough, is trying to shake off at least part of the burden of his
father's memory.

For the 'tenders' of 'affection' made to Ophelia 'of late'—which
can only mean since his return from Wittenberg for the funeral of
his father[26]—show the prince attempting to replace a dead love-
object with a living one. His inky cloak is ambiguous: a mark of
respect for his father, it also indicates his desire eventually to detach
himself from him. As Freud points out in 'Trauer und Melancholie',
mourning has a psychical task to perform: to detach the survivor's

---

[25] *Loss: Sadness and Depression* (London, 1980), 26.
[26] I. iii. 91, 99–100; cf. Anne Barton, introd. to *Hamlet*, ed. T. J. B. Spencer and Stanley
Wells (Harmondsworth, 1980), 24–7.

memories and hopes from the dead.[27] A combination of things prevents Hamlet from effecting that 'severance' which Helena (in a related play of 'remembrance') achieves even before the action of *All's Well that Ends Well* gets under way. Despite her Hamlet-like garb of mourning, her first soliloquy (reversing the prince's) admits that, because of her devotion to Bertram, 'I think not on my father . . . I have forgot him' (I. i. 79–82). Ophelia's apparent rejection is one factor in Hamlet's distress: by returning his letters and refusing him access she throws his love back onto the father who has never (it would seem) emotionally betrayed him. Another is Claudius' refusal to let him return to school in Wittenberg: this leaves the prince surrounded by people and places which remorselessly remind him of the dead king. But most important, of course, is the injunction, 'Remember me!' With this command the ghost condemns Hamlet to an endless, fruitless 'yearning for the lost figure'. In the nunnery and closet scenes, we see the effect on his sanity.

'My lord,' says Ophelia, 'I have remembrances of yours | That I have longed long to redeliver. | I pray you now receive them' (III. i. 92–4). This confirms for Hamlet a suspicion bred of his mother's 'o'er-hasty marriage', that woman's love is brief and unworthy. It seems that Ophelia wants to divest herself of every shred of attachment. In this she is no better than Gertrude, glad to forget her first husband. Moreover, the girl's gesture, 'There, my lord' (III. i. 101), recalls an earlier situation: Old Hamlet, like Ophelia, had pressed on the prince remembrances that were too much his already. In saying her farewells, Ophelia is, in effect, forcing him to remember (and no doubt, though an instrument of Polonius' plots, she *does* want to reclaim his attention). Through the loss of Ophelia, Hamlet feels that of his father—which is why the hysteria which follows is in excess of its apparent object. The sexuality which the prince denounces is that of his mother as well as Ophelia; Claudius, as well as he, is an 'arrant knave';[28] and there is indeed a sad resonance to the question—whether or not Polonius' surveillance is suspected—'Where's your father?' (129). '*Hysterics*', wrote Freud and Breuer, '*suffer mainly from reminiscences.*'[29]

[27] 'Mourning and Melancholia' (1917 (1915)), tr. Joan Riviere (rev. James Strachey *et al.*), in *The Standard Edition of the Complete Psychological Works of Sigmund Freud*, gen. ed. James Strachey, 24 vols. (London, 1966–74), xiii. 243–58. German *die Trauer*, like 'mourning', covers both the affect and the garb of bereavement.   [28] Line 128; cf. I. v. 124.
[29] Sigmund Freud and Josef Breuer, *Studies on Hysteria* (1893–5), tr. James and Alix Strachey, *Standard Edition of Freud*, gen. ed. Strachey, ii. 7.

The queen triggers Hamlet's raving in her bedchamber by calling Claudius 'your father' (III. iv. 9). Forced by this to compare one king with another, Hamlet insists that his mother do the same. As he shows her the counterfeit presentments, the pictures of her two husbands, that tormented, idealizing remembrance which had filled his first soliloquy overwhelms him:

> See what a grace was seated on this brow:
> Hyperion's curls, the front of Jove himself,
> An eye like Mars, to threaten and command,
> A station like the herald Mercury
> New lighted on a heaven-kissing hill,
> A combination and a form indeed,
> Where every god did seem to set his seal
> To give the world assurance of a man.   (55–62)

''A was a man, take him for all in all': the audience is carried back to that almost hallucinatory moment when Old Hamlet drifted into the prince's 'mind's eye'. And this time the ghost, fancied even more vividly, appears, suspended between spiritual and imaginative existence. 'In melancholy men', writes Burton of the phantasy, 'this faculty is most powerful and strong, and often hurts, producing many monstrous and prodigious things, especially if it be stirred up by some terrible object, presented to it from . . . memory'.[30] Hamlet sees a prodigy, but Gertrude, who has forgotten, does not.

It may seem rash to define Hamlet's derangement in terms of remembrance when we have Polonius' warning that 'to define true madness, | What is't but to be nothing else but mad?' (II. ii. 93–4). Yet this is, in fact, encouraging, for by its logic one character is amply qualified to offer a definition. In a tragedy largely dominated by assumed, or partly assumed, insanity, Ophelia's derangement is terminally authentic. And when, in a sequence which parallels the nunnery scene, she gives her brother, like Hamlet before him, remembrances, she says: 'There's rosemary, that's for remembrance; pray you, love, remember. And there is pansies, that's for thoughts.' The language of these flowers is not left to speak for itself; Ophelia provides a gloss. And lest an audience overlook the allusion, Shakespeare spells out the moral. 'A document in mad-

---

[30] *The Anatomy of Melancholy*, ed. Holbrook Jackson (London, 1932), 159 (pt. 1, s. 1, mem. 2, subs. 7).

ness,' Laertes translates, 'thoughts and remembrance fitted' (IV. v. 175–9).

Where does that leave revenge? In the body of the play, as in the first exchange with the ghost, it is far less important to Hamlet than is the impulse to remember. That imbalance is plainly dramatized in the performance of *The Murder of Gonzago*. 'Soliman and Perseda' was staged to effect Hieronimo's revenge, but there is never any question of Claudius being killed in or at 'The Mousetrap'. Perhaps Hamlet does stage the play to test the word of the ghost. Presumably he is not simply rationalizing when he says that it will 'catch the conscience of the King' (II. ii. 605). But the crucial motive is revealed to Ophelia just before the show begins: 'O heavens, die two months ago, and not forgotten yet? Then there's hope a great man's memory may outlive his life half a year, but by'r lady, 'a must build churches then, or else shall 'a suffer not thinking on, with the hobby-horse, whose epitaph is, "For O, for O, the hobby-horse is forgot"' (III. ii. 130–5). Hamlet recovers the orchard as Hieronimo the arbour, but the prince does so because he wants to see his father alive again and to help the 'great man's memory' survive. Revenge is so stifled by remembrance that, when the Player King announces 'Purpose is but the slave to memory' (188), he does more than gird unwittingly at Gertrude's forgetfulness of her husband: ironies spark from the prince's retrospective tardiness to the thought that, precisely by remembering his father, he neglects what Old Hamlet's spirit[31] wants him to do. Only the transformation of 'The Mousetrap''s murderer from brother to nephew—making him the equivalent of Hamlet rather than Claudius—reveals the prince's guilty sense that if he could but abandon himself, become as crude and cruel as 'Lucianus, nephew to the king' (244), he could satisfy the ghost.

With characteristic audacity, Shakespeare gives Hamlet his best chance of killing the king (before the confusions of the denouement) immediately after 'The Mousetrap'. As he goes to see his mother in the bedchamber, the prince comes upon Claudius at prayer. Has he not just seen his father killed afresh, and been persuaded[32] of his uncle's guilt by his reaction to the playlet? Now Hamlet can become

---

[31] The claim that the ghost may be a devil, impersonating the king—see e.g. Eleanor Prosser, *Hamlet and Revenge*, 2nd edn. (Stanford, Calif., 1971), chs. 4–5—impinges on the play's histrionic concerns here, but does not otherwise greatly complicate its mnemonics.

[32] But see above, p. 79.

Lucianus, and he takes up the role with relish, both in resolving to strike—'Now might I do it pat, now 'a is a-praying; | And now I'll do't'—and in deciding against:

> No!
> Up, sword, and know thou a more horrid hent:
> When he is drunk asleep, or in his rage,
> Or in th'incestuous pleasure of his bed,
> At game a-swearing, or about some act
> That has no relish of salvation in't—
> Then trip him, that his heels may kick at heaven . . .
>
> (III. iii. 73–4, 87–93)

Dr Johnson is not the only commentator to have been appalled by this. Others have spoken, more cautiously, of rationalization. What matters, however, is the emergence of these sentiments from thoughts of reciprocity. ''A took my father grossly, full of bread,' Hamlet says, 'With all his crimes broad blown, as flush as May' (80–1). Now that the playlet has recovered the past, showing Old Hamlet asleep in his orchard, 'unhous'led, disappointed, una-nel'd' (I. v. 77), the punitive inadequacy of anything but complete retribution is freshly in mind. Through the Lucianus-like ruthless-ness of his speech Hamlet registers a recognition that revenge is incoherent unless it possesses that recapitulative power which (pace Hieronimo) the passage of experience makes impossible. If the prince found Claudius gaming or swearing, he would want him asleep in an orchard, and not now but then. In other words, his prevarication anticipates problems about punishment in time which I shall discuss in Chapter 11. Here, it is enough to notice that, in so far as The Murder of Gonzago stirs thoughts of the past, it not only compromises action by substituting remembrance for revenge but points up the incoherence of violence by staging a more persuasive recapitulation than stabbing in the back could contrive.

In any case, Hamlet cannot become a Lucianus, and so does not revenge his father. The weapons finally used to kill Claudius (the venomous rapier and celebratory, poisoned drink) mark the attack as spontaneous retaliation, not long-nurtured vengeance. The king dies for the murder of Gertrude and the prince, not for a poisoning in the orchard. Old Hamlet does not return to triumph over the corpses of his enemies, like the satisfied ghost of Andrea at the end of The Spanish Tragedy. Memory being private, the audience cannot even tell whether Hamlet is thinking about his father during these critical minutes. Old Hamlet is simply not mentioned in the turbulent last phase of the play—an omission which seems the more remarkable when Laertes, who is being hurried off by the fell sergeant death with yet more despatch than the prince, finds time to refer to Polonius. Hamlet knows that revenge would gratify the stern, militaristic father whom he loves, and he appears to want to please him; but he cannot overcome his radical sense of its pointlessness. Claudius has killed Old Hamlet and whored the queen. Neither evil can be undone. Revenge cannot bring back what has been lost. Only memory, with all its limitations, can do that.

Nowhere is this lesson brought home more forcefully than in the graveyard scene (v. i). As they delve about in the clay, the gravediggers turn up the past as it really is: earth indistinguishable from earth, skulls, loggat bones. This might be a politician's pate, or a courtier's, says the prince. And might this not be the skull of a lawyer? 'It might, my lord' (81); but, equally, it might not. None of Hamlet's speculations can give life to this bony refuse. The skulls remain, despite his efforts, terrifying, vacant emblems, mouthing the *memento mori* truism: 'Fui non sum, es non eris.'[33] Even if it was inspired by Aeschylus, this sequence is so steeped in Christian *ars moriendi*[34] as to have moved beyond the classicism which consoled and spurred Hieronimo. Only one of the bony relics can, temporarily, escape the bleak commonplaces of piety. When the prince learns that he holds the skull of Yorick, he is able to give it form and feature: 'Alas, poor Yorick! I knew him, Horatio, a fellow of infinite jest, of most excellent fancy. He hath bore me on his back a thousand times' (184–6). Yorick's link with life is fragile, though. Only his small fame, lingering in the minds of gravedigger and prince, shows what a piece of work he was. The rest of him, like every other bone in the cemetery, signifies death: 'Now get you to my lady's chamber, and tell her, let her paint an inch thick, to this favor she must come' (192–4).

[33] 'I am not as I was, you will not be as you are.' For Shakespearean contexts see e.g. Marjorie Garber, '"Remember Me": *Memento Mori* Figures in Shakespeare's Plays', *Renaissance Drama*, NS 12 (1981), 3–25, and Roland Mushat Frye, *The Renaissance 'Hamlet': Issues and Responses in 1600* (Princeton, 1984), ch. 6.

[34] See e.g. Nancy Lee Beaty, *The Craft of Dying: A Study in the Literary Tradition of the 'Ars Moriendi' in England* (New Haven, 1970), and Clare Gittings, *Death, Burial and the Individual in Early Modern England* (London, 1984).

Alexander came to it, and so did 'imperious Caesar'. Even now one might be stopping a bung-hole and the other patching a wall. Why does Hamlet consider the fate of these great men so curiously? Certainly because 'Fui non sum . . . ' has struck home: he recognizes the inevitability of his own death, as his fideistic or fatalistic speech on the fall of the sparrow shows (v. ii. 219–24). But he is also interested in these emperors because they are men remembered.[35] Perhaps it does not matter that their mortal remains have come to base ends: they persist in men's minds none the less. If the graveyard focuses Hamlet's imagination on his approaching end, it also reminds him of the possibility of survival. That is why Horatio is so important to him in the final scene:

> You that look pale, and tremble at this chance,
> That are but mutes or audience to this act,
> Had I but time—as this fell sergeant, Death,
> Is strict in his arrest—O, I could tell you—
> But let it be. Horatio, I am dead,
> Thou livest. Report me and my cause aright
> To the unsatisfied.   (v. ii. 334–40)

Yet, can Horatio report either Hamlet or his cause aright? His brief account to Fortinbras, with its 'carnal, bloody and unnatural acts . . . accidental judgements, casual slaughters' (380–5), suggests that he cannot, for everything that seems essential to Hamlet's tragedy is left out. Honest, compassionate, and intelligent though he is, Horatio is not equipped by circumstance to inform the yet unknowing world about the nunnery scene, Claudius' words to heaven, 'To be or not to be' or, indeed, any of those perplexed soliloquies.[36] Only the play can report such things, which is why the dramatic imagery of Hamlet's speech is so interesting.

When John Pykerying turned to Lydgate's *Troy Book* to find material for *Horestes*, he found a distinctly gloomy view of fame and memory. 'O vnsur trust of al worldly glorie, | With sodeyn chaunge put oute of memorie!', laments Lydgate at the death of Agamenoun, 'O ydel fame, blowe up to þe skye, | Ouer-whelmyd with twyncling of an eye!' (v. 1011–12, 1015–16). The Elizabethan dramatist's attitude could not be more different. For him it is

[35] For some of the variables involved, see Peter Burke, 'History as Social Memory', in Thomas Butler (ed.), *Memory: History, Culture and the Mind* (Oxford, 1989), 97–113.
[36] On the difficulty of Horatio's task see Constantine Cavafy's poem, 'King Claudius'.

Agamemnon's fame which makes him worth revenging. Moreover, it is fame which in his version of the story offers the strongest suasion both for and against the murder of Clytemnestra. Think what evil Oedipus did in killing his parent, Nature urges Horestes, 'And eke remember now what fame of him a brode doth go'; to which Idumeus counters, having encouraged persistence in revenge: 'remembar well the same; | In doing thus you shall pourchas to the[e] immortaull fame, | The which I hope you wyll assaye for to atchife in dede.'[37] Lydgate wrote as a medieval cleric and Pykeryng as an aspiring politician during a period notoriously fascinated by 'fame, that all hunt after in their lives'.[38] But Pykeryng was also dramatizing a story which was merely told in his source. He therefore found himself considering the springs of Horestes' action, his link with his dead father, and Agamemnon's survival through renown.

In the event, fame, the subject of a few lines in the *Troy Book*, seemed so important to Pykerying that he made it into a dramatic character. After the murder of Clytemnestra, Fame comes on stage clutching the gold and iron trumpets through which she announces good and bad deeds to eternity:

A bove eache thinge, kepe well thy fame, what ever that thou lose;
For fame, once gone, th[y] memory with fame a way it gose;
And it once lost, thou shalt in south accomptyd lyke to be
A drope of rayne that faulyth in the bosom of the see.   (830–93)

Or, to put it in Hamlet's terms: unless a man is remembered, he is no more after his death than a 'pate full of fine dirt' (v. i. 107–8). But the most significant connection between *Horestes* and Shakespeare's play lies in Fame's role as presenter. She tells us what is happening both in and just outside the action. So the play which Fame presents dramatizes the fame which she personifies. This is one reason why *Horestes*—though it does not link its revenger with the lost object through meditatively convoluted remembrance—is so unlike Greek tragedy. Pykeryng shows us, through Fame, that what we are seeing is the performance of an action. Aeschylus' actors are the *prattontes* of Aristotle's *Poetics*, a term which John Jones translates well as 'the doers of what is done'.[39] Pykeryng's actors re-enact rather than do. We are made aware that Horestes was, and that he is being played;

[37] *Horestes*, 441, 492–4, in Marie Axton (ed.), *Three Tudor Classical Interludes* (Woodbridge, 1982).   [38] *Love's Labour's Lost*, I. i. 1.
[39] *On Aristotle and Greek Tragedy*, 59.

there is a sense in which the fact that he is being played in itself proves him worth playing. Any performance of Pykeryng's drama constitutes an act of analytical commemoration.

It should now be clear why the tragedians of the city are so prominent in *Hamlet*. Clearly the prince is interested in them because of his obsession with 'seeming' and 'being', and because they can act while divorcing themselves from their actions—which is what Hamlet would have to do if he were to revenge his father. They also interest him, however, because they make remembrance their profession. The prince must struggle to keep his promise to the ghost, to preserve his memory for only a few months against the tide of the world's indifference, but the first player can reach back effortlessly to the crash of 'senseless Ilium' and the murder of Priam (II. ii. 434–522). So vividly does he make the dead King of Troy live, that Hamlet has the players do the same for another dead king—his father—in *The Murder of Gonzago*. The most extended and public act of remembrance in *Hamlet*, 'The Mousetrap' moves on from Troy to dramatize the more immediate past of Vienna and, through that, Denmark, before melting into the present of the larger play, the murder in the orchard being effected and unpunished, the murderer being happily in possession of both crown and queen.

Throughout *Hamlet*, the prince's obsession with actors and acting, together with his allusions to revenge tragedy, work to divorce the character from the actor who represents him. When Burbage or Olivier calls on those who are 'audience to this act', members of the theatre audience are drawn within the scope of the hero's attention as surely as the pale and trembling Danes, but also made aware that, just as the squeaking boy is not Cleopatra,[40] so the actor is not the Hamlet which in another sense he is. The character seems to protest through the imagery that he is too elusively himself to be inhabited by another. Nothing could more clearly mark the difference between ancient and Elizabethan conceptions of dramatic identity than the absence of such imagery from Greek tragedy.[41] Meanwhile, the *Hamlet* audience acknowledges, as it would at a performance of *Horestes*, that it is witnessing, in the dramatic spectacle, both the death of a 'great man' and an act which

---

[40] *Antony and Cleopatra*, v. ii. 219–21.
[41] See Oliver Taplin, *The Stagecraft of Aeschylus*, corr. repr. (Oxford, 1989), 132–3.

celebrates his memory. The duplicity is similar to that created by Shakespeare's Cassius, when, having prepared 'imperious Caesar' to patch a wall, he asks: 'How many ages hence | Shall this our lofty scene be acted over | In states unborn and accents yet unknown!' (III. i. 111–13). And the dramatic imagery invoked by Hieronimo when he, like Hamlet, faces death (making a suicidal gesture which remembers Horatio) might also be compared: 'gentles, thus I end my play: | Urge no more words, I have no more to say. *He runs to hang himself* (IV. iv. 151–2). But if the mechanism at work in *Horestes*, *Julius Caesar*, and *The Spanish Tragedy* is similar to that used in *Hamlet*, its effect is more poignant in the later play. In *Horestes*, the case for remembrance is put by an abstraction, Fame; in *Julius Caesar*, it is sought for the sake of a dead, rather than by a dying, man; and Hieronimo's dramatic imagery—as might be expected from a protagonist who has constantly subordinated remembrance to the revenge which it incites—has a memorial implication which is scarcely more than latent. But in *Hamlet* the appeal for just report has the weight of the play behind it. It comes from a dying hero who, having devoted himself to memory, now asks to be remembered. The appeal is enacted. It is satisfied in its performance.

8. Shakespeare and the Comic

Strain

MAN bites dog. *The Sun* excelled itself a few years ago, when it covered the case of a hooligan 'jailed for two years . . . for biting off a police dog's ear' (Fig. 7).[1] While squabbling with a peanut-seller outside West Ham football ground, Frank Turpin 'CLENCHED his teeth around the dog's ear, SEVERED it and SPAT it on the ground'. Enter, at this point, Hamlet, in the form of Solo's handler. 'But PC Rutter had his revenge. He punched Turpin in the mouth, knocking out two of his front teeth'—the very teeth, a photo-montage indicates, which cropped that very ear. As *The Sun*'s half-comic narrative enters the world of revenge tragedy, Turpin (like the warriors of *chanson de geste*) is magnified by genealogy. His descent from dashing Dick Turpin, the highwayman, is suggested. Indeed, there is a touch of mythic heightening in the way 'Frenzied Frank Turpin', like some latter-day Ajax or Hercules Furens, is said to have 'picked up alsatian Solo by the neck and swung him like a club'. It is through ironies of interchange, however, that vengeance most strikingly constructs the text. In its account of Turpin's first appearance in court, as well as of his subsequent trial, *The Sun* humanizes the dog ('he will be back on the beat when the bandages come off')[2] and represents his attacker as rabidly canine.

Tabloid journalists are expert at finding black humour in violence, but *The Sun*'s account of Turpin stands in a great tradition. Western attitudes to vengeance have for so long been ambivalent that treatments of the subject often develop a comic tonality. Sour wit and giggling sadism are recurrent traits of the revenger. Since antiquity, vengeful showdowns have centred on ludicrous humiliation. When Euripides' Polymestor, for instance, staggers out of Hecuba's tent, after witnessing the slaughter of his sons in revenge

---

[1] Tony Snow, 'Two Years for Fan Who Bit Off Police Dog's Ear', 27 Oct. 1987.

[2] 'Dog Bitten by Man is Feeling Ruff', 11 Apr. 1987.

for the murder of Polydorus, he is forced to scrabble across the stage on hands and knees. Blinded by 'savage bitches'—the Trojan queen and her women—he is now himself reduced to the condition of a hunting-dog or beast of prey, 'running on all fours | to track my quarry down!' (*Hecuba*, 1077, 1058–9). This frantic, wounded quest for revenge reaches, two millenia before Artaud, into the Theatre of the Absurd. As he casts about vainly, trying to snatch at his persecutors and crying 'Where? Where? Here? Where? . . . Where are they hiding, | those bitches of Troy' (1060–5), Polymestor is caught in a hideous game of hide-and-seek or blind-man's buff. His terms of abuse are prophetic. At the end of the play the audience learns that Hecuba will indeed be changed into '*a dog, a bitch with blazing eyes*' (1265). This projected metamorphosis makes concrete the degradation which the queen brings upon herself, through revenge, when she sinks to the level of her enemy, the child-killer Polymestor. There is a tragedy of self-reduction here which deserves closer attention (see Chapter 14); but there is also a comic grotesquerie in this abasement of the tragic queen to the four-legged dogginess of her foe—something which Ovid, characteristically, adumbrates in his account of Hecuba's transformation.[3]

In this chapter I want to think about comic traits in revenge tragedy, using Shakespeare as chief exhibit. My starting-point is a play which is sometimes compared with the *Hecuba*, which certainly owes much to Ovid, and which has touches of tabloid-style black humour: *Titus Andronicus*. I conclude with some reflections on retributive design in *The Tempest*, a work which is as much a revenge play as it is a 'late romance'. Except glancingly, when *The Merry Wives of Windsor* is invoked, Shakespearean comedy will not be discussed. Such plays as *Much Ado About Nothing* and *Twelfth Night* are strongly driven by vengeance—as Malvolio discovers to his cost—and it would be interesting to work out why it should be revenge plots which so often carry tragic materials into comedy. To pursue that question, however, would be to duplicate the work of others,[4] and to stray from the theme of this book. My concern is to identify factors which, individually or in concert, make revenge tragedy hospitable to the comic. More speculatively, I want to

---

[3] *Metamorphoses*, XIII. 565–75.

[4] See e.g. Linda Anderson, *A Kind of Wild Justice: Revenge in Shakespeare's Comedies* (Newark, Del., 1987).

explore the possibility, suggested by *The Tempest*, that the dynamics of revenge action run towards tragicomedy. This claim needs careful testing against pieces of local evidence. But it also requires attention to large elements of dramatic structure, a level of analysis equally desirable in thinking about the wittily rigorous formation of Shakespeare's first tragedy, *Titus Andronicus*.

Such a claim may sound perverse. *Titus* has long been thought laughable in the worst sense. When T.S. Eliot called it 'one of the stupidest and most uninspired plays ever written', complaining of 'a wantonness, an irrelevance, about the crimes', he was only echoing its Restoration adapter, Edward Ravenscroft, who denounced it as 'rather a heap of Rubbish than a Structure'.[5] What Peter Brook showed, however, in his production of 1955, was that the order apparent at the outset—as Saturninus and Bassianus compete for the crown—runs steadily through what follows. Brook's style was ritualistic. Where Deborah Warner (in a more recent Stratford production) 'pre-empt[ed] nervous laughter by showing how often cruelty springs out of dangerous levity',[6] he cut grotesque phrases or smothered moments of potential comedy with taped music.[7] But his, at least, was a *Titus* which respected the formal artistry apparent to Shakespeare's contemporaries. Consider 'the Peacham drawing', a sketch probably made by Henry Peacham, future author of *The Compleat Gentleman*—during the 1590s (Fig. 8). Here Tamora kneels to Titus for the life of Alarbus, her son, and Aaron raises a sword over Quintus and Martius, while two Elizabethan soldiers—odd in doublets beside the toga'd Titus, yet somehow stately—stand guard. There is an overwhelming impression of poise, and space. It might be a scene from Kabuki. To compare the woodcut printed with the seventeenth-century ballad version of *Titus Andronicus* (Fig. 9) is to be reminded how busily atrocious are the events digested by the play. In that vivid, inclusive emblem we see the tabloid side of *Titus*. Far from representing hectic action, Peacham fastens on articulate gestures: the queen's hands joined for grace; Aaron's sinister, pointing finger. No scene corresponds to what he depicts, but the sketch is the more valuable for that. It shows a gifted contemporary looking through, or thinking back

[5] 'Seneca in Elizabethan Translation', in *Selected Essays*, 65–105, p. 82; *Titus Andronicus: Or, The Rape of Lavinia* (1687), A2ʳ.

[6] Michael Billington, 'Cruelty and Grief within Reason', *The Guardian*, 6 July 1988.

[7] See e.g. J. C. Trewin, *Peter Brook: A Biography* (London, 1971), 82.

over, Shakespeare's tragedy, and being struck by a violent orderliness at its heart.

Such a phenomenon would not be possible without the play having an infrastructure more coherent than critics have, up to now, recognized. Take, for instance, Act II, with its apparently chaotic action: Lavinia raped and robbed of her hands and tongue, her husband murdered and dumped in a woodland pit, and her brothers trapped there as Quintus tries to rescue Martius. In the first scene of the play, Titus had ignored Tamora's tearful pleading and sent her son Alarbus to be sacrificed at the tomb of the Andronici. On the family's 'monument', over what Titus calls the 'sacred receptacle' of two and twenty sons (I. i. 92), Tamora's offspring is mutilated then killed. 'Alarbus' limbs are lopp'd', Lucius reports, in text apparently added in revision, 'And entrails feed the sacrificing fire'.[8] When the three surviving Goths find Bassianus and Lavinia at their mercy, they take Alarbus' revenge. But they do it by artful division, in a kind of dramatic montage. Despite her tears, Lavinia is raped and—in Marcus' telling echo—'lopp'd', while her husband's corpse is thrown into a pit associated with the Andronicus tomb. It is also called a 'receptacle'; full of roots like 'entrails', it is lit by a ring on Bassianus' finger that burns with light 'like a taper in some monument' (III. iii. 226–30, 235).

The pit is, then, a tomb—a dark refiguring of that 'receptacle' which had dominated Act I. Yet it is also, in its hideous way, anatomical, and, being so, it relates the death of Bassianus to Lavinia's rape. The sexual assault was unstageable, but Shakespeare rose to the challenge by implying it parodically, with a dead husband and two brothers crammed unceremoniously into a hole while Chiron and Demetrius set to work backstage. 'Unhallow'd', 'As hateful as Cocytus' misty mouth' and, in practical terms, the stage-trap, the pit is a theatrical 'hell', and 'hell' in Elizabethan slang meant the female genitals (III. iii. 210, 236). After condemning Lavinia to rape on the morning after her marriage, Tamora had said: 'Now will I hence to seek my lovely Moor, | And let my spleenful sons this trull deflow'r' (190–1). Scornfully suggesting that Bassianus did not consummate his nuptials, Tamora raises, in the word 'deflower', distinctly unfloral implications which carry

---

[8] Lines 143–4; see e.g. the notes to I. i. 35, 96–149, in *Titus Andronicus*, ed. Eugene M. Waith (Oxford, 1984).

across to the blood-dewed 'flowers' in Quintus' description of the 'loathsome pit'. 'What subtle hole is this', he asks,

> Whose mouth is covered with rude-growing briers,
> Upon whose leaves are drops of new-shed blood
> As fresh as morning dew distilled on flowers?
> A very fatal place it seems to me.   (198–202)

One answer to Quintus' question would be that the place is Lavinia's genitalia, after her marriage night and before the lustful brothers tumble in. Like Tennyson at the start of *Maud*, the dramatist makes sexual anxiety part of the landscape of death: 'I hate the dreadful hollow behind the little wood, | Its lips in the field above are dabbled with blood-red heath . . . there in the ghastly pit long since a body was found . . . '[9]

However, Shakespeare could develop this pit by means unavailable to Tennyson, mingling deathly-erotic dread with those rather different appetites which grant the protagonist his revenge. When Quintus, peering into the stage-trap, speaks of 'the swallowing womb | Of this deep pit' (239–40), he may clinch its sexual status, but he also extends its significance into the digestive tract. In early modern English 'womb' could mean 'gut' or 'stomach'. 'My womb, my womb, my womb undoes me', Falstaff laments in *2 Henry IV* (IV. iii. 22). This registers in Quintus' lines, and not only because the 'womb' that he describes is 'swallowing'. The pit has 'ragged entrails'; it is 'dark' and 'blood-drinking'; this 'receptacle' is 'fell' and 'devouring' (230, 224, 235). Entering the play in the reported form of the 'entrails' burned on the Andronicus tomb, intestines develop an extended, figurative life. 'For now I stand as one upon a rock,' Titus cries,

> Environ'd with a wilderness of sea,
> Who marks the waxing tide grow wave by wave,
> Expecting ever when some envious surge
> Will in his brinish billows swallow him.   (III. i. 230–3)

By means of speeches like this, Shakespeare prepares for revenge. Through the intensity and amplitude of such imagery he anticipates the Thyestean banquet, where 'swallowing', 'devouring', and the 'drinking' of 'blood' once more become stage concerns.

---

[9] *Maud*, lines 1–2, 5, *The Poems of Tennyson*, ed. Christopher Ricks, 2nd edn., 3 vols. (London, 1987).

Crucial, here, is Titus' speech to Chiron and Demetrius at the end of the penultimate scene. With the brothers now in his power—brought to his house by Tamora, disguised as Murder and Rapine—Titus drolly promises to punish them as their assumed but accurate names suggest they deserve. The violence proposed is so purposeful that, as Titus threatens the pair, he might almost be rehearsing his own grievances: the coffins of his dead sons brought to Rome; the heads of Quintus and Martius carried from execution; the 'blood-drinking' pit in the woods. 'Hark, villains, I will grind your bones to dust,' he says,

> And with your blood and it I'll make a paste,
> And of the paste a coffin I will rear,
> And make two pasties of your shameful heads,
> And bid that strumpet, your unhallowed dam,
> Like to the earth swallow her own increase. (v. ii. 186–91)

It should by now be clear why Titus goes to the trouble of slaving over a hot stove. Whether or not his 'crimes' are (as Eliot puts it) 'wanton', they can hardly be accused of 'irrelevance'. As she devours 'the flesh that she herself hath bred' (v. iii. 62), Tamora becomes a 'swallowing womb', both reproductive and ingestive. With hideous aptness, Chiron and Demetrius are repaid for their villainy at the 'unhallowed' and 'blood-drinking' pit by being themselves devoured. 'Like to the earth', Tamora 'swallow[s] her own increase' and becomes a 'fell devouring receptacle', a greedy 'monument' to the doomed house imprisoned in her 'entrails'.

Deliberately or not, Ravenscroft squandered the effect. More concerned to warn about the perils of civil strife[10] than to relish the paradoxes of violence, he assumed a state of chaos wherever he found bloodshed. To bring a semblance of order to Shakespeare's 'heap of Rubbish', he decided, in particular, to correct Aaron's exclusion from the bloody banquet by having him '*discover'd on a Rack*' as the feast proceeds. Eager to save the life of the child whom he fathered on the adulterous Tamora, the post-Restoration Moor confesses his part in the horrors of Act II. When the empress stabs the infant in retaliation for this betrayal, Aaron is appalled—not so much out of tenderness (it seems) but because 'She has . . . Out-

---

[10] See Ravenscroft's 'To the Reader', A2ʳ⁻ᵛ, on the Popish Plot, and, for contexts, Matthew H. Wikander, 'The Spitted Infant: Scenic Emblem and Exclusionist Politics in Restoration Adaptations of Shakespeare', *Shakespeare Quarterly*, 37 (1986), 340–58.

done me in Murder . . . Give it me', he cries, 'I'le eat it' (H4ᵛ).
Though the filicide is out of character, its competitiveness is not. It
is of a piece with the vaunting speech provided for the Moor by
Shakespeare (and appreciatively transcribed by Peacham beneath
his sketch) in which this Grand Guignol version of Frank Turpin—
this 'black dog', this 'inhuman dog'"—boasts of the 'thousand
dreadful things' which he has done, and adds, 'nothing grieves
me heartily indeed, | But that I cannot do ten thousand more' (v.
i. 141–4). What Ravenscroft's revision does obscure, however, is
Shakespeare's structural wit. In the Elizabethan text, Lucius sets
up a punishment which acknowledges the Moor's apartness (he is
neither a Roman nor a Goth) while cleverly meshing his fate with
that of Tamora and her sons. 'Set him breast-deep in earth and
famish him,' he commands: 'There let him stand and rave and cry
for food' (v. iii. 179–80). As in the murder of Quintus and Martius,
planned by Aaron, the victim is put into a pit alive in order to make
him dead. Devoured by a 'swallowing' hole, the solitary Moor is
forced (Tamora-like) to consume his own flesh by dwindling, to be
consumed (in the manner of Quintus and Martius) by the 'earth'.

Ravenscroft was equally free with the minutiae of Shakespeare's
verse. This is particularly damaging to the couplets which orchestrate the denouement. In the original, rhyme orchestrates action to
heighten both violence and order. When Titus stabs his daughter,
for instance, Saturninus' wild question, 'What hast thou done,
unnatural and unkind?' is countered by mad logicality in the
strongly rhymed reply: 'Kill'd her for whom my tears have made
me blind' (v. iii. 48–9). Couplets then accumulate, until, at the
climax of the sequence (64–6), a powerful consonance is contrived. So strong is the effect of rhyming that even breaks in the
pattern signify—as when, after five consecutive couplets, Titus
rounds on Tamora with the words, ''Tis true, 'tis true, witness
my knive's sharp point', and a gestural rhyme (only) is provided
when '*He stabs the Empress.*' Dramatic couplets then resume, with
Saturninus killing Titus on the words, 'Die, frantic wretch for this
accursed deed!' 'Can the son's eye behold his father bleed?' Lucius
responds: 'There's meed for meed, death for a deadly deed.' As
'meed' repays 'meed' (in phonetic revenge), and 'death' turns, via
'deadly', to a repeated rhyme, atrocity climaxes in a syzygy of

---

" v. i. 122 and v. iii. 14.

uttered 'deed' and the done. The stage is piled with corpses, yet the horrible dance of violence has a viciously playful beauty—the product of a wit which tropes persons along with language, which uses rhyme and word-play to freeze-frame, slow-motion, and (the peculiar gift of revenge) action-replay killing as a sequence of bloodthirsty conceits.

*   *   *

At this point, I must return to where my book started from: to A and B, still at odds, out on the open stage. This time, however, they are circus clowns, being watched by the philosopher Bergson, who is researching the causes of laughter:

There came on the stage two men, each with an enormous head, bald as a billiard ball. In their hands they carried large sticks which each, in turn, brought down on to the other's cranium. . . . After each blow, the bodies seemed to grow heavier and more unyielding, overpowered by an increasing degree of rigidity. Then came the return blow, in each case heavier and more resounding than the last, coming, too, after a longer interval. The skulls gave forth a formidable ring throughout the silent house. At last the two bodies, each quite rigid and as straight as an arrow, slowly bent over towards each other, the sticks came crashing down for the last time on to the two heads with a thud as of enormous mallets falling upon oaken beams, and the pair lay prone upon the ground.[12]

On paper this sounds savage. So why do audiences (as Bergson testifies) find it amusing? Partly, no doubt, because it licenses sadism by allowing a half-conscious awareness that the violence has no real effect. The false headpieces which make the clowns inviting targets simultaneously protect them from injury. The stylized exaggeration of the contest is itself the cue to this being registered. Those huge blows are too devastating to be true, so that, paradoxically enough, the more brutal they become the more entertaining they will seem.

Bergson, however, is more interested in the metamorphosis of the clowns. At the 'instant' of their fall, he says, 'appeared in all its vividness the suggestion that the two artists had gradually driven into the imagination of the spectators: "We are about to become . . . we have now become solid wooden dummies"' (p. 99). It is central to Bergson's theory of laughter that '*We laugh every time a*

---

[12] 'Laughter', in Wylie Sypher (ed. and tr.), *Comedy: George Meredith, 'An Essay on Comedy', Henri Bergson, 'Laughter'* (New York, 1956), 61–190, pp. 98–9.

person gives us the impression of being a thing' (p. 97). This can hardly
mean that Lot's wife is hilarious when she turns into a pillar of salt.
As Bergson is usually careful to point out, for laughter to thrive
there has to be some play between the innately flexible and the
fixed. In any case—to develop his analysis—what makes the two
clowns comic is not so much their resemblance to things as the fact
that their rigidity is seen to be a consequence and expression of
their being trapped in avoidable behaviour-patterns. Like Titus,
Saturninus, and the rest, constrained by vengeful couplets, they
make themselves subject to that which articulates violent reciprocity.

The idea that laughter derives from rigidity crops up so often in
Le Rire that it can seem the kind of obsession which, if it figured in a
play, would be regarded by Bergson as comic. Yet he argues rather
convincingly that the Jonsonian character dominated by his
humour, the man ridden by a hobby-horsical notion, and the
person who is slave to a catch-phrase are all suffering from the
same *raideur*. It is a principle which encompasses vengeance. When a
revenger accepts the task imposed on him, he limits the flexibility of
his life-responses in order to focus on a single aim. Like one of those
stick-wielding clowns, the revenger sets out, with foreshortened
purposefulness, to inflict upon another a hurt which has already
afflicted him. The repetitive nature of the process is, of course,
important here, because, as Bergson notes, '*repetition*' is 'one of the
usual processes of classic comedy' (p. 107). Even in the circus
routine, comic excitement flows from repetition. The crescendo of
violence is comic, but only because it gives repetition a plot. The
movement towards greater force climaxes in thumping simultaneity
('the sticks came crashing down for the last time on to the two heads
. . . and the pair lay prone'), and what an audience senses at the
'instant' of collapse is that A has turned into B, the man has bitten
the dog, and the clowns might as well have been hitting themselves
so assured were their mutual responses.

Le Rire was published in 1900 and some of its limitations, as
theory, can be traced to that historical moment. Encouraged by
nineteenth-century anxieties about the mechanization of human
experience, Bergson identifies a kind of laughter which is better
exemplified by *Modern Times*, where Charlie Chaplin wrestles with
the demands of a production line, than by *The Wasps* or *As You Like
It*. Culturally, moreover, his theory is rooted in Western assumptions

about individual freedom. Japanese audiences do not regard the juxtaposition of fluid manipulation and fixed posturing in Bunraku, where large-sized puppets are moved about by visible, black-clad puppet-masters, as laughable. Ignorant of Bergson's dictum that an image 'is generally comic in proportion to the clearness, as well as the subtleness, with which it enables us to see a man as a jointed puppet' (p. 80), they admire the capacity of Kabuki actors to emulate the movements of Bunraku. During the *Toyata Monogatari*, for instance, while one actor 'performs precisely as a puppet in faithful obedience to its irregular and jerky movements' another 'dressed in black like an old-fashioned puppeteer . . . goes through the simulated motions of manipulating the human "puppet"'.[13]

In revenge tragedy, the point of maximum stylization is often the moment of repetition. It is also that phase of an action in which characters most behave like puppets. The shows and bloody banquets which end such works as *The Spanish Tragedy* and *Titus Andronicus* have a manipulative and recapitulative force which gives them a comic potential. 'A really living life should never repeat itself,' says Bergson: 'Wherever there is repetition or complete similarity, we always suspect some mechanism at work behind the living' (p. 82). This 'mechanism' can be humanly contrived, but often, as *Le Rire* intuits, comedy springs from a sense that providence itself reduces persons to puppets (pp. 111–12). Given the providential ideology of much post-Reformation drama—its belief that punishments enacted in the world are an expression of heavenly wrath[14]—it is hardly surprising that comedy of this sort should flourish in Jacobethan tragedy. Paradoxically, the effect is heightened when what is presented as providence is exposed as human contrivance. This is what happens in *The Revenger's Tragedy*, when Vindice's dancing masque—that gyration of vengeful puppets—provokes a peal of thunder so patly disapproving that it registers as half-parodic (v. iii. 41). In a play which is full of grisly jokes,[15] an audience will not register the import of this heavenly message without relishing the technical means which create such a stagey racket.

Writing about Bunraku, Roland Barthes remarks: 'the Western

[13] Faubion Bowers, *Japanese Theatre* (Rutland, Vt., 1974), 190.
[14] Above, pp. 120–1 and n. 25, below, 217–18.
[15] See Nicholas Brooke, *Horrid Laughter in Jacobean Tragedy* (London, 1979), ch. 2.

theater of the last few centuries; its function is essentially to manifest what is supposed to be secret ("feelings", "situations", "conflicts"), while concealing the very artifice of such manifestation (machinery, painting, makeup, the sources of light)."[16] When nemesis bears down in such works as *The Revenger's Tragedy*, however, Western theatre turns inside-out: technologies of artifice, and especially devices of concealment (curtained discovery spaces, masque costumes), are visibly put to use, themselves revealed. Language is similarly wrested out of self-effacing artfulness. Denied transparency, it fragments into a playlet of sundry languages, or stiffens into *Titus*-like couplets. Examples of mobilized artifice can be found in revenge plays from other cultures. But when, at the end of *The Chushingura* (for instance), the forty-seven loyal samurai storm the house of Moronao marked with the forty-seven characters of the Japanese syllabary, there is no perverse extraversion. Language is not running wild here, as in that 'fall of Babylon', 'Soliman and Perseda'.[17] Seventeenth-century Japanese attitudes were not (to think of Bergson) the proto-industrial ones which precipitate the farcically misconducted masque with flaming gold and spiked mantrap of Middleton's *Women Beware Women*, or the dialectic of *élasticité* and *raideur* played out in *The Broken Heart* when Ithocles is tragically but absurdly trapped in a trick chair and stabbed by the angry Orgilus.

The drama of extroverted concealment is concentrated on the revenger. Vulnerable to counter-measures, he is forced to adopt a disguise. This may be physically assumed, but it can also be psychological, as when Yuranosuke in *Chushingura* passes his days in dissipation, seemingly forgetful of his dead master. The deceptively idle revenger need not be comic, but Dr Johnson was right (and not insensitive) to say that the 'antic disposition' of a Hamlet can cause 'much mirth'.[18] It should be no surprise to find the protagonist of *Antonio's Revenge*—a play based on the same source-material as *Hamlet*[19]—donning a cap and bells. Hypocrisy, deception, and mild derangement (standard instruments of comedy for a clown) are natural adjuncts of the revenger. Dissimulation assists intrigue, and intrigue itself breeds laughter, especially when the aim

[16] *Empire of Signs*, tr. Richard Howard (London, 1983), 61.
[17] Thomas Kyd, *The Spanish Tragedy*, IV. i. 195.
[18] *Selections from Johnson on Shakespeare*, ed. Bertrand H. Bronson and Jean M. O'Meara (New Haven, 1986), 344.
[19] See Marston, *Antonio's Revenge*, ed. Gair, 12–19.

of its complexity is as simple, and reductive, as revenge. The schemes of a Vindice would be less diverting if he were not so much the master of deception as to be employed, in his own person, to murder himself in disguise (IV. ii). As for his lethal masque: such displays mock Renaissance courtliness by making the devices of mystery opportunities for duplicity; they exploit the Bergsonian comedy latent in all public ceremony, which is 'to the social body what clothing is to the individual body' (p. 89). This helps explain the comic buoyancy of the gesture of revelation, the gesture which Marston's conspirators make when they throw off their masquing costumes before Piero 'and triumph over him' (V. v. 33).

The comic lift of this moment owes something to that '*Sudden Glory*' which (according to Hobbes) 'maketh . . . Laughter' when people vaunt over others' inferiority.[20] Certainly Hobbesian glorying contributes to the hostile mirth which rings out in *Antonio's Revenge*. Ethologists have pointed out that the grimace of both placatory and hostile dogs is similar, that laughter shows your fangs. But this insight (or misleading analogy) was already available to Marston, who has Pandulpho cry to the cornered Piero, 'Grinn'st thou, thou snurling cur?' (V. v. 40). The psychology of vengeful laughter here merges with that of aggression and victimization in general. Reflecting on human nastiness, the TV prankster Jeremy Beadle once admitted that, in order to hone his skills as a comedian, he had 'spent years studying revenge'.[21] His private library contains many volumes 'about murder, and the variegations of human wickedness. "I'm into sublime ingenuity, so I love really brilliant villains".' Like Marlowe's Jew of Malta, Beadle recognizes that a good revenge is a form of practical joke, and that coping with other people is a matter of paying them back—preferably in advance: 'We're told to turn the other cheek, but if you do, a bigger fist comes and whacks you. Comedy lets us get in first. A lot of comedy is about ambush.'

Group violence makes for lively theatre because its ambushes are spectacular, but Elizabethan revengers—much given to soliloquy—are often individual and isolated. Even those with comic side-kicks[22] tend to lose or sacrifice them (as Barabas does Itha-

---

[20] *Leviathan*, ed. C. B. Macpherson (Harmondsworth, 1968), 125.
[21] Peter Conrad, 'Revenger's Comedy', *Observer Magazine*, 15 Dec. 1991, 34–9, p. 36.
[22] Cf. Douglas Cole, 'The Comic Accomplice in Elizabethan Revenge Tragedy', *Renaissance Drama*, 9 (1966), 125–39.

more). Alienation of this sort can dramatize the moral apartness of those forced to recognize, where others can or will not, that society enshrines a wrong. There is something rotten in the state of Denmark, though ministers and courtiers ignore it. Set apart by this apprehension, and by a dangerous knowledge of where guilt lies, the Elizabethan revenger sees life's civilized surface as a veneer. Like a Juvenalian satirist, he is hypersensitive to corruption and given to threatening condign punishment. Marston's *Certain Satyres* and *The Scourge of Villainy* are based around the persona of a 'barking Satyrist',[23] a turbulent cynic whose rage owes more to Frank Turpin ('cynic' is from *kunikos*, 'dog-like') than to the urbanities of Horace. No doubt this sort of figure would have merged, in due course, with that of the stage revenger, but osmosis was positively encouraged by the official banning and burning of verse satires (including Marston's) in 1599. During the last years of Elizabeth's reign, satire was directed the more forcefully into such plays as Jonson's *Poetaster*,[24] a work so combative in its literary infighting that it shows Marston (in the character of Crispinus) being forced to puke up bits of his own jargon. Such texts 'are revenge comedies in the sense that they were written at least in part as instruments of revenge'.[25] But a similarly satiric intonation can be heard in tragedies like *Hamlet*, where the revenger's shafts of hostility—speaking daggers when using none—broach grievances which apply to more than the world of the play. 'To be or not to be . . .' springs out of a particular revenger's situation, but its catalogue of social complaints ('the law's delay, | The insolence of office . . .')[26] draws on the commonplaces of 1590s verse satire.

'Grinn'st thou, thou snurling cur?' Revenge tragedy knows that, while the aggressor vaunts, the victim titters with fright. But it is also interested in staging Blake's proverb, 'Excess of sorrow laughs.'[27] When, for instance, the Andronici are brought the heads of Quintus and Martius—together with the hand of Titus, chopped off as the supposed price of saving them—Marcus copes with his

[23] 'The Authour in prayse of his *precedent Poem*', line 46, from *Certaine Satyres*, in *The Poems of John Marston*, ed. Arnold Davenport (Liverpool, 1961).

[24] For a strong version of this thesis see O. J. Campbell, *Comicall Satyre and Shakespeare's 'Troilus and Cressida'* (San Marino, 1938), modified by e.g. Anthony Caputi, *John Marston, Satirist* (Ithaca, NY, 1961), 80–1, David G. O'Neill, 'The Commencement of Marston's Career as a Dramatist', *Review of English Studies*, NS 22 (1971), 442–5.

[25] Anderson, *A Kind of Wild Justice*, 173 n. 14.   [26] *Hamlet*, III. i. 55–89.

[27] *The Marriage of Heaven and Hell*, plate 8, in *The Poems of William Blake*, ed. W. H. Stevenson and David V. Erdman (London, 1971).

horror (as when faced with the lopped Lavinia) by finding rhetorical consolation in an elaborate display of grief. Lavinia herself, being tongueless, must communicate with disabled embraces. Titus, however, laughs. His 'Ha, ha, ha!' (III. ii. 264) can be electrifying. In Peter Brook's production, Olivier's 'slow, answering laugh was like the menace of a tide upon the turn'.[28] Yet more is involved than an advance from anguish through laughter to thoughts of revenge. Titus' hollow mirth does not burlesque the scene; it defuses a laughing reaction against horror in the audience, accommodating discordant grotesquerie by making it explicit. Because of this, Marston could appropriate Titus' reaction, in *Antonio's Revenge*, without (in any reductive sense) 'sending it up'. For when Pandulpho, faced with the body of his son, cries 'Ha, ha, ha', and, rebuked that 'this laughter ill becomes . . . grief', declares

> Wouldst have me turn rank mad,
> Or wring my face with mimic action,
> Stamp, curse, weep, rage, and then my bosom strike?
> Away, 'tis apish action, player-like. . . .   (I. v. 74–80)

the part sees round the character. Resolving not to be histrionic, Pandulpho apes those actors who have taken the role of Titus. Steeped in Shakespeare as well as Kyd, and sharing that knowledge with his sophisticated, indoor-theatre audience, Marston is able to pay a tribute which, in another genre, would collapse into travesty, but which here has the quasi-Pirandellesque effect of enforcing psychological truth by theatrical overdetermination.

A great deal of Renaissance revenge tragedy sparkles with self-reference. The phenomenon owes much to the effect of the inherited scenario (above, pp. 12–15), to that sense which revengers have of being characters in others' plots. Metadramatic allusion makes the burden of responsibility more manageable. Marston, however, elaborates this, rendering the comedy which flows from reflexivity integral to his dramaturgy. In Act II of *Antonio's Revenge*, for instance, the foolish gentleman Balurdo has an entry *'with a beard half off, half on'* (II. i. 20). This makes hay with tragic decorum by showing the audience an actor having trouble with his costume: 'the tiring man hath not glued on my beard half fast enough', he says, 'God's bores, it will not stick to fall off' (30–2). A loose ruff or tight boot might as easily have inconvenienced the performer. To have a beard in disarray stresses the lack of fit between child actor and adult role, and it does so with special perversity because, by convention, the boy players did not use beards. This joke has to be resonant in a play which depends on vengeful disguise. Equally interesting, however, is the fact that, just as Pandulpho's laughter unwittingly plagiarizes Titus', so Balurdo's predicament derives from the last act of *The Spanish Tragedy*, where Balthazar is caught, half-bearded, before a performance of 'Soliman and Perseda' (IV. iii. 18–19). The mimetic impulse of revenge tragedy is wittily troped by this foregrounding of the artifice of a main, as against an inset, action.

Piero is bewildered when Balurdo mentions 'the tiring man'. 'Dost thou know what thou hast spoken all this while?' he asks, to which Balurdo sagely replies: 'Many men can utter that which no man but themselves can conceive; but I thank a good wit, I have the gift to speak that which neither any man else nor myself understands' (33–7). In a play where characters are insulated from themselves as well as from each other by linguistic eccentricity, this observation is pregnant. Given lines which are patched together with scraps from Shakespeare, Kyd, or Seneca, and studded with baffling neologisms, they speak a dramatic language half off, half on. A few lines later, for instance, Piero asks Balurdo to see the Princess Mellida to prison, adding: 'Bid Forobosco and Castilio guard; | Endear thyself Piero's intimate' (47–8). According to the *Oxford English Dictionary*, 'endear' and 'intimate' were novel in 1600. Balurdo cannot resist their modish allure, and, by using them uncomprehendingly, he recalls his earlier reply to Piero: ' "Endear" and "intimate"—good, I assure you. I will endear and intimate Mellida into the dungeon presently' (49–50). Though verbally imitative clowns are plentiful in Elizabethan comedy, they are rare in tragedy. But Balurdo's fixation is right for a play driven, even in its high plot, by vindictive automatism. A couple of scenes later, Antonio himself uses 'endeared' and 'intimate' (II. iii. 28). Balurdo's way with words may be more evidently mechanical, more open to Bergsonian laughter. Such neologisms as ' "retort" and "obtuse" ' lodge fast in his vocabulary, and their repetitions (e.g., I. iii. 22, II. i. 52–3) display the workings of his mental clockwork. But his presence in Antonio's masque, where he joins in the abuse of Piero by shrieking 'Thou most retort and obtuse

rascal!' (v. v. 67), makes a larger point about the emotional inflexibility which goes with the scoffing violence of revenge.

An inclination to verbal comedy, touching on self-parody, is as old
as the genre. The Nurse in *The Libation Bearers* is the only comic role
extant in Aeschylus. In Euripides' savage yet 'whimsical'[29] *Orestes*,
the Phrygian Slave who rushes out of the *skēnē* to babble of the
avengers' attack on Helen is 'a semi-comic character, ludicrous in
his unmanly fear and his native lack of dignity'.[30] The heroine of his
Electra is married to a farmer whose homely, aphoristic idiom flouts
tragic expectations. Much discordant comedy is associated with the
pair. Electra makes her grand entrance carrying a water-pot.
Orestes asks if the (modest and honourable) farmer has respected
his sister's virginity because he finds her too ugly to sleep with.
Noticing such things, the Chicago translator 'suspects an entire
parody of tragedy in the high style' (p. 390) and Bernard Knox
identifies 'social comedy'.[31] Certainly, here as in Marston, the
disruptive verbal touches are 'harmonics' in Bergson's sense (pp.
95–6): translations of the comic potential of an action into motifs in
a work's linguistic superstructure. It is to the shape of the grounding
action, to the dispositions of revenge, that I must finally turn.

*   *   *

Renaissance scholars were interested in Euripides' *Orestes* and *Electra*
because the actions of both flout Aristotle's rules for tragedy.
Chapter 13 of the *Poetics* describes

> the sort of arrangement that some people say is the best: this is the one that
> has a double arrangement of the action like the *Odyssey*, and ends with
> opposite fortunes for the good and bad people. It is thought to be the best
> because of the weakness of the audiences; for the poets follow the lead of
> the spectators and make plays to their specifications. But this is not the
> pleasure proper to tragedy, but rather belongs to comedy; for in comedy
> those who are most bitter enemies throughout the plot, as it might be
> Orestes and Aegisthus, are reconciled at the end and go off and nobody is
> killed by anybody. (1453a)

Aristotle strains assent when he compares the ending of the *Odyssey*
to a reconciliation between Orestes and Aegisthus. The suitors and

[29] *Euripides: 'Orestes'*, ed. C. W. Willink (Oxford, 1986), pp. xxv, xxvii.
[30] *Euripides: 'Orestes'*, ed. M. L. West (Warminster, 1987), 277.
[31] 'Euripidean Comedy', repr. in his *Word and Action*, 250–74, p. 254.

Odysseus are hardly reconciled. Yet his analysis is suggestive because its inadequacy points up the isomorphism between revenge and 'a double arrangement' in drama. A work which concludes with the punishment of a wrongdoer can only be comprehensively tragic if the agent of retribution is brought down by what he does. Outside a world which believes in Furies, however, there is no necessary reason for B or his accomplices to be damaged by their revenge upon A. And if tragicomic dividedness is the logical outcome of vengeance, such plots can lead as readily towards general reconciliation as towards carnage. Certainly, during the Renaissance the *Odyssey* became a model for *duplex* tragedy, for *tragedia mista*—the 'mixed tragedy' with double ending—favoured by Cinthio and his followers, while humanists found much to admire in the sort of denouement which reconciles Orestes with his enemies. Discussing the finale imposed by Apollo on Euripides' *Orestes* (Menelaus and the protagonist made friends, the latter told to 'marry Hermione, | the girl against whose throat your sword now lies' (1653–4)), the commentator Robortellus noted that 'The argument of this tragedy is as similar as may be to the comic.'[32] He related its catastrophe to that of the *Electra*, which is managed by the Dioscuri. As his fellow scholar Victorius wrote: 'The outcome of the plot [of *Electra*] "from the machine" (*apo mēchanēs*), therefore, is very similar to the resolution of *Orestes* . . . The ending of either play, since it is in no wise sad . . . seems more proper to comedy than to tragedy.'[33]

The impact of such catastrophes was felt in Shakespeare's England, and not just in the academic tradition which (at its most brilliant) produced William Gager's *Ulysses redux* (1592).[34] *Antonio's Revenge*, for instance, reveals its debt to *tragedia mista* by having Piero stabbed to death while the conspirators are offered thanks and handsome rewards by the Venetian senate. It is often supposed that Elizabethan revengers are required to die. The strength of providential retributivism did mean that even well-intentioned Hamlets were not usually allowed to get away with murder. But the survival of Antonio and his fellows, 'In holy verge of some religious order' (v. vi. 35), is evidence not just of the sympathy

---

[32] Quoted by Marvin T. Herrick, *Tragicomedy: Its Origin and Development in Italy, France, and England* (1955; Urbana, Ill., 1962), 14.   [33] Ibid. 15.
[34] On Gager's defence of the play's tragicomic features, see J. W. Binns, *Intellectual Culture in Elizabethan and Jacobean England: The Latin Writings of the Age* (Leeds, 1990), 128–31.

which could flow to outrageously provoked revengers[35] but of the
pressure towards tragicomic outcomes created by vengeful plotting.
Hence the significance of that false climax which precedes the
assassination of the Duke. A few lines before the conspirators'
blades are thrust home (with a flurry of gestural and internal
rhyming patently derived from *Titus*), '*They offer to run all at* PIERO
and on a sudden stop' (v. v. 73). The comic impact of this hiatus bears
out Kant's claim, noted by Bergson, that 'Laughter is the result of
an expectation which, of a sudden, ends in nothing' (p. 116). But its
larger importance becomes clear when one turns tò Marston's *The
Malcontent*, to find a plot which roughly shadows that of *Antonio's
Revenge* but which has Malevole and his fellow-conspirators let Duke
Mendoza off in their vengeful masque:

> *Cornets sound the measure over again; which danced,*
> *they unmask.*

MENDOZA Malevole!

> *They environ Mendoza, bending their pistols on him.*

MALEVOLE No.
MENDOZA Altofront! Duke Pietro! Ferneze! Ha![36]

It is true that, unlike Piero, Mendoza is not guilty of murder
(though he does his best to be). Closer to Antonio in *The Tempest*,
he is merely a usurper. Yet this underlines the ease with which the
movement of tragic events towards reconciliation can be sustained
by the logic of revenge. For, judged by his acts, Mendoza gets what
he deserves. With this in mind we can go back to Shakespeare and
find, in *The Merry Wives of Windsor* and *The Tempest*, genre-stretching
variants on revenge tragedy more explicitly 'comic' than *Titus
Andronicus*.

It might sound briskly sophistical to put these plays into the same
category as *Hamlet*. But the tragic shaping of *The Merry Wives* is
impeccable. Ford is a jealous revenger, a man who, like the Moor of
Venice, groundlessly thinks himself a cuckold. 'The green-eyed
monster' (in Iago's phrase) infects his whole life, making him cruel
to his wife and mistrustful of all around him. In the hands of an
actor such as Ben Kingsley (in the 1979 RSC production), Ford can

---

[35] See e.g. Philip J. Ayres, 'Degrees of Heresy: Justified Revenge and Elizabethan
Narratives', *Studies in Philology*, 69 (1972), 461–74.
[36] *The Malcontent*, ed. George K. Hunter (London, 1975), V. vi. 112–15.

be convincingly frightening. As an avenger, he goes in disguise, visiting Falstaff, his enemy, as Master Brook, to find out what is going on in his own bed. Moreover, he goes mad. He may not fall into epilepsy like Othello; but he is 'horn mad' by his own admission, and, according to Evans the schoolmaster, becomes 'as mad as a mad dog'—as mad, in fact, as Frank Turpin. Shakespeare never read *The Sun*, but he put something of its rough-house comedy into the skimmington laid on for Falstaff by the Windsor community in Act V. This ending is shaped by revenge, however, as much as by popular festivity. Critics often regard the final scene as being hastily copied from *A Midsummer Night's Dream*, with Evans's pupils dressed up as Oberon's fairies, pinching and prodding a Falstaff disguised as Herne the Hunter. Yet the pageant is shrewdly adjusted to the demands of retribution. As he is tweaked and pricked with pins, Falstaff is like the victim of a revenge masque, punched and stabbed with poinards, except that the punishments have been reduced because he never committed the debaucheries which he so ambitiously intended. The fairies speak a babble which is the childish equivalent of Hieronimo's Babel. And those ludicrous antlers, perched on Falstaff's head—most immediately a disguise adopted for his nocturnal assignation in the forest—not only punish him for deer-stealing but repay him for the cuckold's horns which he sought to put on Ford and Page.

The revenge dynamics of *The Tempest* more evidently resemble those of *Hamlet*, a play so steeped in remembrance that it is eventually doubtful whether it ends in vengeance or not. Prospero enters the play with speeches uncannily close to the ghost's. Repeatedly asking Miranda whether she can 'remember | A time before we came unto this cell?', what her 'remembrance' holds of 'house or person', if she 'rememb'rest aught' of the past (I. ii. 38–9, 42–4, 51), he tells his daughter a story which might have come from Elsinore. Twelve years ago, the Duke of Milan was ousted by his brother, Antonio, and left for dead on a rough sea in a frail boat clutching his baby daughter. Like Claudius, the usurper thinks his brother gone for good. But the play will recover, and resolve, the past. As though to point up this obsession, Ariel enters and requests his freedom by saying 'Let me remember thee what thou hast promis'd' and 'Remember I have done thee worthy service' (243, 247). The imputation of forgetfulness and ingratitude is too much for Prospero, and he turns both charges back: 'Dost thou forget | From

what a torment I did free thee?' (250–1). As in the exchange with
Miranda, dialogue then gives way to narrative. Prospero provides
the audience with a great deal of necessary information about what
Sycorax and Caliban once did, and betrays a series of ironic
relations between his own experiences of exile and entrapment
and those of others on the island. However, his narrative also,
and more comically, has a punitive dimension. Prospero bludgeons
Ariel with what the spirit already knows, then offers more of the
same. Urging Sycorax again and again ('Hast thou forgot her?'), he
threatens to torment Ariel with insistent, repetitive remembrances:
'I must | Once in a month recount what thou hast been, | Which
thou forget'st' (258, 261–3).

The threat is symptomatic. A strategy of corrective remembrance
guides Prospero through the play. While Hieronimo secures his
revenge by theatrically reconstructing the past and subjecting his
enemies to it, Prospero seeks to punish by awakening guilty memories. That is why the first scene which he shares with his opponents
(III. iii) takes the form of a vengeful masque which is more interested
in tantalizing than stabbing. '*Enter several strange* SHAPES *bringing in a
banket; and dance about it with gentle actions of salutations*' (19). The
resemblance between this 'living drollery' (as Sebastian calls it)
and the kind of court entertainment staged by Marston's Antonio
is plain, and the show takes a punitive turn when Ariel '*like a harpy*'
snatches the banquet away from Alonso, Sebastian, and Antonio
(52). Editors rightly refer this intervention to an episode in the *Aeneid*
(III. 225–57), but they overlook a significant feature when they ignore
the vengefulness of Virgil's harpies. Entering the scene to punish,
Ariel arrives (like the masquing Vindice) against a background of
'*Thunder and lightning*', and claims the authority of providential
retribution (52, 60–1). The purpose of his appearance, however, is
not physical injury but the stirring of memory:

> But remember
> (For that's my business to you) that you three
> From Milan did supplant good Prospero,
> Exposed unto the sea (which hath requit it)
> Him, and his innocent child; for which foul deed
> The pow'rs delaying (not forgetting), have
> Incens'd the seas and shores . . .   (68–74)

Ariel is less interested in the elements' retributive violence than in
'the pow'rs . . . not forgetting'. Very nature prompts remembrance.

And if Gonzalo can be believed, Alonso, Sebastian, and Antonio are distressed by the past. 'Their great guilt', he says, '(Like poison given to work a great time after) | Now gins to bite the spirits' (104–6).

When Davenant read *The Tempest*, with a view to adaptation, he recognized its affinities with *Hamlet*. Indeed, he developed its vengefulness. Together with his collaborator Dryden, he made Alonso and his companions penitent from the outset. This left Prospero's harsh treatment of them looking the more retributive. Davenant and Dryden also added an intrigue centred on Hippolito: a male equivalent of Miranda, who has never seen a woman before the play begins, and who, in excitement at the prospect of polygamy (since Miranda has a sister called Dorinda), gets into a duel with Ferdinand. His apparent death in the sword-fight gives Prospero an opportunity to debate with Miranda the topically post-Restoration question of whether the punishments of God's magistrate should be Pauline in their rigour,[37] but there is no doubting his own conviction that—as he tells Alonzo—'Blood calls for blood; your *Ferdinand* shall dye'.[38] By comparison, Shakespeare's Prospero is opaque. Though clearly looking to punish, he is more likely to talk about art than about blood and death. The traumas which he should conventionally pass through are displaced from him onto others. The madness of the revenger is not inflicted upon him (though he has his instabilities) but *by* him on Antonio, Sebastian, and the rest. He does not shift shapes by adopting disguises: that is left to his agent, Ariel, or, on a lower level, to Stephano and Trinculo in the gaudy apparel they steal from near his cell. Yet the contours of vengeance remain. Only the success of Ariel in rousing Hippolito from his coma turns the course of the Restoration *Tempest* from tragedy to comic romance. In Shakespeare's play, by contrast, the structures and dynamics of revenge tragedy are active right to the end.

It is true that, early in Act V, Ariel so eloquently describes the distraction of Alonso, Sebastian, and Antonio—and Gonzalo's 'sorrow' for them—that Prospero declares,

[37] For emerging alternatives see e.g. Hobbes, *Leviathan* (1651), I. xv, II. 26–8, John Locke, *Two Treatises of Government* (pub. 1690), II. 2, 7–9.

[38] *The Tempest: Or, The Enchanted Island*, ed. Maximillian E. Novak and George R. Guffey, in *The Works of John Dryden*, gen. ed. H. T. Swedenberg, Jr. (Berkeley, 1956–), x; v. i. 1–34, IV. iii. 150.

> Though with their high wrongs I am strook to th' quick,
> Yet, with my nobler reason, 'gainst my fury
> Do I take part. The rarer action is
> In virtue than in vengeance. They being penitent,
> The sole drift of my purpose doth extend
> Not a frown further.   (V. i. 25–30)

But this is problematic. Prospero's 'They being penitent'—poised between 'Since they are . . .' and 'If they are . . .'—suspends judgement. Nor is it simply a matter of him distrusting the ambiguity of report. In a play where punishment works through conscience, rather than by means of dagger-thrusts, it is hard to distinguish between retributive guilt and the symptoms of something else. How 'penitent' did the masque of III. iii, for instance, render Prospero's enemies? Despite Gonzalo's diagnosis, Sebastian and Antonio seem closer to bravado than 'great guilt', as they wave their swords at the spirits, and Alonso, awkwardly enough, appears more distressed by the lie that Ferdinand has been drowned than by the truth of his betrayal of Prospero. The masque produces signs of distress without guaranteeing their causes.

This helps explain the volatile mixture of cynicism and longing for justice in Prospero, given that his theatrical powers make deception (including self-deception) easy. When the roughly treated Ferdinand, for example, draws his sword against the magician, and is '*charmed from moving*', Prospero takes this as evidence that, as he has himself claimed, the young man is a spy intent on usurping the isle: 'Put thy sword up, traitor, | Who mak'st a show but dar'st not strike, thy conscience | Is so possess'd with guilt' (I. ii. 470–2). That the charge is not true, and that Prospero can scarcely believe it, is not the point: he is relieving his anger at Antonio's treachery in Milan by playing out a scene which facilitates a display of rage against an appearance of guilt. If, as critics used to argue, some form of disillusionment with drama helped motivate the composition of *The Tempest*, Shakespeare's last non-collaborative play, the subject was wisely chosen. For the inset performances of revenge show how guilt and justice can be staged without anything being changed. Lorenzo is no less a villain, no more like Horatio, for acting that gallant youth's part in 'Soliman and Perseda', and it is impossible to tell, in Act V of *The Tempest*, how spontaneous are the mental torments endured by those held in Prospero's magic circle. When the magus reminds the frantic and charm-tranced Sebastian

of his plots against Milan, saying, 'Thou art pinch'd for't now'—
then finds a stricter justice in the fact that, having conspired against
Alonso as well as Prospero, Sebastian's 'inward pinches therefore
are most strong' (74, 77)—the audience cannot know what lies
behind 'therefore': whether the cramps and dry convulsions arise
from guilty remembrance, or are magically imposed, like those
inflicted on the island's other conspirators, Stephano, Trinculo,
and Caliban (IV. i. 258–62).

The dramaturgy of this sequence shows Shakespeare at his most
Japanese. When Prospero draws his enemies into the magic circle,
making them puppets of his power, revenge (even more than at the
end of *Titus*) moves towards stasis. Prospero becomes a narrator,
commenting on a framed set of stage attitudes, as in the *monogatari*
of Kabuki. But there is a nearer model, pointed up by his words to
(it seems) Alonso: 'thy brains, | Now useless, boil within thy skull!'[39]
The brain-seething denouement of Chettle's *Hoffman* is also played
out by characters who assemble at the revenger's cell. In another
play, the circle would be the scene of a bloody banquet; there would
be skulls backstage, or a body hanging, like that of Hieronimo's son,
in the discovery space. Prospero, however, circumscribes his enemies only to go through the motions. The fairy pinchings and
gastronomic deprivations inflicted on the island turn out to be
proportioned punishments, like those in Windsor forest, rather
than taunting preparations for a bloodbath. 'You, brother mine,'
says Prospero to the Claudius of the play, 'I do forgive thee, |
Unnatural as thou art' (75–9). Far from assaulting his enemies,
Prospero joins them in their tableau, calling for the 'hat and
rapier' which he wore in Milan. He does not recover his old
trappings to reprise, like Hieronimo, his resentments. Moreover,
when he opens the discovery space the audience sees, not the
corpse of a child, but an image of the future: Ferdinand and
Miranda playing chess. All this is too positive for revenge tragedy.
Yet the principle of requital is still registered, as Prospero pulls aside
the curtain and says to Alonso, 'My dukedom since you have given
me again, | I will requite you with as good a thing' (168–9).

Shakespeare cannot be reduced to order. The final scene of *The
Tempest* resists generic summary. If dark memories lift when Pros-
pero says to Alonso, 'Let us not burden our remembrances with | A

---

[39] v. i. 59–60, preferring the Folio's 'boile' to 'boil'd'.

heaviness that's gone' (v. i. 199–200),[40] they continue to hang over what he says about Antonio and Sebastian. Even the future of the lovers cannot exclude the possibility of betrayal. 'Sweet lord, you play me false', Miranda says to Ferdinand (172), over the kings, queens, and castles. Intricacies of this sort, however, depend on more than individual genius. The shifting, tonal complexity of what Shakespeare achieves in the genre, from *Titus Andronicus* onwards, points up the sheer variety of factors which make vengeance hospitable to the comic. Other kinds of tragedy have light-hearted interludes, subplots, and surprises. Criticism typically attempts to show that these elements work together. There is a difference, however, between components which have to be integrated by the playwright and those which spring spontaneously from tragic action. Repeatedly, vengeance generates, from out of its dramaturgic potential, a strain of awkward comedy which raises laughter, and kills it.

[40] Cf. James Black, 'The Latter End of Prospero's Commonwealth', *Shakespeare Survey*, 43 (1991), 29–41, p. 40.

9. Playing with Fire: Richardson to Mozart

In December 1752, fire broke out in the home of Samuel Richardson, novelist and printer. 'It was occasioned by the carelessness of a boy,' he wrote to Thomas Edwards,

whose business was in the warehouse; and who setting some loose papers in a blaze in the warehouse room behind the parlour, it caught the books, that hung upon the poles, as we call them, just under the ceiling; and, had it not been extinguished, would, in a quarter of an hour more, have destroyed the whole house. . . . It luckily happened about seven o'clock in the evening. I was at home drinking tea, two young ladies with me; and, I bless God, had presence of mind to give the necessary orders: but twice I gave up all for lost. . . . I am so thankful for the stop of the fire, and for a deliverance from a total destruction, that I make light of what did happen: and still the lighter, as I was insured . . .¹

Readers of the fiction will find this scene iconic. That sudden blaze among books and papers, as unexpected as *Pamela* amid the exemplary *Letters*,² seems a reflex of the author's imagination. Great heaps of words are bound and stored here as property; the material context is vividly realized, down to the 'poles' beneath the ceiling; female admirers court the author; and an epistle reconstructs what occurred. Above all, there is the unselfconscious modulation into thankfulness to God. With retrospective piety, 'presence of mind' is associated with divine 'deliverance', and prudently, God be praised, the author was insured.

This is the idiom of bourgeois protestantism: literate, industrious, and metaphysically volatile. Partly encouraged by Romans 12, post-Reformation Englishmen looked about them for signs of divine

¹ *The Correspondence of Samuel Richardson*, ed. Anna Lætitia Barbauld, 6 vols. (London, 1804), iii. 49–50.
² For the inception of *Pamela* (1740) during the preparation of *Letters Written to and for Particular Friends, On the Most Important Occasions* (1741), see *Selected Letters of Samuel Richardson*, ed. John Carroll (Oxford, 1964), 40–1.

intervention. Earthquakes, fires, and famine were evidence of God's vengeance; a good harvest showed His approval. In diaries, sermons, and chapbooks, and in such encyclopaedic volumes as Thomas Beard's *Theatre of Gods Judgements* (1597, etc.), instances of providential judgement were collected. Such texts fostered a world-view hospitable to revenge tragedy because they aligned the actions of righteous avengers with the punitive designs of God, while making it provocatively possible for protagonists to lay false claim to the Pauline sword. After the Civil War, the influence of St Paul was modified by that of Hobbes and Locke.[3] Theories of punishment were grounded in principles of deterrence, correction, and social prudence, rather than posited on the retributive duty of God's minister, and revenge tragedy lost cultural centrality. Though providentialism waned, however, in seventeenth-century England (and elsewhere), it was by no means extinguished. Because notions of providential intervention could be reconciled with the idea of God's working through the laws of nature,[4] a residual sense of the world as divine theatre proved persistent. Across eighteenth-century Christendom, believers resisted Deism by arguing that God would not abandon what he had created. If divine love appeared erratic, Heaven could be permitted to move in a mysterious way. As William Sherlock explained, in Richardson's periodical *The Christian's Magazine*, to trust in providence 'is not to trust in God, that he will do that particular thing for us which we desire; but to trust our selves and all our concernments with God, to do for us in every particular course which we recommend to his care, what he sees best and fittest for us in such cases.'[5]

With God allowed such latitude, providentialism became asymmetrical, in that the punishment of wrong confirmed what the sufferings of virtue might nevertheless support. This made it hardy as a view of life, and more productive of tragic writing than has usually been recognized. Richardson offers a counter-example to the familiar, half-persuasive thesis that Christianity is inimical to tragedy.[6] Whatever one makes of his beliefs, he was freed by them into an acceptance of earthly misery. When Lady Bradshaigh

---

[3] Above, p. 213 and n. 37.

[4] See e.g. Thomas, *Religion and the Decline of Magic*, 93, 110.

[5] Ch. 21; quoted by James Louis Fortuna, Jr., *'The Unsearchable Wisdom of God': A Study of Providence in Richardson's 'Pamela'* (Gainesville, Fla., 1980), 20. Cf. Tom Keymer, *Richardson's 'Clarissa' and the Eighteenth-Century Reader* (Cambridge, 1992), 199–214.

[6] For an eloquent account of Christianity as 'an anti-tragic vision of the world' see George Steiner, *The Death of Tragedy* (London, 1961), 331–3.

requested that Clarissa be rewarded after her tribulations, Richardson replied:

A Writer who follows Nature and pretends to keep the Christian System in his Eye, cannot make a Heaven in this World for his Favourites; or represent this Life otherwise than as a State of Probation. Clarissa I once more averr, could not be rewarded in this World. To have given her her Reward here, as in a happy Marriage, would have been as if a Poet had placed his Catastrophe in the Third Act of his Play, when the audience were *obliged* to expect two more.[7]

As often in his critical statements, Richardson courts the charge of naïvety. Yet his gist is clear and enabling, and spelled out in the 'Postscript' to his 'dramatic narrative'—as he called it—*Clarissa* (1747–8).[8] 'Shall man', he asks, 'presuming to alter the common course of nature . . . imagine, that he can make a better dispensation; and by calling it poetical justice, indirectly reflect on the divine?' (iv. 557). Significantly, Richardson has no sooner said this than he plants an ample tradesman's thumb on the scales of justice, and points out that, though virtue suffers in his novel, villainy is also punished. Is the rake not driven half-mad with remorse for raping the heroine, he asks? And Mrs Sinclair, the bawd, with the whores, 'exemplarily punished'? It is a perfect example of asymmetrical providentialism generating tragedy, and it shows how the ending of *Clarissa* can incline towards the tragic for Lovelace as well as the heroine, while preserving a metaphysical consistency not entirely at odds with experience.

Richardson's dramatic analogy is revealing. Though hostile to playhouses in his pamphleteering,[9] he cultivated theatrical friends, printed tragedies (including Edward Young's *The Revenge*), and, in his novels, cultivated effects which owe a great deal to the stage. Lovelace's letters are threaded with quotations from Restoration drama; dialogue is intermittently laid out as though in a playbook; disguise and role-playing are prominent. The fate of Clarissa, indeed—wheedled and snatched from her family, drugged, raped, and escaping into death—seems to have been inherited

[7] *Selected Letters of Samuel Richardson*, ed. Carroll, 108.
[8] *Clarissa: Or, The History of a Young Lady*, introd. John Butt, 4 vols. (London, 1932), iv. 554. This text is based on Richardson's revised, 3rd edn. (1751).
[9] See e.g. *A Seasonable Examination of the Pleas and Pretensions of the Proprietors of, and Subscribers to, Play-houses* (1735).

from Charles Johnson's *Caelia* (perf. 1732).[10] Like the heroine of that
melodrama, some fifteen years later, Clarissa finds herself confined
to a brothel; she, like Caelia, dies of something nameless compounded from grief; and there is even, in the play, the double
catastrophe of the novel, with Johnson's perjured rake, like Lovelace, killed in a duel by a relative of the woman he has wronged.
Other tragedies are cited. Clarissa recognizes that *Venice Preserved*,
which she and Lovelace go to see at a stable point in their relationship, relates to her own plight, and she reminds Anna Howe that
'You have my remarks upon it in the little book you made me write
upon the principal acting plays' (ii. 372). Immediately after the rape,
when Clarissa's identity fragments, and her prose becomes a scatter
of scraps, lines from *Hamlet*—'I could a Tale unfold | Would
harrow up thy soul!' and 'Oh! you have done an act | That blots
the face and blush of modesty'—intimate what she cannot commit
to paper (iii. 209). Then again, *The Fair Penitent* is invoked near the
end of the story, when Lovelace contrasts the 'virtuous, noble, wise,
and pious mien' of Clarissa with that of Rowe's suicidal heroine (iv.
118–19).[11]

What the Otway, Shakespeare, and Rowe have in common is, of
course, revenge. Though *Clarissa* has often been discussed as a
'dramatic narrative',[12] its affiliations with revenge tragedy have
been neglected. Yet Clarissa's family, the Harlowes, is (as surely as
the Atreidae) torn apart by internal feuding, and Lovelace pursues
the heroine with vengeful designs of his own. *Vindication*, in its triple
eighteenth-century sense, provides the matrix of interest, and links
between its meanings ensure that *Clarissa* brings something new to
the genre, while drawing on values which run deep through
Hanoverian England. Most obviously, *vindication* is vindictive action
(sense 1a in the *Oxford English Dictionary*). The book starts with a
skirmish between Lovelace and Clarissa's brother, and the rake
vows 'revenge' when James, on this account, bars him from Harlowe Place (i. 19). He will not seek legal redress, for 'how, he asks,

[10] See Ira Konigsberg, *Samuel Richardson and the Dramatic Novel* (Lexington, Ky., 1968),
40–5.
[11] On Richardson's more glancing and opportunistic use of dramatic quotations from
Edward Bysshe's *Art of English Poetry*—and for the heading 'Revenge'—see Michael E.
Connaughton, 'Richardson's Familiar Quotations: *Clarissa* and Bysshe's *Art of English
Poetry*', *Philological Quarterly*, 60 (1981), 183–95, p. 187.
[12] See esp. Mark Kinkead-Weekes, *Samuel Richardson: Dramatic Novelist* (London, 1973),
pt. 2.

can a man of honour go to law for verbal abuses given by people entitled to wear swords?' (i. 121–2). Such threats, routine in the honour community of the eighteenth-century gentry, encourage Clarissa to begin the secret correspondence with Lovelace which she considers, to the end of her life, her great mistake. There is no one in the narrative willing to overrule revenge by bravely refusing to fight, as Sir Charles Grandison does in Richardson's later novel. Yet when Cousin Morden takes up the sword for Clarissa, after the rape, it is against her clear advice. 'There is no necessity for you to attempt to vindicate my fame' she declares (iv. 461)—and rightly, since the letter itself, in its stern morality, vindicates her reputation. *Vindication*, then as now, is 'justification, explanation, documentation', and in the vindicative epistolary medium, Clarissa is a practised performer. Lovelace justifies himself to Belford, Anna to Clarissa, and Clarissa to almost everyone. Not all the epistles in the novel overtly justify, but many invoke means and circumstances to bolster what is written. For the vindicating persuasiveness of a letter rests on more than what it says. Its being smudged, torn, forged, interceptable, tiring and/or pleasurable to write, inscribed in inky gall, or scribbled with evident difficulty on a bent knee in some dank copse by night—these are integral to the risk, ardour, or plausibility of what is communicated. The physicality of the written therefore looms large in *Clarissa*. Language is metonymically endowed with substance; its emotional burden registers (incrementally) as mass. Letters have the properties of property, and they are locked in drawers because they have value as well as renewable suasive force.

If letters, however, are property, reading and writing them is a coming into possession, and thus a vindictive act. For *vindicate* has this third Augustan sense: 'To claim as properly belonging *to* oneself . . . to assert or establish possession of (something)'.[13] This makes the link between violence and wealth, particularly in *Clarissa*, clearer. The pattern of economic rivalry which Christopher Hill has traced in the Harlowe household,[14] through which James's social ambitions are blocked by Clarissa's inheriting her grand-father's, and perhaps her uncle's, property, is bound up with revenge. James acts vindictively in every sense, but he vindicates

---

[13] *OED,* 5a and b.
[14] 'Clarissa Harlowe and her Times', *Essays in Criticism,* 5 (1955), 315–40.

himself as a man of property by taking possession of the patrimony, with Clarissa's expulsion from the house, and eventually her death. Moreover, before the rape, the heroine calls Lovelace 'the man, who has had the assurance to think me, and to endeavour to make me, his *property*' (iii. 17). By raping her, Lovelace possesses Clarissa, and vindicates himself—not only against the Harlowes but, as I shall argue, against the inadequacies which being what he is entail. This might sound like heartless quibbling, but it is out of the conceptual coincidence of sexual possession and vindication, so ingrained in the language of the period as to seem a natural congruence, that the tragedy of the novel emerges.

So does its epistolary medium. Writing is Clarissa's defence against an assault from Lovelace which fluctuates between active coercion and the more subtle coming-into-ownership which his writing to and about her permits. For his subtleties as reader, re-reader, and correspondent, have an acquisitive dimension. His analysis of Clarissa's prose puts one in mind of Malraux's remark: 'Attempts to analyse a woman always have something erotic about them. . . . To try and unravel a woman's character is surely always a method of possessing or of taking one's revenge upon her.'[15] The field of their combat, at once amorous and hostile, puts language into a state of dramatic activity because writing is not a record only but the means to vindication. Surges of passion, frustration, and decision are marked by Richardson the printer with all sorts of typographical devices (many not matched in modern editions)— italic, capitals, dashes, emphases thrown in as though created by thoughts being realized. When Lovelace forwards an intercepted letter to Belford, having indicated 'the places devoted for vengeance or requiring animadversion', Richardson marks the phrases in question with printer's hands (i.e. indices) in the margin. At points the text is even set in a type which looks like manuscript.[16] The use of theatrical quotation, and of letters set as dialogue, are only the most extreme manifestations of a dramatic vitality which runs through words which are galvanized *as* signifiers as well as telling a story.

From the start, Lovelace's desire is inseparable from vengeance. 'I have boasted that I was once in love before', Letter 31 tells Belford:

[15] André Malraux, *Man's Estate*, tr. Alastair Macdonald (Harmondsworth, 1961), 211.
[16] Cf. Geoffrey Day, *From Fiction to the Novel* (London, 1987), 94–5.

and indeed I thought I was. It was in my early manhood—with that quality-jilt, whose infidelity I have vowed to revenge upon as many of the sex as shall come into my power. I believe, in different climes, I have already sacrificed an hecatomb to my Nemesis, in pursuance of this vow. (i. 145)

In the course of this, his first, epistle, Lovelace identifies Clarissa as an object of both the 'gentle fire' of love, and the 'raging flames' of revenge. Is she not desirable yet, as a Harlowe, deserving of vengeance? Her reaction to his contrivances is insistent, literally italicized, yet passive. 'If *I* am to be singled out to be the *punisher* of myself and family,' she writes to Anna:

pray for me, my dear, that I may not be left wholly to myself; and that I may be enabled to support my character, so as to be *justly* acquitted of wilful and premeditated faults. The will of Providence be resigned to in the rest: as *that* leads, let me patiently and unrepiningly follow! I shall not live always. May but my *closing* scene be happy! (i. 420)

This providential doctrine remains hers throughout, but Lovelace parodically claims it for vindictive ends, calling his schemes against her '*providences*'[17] and mocking the idea of Divine intervention by stage-managing the appearance of characters such as Captain Tomlinson. Desire and vengeance together govern his plotting, though Belford warns that the Harlowes will avenge themselves if Clarissa comes to grief, and the sententious Lord M. declares, 'let him remember that *vengeance, though it comes with leaden feet, strikes with iron hands*' (ii. 323).

Conflagration is the *peripeteia*. When Clarissa is lodged in the brothel by Lovelace, Mrs Sinclair's maid, reading late in the attic, carelessly sets the curtains ablaze and the house is thrown into uproar by the cry of 'Fire!' (ii. 500). With as much 'presence of mind' as Richardson in his warehouse, the maid extinguishes the flames by thrusting her curtains into the hearth; but not before Lovelace has burst into the heroine's bedroom and almost overwhelmed her with help. Should the episode be allegorized? In his opera based on Richardson, *Clarissa* (1976), Robin Holloway treats the flare-up as an outbreak of collective passion: beguiling, mischievous, and sexual. It is natural to think of the flames as imaging the 'gentle fire' of Lovelace's desire, roused to sudden ferocity after

---

[17] e.g. ii. 115, iii. 98.

weeks of restraint. Bachelard is doubtless right to contend that
sexuality has ancient links with the making and spreading of
flame.[18] Fire suggests the warmth, the risk, and alacrity of eros.
But the 'raging flames' of vengeance must also be remembered: the
rake's advances in the bedroom are alarmingly aggressive. Even
Lovelace is forced to admit, the next morning, 'that the violence of
my passion for you might have carried me beyond fit bounds' (ii.
500). When Clarissa flees the house, a few hours later, Lovelace's
reaction is revealing. His letter to Belford, starting *'Oh, for a curse to
kill with!'* is (to extend the image) so scorching as to become
unreadable. The 'raging flames' of vengeance seem to burn a
hole in the text as Richardson intervenes with a note: *'Here Mr
Lovelace lays himself under a curse, too shocking to be repeated, if he revenge not
himself upon the lady, should he once more get her into his hands'* (ii. 517, 525)

Lovelace's vindictive love has an intensity which exceeds his
combined hostility towards the Harlowes and desire for Clarissa.
When he writes to Belford, 'O Jack, the rage of love, the rage of
revenge, is upon me!' (iii. 194) the rising isocolon stresses the violent
vulnerability of a man whose identity depends on others' perceptions of him. The honour code of eighteenth-century England, as
opponents of duelling (including Richardson)[19] never ceased to
point out, forced men to struggle for status rather than follow
inner conscience. The man who did not meet his gambling debts,
or who could not consume and control large quantities of liquor,
and women, lost honour. He became a sort of social ghost. Restless
until his position had been vindicated (like the spirit of a revenge
play), he sought situations in which his control could not only be
asserted but be seen to be so. It misconstrues Clarissa's suffering to
think that Lovelace drugs and rapes her in front of Mrs Sinclair and
the whores to satisfy some oblique impulse to voyeurism (which is
not to deny the scene's pornographic potential). Lovelace acts
before others because his sexual vindication needs witnesses. He
must complete the business of controlling Clarissa which has, before
the rape, been exercised through dialogue, theatrical scheming, and
epistolary intervention. Lovelace has been censoring Clarissa's

---

[18] Gaston Bachelard, *The Psychoanalysis of Fire*, tr. Alan C. M. Ross (London, 1964), ch.
4.

[19] See his 'Six Original Letters upon Duelling', *Candid Review and Literary Repository*, 1
(1765), 227–31 and, for contexts, Donna T. Andrew, 'The Code of Honour and its Critics:
The Opposition to Duelling in England, 1700–1850', *Social History*, 5 (1980), 409–34.

letters to such friends as Anna Howe. Now he reduces her entirely
to an instrument of his status, and writes what he wants upon her.
'Rape', as Angela Carter puts it, 'is a kind of physical graffiti.'[20]

*   *   *

The pattern of Lovelace's violence would be less striking if it were
unique. Throughout eighteenth-century fiction, and in stage versions of the rake-plot, much resembling it can be found. Turn to an
epistolary novel such as *Les Liaisons dangereuses* (1782), and you find in
Laclos's Valmont another attractive dissolute with the same vindictive psychology. Only here the feelings of the rake for Cécile are
whetted by the fact that it is his friend and rival, Madame de
Merteuil, who seeks revenge, through her, upon a previous lover,
the Comte de Gercourt. When de Merteuil persuades Valmont to
help her get even with the Comte, it might be the Lovelace of Letter
31. In seducing Gercourt's proposed spouse, she writes, 'vous
servirez l'amour et la vengeance'.[21] The similarity will seem the
greater when it is remembered that Madame de Merteuil has, like
Lovelace, declared war on the opposite sex. She was, she admits to
Valmont, 'née pour venger mon sexe et maîtriser le vôtre' (*Lettre*
LXXXI). When he forcefully possesses Cécile, what *Lettre* LXXI
calls 'une vengeance de l'amour' is effected, and—such is the suave
depravity of the book—the victim finds it exciting. This in itself
brings *Les Liaisons dangereuses* into risky conjunction with pornography. In his plots against the virtuous Madame de Tourvel, as well as
against Cécile, Valmont is spurred, and the reader titillated, by
conjunctions of eroticism and revenge.[22] Her reading in *Clarissa*—
a novel which Valmont has also perused[23]—cannot protect her from
his Lovelacean designs. It was that 'Lovelace en femme',[24] Madame
de Merteuil, however, who fascinated and scandalized contemporaries. To judge from her sympathetic treatment in Christopher
Hampton's stage version (1985), later filmed by Stephen Frears,
she remains a compelling figure. A female rake, an intriguer, she
turns the tables on men by using the instruments of male dominance. In Laclos (though not in Hampton) she is punished for her

---

[20] *The Sadean Woman: An Exercise in Cultural History* (London, 1979), 6.
[21] *Les Liaisons dangereuses*, introd. René Pomeau (Paris, 1989), *Lettre* II.
[22] e.g. *Lettres* XLIV, LXX, C.   [23] *Lettres* CVII, CX.
[24] Wilhelm Karl Grimm, quoted in Choderlos de Laclos, *Œuvres complètes*, ed. Maurice
Allem, 2nd edn. (Paris, 1943), 722.

presumption: defaced by the smallpox, as well as ostracized by society. Both her intellectual brilliance and the wilfulness of Laclos's retribution tempt the modern reader to admire de Merteuil. But the fact that she employs phallic humiliation to get even raises doubts about what has been called, by Susanne Kappeler, equality of opportunity to exploit.[25] These doubts would not surface if Laclos's novel were not structured by that impulse to balanced coercion which goes under the name of 'vindication' and which seduces as much by its ostensible even-handedness as by its violence. To put this another way: Laclos was not the only Enlightenment author to be in favour of education for women. So was the Marquis de Sade. The issues raised by Lovelace's conflagration are inseparable from those indicated by Simone de Beauvoir's incendiary title, 'Must We Burn Sade?'[26]

In her study of *Pornography and Silence* Susan Griffin goes some way towards clarifying this. We all, she argues, live with vulnerability, imperfection, fear of death, and deeply wish to resist accepting that they bear upon us. For men, in a dominant cultural position, able to determine and propagate images, 'woman' comes to signify the natural: those feelings of incompletion and decay that put everyone at risk. This pattern is reinforced by the bodily, nurturing roles which culture allots to women, a pattern (it could be added) in which the feminine can never give enough and thus can always be condemned. Understood in those terms—and others are, of course, conceivable—pornography is a display of power which lends the illusion of invulnerability to men, because it purports to master the natural. 'We invent the perfect revenge', as Griffin puts it: 'the pornographic mind gives itself power and diminishes the power of nature. It opposes itself to nature. And it erects culture as an act of revenge against nature.'[27] In this sense the rake's mind is pornographic because it reduces distinct women to a generality, a schedule, even (as Lovelace says) 'a hecatomb'. For 'It is only dead flesh that the pornographer controls', as Griffin says, 'Only a body without life, which has no desire or will' (p. 69). Hence the drugged state of Clarissa, alive but dead to the world. Heterosexual rape can be seen, along these lines, as an assertion of the invulnerability of

[25] *The Pornography of Representation* (Cambridge, 1986).

[26] 'Faut-il brûler Sade?', in her *Privilèges* (1955; Paris, 1964), 11–89.

[27] Susan Griffin, *Pornography and Silence: Culture's Revenge Against Nature* (London, 1981), 66.

the rapist—male, his body unpenetrated—in which the feminine becomes his vulnerability, punished by an exercise of force in which the phallus might be a dagger, or broken bottle, or (for the psychoanalytically minded) a pen. Lovelace's having been jilted, even though only once, is crucial because Clarissa continually reminds him of that failure of his will (irretrievably, except in fantasy) to impose its terms on nature. 'This is a familiar refrain in pornography', Griffin writes, 'The hero . . . makes a doll as revenge against the women who rejected him. Or he kidnaps a woman and keeps her in bondage' (p. 97). For 'when a woman rejects a man, he must face the reality that he does not control her. And that therefore he does not control nature' (p. 144).

Once the fantasy of possession is over, Lovelace has coerced but not controlled Clarissa. Like the pornographer he is frustrated by what whets his appetite; the forbidden fruit tastes of ashes not knowledge. This is intimate with vengeance because retribution is intellectually foreshortened. Even when Machiavellian in its calculation, vengeful intelligence does not set out to understand the quality and value of what it attacks, only how what has been done by what it attacks can be redone, or, in fantasy, undone. One of the most contentious arguments in eighteenth-century moral philosophy, as providentialism came under terminal strain, confronted just this problem. Since other minds have an opacity which makes punishment in proportion to intent impossible to determine, should one give up the right to punish—a line of argument advanced by Beccaria, and developed by Godwin—or should one insist on full retribution as the only principle which stands free enough of personal complexity to answer crime with some earnest of the gravity which its having been committed by and upon an uniquely valuable individual requires? The latter view leads to Kant, but also, as I want to show (with some help from Sade), to the kind of moral blindness which would justify Lovelace's amorous vindictiveness. For it is no accident that, when Griffin describes phallic desire, she reproduces—with no sign of deliberation—the shape, and many of the features (madness, an inset drama, persons reduced to mannequins) of revenge drama. 'Culture presents' the pornographic hero, she says, 'with a stage on which to revenge nature. On the stage are dolls who do not have a soul such as he has. Engraved into the scenery behind him are countless shapes of violent acts inflicted on women's bodies' (p. 102).

If anyone acts on this stage, it is Lovelace. It is an observable effect of rape, however, that the victim often blames herself. Clarissa thinks herself punished by Lovelace's violence for being 'a vain, proud, poor creature—full of secret pride' (iii. 212). She tries to come to terms with the assault by giving it meaning; she needs her own mental theatre, because any meaning is better than none. Yet can the reader be sure that her humility is not, as Anna later hints, tainted with masochistic vanity? Here the analysis of a critic such as Griffin must be sympathetically neglectful because it sees the pornographic victim as so utterly constructed by men that there is no room for female self-regard. When Clarissa seeks to leave the brothel on the stagey line 'Hinder me not from going whither my mysterious destiny shall lead me' (iii. 232), is the self-hurting providentialism extricable from the pride of thinking one's destiny of special interest to God? It is true that Clarissa's belief in providence leads her to resist revenge against Lovelace. Indeed, she warns her brother, James, not to 'arrogate to yourself God's province, who has said: *Vengeance is Mine, and I will repay it*', and repeats this in a letter to Morden: 'Remember, my dear cousin, that vengeance is God's province, and He has undertaken to repay it' (iv. 362, 461). That repeated, retributing 'it' is more severe than anything to be found in eighteenth-century Bibles. Those who take revenge, according to Clarissa, are liable to *its* being repaid, and the Epistle to the Romans is more stringent than St Paul knew.

Even so, her providentialism does not place Clarissa outside revenge tragedy. On the contrary, her situation, under the eye of a retributive deity, resembles that of Hieronimo or Hamlet. After the wrong committed against her comes a phase of derangement, dense with echoes of earlier texts. Renouncing violence, Clarissa then creates a playlet, complete with coffin and pious mottoes, in which to make exemplary her 'destiny'. She may reject Lucretia's suicide as 'faulty revenge' (iii. 220, 522), but her movingly staged death-bed forgiveness of Lovelace functions like Lucrece's condemnation of Tarquin, in that the male members of her family are whipped into vengeful passion. Lovelace certainly comes to feel that Clarissa is exacting '*Christian Revenge*' (iv. 86). 'So this lady, as I suppose,' he writes,

intended only at first to vex and plague me; and, finding she could do it to purpose, her desire of revenge insensibly became stronger in her than the desire of life; and now she is willing to die, as an event which she thinks will cut my heart-strings asunder. And still the *more* to be revenged, puts on the Christian and forgives me.   (iv. 326)

'I suppose' shows that even Lovelace cannot fully credit what he says; but Clarissa's posthumous instruction to Morden, 'Let the poor man's conscience, then, dear sir, avenge me', points up a partial truth in the charge.[28] Conscience does torment him, like a fury, after Clarissa's death. Indeed, the heroine haunts his delirium. Already compared by Anna Howe to the ghost in *Hamlet*, Clarissa appears to the dying Lovelace in the last letter of the book like 'some frightful spectre' at the end of a revenge play (iv. 530), witnessing the destruction of his foe. Even before the deaths of Tomlinson and Mrs Sinclair, Lovelace complains that 'something has been working strangely retributive'; neurotic and dejected, he feels God's anger blighting his life: 'I never was such a fool as to disbelieve a Providence' (iv. 438). In this epistolary novel, though, divine graffiti is the clearest sign of doom. 'Seest thou not,' Belford demands, 'in the deaths of two of thy principal agents, *the handwriting upon the wall against thee?*' (iv. 517). What the moving finger writes is a death sentence for the rake, and if he embraces it in a spirit of melodrama—crying 'There is a fate in it! . . . a cursed fate!' and 'LET THIS EXPIATE!' (iv. 529–30)—the tragic effect is not diminished as asymmetrical providence bears down.

The danger of this claim is that it facilitates a merger between the moral myopia of retributivism and the consoling form of tragedy; Lovelace's death is allowed to satisfy the reader when 'fate' (or, more piously, 'a Providence') legitimates the vindictiveness of a closure which Clarissa partly resists. That he challenges this conjunction is one reason why Sade is difficult to stomach, even for readers who believe that they have put providentialism behind them. He presents a chemistry of passions close to that found in Richardson and Laclos—both of them authors he admired; yet he eschews the poetic justice to which even the latter, when he defaced Madame de Merteuil, succumbed. Certainly the fire of the erotic is, in Sade, as in *Clarissa*, associated with retributive violence. Monsieur Rodin in *Justine* (1791) whips children in his schoolroom, and dissects them in the cellar. 'Blood appears', Sade writes, 'Rodin is in

---

[28] iv. 462; cf. 'Revenge' in the table to the 3rd edn.

ecstasy; his delight is immense as he muses upon the eloquent proofs of his ferocity. He can contain himself no longer, the most indecent condition manifests [the fire of his passion].'[29] It is the appearance of 'proofs' in that blow-answering visibility which drives the action forward. Punishment makes cruelty purposeful, but without meaning. Retribution gives violence definition. It identifies a judge and victim, articulates the exercise of power. In Rodin's school mere instinct provokes vindictive wrath. '"Ah, I am going to make you pay for this stupidity!"', he tells a 15-year-old whom he has masturbated into arousal, '"I must avenge myself upon the illusion [of innocence] you create in me!"' (p. 539). These cruelties reach their apogee in the monastery of Sainte-Marie. Run according to the strictest principles, parodic of the Benedictine rule which the monks ostensibly follow, this institution is governed by laws which are ultimately known only to those who apply them. Justine and the other conventites are thus liable to be punished for breaking rules which are simply extensions of their rulers' wills. Each day, the libertines' appetite for retribution stimulates them to multiply the number of possible offences.

The structure of Sade's narratives reflects this viciously local orderliness in a random, incremental story-line which, constituting evacuated tragedy, lacks an overall rationale. Permutations of sexual relations, all involving power exchanges, contrive plots from which large structures are as absent as the providence they might adumbrate. 'The Sadian relationship (between two libertines)', Barthes notes,

is not one of reciprocity but of revenge (Lacan): revenge is a simple *turn*, a combinative movement: 'Now a temporary victim, my angel, and soon a persecutor . . .' This gliding (from recognition to mere availability) ensures the immorality of human relationships (libertines are complaisant, but they also kill one another): the line is not dual, but plural . . . for the *couple*, whenever possible, is substituted the *chain* . . .[30]

The validity of this analysis comes from its recognition that libertine couples tend to sameness in Sade—despite their belonging to a

---

[29] '. . . l'état le plus indécent manifeste sa flamme'. *Justine, or Good Conduct Well Chastised*, in *The Complete 'Justine', 'Philosophy in the Bedroom' and Other Writings*, ed. and tr. Richard Seaver and Austryn Wainhouse (New York, 1965), 537; *Œuvres complètes du Marquis de Sade*, ed. Annie Le Brun and Jean-Jacques Pauvert, 15 vols. (Paris, 1986–), iii. 105.

[30] Roland Barthes, *Sade, Fourier, Loyola*, tr. Richard Miller (London, 1977), 165.

chain which relies on full plurality—so that relations are levelled to the A and B, or C for B, equivalence which makes bad revenge drama reductive. A mutual lack of mutuality polarizes couples as alternately persecutor and victim, like the agents of an agon who strike and are then struck. This dynamic helps explain the discrete quality of Sade's narrative episodes, the *tableau vivant* nature of the scenes, and scenes within scenes, which punctuate his writing, because the other is always instrumental to the staging of vindictive sexuality. It also clarifies our sense that the libertine, even in orgies, suffers from quasi-theatrical solitude, as he becomes the mere enactor of his desires. Locked into his 'revenge', his 'simple *turn*', the 'persecutor' plays out a banal tragedy of isolation through the exercise of appetites conventionally considered bonding.

Meanwhile, Sade's theory of vengeance makes him a recognizably modern phenomenon. Hobbes and Locke locate the origin of society in a contract designed to protect individuals from the depradations of the mass. Hume, writing in the decade of *Clarissa*, revises this by arguing that society was created for the preservation of 'property'. Justice becomes an artificial virtue almost interchangeable with the politics of ownership,[31] and *vindication* takes on Richardsonian scope. Sade rejects both views, arguing in *Aline et Valcour* that a social contract was established, if at all, so that the strong could dominate the weak. 'Going back to the origin of the right of property', he says, 'we come necessarily to usurpation.'[32] Punishment finds reasons to condemn and is the expression of a will to power. The indolence of legislators, not God, invented 'the law of the talion. It was much easier to say, "Let us do to him what he has done," than to proportion spiritually and equitably the punishment to the crime.'[33] As for virtue, that must be its own reward, since Heaven will not heed it. Time and again, Justine acts well, only for misery to afflict her. Juliette, her sister, accepts the world as she finds it and goes from pleasure to pleasure. As sorrows crowd in upon Justine, she is forced to admit her folly. 'It was inscribed in the great book of fate', she declares, 'that upon those who had tormented me, humiliated me, bound me in iron chains, there were to be heaped unceasing bounties and rewards for what they had done with regard

[31] David Hume, *A Treatise of Human Nature* (1739–40), bk. III, pt. iii.
[32] *Juliette*, tr. and quoted by Geoffrey Gorer, *The Life and Ideas of the Marquis de Sade*, rev. edn. (London, 1953), 113.   [33] Ibid. 125.

to me, as if Providence had assumed the task of demonstrating to me the inutility of virtue.' These 'Baleful lessons', however, she confesses, 'did not correct me' (p. 621).

Incorrigibly, Justine staggers from misfortune to ill-luck. 'You constantly talk about Providence', complains la Dubois, an ex-bandit now become a Baroness, 'ha! what proves to you this Providence is a friend of order and consequently enamored of Virtue? Does It not give you uninterrupted examples of Its injustices and Its irregularities?' (p. 695). Fire provides a memorable instance when Justine rushes into a blazing inn to rescue a baby left in the panic:

I fly to our chamber, having to pass through the conflagration and to sustain burns in several places: I snatch up the poor little creature, spring forward to restore her to her mother: I advance along a half-consumed beam, miss my footing, instinctively thrust out my hands, this natural reflex forces me to release the precious burden in my arms . . . it slips from my grasp and the unlucky child falls into the inferno before its own mother's eyes . . . (p. 712)

In this typically crushing passage—as against, say, Richardson's account of fire in his warehouse—there is no slippage from 'presence of mind' to 'I bless God'. Nor is there 'deliverance'. A reflex betrays Justine, virtue brings her blame, and la Dubois's insistent counsel—'You count upon an avenging God; cease to be a gull' (p. 713)—strikes home the more forcefully. 'Richardson and Fielding taught us', Sade remarks, 'that virtue's continual triumph is not always interesting.'[34] Recalling Aristotle, he adds: 'From what can *terror* spring, save from pictures of crime triumphant, or *pity* save from virtue in distress?'[35] Yet his relentlessly scripted discourse (with only 'It was inscribed in the great book of fate' for transcendence) resists any freedom in the cause of good. Terror and pity are disabled when a heroine kills by a 'natural reflex'. Sade makes you wonder, contrary to the usual wisdom, whether Atheism, rather than Christianity, spelled the 'death of tragedy'. He also brings out, however, the peculiar difficulty which faced revenge tragedians at the end of the eighteenth century, in that the structures which lent coherence (which gave their works the shape of revenge) were complicit with a providentialism which it was, philosophically, increasingly hard to

[34] *Les Crimes de l'amour*, tr. and quoted by Gorer, *Marquis de Sade*, 64.
[35] Ibid. 66.

credit. This makes it the less surprising that the one outstanding rake tragedy of the closing phase of the century—Mozart's *Don Giovanni*—should orchestrate its punitive denouement by combining the immediacy of music with the stylized conventions of Italian opera, and, even so, raise as many questions as it answers.

*   *   *

The rake is most attractive when advancing his mercurial designs. His brilliance dwindles as, and even more after, his vindictive amours are realized. An open, appetitive gusto is lost; yet another conquest is added to a sum which, huge to prove his invulnerability, reduces by its scale the significance of any seduction. Barthes shrewdly notes that Juliette, as a libertine, is a bookkeeper, and that Sade plays games on paper with a kind of sexual arithmetic (pp. 28–9, 179). The 31st letter of *Clarissa*, 'I believe, in different climes, I have already sacrificed an hecatomb' implies not just piles of bodies but a specific total of them. Place, 'in different climes', has more to do with what has been demonstrated, quasi-mathematically, than with what has been seen and enjoyed. While Barthes is subtly perverse when he says that 'the cruiser—if one wishes, Don Juan—travels in a basically more disinterested way than the tourist' (p. 150), his analogy is worth pursuing. For when we read Lovelace's letter about mistresses 'in different climes', we half expect him to launch into the catalogue aria from *Don Giovanni*:

> Madamina, il catalogo è questo
> delle belle che amò il padron mio:
> un catalogo egli è che ho fatt'io;
> osservate, leggete con me.
> In Italia seicento quaranta,
> in Almagna duecento trentuna,
> cento in Francia, in Turchia novantuna,
> ma in Ispagna son gia
> mille e tre . . .[36]

Leporello's aria is so document-centred that it bears comparison with the letter scenes in Tchaikovsky's *Eugene Onegin*, Berg's *Lulu*, and

[36] 'Little lady, this is the list | of the beauties my master has courted, | a list I've made out myself; | take a look, read it with me. | In Italy six hundred and forty, | in Germany two hundred and thirty-one, | a hundred in France, ninety-one in Turkey; | but in Spain already | a thousand and three.' Libretto by Lorenzo da Ponte, tr. Lionel Salter, with Sir Colin Davis's 1973 recording with Wixell, Ganzarolli, Arroyo, etc., and the Chorus and Orchestra of the Royal Opera House, Covent Garden (1973), 12.

(come to that) Holloway's *Clarissa*. The palpably scripted catalogue makes substantial—and suitably reductive—the erotic life of the hero. '*Read* it', sings Leporello: 'leggete con me'. Commentators sometimes try to distinguish the insouciance of the Don from the list-minded mentality of his valet, yet Giovanni sings in the Champagne aria of adding 'una decina' to 'la mia', not *la tua*, 'lista'. In a famous passage of *Either/Or*, Kierkegaard cites the number one thousand and three as the clue to Giovanni's nature because it figures endless yearning,[37] but this is to overlook his blunt tendency to think of women in lots of ten ('una decina'); it neglects the accurate randomness of a number which exposes his conquests as incremental and arbitrary.

But then, Kierkegaard's analysis has a way of minimizing all the other agents in the opera, including the Commendatore.[38] Since he, or his statue, brings blazing retribution onstage, and since both Donna Anna and Elvira enter the opera actively, burning with vengeance and something like desire, this is to misconstrue the drama in which the role of the Don takes shape. What it neglects, in short, is the logic of revenge tragedy, inherited by Mozart's well-read librettist, Lorenzo Da Ponte, from such texts as *Clarissa* and Laclos, and, ultimately, from Tirso de Molina's *El Burlador de Sevilla*. At bottom, this late-Enlightenment masterpiece (first performed in 1787) rests on a seventeenth-century potboiler about honour. If identity thins here, beside, say, *The Marriage of Figaro*, that is not because Giovanni personifies the erotic vitality of music (as Kierkegaard believed) but because of the drift in honour tragedy towards the social determination of status. Romantic accounts have a way of making whole tracts of the work, such as Elvira's 'Mi tradì', dismissable. These female arias have been rejected as Handelian, or Metastasian; but the peculiar brittleness of feminine assertion, and its concomitant tendency to dissolve in flows of abandoned, Heroidean rhetoric, have to do with the difficulty which women confront in establishing their own positions in the honour code. Honour can be taken from women without their choice or submission, and, where sexual disgrace is at issue, it can hardly be reclaimed (Mozart's letters to his wife are eloquent on this topic).[39] Anna and Elvira cannot challenge Giovanni to pistols

---

[37] Tr. David F. Swenson *et al.*, rev. Howard A. Johnson, 2 vols. (Princeton, 1959), i. 93–5.   [38] See e.g. *Either/Or*, i. 123.

[39] See e.g. those of 29 Apr. 1782 and Aug. 1789, in *The Letters of Mozart and his Family*, ed. and tr. Emily Anderson, 3rd edn. (London, 1985), 802–3, 932–3.

at dawn, and even if they could, the sexual smirch would not be erased in the way an affront to a man might be. Without a protective male to vindicate her, Elvira is doomed to ineffectual, embarrassing outbursts. With the stolid loyalty of Ottavio to rely on, Anna has the possibly worse fate of being grateful to a mediocrity. One of the most ruthless but intelligent features of *Don Giovanni* is Mozart's refusal to give Elvira (in any extended way) the dignity she deserves but cannot have, and his steady leeching of musical inventiveness away from Donna Anna.

In the most persuasive part of his argument, Kierkegaard traces eroticism through the other Mozart operas. Don Giovanni, for him, is Cherubino grown up, a sophisticated version of Papageno. Yet this is not the only line of development which can be detected. Mozart's sympathy with wronged female honour, for example, goes back through *The Marriage of Figaro* to his earliest opera, *La finta giardiniera* (1775). This work constitutes a link with Richardson since, along with its model, Piccinni's *La buona figliuola* (1760), it derives, via Goldoni, from *Pamela*. Operas based on Richardson's novel were hugely popular in the mid- to late eighteenth-century.[40] The pathos of the heroine's situation, at once wooed and bullied by her master, gave composers ample opportunity to write plangent arias, while her success in converting and marrying her persecutor helped defuse and resolve, at the level of romance, the social tensions which animate the story. It has been said that Mozart's '*Pamela* opera . . . places its young composer at the centre of the mid-eighteenth-century European bourgeois culture largely influenced by English models',[41] and there is no doubt that his dependent status, first as a travelling virtuoso (paid entertainer of the nobility), and then, in the household of the Archbishop of Salzburg, as a servant who dined with valets and kitchen staff,[42] made him sympathetic to certain anti-aristocratic, if not 'bourgeois', attitudes. When Mozart was dismissed from the Archbishop's service in 1781, he told his father, in the language of Sensibility, 'I have but to consult my own feelings and judgment and therefore do not need

[40] Cf. Mary Hunter, '"Pamela": The Offspring of Richardson's Heroine in Eighteenth-Century Opera', *Mosaic*, 18/4 (1985), 61–76.
[41] Nicholas Till, *Mozart and the Enlightenment: Truth, Virtue and Beauty in Mozart's Operas* (London, 1992), 24.
[42] See his letter to Leopold Mozart, 17 Mar. 1781, *Letters of Mozart*, ed. and tr. Anderson, 713–14.

the advice of a lady or a person of rank to help me to do what is right and fitting . . . It is the heart that ennobles a man; and though I am no count, yet I have probably more honour in me than many a count.'[43]

It would be false to assimilate Mozart, however, to the values of *Pamela*. Quick to hand out insults and to take offence, he was too fond of gambling, finery, and (like Da Ponte) women[44] to become a respectable burgher. Indeed, the letter which I have just quoted shifts from 'bourgeois' self-righteousness to a prickliness which would do credit to a Lovelace: 'For when I am insulted, I must have my revenge.' The enemy in view here is Count Karl Arco, one of the principal members of the Archbishop's household. It was Arco who, a few weeks earlier, had turned Mozart out of his Grace's service with an undignified 'kick on his arse'.[45] 'I only refrained from taking my revenge on the spot', the composer wrote to Leopold Mozart, 'because you, my most beloved father, were ever before my eyes.'[46] 'That arrogant jackass will certainly get a very palpable reply from me,' he vowed, 'even if he has to wait twenty years for it', and 'I shall feel bound to assure him in writing that he may confidently expect from me a kick on his behind and a few boxes on the ear in addition.'[47] To judge from the correspondence—which reads as grippingly, at this point, as an epistolary novel—Leopold Mozart put a stop to his son's vindictive *dramma giocoso* (as *Don Giovanni* would be called), but Count Arco's affront continued to rankle.

Revenge—and its comic potential—is, in fact, a more consistent preoccupation for Mozart than what Kierkegaard calls the growth of 'ethical consciousness' out of 'The Immediate Stages of the Erotic'. From an early aside in his letters about *Idomeneo* and the ghost in *Hamlet*,[48] to the operatic *Tempest* which he was planning when he died, Mozart remained fascinated by the theme. Indeed, it

[43] 20 June 1781; ibid. 747.

[44] On Mozart's 'marked sensuality' (as his first biographer, Friedrich Schlichtegroll, put it), see Wolfgang Hildesheimer, *Mozart*, tr. Marion Faber (London, 1983), 340–2. For Da Ponte's exploits, his friendship with Casanova, and the compositional circumstances of *Don Giovanni* (assisted by a nubile mistress), see Sheila Hodges, *Lorenzo Da Ponte: The Life and Times of Mozart's Librettist* (London, 1985), chs. 2–3 and pp. 80 ff.

[45] Letter to Leopold Mozart, 9 June 1781, *Letters of Mozart*, ed. and tr. Anderson, 741.

[46] 9 May 1781, ibid. 727.

[47] Letters to Leopold Mozart, 16 and 20 June 1781, ibid. 746, 747.

[48] Letter to Leopold Mozart, 29 Nov. 1780, ibid. 674.

is possible to guess how, during the decade of *Les Liaisons dangereuses* and *Justine*, vengeful tensions in his life left marks upon his work. *Die Entführung* (1782), for example, composed shortly after the Arco affair, compounds the question of parental authority and revenge with Konstanze's rescue, by Belmont, from the Clarissa-like plight of being immured in a Turkish seraglio. At just this time, Mozart was trying to persuade his father that marriage to Constanze Weber would be advantageous for him. In the event, wedlock occurred before grudging consent arrived, opera having created the emotional circumstances which made it possible. At the end of *Die Entführung*, that is, despite the captured Belmont's admission that, were the tables turned, *his* father would not pardon the Pasha for rescuing a girl from Spanish custody, Selim bursts out with the noble sentiment: 'tell your father that it is a far greater pleasure to repay with good deeds an injustice suffered, than to erase evil with evil'. 'Nothing is as ugly as revenge,' the lovers chorus (as though with Leopold in mind), 'to forgive mercifully, | is the quality only of great souls.'[49] As late as *The Magic Flute*, his last opera (1791), the same configuration is being explored. Much of the confusion imputed to the work disappears when it is realized that its chief librettist, Schikaneder, was one of the best German Hamlets and the author of an entertainment called *Revenge for Revenge*. The concealed motives, especially of the Queen of the Night, and overheated outbursts in contained situations, owe much to the conventions of revenge plotting. 'Hört! Rachegötter!' is the Queen's revelation of her true hostility to Sarastro—'Hear me, gods of vengeance! Hear a mother's vow!' —while he replies, with reassuring poise, 'In these sacred halls | we know no revenge . . . Within these sacred walls . . . we forgive our enemies.'[50]

The turn towards forgiveness in *Die Entführung*, *Die Zauberflöte* and, come to that, *Figaro*—to say nothing of the Metastasian tradition to which *La Clemenza di Tito* is a coda—is not repeated in *Don Giovanni*. There, the logic of revenge tragedy, carried through Bertati from Molière and de Molina, persists. That Mozart allowed his work the

[49] Libretto by Gottlieb Stephanie, tr. Peter Branscombe, with Sir Thomas Beecham's 1957 recording with Marshall, Holweg, Simoneau, etc., and the Royal Philharmonic Orchestra (1966), 21–2.
[50] Capitol Records tr., with Bernard Haitink's 1981 recording with Popp, Gruberova, Lindner, etc., and the Chor des Bayerischen Rudfunks and Sinfonie-Orchestre des Bayerischen Rudfunks (1964), 32.

label *giocoso* might seem at odds with that, but its mirth is of a piece with the vindictive pleasure of, say, kicking a count on the backside, or (as in Zerlina's 'Razor Duet')[51] with the vaunting hostility which threatens a rapist with castration. The best gloss on Mozart and Da Ponte's often cruel humour is Schikaneder's description of *Rache für Rache*: 'seasoned with the best comical salt'.[52] This condiment has long been essential to the cuisine of such avengers as Titus Andronicus. The honour plays of Tirso and his contemporaries bristle with sadistic gibes. Droll accomplices resembling Leporello proliferate in Renaissance revenge tragedy. In the play which most influenced Richardson's depiction of Lovelace[53]—Shadwell's *The Libertine* (1675)—the mischief of the Spanish *burlador* acquires a nihilistic edge, as the rake becomes a dangerous free-thinker. When piqued, Shadwell's Don John amuses himself by setting fire to a convent in order to flush out and rape the nuns. Yet even here, vindictiveness has a comic brio, endorsing Octavio Paz's claim that 'The humour of the *macho* is an act of revenge.'[54] Mozart's Giovanni, rather similarly, is a seventeenth-century *burlador* under the skin of an Enlightenment libertine. Leporello gets thrashed, is tantalized with food. Elvira is mocked for her constancy. The statue is teased by the Don. Much of the opera's humour comes from dominance and humiliation, and is the gay side of a power struggle in which punishment may be brutal but cannot be entirely serious. The stony, walking Commendatore is the final jape of a *dramma giocoso* which is not (strictly speaking) called *Don Giovanni* but *Il Dissoluto punito*.

In musical terms this means D minor. Mozart's 'tragic key', the tonality of the *Requiem*, frames the opera. The opening chords of the overture are in it. The Commendatore, challenging Giovanni after his assault on Donna Anna, duels in D minor. His statue, unnervingly, accepts the Don's defiant invitation to dinner in the same key, and arrives with one flat and C sharp. While Anna's plots against the rake wax and wane from major to minor, through pastoral and courtly musical languages, the statue remains inflexibly constant to

<hr/>

[51] Added by Mozart to the 1788 Vienna production.

[52] Hildesheimer, *Mozart*, 313.

[53] Cf. Jocelyn Harris, 'Richardson: Original or Learned Genius?', in Margaret Anne Doody and Peter Sabor (eds.), *Samuel Richardson: Tercentenary Essays* (Cambridge, 1989), 188–202, pp. 198–201.

[54] *The Labyrinth of Solitude*, tr. Lysander Kemp (1961; Harmondsworth, 1985), 73.

a key which is, musically, that of *Idomeneo* with a vengeance. His oracular voice, fetched from Gluck's *Alceste*, and Rameau further back, and linked for Mozart (through that passage in the letters) with the ghost in *Hamlet*, and so, perhaps, with Leopold Mozart (for he died while the opera was being written),[55] speaks at the climax of *Don Giovanni* as though from beyond the opera. But to explain its tenebrous authority in terms of musical allusion is to recall those more light-footed echoes which play through the denouement. For the penultimate scene of *Giovanni* develops from quotation to conflagration. Like many revenge tragedies, that is, it ends with an inset drama which both concedes derivativeness and secures an effect of fatality. Giovanni's supper, as surely as the banquet in *Titus Andronicus*, alluding to Seneca and Ovid, is a scene contrived for punishment. The *Tafelmusik* provided by the onstage band amusingly passes the time; but, with each jaunty melody, the empty place provided for the statue comes to seem more ominous. The musicians quote Martin y Soler's *Una cosa rara*, and Leporello is delighted. They play Giuseppe Sarti's *I due litiganti*, and this gives further pleasure; the music, however, has shifted from D major to D minor. A passage from *Figaro* follows, yet its troubling message is 'Non più andrai . . .'. Giovanni's days of philandering are over, and the statue comes to quote him his fate, surrounded by smoke and flame.

The use of quotation and key signature to suggest a 'mysterious destiny' (in Clarissa's phrase) can be immensely potent in the opera-house; yet there remains a pantomimic undercurrent which prevents audiences from moralizing Giovanni's doom. Indeed, there is a subversive jocosity in the way, at almost every performance, the opera modulates into G major and ends in a fatuous chorus. 'Questo è il fin di chi fa mal' the cast sings, *tutti*: '. . . Sinners finally meet their just reward, | and always will'—a sentiment somewhat discounted by their insistence that Giovanni will be visiting not Satan but 'Proserpina e Pluton'. That Mozart was by no means sure of how to handle the Don's perdition can be deduced from a libretto of 1788, as well as the Florentine score, which finish with Giovanni being swept into the blaze of stage sulphur without reference to this chorus. Not surprisingly, nineteenth-century pro-

[55] Cf. Brigid Brophy, *Mozart the Dramatist: The Value of His Operas to Him, to His Age and to Us*, 2nd edn. (London, 1988), chs. 18–21.

ductions took this option further. Giovanni was judged an erotic Faust, for whom hell was as much a final thrill, a realm of discovery, as a punishment. The final sestet was excluded. In the Romantic literature of Don Juan, from E. T. A. Hoffmann to George Bernard Shaw, the incendiary fate of Mozart's protagonist becomes increasingly private. The 'fire' of passion, in Lovelace's image, and the 'raging flames' of retribution, are alike internalized.

While Mozart's *Don Giovanni* is not Hoffmann's or Shaw's, his ambivalence in scoring the denouement shows how far revenge tragedy had travelled between Richardson and 1787. What the audience is shown at the end of the opera lacks metaphysical resonance because Mozart's Christian piety, though real enough, cannot digest the providentialism which had, earlier in the century, held sway. He is closer to Laclos, in the sense that the chorus's judgement of the libertine, like the smallpox which afflicts Madame de Merteuil, is provocatively superogatory and smacks of poetical justice. There is even something of Sade in the triumph which surrounds Giovanni's refusal to acknowledge the authority of the statue and the eschatological import of the fire which rages about him. 'Whence come these hideous | spurts of flame?', he asks, as though the blaze were as literal as an outbreak in a printer's warehouse. He calls the flames 'un inferno', but translators miss his vacillation when they render this, theologically, just 'Hell'.[56] 'No' is his cry, when invited to repent: a triumph of the will, however comically obtuse. While Mozart's fire is musically convincing, and supported by the traditions of revenge tragedy, the relations which it suggests between providence and retribution are complicated by a feeling that what is at stake in this ending is not quite heaven and hell but a view of punishment which, yet again, looks to intimidate, and against which the protagonist becomes a hero by refusing to be coerced. The statue's power is amplified by a full-throated orchestral roar, but Giovanni's mocking resistance also makes him look like a figure in papier mâché armour taken from some old play. Don Juan 'would consider it normal to be chastised. That is the rule of the game', Camus perceptively writes: 'Yet he knows he is right and that there can be no question of punishment. A fate is not a punishment.'[57] The imposition of revengeful symmetry, in other words, does not quite underpin

---

[56] Salter finds 'Hell' here, as e.g. Norman Platt and Laura Sarti do, at 'Di fuoco pien d'orror', in *Don Giovanni*, ed. Nicholas John (London, 1983), 104.

[57] Albert Camus, *The Myth of Sisyphus*, tr. Justin O'Brien (1955; Harmondsworth, 1975), 71.

retribution at the moment when all hell breaks loose. Music enables a tragic intensity which neither the novel nor the drama could, by this date, in this genre, effect, but it is a mode of tragedy which would find its fruition in the absurdism of late twentieth-century literature.

10. Revolution, Revenge, and Romantic Tragedy

THE summer of 1820 found Byron in Ravenna, distracted by the attentions of his mistress, Teresa Guiccioli, but working with unusual steadiness on his first historical drama. The politics of *Marino Faliero* interact so richly with the events of that year[1] that it is hard to determine which factors stimulated, and which merely lent significance to, the evolving text of a play which had been on Byron's mind since 1817. Thus the spark which ignites its action— the arrest and brief confinement of Michel Steno for writing '*Marin Falier, the husband of the fair wife; others kiss her, but he keeps her*'[2] on the Doge's throne—recalls (as others have noted) the imprisonment of Hobhouse for political libel during the winter of 1819–20, but it also chimes with the appearance of seditious graffiti on the streets of Ravenna (April 1820), inscriptions which Byron compared to obscenities scribbled on Hyde Park wall.[3] Provoked by the lightness of Steno's sentence, Faliero joins forces with a group of patriotic assassins and plots a 'sweeping, whole revenge' against the Venetian élite (III. ii. 420). The rebels, betrayed and executed in the tragedy, share the fate of the Cato Street conspirators, hanged on 1 May. Byron deplored the London conspiracy, but his view of such plots grew more perplexed as he himself became involved in the plans of the most plebeian faction of the Carbonari to rise against the Austrians in Italy. Equally overdetermined is the role of the heroine, Angiolina. Her eloquence on the theme of female honour, when the Doge, her husband, is sentenced to death, could be, and was, interpreted as propaganda for Queen Caroline, dishonoured

[1] Cf. e.g. E. D. H. Johnson, 'A Political Interpretation of Byron's *Marino Faliero*', *Modern Language Quarterly*, 3 (1942), 417–25.

[2] Quoting Byron's chronicle source—in the play, the insult is interrupted before it is spoken (I. ii. 62)—from *Byron: Complete Poetical Works*, ed. McGann, iv. 532.

[3] *Byron's Letters and Journals*, ed. Leslie A. Marchand, 12 vols. (London, 1973–82), vii. 84; hereafter, *BLJ*.

and rejected by George IV, and put on trial in late 1820. But this strand in the play is also entangled with Byron's love-life, since Teresa's husband abused and slandered her in the course of a marital break-up which Byron called 'The Guiccioli revolution', and which he, rather flippantly, said was 'the consequence of the revolution in Spain' (*BLJ* vii. 36).

Certainly the affair with Teresa—a woman married, like Angiolina, to a much older man—took a bad turn in 1820. Threatened by her husband, Byron kept in practice with his pistols. Yet he does not seem to have resented being subject to Guiccioli's, and Faliero's, honour code. It was understandable, he told John Murray, that the Count should seek his life: 'assassination—what is it but the origin of duelling—and "a wild Justice" as Lord Bacon calls it' (*BLJ* vii. 184). Byron had recently been picking out 'slips' and 'inaccuracies' in Bacon's apophthegms. A list of his corrections garnishes the fifth canto of *Don Juan*. Given that, his distorting curtailment of the *Essays*, both here and, later, in a letter to Lady Byron (*BLJ* vii. 249), is striking. Bacon writes, rather cautiously: '*Revenge* is a kinde of Wilde Iustice; which the more Mans Nature runs to, the more ought Law to weed it out.'[4] Byron acknowledges that Guiccioli's plots are vindictive, but he does not seem to think that they should be countered by the power of the 'Law'. Sympathetic to the conspirator in Faliero, Byron also respected his vengefulness. In May 1820, while correcting Bacon, he challenged Henry Brougham to a duel for spreading scurrilous rumours about Byron's own marriage (*BLJ* vii. 95–6). His devotion to the honour code brings him closer to Pushkin and Lermontov than to his English Romantic contemporaries. When Shelley told Medwin that Byron resembled Mozart's Don Giovanni, with Fletcher, his man, as Leporello,[5] he caught at once the flaring energy, the touchiness about honour, and the sense of impending retribution which hung about the poet.

Byron had his own ideas regarding the punishment of the Don. In a letter partly concerned with the publication of *Marino Faliero*, he told Murray that he remained uncertain whether the hero of *Don Juan* would 'end in Hell—or in an unhappy marriage' ('probably only an Allegory of the other state'), or would 'finish as *Anacharsis*

---

[4] *The Essayes or Counsels, Civill and Morall*, ed. Michael Kiernan (Oxford, 1985), 16.
[5] Thomas Medwin, *Medwin's 'Conversations of Lord Byron'*, ed. Ernest J. Lovell, Jr. (Princeton, 1966), 5.

Cloots—in the French revolution' (*BLJ* viii. 78). Jean Baptiste, Baron de Clootz, was a Prussian aristocrat who came to Paris, joined the Jacobins, and voted with the regicides. When he attracted the displeasure of Robespierre, he was implicated in a plot and guillotined. To cast Juan as Clootz would be to make him, like Faliero, a noble rebel punished for leading plebeians against the class which bred him. It is characteristic of the poet's Carbonari phase that he should think of developing Juan in this way. Byron looked at the politics of Italy through the spectacles of pre-revolutionary France, just as, when he thought of London, he dreaded an impending Terror. This was what troubled him when Whigs like Hobhouse sided with '[Orator] Hunt and Cobbett—and the bones of Tom Paine' (*BLJ* vii. 50). What would become of gentlemanly reformers if they conspired with such 'ruffians', compared with whom 'Robespierre was a Child—and Marat a quaker'?[6] In the tragedy of Faliero, Byron looked for an answer. As much because of as despite its relations with the politics of 1820, the play endorses what Shelley once wrote to his friend, that the French Revolution 'may be called the master theme of the epoch in which we live'.[7] In this, I want to argue, *Marino Faliero* is typical of much that is lasting in Romantic tragedy. Like *The Borderers, Osorio,* and *The Cenci,* Byron's play explores the revolutionary aftershocks of 1789 through a plot about 'wild Justice' which involves the dramatist in highly charged relations with violence and remorse.

There is an aptness in Byron's using revenge drama to descant upon this 'theme'. As various studies have demonstrated, the turbulence of revolutionary France had from the outset a theatrical dimension,[8] and the dynamics which drove events were often interpreted as vengeful. Paine justifies the violence of the Parisians by writing, 'They learn it from the governments they live under, and retaliate the punishments they have been accustomed to behold.'[9] In *Vindiciae Gallicae,* James Mackintosh suggests that *chateaux*-burning peasants 'had oppressions to avenge'.[10] Recognizing the ferocity of

---

[6]   *BLJ* vii. 44–5; cf. viii. 240, where Major Cartwright, Hunt of Bristol, and Samuel F. Waddington are described as 'very low imitations of the Jacobins'.

[7]   *The Letters of Percy Bysshe Shelley,* ed. F. L. Jones, 2 vols. (Oxford, 1964), i. 504.

[8]   See e.g. Marvin Carlson, *The Theatre of the French Revolution* (Ithaca, NY, 1966), Peter H. Melvin, 'Burke on Theatricality and Revolution', *Journal of the History of Ideas,* 36 (1975), 447–68, Marie-Hélène Huet, *Rehearsing the Revolution,* tr. Robert Hurley (Berkeley, 1982).

[9]   Thomas Paine, *Rights of Man,* ed. Henry Collins (Harmondsworth, 1969), 79.

[10]   *Vindiciae Gallicae: Defence of the French Revolution* (London, 1791), 180.

what he sought to palliate, he negotiated his anxiety by appealing, like Byron, to Bacon. Is the rage of the people, he asked, worse in anything but appearance than the violence of the state? 'The massacres of war, and the murders committed by the sword of justice, are disguised by the solemnities which invest them. But the wild justice of the people has a naked and undisguised horror' (p. 174). After the killings of 2 September 1792, the 'horror' of popular fury was conceded even by radicals. In her *Letters from France*, Helen Maria Williams cannot bring herself to deal with these massacres in the course of her main narrative. After deferring discussion, she insists that the Parisians did not kill out of malice but in 'dreadful vengeance' for the death of loved ones.[11] Time and again appealing to 'revenge' to explain events in the revolutionary 'theatre of crimes',[12] she turns, like Mackintosh, to Bacon, for help with this particular atrocity: 'the affair of the second of September was not a mere indiscriminate massacre, but a kind of *savage justice*, executed by a people frantic at the moment with fear, jealousy, and thirst of vengeance' (iv. 202).

In the confusions of the time, talk of conspiracy was rife. 'It is supposed by some,' writes Williams, 'that the second of September was the result of a deep and long-premeditated plan, formed by certain persons in high authority, with a view to place all the power of the state in the hands of their own party, and at the same time to revenge their private quarrels' (iv. 184). Like Mary Wollstonecraft in her *Origin and Progress of the French Revolution* (1794), Williams is sceptical about the more exaggerated conspiracy theories. But she does not hesitate to depict Robespierre, in luridly Miltonic terms, as the Satanic leader of a 'band of conspirators' (iii. 7), and even Wollstonecraft, in sober hindsight, maintains that the March on Versailles was orchestrated by the Duke of Orleans 'to revenge himself on the royal family'.[13] Whatever the actual extent of factional scheming, perceptions of its existence helped shape political events. The Girondists opposed Robespierre, after the September massacres, by claiming that his party was riddled with crypto-royalists, aristocratic sympathizers who sought to avenge

---

[11] Helen Maria Williams, *Letters from France*, facs., introd. Janet M. Todd (Delmar, NY, 1975), vol. i of 2 vols, iv. 192; cf. iv. 194, 196, 205–6.

[12] e.g. i. 81; iv. 20, 23, 35; iv. 212.

[13] *The Works of Mary Wollstonecraft*, eds. Janet Todd and Marilyn Butler, 7 vols. (London, 1989), vi. 198.

class injuries and to reinstate tyrannical power. Propaganda of this sort found a ready reception abroad. English newspapers of the time are full of it,[14] and politicians shaped their counsels accordingly. 'It is the system you must reform, not wreak your revenge upon individuals', John Thelwall warned fellow-radicals in 1795, adding that the 'misfortunes' of France had arisen from its being 'less influenced by principle than by faction'.[15]

Contexts such as these, long predating 1820, bring *Marino Faliero* into focus as a play about revolution. The conspirators, led by Israel Bertuccio, do not rebel from abstract principle. Struck in the face by a patrician, Bertuccio is moved to 'vengeance' by the insult to his honour (I. ii. 356–9, 497). Retaliating the punishments he has been accustomed to behold, he seeks, like the Doge, 'wild Justice'. Neither is willing to stop, however, with the punishment of individual patricians. As at the height of the Terror, revenge seeks a general tyranny. To win Faliero to the conspiracy, Bertuccio offers him the crown: like the Jacobins of Girondist myth, he sets out to destroy a republic in order to introduce monarchical government (I. ii. 417–23). Meanwhile, from his fellows, we hear the voice of Robespierre and Marat. The patricians, according to Calandro, 'Revel, and lie, oppress, and kill in concert,— | So let them die as *one!*' (III. ii. 36–7). Death comes by association, or suspicion. To disable future reaction, the revolution must deracinate an ethos, the 'spirit' of the élite (37–41). Faliero is, naturally, less positive. The class loyalty which stirred in Byron when he heard what the 'butchers' of Cato Street plotted (*BLJ* vii. 62) finds an echo in the Doge. 'You never broke their bread, nor shared their salt', he tells Bertuccio:

> You never had their wine-cup at your lips;
> You grew not up with them, nor laugh'd, nor wept,
> Nor held a revel in their company; . . .
> And can I see them dabbled o'er with blood?
> Each stab to them will seem my suicide. (III. ii. 459–72)

Israel's response to the Doge's distress, 'I feel no such remorse' (500), is socially unimaginative, but significant in a Romantic tragedy, where the mastery of remorse links villains and anti-

---

[14] See e.g. Alan Liu, *Wordsworth: The Sense of History* (Stanford, Calif., 1989), 144–5.
[15] Quoted by Nicholas Roe, *Wordsworth and Coleridge: The Radical Years* (Oxford, 1988), 173.

heroes. In order to rebel, Faliero must overcome remorse. Doing so he becomes a figure of tragic ambivalence. As I shall show, that development brings him closer than might be expected[16] to the most remarkable protagonist of Romantic tragedy: Beatrice Cenci. Before turning to her, however, I want to think more closely about relations between 'wild Justice' and the *égalité* and *fraternité* of 1789, between the logic of revenge tragedy and the politics of Tom Paine's bones.

*   *   *

Every student of Romanticism knows that fraternal treachery cheats the hero of Schiller's *Die Räuber* of his father's love and his inheritance. Outcast, like Edgar in *King Lear*, Charles Moor finds a new life among the oppressed and becomes an egalitarian bandit with a cause. What has been neglected, however, is the motive which articulates his revolutionary rage: 'my trade is the *lex talionis*; Like for like:—Vengeance is my trade!'[17] An increasingly megalomaniac pursuit of justice ('Vengeance belongs exclusively to me' (p. 167)) leads him back home. When he finds his father starving in a tower, and his mistress, Amelia, deranged, 'Revenge! revenge! revenge' is his cry against the brother who has caused this misery (p. 177). Though his robber band unites against the wickedness of Francis Moor, the claims of Amelia prove divisive. Charles's remorse for his criminal life is almost enough to keep the lovers apart. The robbers ensure a tragic outcome, however, by insisting that their leader keep his promise 'never to desert those who have been true to thee' (p. 212). In a *coup de théâtre* which made late eighteenth-century pulses race, Charles frees himself from his vows by running Amelia through with his sword. He urges his followers to 'Go, serve a gracious king, who wages war to vindicate the rights of man!' (p. 218) and resolves to give himself up to an indigent and hardworking officer, one representative of the law who deserves the price on his head.

The influence of *The Robbers* on Wordsworth and Coleridge has often been discussed, but new light can be shed on the conjunction by concentrating on revenge. Certainly, in *The Borderers*, the outlaw-

---

[16] Expressing reservations about *The Cenci*, Byron sent Shelley a copy of *Marino Faliero* and urged him to 'revenge [him]self upon it' (*BLJ* viii. 103). Shelley exacted his retribution tactfully, in a letter written to Leigh Hunt (*Letters*, II. 345).

[17] *The Robbers*, tr. Alexander Tytler (London, 1792), 97.

leader Mortimer inherits Charles Moor's ardour, while his sardonic amorality goes to the cynical anti-hero Rivers, who was once partly tricked into murder, and who now combines Godwinian philosophizing against remorse[18] with the sort of revolutionary psychology which Wordsworth observed in action 'During my long residence in France, while the Revolution was rapidly advancing to the extreme of wickedness'.[19] Falsely persuading his leader that old Herbert intends to prostitute his daughter, whom Mortimer loves, to the villainous nobleman Clifford, Rivers stirs Mortimer to vengeful homicide. Much of the interest lies in Wordsworth's showing how difficult it is for the innately virtuous outlaw to take Herbert's life, even though he thinks him guilty of gross depravity. 'Is not the depth | Of this man's crimes beyond the reach of thought?', he asks, 'And yet in plumbing the abyss of vengeance | Something I strike upon which turns my thoughts | Back on myself' (II. iii. 59–63).

Yet the conflict between just ire and mercy is a commonplace of revenge tragedy. The energies of retribution elicit a stranger, more innovative drama out of the relations between Rivers and Mortimer. Though Rivers, being ambitious to lead the robber band, has some reason to hate his chief, he has none to punish him; and yet, as though driven by a desire to cast off, or at least make over to another, the effects of a murder which makes him differ, he shapes Mortimer in his own image by provoking the action against Herbert. Annexing the other's freedom, subjecting Mortimer to what once subjected him, he calls up his own past in a recapitulative action (a Romantic version of Hamlet's 'Mousetrap') which has the shape of revenge. Rivers's spot of crime, we eventually learn, consisted in his abandoning a sea-captain on a naked island, alone and—a Schillerean echo—without food. Mortimer is to be dragged down, or forward beyond remorse, by likewise killing another man. Yet when Rivers divulges the nature of his own crime to Mortimer, forging 'a chain of adamant' between them (IV. ii. 187), he cannot know that the past has uncannily declared itself to the extent of inciting not the immediate death of Herbert but his abandonment on the heath—without, as only later hits Mortimer's forgetfulness, his scrip of food.

In chapter 2 of *Violence for Equality*, the philosopher Ted Honder-

---

[18] III. v. 82–8, citing 'The Early Version (1797–99)' in William Wordsworth, *The Borderers*, ed. Robert Osborn (Ithaca, NY, 1982).   [19] *The Borderers*, 33.

ich investigates injurious omissions. He contends that we all (in effect) resemble Mortimer when we deny the starving that scrip of food which a contribution to Oxfam would provide, and that we should correct the consequences of our wrongdoing by working towards equality. This will assist, pre-empt, or even render redundant the not entirely indefensible violence of the deprived towards their oppressors. Honderich is relatively unconcerned to determine what kind of equality should be our aim, because the philosophical issues involved are not only of some complexity but also largely irrelevant when the world is so far from equality by any measure. He does state, however, that by 'the *Principle of Equality*' he means 'movement towards equality of well-being'.[20] This is a philosophical position with roots, of course, in the Enlightenment. But the *égalité* of 1789 was, or quickly became, confused. Helen Maria Williams laments that the revolutionaries exposed themselves to 'many severe and ill-grounded censures . . . for want of taking pains enough to explain what they meant by the term EQUALITY'.[21] She, at least, is clear that the Revolution did not seek to introduce the communistic or primitive-Christian egalitarianism which such Pantisocratists as the young Coleridge and Southey argued for in the mid-1790s. But almost any degree of equality could follow from Paine's observation: 'Every history of the creation, and every traditionary account . . . all agree in establishing one point, *the unity of man*; by which I mean, that men are all of *one degree*, and consequently that all men are born equal, and with equal natural right.'[22]

This relates to tragedy because revenge creates violent equality, correcting A's oppression of B by striking back and levelling the odds. The ironies of vengeful equivalence have always been potentially more interesting than the injuries which generate them. During the Romantic period, however, the philosophically heightened attention which attached to revenge's equivalencing began to engage with and inform not only accounts of revolutionary 'wild Justice' but of that quintessential early nineteenth-century motif of social confusion and psychological turmoil, the *doppelgänger*. Classic revenge situations started to reform as fables of doubling—in the manner of Poe's 'William Wilson', where 'equality' provokes

[20] Ted Honderich, *Violence for Equality: Inquiries in Political Philosophy*, rev. edn. (Harmondsworth, 1980), 55.   [21] *Letters from France*, iv. 248.
[22] *Rights of Man*, 88.

'Wilson's retaliations in kind' against Wilson, and leads to uncanny self-revenge.[23] In drama, as in *The Borderers*, emphasis similarly fell on those absorptions of mind which remake the other in terms allowing self-examination. Consider the confusions of identity which organize Browning's early tragedy of revolution, *The Return of the Druses*. Instead of starting out from the levelling of A and B, this play centres its action on instinctive empathy between antagonists: on the one hand, the insurgent Druse leader, Djabal, who has returned to the Sporades 'to take revenge, lead back [his people] to Lebanon',[24] and, on the other, Loys de Dreux, Knight-Novice of the Templars, who loves the same woman as Djabal, and like him, though with imperialistic and Christian support, is about to claim command of the Druses. Djabal and de Dreux turn out to have been brought up together, like brothers, in the south of France. Indeed, it is warmly suggested that they might descend from a certain Frenchman who, crusading through the Lebanon many years ago, started a branch of the de Dreux family now tribally known as the Druses.

Browning's tragedy has learned (it seems to me) from Coleridge's *Remorse*, and through that from *The Robbers*. In both those plays, fraternal rivalry for a woman precipitates, through a revenge structure, a psychodrama of likeness and difference. Coleridge is particularly subtle about the ramifications of this A/B relationship, making much of disguise, substitution, and the rebirth of identity through guilt. In both versions of his play—the unpublished *Osorio* of 1797 and more conservative *Remorse* of 1813—Albert (Alvar) returns to reclaim his lands from his pernicious brother Osorio (Ordonio) and to win his beloved, Maria (Teresa), back from what he fears must be Osorio's seduction. Disguised as an Arab, Albert signals his sympathy with the Moorish minority in Spain as they struggle against the tyranny of his brother and the tortures of the Inquisition. But though Albert is a rebel and a free-thinker, he is not a Charles Moor crying 'Revenge!' He returns to Granada determined to awaken 'Remorse' in those who have wronged him,[25] while revolutionary vengeance is displaced onto the

[23] *Edgar Allan Poe: Poetry and Tales*, ed. Patrick F. Quinn (New York, 1984), 337–57, pp. 342–3, 356–7.
[24] II. 22–3, in *The Poetical Works of Robert Browning*, ed. Ian Jack and Rowena Fowler, iii (Oxford, 1988).
[25] I. i. 319, in *The Complete Poetical Works of Samuel Taylor Coleridge*, ed. Ernest Hartley Coleridge, 2 vols. (Oxford, 1912) ii.

Moors. For the hostility which Albert might feel towards Osorio, Coleridge substitutes the rage of Alhadra, who seeks the tyrant's life for killing her husband. She and her followers inherit the language of revenge associated with revolutionary struggle in Coleridge's early collaboration with Southey, *The Fall of Robespierre* (1794).[26] They are touched by that 'kind of wild Justice' which the poet identified in a section of the English poor in *Conciones ad Populum* (1795).[27] Osorio, by contrast, is converted from a Rivers-style contempt for 'Remorse! . . . that fool's word' (v. i. 199–200) to an acceptance of its power. When his brother reveals himself, Osorio attempts suicide, '*Throws himself at* ALBERT'S *feet*', develops a charged pronominal simplicity in speaking of himself and Albert—'Thou said'st thou didst not know him. That is he! | He comes upon me!'—and calls for retribution: 'Let the eternal Justice | Prepare my punishment in the obscure world. | I will not bear to live—to live! O agony! | And be myself alone, my own sore torment!' (v. v. 251–66).

These pangs are important to Coleridge in 1797, and they will become more so. They demonstrate an access of vulnerable new consciousness through guilt: a familiar Protestant theme, but given fresh valency and extension by the poet's subsequent reading in German Idealism. Even a few months earlier, Coleridge would have resisted Osorio's remorse. '*Guilt* is out of the Question', he wrote to Thelwall in 1796: 'I am a Necessarian, and of course deny the possibility of it.'[28] But the poet who was thinking his way towards *The Ancient Mariner* (1798) was changing his perception of arbitrarily cruel acts and of how they invite from above what that work's marginal glosses (in 1817) call 'vengeance'. Like the Wordsworth of *The Borderers*, the Coleridge of *Osorio* used drama to disengage himself from *Political Justice*. 'I employ myself now on a book of Morals in answer to Godwin, and on my Tragedy', he announced in April 1797.[29] The measures in question would involve thinking through Kant on duty and Fichte on identity. At a theological level, there would be a rejection of Unitarianism, and exploration of the unitrine nature of God through trichotomy: 'I + {it + i = he} = Thou'.[30] Eventually, the

---

[26] Cf. Julie A. Carlson, *In the Theatre of Romanticism: Coleridge, Nationalism, Women* (Cambridge, 1994), 100–1.

[27] *Lectures 1795 on Politics and Religion*, ed. Lewis Patton and Peter Mann (Princeton, 1971), 38; cf. 9–10.

[28] *The Collected Letters of Samuel Taylor Coleridge*, ed. Earl Leslie Griggs, 4 vols. (Oxford, 1956–9), i. 127.   [29] Ibid. 183.

[30] *The Notebooks of Samuel Taylor Coleridge*, ed. Kathleen Coburn, iii. (1808–19) (London, 1973), s. 4426.

thought that 'the becoming conscious of a conscience, partakes of . . . an act' would be found near the root of all: 'It is an act, in and by which we take upon ourselves an allegiance. . . . It is likewise the commencement of experience.'[31] And this 'act'—inherently dramatic, though inward—would be found to comprise 'an allegiance' because it involves the inter-activeness of I and Thou and He, the awesomely other Thou or He (to think of Osorio on Albert) without which there could be no 'conscious' I.[32] This is why living a non-relational life ('and be myself alone') would be a torment for the remorseful Osorio.

All this is made explicit in Coleridge's later writings. 'The third person', he declares in the *Opus Maximum*,

could never have been distinguished from the first but by means of the second. There can be no He without a previous Thou. . . . This is a deep meditation, though the position is capable of the strictest proof,—namely, that there can be no I without a Thou, and that a Thou is only possible by an equation in which I is taken as equal to Thou, and yet not the same. . . . I do not will to consider myself as equal to myself, for in the very act of constituting myself *I*, I take it as the same, and therefore as incapable of comparison, that is of any application of the will.[33]

Here, rather indirectly, with more attention to grammar and metaphysics than politics, is Coleridge's answer to the egalitarianism of 1789. There is no original '*unity of man*', but an equality derived from difference. A revenge situation in which a wronged agent stirs painful remorse in a wrongdoer develops consciousness out of conscience because its equivalencing dynamic shadows the structure which, for Coleridge, defines conscience itself. 'The equation of Thou with I, by means of a free act, negativing the sameness in order to establish the equality,' he adds, 'is the definition of conscience . . . the precondition of all experience.' This is, indeed, 'a deep meditation'—too profound to be more than distantly signalled on any stage; but it suggests that the revenge drama in *Osorio* mattered to Coleridge partly because it began to

[31] Quoted by e.g. Thomas McFarland, *Coleridge and the Pantheist Tradition* (Oxford, 1969), 238.

[32] e.g. *Notebooks of Coleridge*, ed. Coburn, ii. (1804–8) (London, 1962), s. 3231 and iii. ss. 4426–7. For analysis, see Lawrence S. Lockridge, *The Ethics of Romanticism* (Cambridge, 1989), 115.

[33] Quoted by e.g. McFarland, *Coleridge and the Pantheist Tradition*, 238–9.

articulate problems, grounded in the French Revolution, which would be pursued in some of his richest philosophical writing.

The fraught, affecting confrontation between Osorio's I and the I-based otherness of Albert is not, in fact, the end of the play. In 1797, as though to answer his cry for 'punishment in the obscure world', the bad brother is swept offstage by the Moors—like Francis, by the robbers, in Schiller—to meet his horrible doom, despite Alhadra's Albert-like thought that he might be spared and left to remorse; and the tragedy finishes with the Moorish heroine declaring, in Jacobinical vein, that, if she could find a hundred despairing men not yet palsied by their griefs, she could 'shake the kingdoms of this world' (v. v. 311–13). The more-or-less Tory author of *Remorse* is careful to blacken Alhadra by depriving her of those lines in which she thinks 'to let [Osorio] live— | It were a deep revenge!' (299–300). Instead, he has her recall her dead husband ('Isidore's spirit unavenged?') and stab Ordonio on stage.[34] In other respects, however, human vengeance is played down in 1813. Ordonio cries 'Atonement!' when he is struck, as though a metaphysical blow had fallen, while Alvar, equally pious, denies Alhadra's hand its agency, and cries: 'Arm of avenging Heaven | Thou hast snatched from me my most cherished hope—' (254–6). Moreover, mention of 'dire Remorse'—now an authoritarian force which 'scares us, goads us'—is kept back until Alvar's epilogue-like closing speech, dissociating Alhadra from the principle and denying her final, rebellious lines the prominent position which they had enjoyed in 1797. These changes point to a Coleridge determined to subdue what had remained of a Schillerean revenge plot in *Osorio*, and to substitute divine retribution. In a notebook entry for 1809, which might show Kantian influence, he had reminded himself to devote an issue, or at least a part-issue, of his journal, *The Friend*, to 'that aweful Text—"Vengeance is mine saith the Lord—I will award it."' Coleridge is troubled that 'because Vengeance is most wisely & lovingly forbidden to us, hence we have by degrees under false generalizations & puny sensibilities taken up the notion, that Vengeance is No where— that there is no Vengeance in Deity—'.[35]

Similar anxieties worked themselves out in Coleridge's literary

---

[34] v. i. 253, in *Complete Poetical Works of Coleridge*, ii.

[35] *Notebooks of Coleridge*, ed. Coburn, iii. s. 3560, and, on Kant, Coburn's commentary.

criticism, most vehemently in the attack on *Bertram* in *Biographia Literaria*. Though he insists that his own attitudes have never been infected by the literary Jacobinism which (in his view) disfigures Maturin's tragedy, there is little doubt that Coleridge's hostility owes much to his confronting and rejecting the staining elements of *The Robbers*—now declared 'a monster not less offensive to good taste, than to sound morals'[36]—which link *Remorse* to *Bertram*. Hence the importance of the comparison which Coleridge mounts between Maturin's plotting and that of traditional stage (and puppet-play) versions of Don Juan. All the works in question are revenge tragedies; but where the Don Juan dramas end, like *Remorse*, in divine retribution, and are therefore 'susceptible . . . of a sound moral' (ii. 220), *Bertram* does not. Implying, in effect, 'that there is no Vengeance in Deity', Maturin would betray his audience into fascination with wickedness. Coleridge was shocked by Bertram's adultery with Imogine, unhappily married to Aldobrand, his enemy. But the real scandal lay in the fact that, while Imogine then runs 'mad with horror and remorse',[37] her lover remains defiant. Sustained by desire for revenge, Bertram rises above his anguish to stage a finely amoral death. The forces of virtue may gather. When the Prior learns of Aldobrand's murder, he urges the assembled knights and monks to 'Arise, pursue, avenge' (p. 366). In the gloriously stagey finale, however, 'Bertram disarmed, out-heroding Charles de Moor in the Robbers'—as Coleridge puts it (ii. 233)—faces them down: 'Cease, triflers, would you have *me* feel remorse?' (p. 372). Neither their virtue nor his guilt, but the sight of Imogine wilting to death, impels him to suicide. Bertram's revenge against Aldobrand is satisfied, while the 'Vengeance' of heaven remains doubtful.

*　　*　　*

Though they had their differences over the validity of 'wild Justice' in human affairs, Byron and Shelley were agreed in challenging the morality of divine retribution. Faliero, under intense strain, worries that the disrespect which he once showed the communion wafer might have led to the defeat of his conspiracy (v. ii. 15–41), but he

---

[36] *Biographia Literaria*, ed. James Engell and W. Jackson Bate, 2 vols. (Princeton, 1983), ii. 210.

[37] Quoting the text in *Seven Gothic Dramas 1789–1825*, ed. Jeffrey N. Cox (Athens, Ohio, 1992), 315–83, p. 353.

refuses to be intimidated (50–1), and then, willing a different interpretation, finds 'a comfort in | The thought, that these things are the work of Fate', because it is better to 'cling to any creed of destiny' than believe that the Venetian nobility have deserved to overcome him (65–74). Byron's sympathies would be with Camus's rebellious Don Juan[38] rather than with Coleridge on Heavenly punishment. He was, of course, responsible for having *Bertram* staged at Drury Lane, and it has been plausibly suggested that his own open-ended, non-providential version of the Don Juan story was inspired by a reaction against chapter 23 of *Biographia Literaria*.[39] Though fascinated by the idea of 'Vengeance in Deity', and, in his more Calvinistic moods, willing to entertain thoughts of its fated nature, Byron felt the absurdity and injustice of God's making man in the knowledge that he would disobey Him, and then exacting a penalty for sin. Such considerations put divine revenge in a far less favourable light than the 'wild Justice' of a Guiccioli. As a result, when the Abbot in Byron's *Manfred* quotes 'Vengeance is mine alone!', the biblical injunction enters an argument bold enough to spit it out. 'Must crimes be punish'd but by other crimes?' Manfred asks, as the spirits make to claim him:

> —Back to thy hell! . . .
> What I have done is done; I bear within
> A torture which could nothing gain from thine:
> The mind which is immortal makes itself
> Requital for its good or evil thoughts
> Is its own origin of ill and end—
> And its own place and time[40]

At this point, with the language of Milton's Satan ringing in our ears,[41] we can turn from Byron to Shelley and find revenge tragedy unlocking some defiant metaphysics. For the '*terror and pity*' which Byron experienced when reading Milton's account of Satan (*BLJ* viii. 115) was more than matched by Shelley's approbation. 'Milton's Devil as a moral being', he wrote, 'is as far superior to his God as one who perseveres in some purpose which he has conceived to be excellent . . . is to one who in the cold security of undoubted triumph inflicts the most horrible revenge upon his enemy.' These

[38] Above, p. 240.   [39] *Byron: Complete Poetical Works*, v. 668.
[40] III. i. 63, III. iv. 123–32, in *Byron: Complete Poetical Works*, iv.
[41] Cf. *Paradise Lost*, I. 254–5.

words are familiar from the 'Defence of Poetry', but they first appeared in the 'Essay on the Devil and Devils'.[42] There Shelley identifies vengeance with the retributive Deity, and so God with injustice. Persuaded by Locke, Beccaria and, above all, Godwin that retributive punishment is irrational, Shelley found evil at the heart of received belief. After the fall of Lucifer, he relates, 'God was considerably puzzled to invent what he considered an adequate punishment'. Having 'exhausted all the varieties of smothering and burning and freezing', he imposed a 'terrible vengeance' by transforming Lucifer's 'good into evil' and making him 'a minister of those designs and schemes of which he was the chief and the original victim' (p. 270). Hostile to 'wild Justice' even when provoked by political oppression, Shelley carried Byron's blasphemy to more extreme, and more lyrical, ends. They are realized in *Prometheus Unbound*, where, as the Preface announces, a purified version of Satan is found 'exempt from the taints of ambition, envy, revenge', overthrowing by endurance and not retribution a God whose powers are identified with 'vain revenge . . . revenge | Of the Supreme . . . dread revenge [which] is defeat . . . not victory'.[43]

It is in the philosophically conflicted world of *The Cenci*, however, that Shelley's resistance to 'wild Justice' reaches a dramatic climax, for the inward shape of Beatrice's action is at odds with the inherited conventions of revenge tragedy. According to Trelawny, Shelley disparaged his play for being, oddly, 'a work of art'. 'It is not', he is reported as saying, 'obscured by my metaphysics. I don't think much of it. It gave me less trouble than anything I have written of the same length.'[44] Trelawny's *Records* always need reading with pinches of salt, but it is possible to imagine what lies behind these remarks. Written with astonishing speed between Acts III and IV of *Prometheus*, *The Cenci* enforces, where the long poem arduously transcends, the fable of the 'Essay on the Devil'. At times only too evidently fabricated from the materials of Jacobethan tragedy, and thus driven towards a denouement which, through quasi-providential accidents and ironies, would purport to punish what looks like

[42] *Shelley's Prose: Or, The Trumpet of a Prophecy*, ed. David Lee Clark (1954; London, 1988), 290, 267.
[43] Quoting *Shelley's Poetry and Prose*, ed. Donald H. Reiman and Sharon B. Powers (New York, 1977), 133, and *Prometheus Bound*, I. 11, 215–16, 641.
[44] Edward John Trelawny, *Records of Shelley, Byron and the Author*, ed. David Wright (Harmondsworth, 1973), 121.

the retributive plotting of its protagonist, it is (merely) 'a work of art'; yet its analysis of vindictive teleology runs so cogently from Count Cenci, through the Pope, to God, that it registers a critique of its own structurally retributive assumptions. As George Bernard Shaw observed, more abruptly, 'Count Cenci . . . is really a personification of the . . . God whose attributes convicted the average evangelical Briton in Shelley's eyes of being a devil worshipper'.[45] When younger, Cenci says, 'lust was sweeter than revenge'.[46] Now vindictiveness is his passion, and he indulges this by destroying his sons and defiling his daughter. Against his Godlike malice, Beatrice, resembling the 'benevolent and amiable' Lucifer, rebels.[47] Lust then leagues with vengeance to punish her not only with incestuous rape but with the corrupting ingenuity that God turns against Satan:

> She shall become (for what she most abhors
> Shall have a fascination to entrap
> Her loathing will), to her own conscious self
> All she appears to others . . .
> A rebel to her father and her God . . .   (iv. i. 85–90)

By resisting him, Cenci says, Beatrice will internalize the vindictive hatred which oppresses her. Much criticism assumes that this is indeed what happens when she contrives her father's death and then stubbornly denies complicity. Such a reading squares with Shelley's view of revolutionary vengeance. 'Again and again in his comments on the French Revolution', writes P. M. S. Dawson, 'he argued that the attempt to overthrow the old order by violent revolution merely perpetuated the spirit of that order'.[48] Like Paine's Parisians, Beatrice retaliates the punishments she has been accustomed to behold, perpetrating what Shelley's preface calls 'Revenge, retaliation, atonement . . . pernicious mistakes'. Within the play, however, the language of revenge is concentrated on Beatrice's mother, Lucretia, and on the treacherous cleric, Orsino. What the audience witnesses most painfully, after IV. i, is that 'execrable passion of vengeance' which is integral (for Shelley)

[45] 'Art Corner', in *Our Corner*, 1 June 1886, 370–3, repr. in *Shaw Review*, 15 (Jan. 1972), 35–8, p. 37.   [46] I. i. 98, quoting *Shelley's Poetry and Prose*, ed. Reiman and Powers.
[47] 'Essay on the Devil and Devils', in *Shelley's Prose*, ed. Clark, 270; cf. Stuart Curran, *Shelley's 'Cenci': Scorpions Ringed with Fire* (Princeton, 1970), 137–8.
[48] *The Unacknowledged Legislator: Shelley and Politics* (Oxford, 1980), 6.

to 'criminal justice'[49] taking over where Cenci left off in its persecution of Beatrice. Those who look for the Count in his daughter are liable to rationalize the Count in themselves. Henry Crabb Robinson, for instance, wrote of the trial scene: 'At first I objected to her wilful denial of the truth, but her motive is the allowable infirmity of noble minds. To save the family honour she lied to the last.'[50] This is cruelly inept, taking as primary one of Beatrice's virtuously inadequate attempts at worldly-wise evasiveness instead of registering the will to life which shines out of her performance:

> O white innocence,
> That thou shouldst wear the mask of guilt to hide
> Thine awful and serenest countenance
> From those who know thee not!   (v. iii. 24–7)

Even these notorious lines strike the ear as having overgone hypocrisy. If 'innocence' or 'guilt' must be chosen (the only terms understood by the court), it is clear which it should be, and how passionately. Michael O'Neill maintains that 'The distinction between "white innocence" and the "mask of guilt" strikes one as self-deceivingly casuistical.' He feels compelled to add, however: 'And yet here the spectator or reader is out on his or her own, at once aware of Beatrice's sense of righteousness and recognizing that, for her, there is no other course to take.'[51] This can be put more positively. Beatrice bravely chooses the course which she must take; she makes it her own by an act or play of will. The histrionic inflation of her language indicates a desire to find roles beyond good and evil, beyond 'innocence' and 'guilt'. Nietzschean overtones are unavoidable here, not least because the stresses of Act V owe much to Shelley's sympathy with those noble aspects of Beatrice's defiance which have to do with resisting remorse.[52] Seamus Deane has shown that the poet inherits from La Mettrie the idea that remorse is a form of psychological revenge, a mode of torture imposed by society on the criminals which it creates.[53] By setting out to stage what the Enlightenment had described, by contriving a

---

[49] 'A System of Government by Juries', in *Shelley's Prose*, ed. Clark, 262–3, p. 263.

[50] *Henry Crabb Robinson on Books and Their Writers*, ed. Edith J. Morley, 3 vols. (London, 1938), 652.

[51] *The Human Mind's Imaginings: Conflict and Achievement in Shelley's Poetry* (Oxford, 1989), 87.   [52] See e.g. Friedrich Nietzsche, *Beyond Good and Evil*, s. 260.

[53] *The French Revolution and Enlightenment in England 1789–1832* (Cambridge, Mass., 1988), 110–29.

drama of the will, Shelley anticipates a significant body of late nineteenth-century thought about justice, remorse, and vengeance. A Godwinian account of Beatrice—one close to Shelley in 1819—would 'doubt universally of the propriety of punishment'.[54] For the author of *Political Justice*, restraint of a wrongdoer to prevent future wrongs is 'punishment upon suspicion' and the 'most abhorrent to reason . . . that can be devised' (p. 644). But then, justice as 'reformation' is 'built upon a very obvious mistake', because 'All coercion sours the mind' (pp. 645–6). Similarly, deterrence inflicts suffering not for what the criminal has done but to serve other ends, while its punishments are proportioned to their social effect rather than to the crimes committed. Not that the latter kind of proportion could ever be achieved. As Godwin sees it, punishment is finally irrational because of the impossibility of judging what is commensurate, not only along the axis of retribution—take 'eye for eye', yet are both eyes equally valuable?—but between offenders charged with the same offence. 'No two crimes were ever alike; and therefore the reducing them, explicitly or implicitly, to general classes . . . is absurd. Nor is it less absurd to attempt to proportion the degree of suffering to the degree of delinquency, when the latter can never be discovered' (p. 649).

The author of *Political Justice* being the same as that of *Caleb Williams*, this thesis is developed with psychological brilliance, so that the reader is almost persuaded that, without a complete account of motives and intention, no punishment could be just, and that the uniqueness and opacity of the individual is such that his or her humanity lies in such an account being impossible. Yet this is more or less the juncture from which Kant insisted that, to respect the individuality of agents, punishment must retribute wrongs. 'The real morality of actions,' Kant admits in the *Critique of Pure Reason*,

their merit or guilt, even that of our own conduct . . . remains entirely hidden from us. Our imputations can refer only to the empirical character. How much of this character is ascribable to the pure effect of freedom, how much to mere nature, that is, to faults of temperament for which there

---

[54] William Godwin, *Enquiry Concerning Political Justice*, 3rd edn. (1798), ed. Isaac Kramnick (Harmondsworth, 1985), 642. All passages cited agree with Godwin's 1st edn., 2 vols. (London, 1793), ii. 705 ff., except this one, which originally read, with libertarian rigour, '. . . propriety of coercion'.

is no responsibility, or to its happy constitution (*merito fortunae*), can never be determined; and upon it therefore no perfectly just judgments can be passed.[55]

What follows from this, by a greater insistence than Godwin's on the collective reach of the individual will in the founding of a civic community (the influence of Rousseau can be felt), is an appeal to the categorical imperative—'that is to say, I ought never to act except in such a way *that I can also will that my maxim should become a universal law*'[56]—and, through the Enlightenment 'principle of equality',[57] to strict reciprocity in punishment. Kant concedes a tempering role to deterrence and rehabilitation, but the basis of his code is retributive. With utilitarian arguments sapped by an intense regard to the criminal's, as well as the victim's, uniqueness, he ends up with conclusions as divergent as could be from Godwin's, arguing, from equality, that 'the Law of retribution (*jus talionis*)' is the rational foundation of punishment.[58]

In the *Groundwork of the Metaphysic of Morals*, pondered by Coleridge in 1803,[59] Kant maintains that punishment cannot address the matter of social good until it has respected the offender enough to exact retribution *from him*. In the *Philosophy of Law* and elsewhere, however, he comes close to the view associated with some of his disciples, such as Fichte and, in this regard, Hegel, that the criminal has a right to punishment indistinguishable from his right to freedom in the ethical community, the *Sittlichkeit*. Crime cancels itself as by a reflex within the 'general mind', a turning back of the crime (implicitly universalized as a law) which is an expression of the criminal's will. 'The injury [the penalty] which falls on the criminal is not merely *implicitly* just—as just, it is *eo ipso* his implicit will, an embodiment of his freedom, his right.'[60] Clearly, the differences over this subject between Godwin, Kant, and Hegel are immense. Yet continuities in their attitudes to deterrence and restraint ensure

[55] Tr. Norman Kemp Smith (London, 1929), 475 n.

[56] *The Moral Law: Kant's 'Groundwork of the Metaphysic of Morals'*, tr. H. J. Paton (London, 1948), 67.

[57] *The Metaphysical Elements of Justice: Part I of The Metaphysics of Morals*, tr. John Ladd (Indianapolis, 1965), 101.

[58] Ibid.; for analysis see e.g. Roger J. Sullivan, *Immanuel Kant's Moral Theory* (Cambridge, 1989), 243–4.

[59] *Notebooks of Coleridge*, ed. Coburn, i. (1794–1804) (New York, 1957), ss. 1705, 1710–11, 1717, 1723.

[60] *Hegel's Philosophy of Right*, tr. T. M. Knox (Oxford, 1942), s. 100; cf. s. 101.

that any line of argument run between their theories will have, from one perspective, considerable consistency, though from others it will appear tangled or contradictory. Something similar can be observed in the work of those poets who, early in their careers, come under Godwinian influence, who then shift their allegiances, but who nevertheless keep faith with key elements of their youthful beliefs.

Certainly the Wordsworth who published *Guilt and Sorrow* in 1842 was a very different poet from the one who, nearly half a century earlier, had left unfinished its earlier version, *Adventures on Salisbury Plain*. Like the 1842 text of *The Borderers*, worked up from the manuscript of 1797, the late recension of Wordsworth's most Godwinian poem is steadily and gravely Christian. Yet it shows at least as much anxiety about deterrence as its 1795–9 precursor. Both poems end with a man who has been driven by circumstance to murder, and then racked by guilt, finding relief in execution. However, where the *Adventures* ends with a repulsive image of this man 'hung in iron cage' to set an example to the multitude (which promptly turns him into a holiday attraction), *Guilt and Sorrow* denies—as though countering its unpublished self—that this could have happened: 'Him in iron case | (Reader, forgive the intolerable thought) | They hung not:—no one on *his* form or face | Could gaze, as on a show by idlers sought.'[61] The weight of the endings has shifted. In 1795–9, the poet welcomes the death penalty, on behalf of the guilt-wracked murderer, as a release, but he makes it clear, with Godwinian qualms, that this case is exceptional ('Blest be for once the stroke . . .') and that 'Justice', which operates out of 'halls of terror', bears a 'violated name' (817–19). In 1842, the murderer himself expresses gratitude for the 'welcome sentence' (655), and the prospect of death concentrates his mind on religion. Throughout both texts, however, Wordsworth's sense of how awesome it is to take a life, in execution as in murder, remains consistent, as does his distaste for the element of public exhibition encouraged by theories of deterrence.

During the 1830s the relationship between vengeance and capital punishment had been heavily debated. Acts of Parliament passed in 1837 removed the death penalty from about 200 offences, and pressure for its abolition grew. At this point, while revising *The*

---

[61] *Adventures*, 820, *Guilt and Sorrow*, 658–61, in *The Salisbury Plain Poems of William Wordsworth*, ed. Stephen Gill (Ithaca, NY, 1975).

Borderers and the *Adventures*, Wordsworth published a cycle of poems which in the stress they place on full retribution, the dignity of the state, and something called 'the general mind', strike a firmly Christian yet also intuitively Hegelian note:

> Lawgivers! beware
> Lest capital pains remitting till ye spare
> The Murderer, ye, by sanction to that thought
> Seemingly given, debase the general mind . . .

Wordsworth's *Sonnets upon the Punishment of Death*—of which this is number IV[62]—could not be further from Shelley's Godwinian arguments against execution (as a form of 'revenge') in his 'Essay on the Punishment of Death'. Even in these late poems, however, reservations which Godwin and Shelley would recognize persist. Wordsworth admits the impossibility of determining degrees of criminal responsibility. 'Fit retribution by the moral code | Determined, lies beyond the State's embrace', he says. But that does not urge abolition. Without capital punishment, he warns (with a final glance at Bacon), 'Passion . . . might plead | In angry spirits for her old free range, | And the "wild justice of Revenge" prevail' (VIII).

Like the later writings of Coleridge, these poems contribute to a strain of thought about justice and vengeance which runs strongly through the nineteenth century. Its roots can be found in the scriptural precept—important to Kant, and quoted in Wordsworth's Sonnet VII—'*Eye for eye and tooth for tooth*'. Morality in this vein regards punishment as 'a point of religious obligation',[63] and it finds much justification in the stirring of 'conscience' by 'remorse'. In Byron and Shelley, by contrast, we find a train of argument which leads, eventually, to Nietzsche. The probing of retributive fatalism in the closing scene of *Marino Faliero* is carried further in *The Cenci*, where society vindicates its beliefs on its victims with no rational recession to Necessity but a superstitious appeal to God: 'first cause' of that punitive teleology which maps the values in Beatrice's world but also the dynamics of her revenge play. It is not until the publication of *The Genealogy of Morals* (1887) that a sceptic committed to determinism draws this system with acid clarity, showing how narratives in life and art can be complicit

---

[62] Quoting the texts as first published, with commentary, in Sir Henry Taylor, 'The Sonnets of William Wordsworth', *The Quarterly Review*, 69 (1841–2), 1–52, pp. 39–49.
[63] Ibid. 44.

with an idol-Divinity from whom depends 'terror, madness, crime, remorse . . . the great chain of things'.[64] But the shocks which run through the quasi-providential foundations of *The Cenci*, from Beatrice's defiance in Act V, are pre-echoes of the revolution in ethics announced by Nietzsche. While historical change has obscured the gravity and distinction of *The Borderers* and *Remorse*, Shelley's tragedy remains disturbingly alive, engaging with arguments about punishment and revenge which flow out of the Enlightenment into modernity and post-modernity.

[64] *Prometheus Unbound*, II. iv. 19–20.

Part IV

MODERNITY AND POST-MODERNITY

11. Killing Time: Nietzsche,

Job, and Repetition

WHY does Raskolnikov, in part II of *Crime and Punishment*, yet again
thread his way through the darkening streets of Petersburg, climb
the eery stairs to the moneylender's fourth-floor flat, jangle the bell,
repeatedly, sending shivers down his spine, and feel oddly resentful
at changes made to the room since his killing of Alyona Ivanovna
and Lisaveta?[1] To make this journey before the murder, as a kind of
dress rehearsal for the deed which should fill his pockets with
roubles and free him from futile poverty, makes dreadful, commonplace sense. But to repeat the venture, and in returning arouse
suspicion in the decorators at work in the flat, in the caretaker,
and others, smacks of a compulsion. It falls into the same obsessive
category as Raskolnikov's harping on the stone which hides the
spoils of his crime, that massy stone which—not pushed away
until the murder is confessed to the police—comes, through
Sonia's heartfelt recitation from the New Testament in part IV
(ch. 4), to recall the stone rolled aside at Christ's command from
the tomb of Lazarus. Dostoevsky's notebooks show Raskolnikov
beginning life as a reductive utilitarian, convinced that the murder
of a mean and haggish pawnbroker can be morally outweighed by
the philanthropic application of her funds. By the time the novel
was finished, this unscrupulously rational view had been attributed
to the unnamed student who, overheard by the future murderer,
becomes one of the voices of coincidence which give his intentions
the shape of fate (pt. I, ch. 6). Raskolnikov, meanwhile, had evolved
into a philosophically more alarming type: Nietzschean in aspira-
tion,[2] insisting on an absolute difference between the herd of law-

---

[1] *Crime and Punishment*, tr. David Magarshak (Harmondsworth, 1955), pt. II, ch. 6.
[2] See e.g. Richard Peace, *Dostoevsky: An Examination of the Major Novels* (Cambridge,
1971), 24, who also notes, however, the importance of Louis Napoleon's *The History of
Julius Caesar* (1865) in forming Raskolnikov's 'concept of the "superman"'.

abiders and the extraordinary few who (in the spirit of Napoleon) transcend conventional measures of good and evil. How—to complicate the question—does Raskolnikov's compulsion to return, to reprise, to repeat, connect with his ethical development? Though clues to an answer are scattered through much nineteenth-century fiction, they concentrate in Nietzsche, who called Dostoevsky 'the only psychologist . . . from whom I had something to learn'.[3]

Nietzsche broke with much that was believed in the long, Christian centuries discussed in Part III of this book. His modernity lies not just in his willingness to challenge received ideas, however; it is involved, even paradoxically, with an insistence that 'in intellectual matters . . . we are *historical* through and through'.[4] Certainly, when his remarks about vengeance are set in a nineteenth-century context, family likenesses emerge which help clarify his position as the first philosopher of the modern epoch. Kierkegaard's existentialist critique of Christianity, for instance, developed in the 1840s, anticipates elements of Nietzsche's thought in the 1870s and 1880s. Over that same period—and especially in the decade and a half which brackets *Crime and Punishment* (1866) and *The Brothers Karamazov* (1879–80)—Dostoevsky worked out his anxieties about the irrationality of Christian belief through doubts about the justice of a God who permitted worldly suffering. How deeply Nietzsche was familiar with either writer is uncertain. Various works of Kierkegaard were available in German before the composition of *Also sprach Zarathustra* (in 1883), and, if Lou von Salomé did not introduce him to Kierkegaard in the early 1880s,[5] Nietzsche heard about him from the Danish critic, Georges Brandes, in 1887–9.[6] Brandes also knew the novels of Dostoevsky. While corresponding with Nietzsche, he published a book which described the author of *Crime and Punishment* as 'a colossal example' of 'slave morality'.[7]

---

[3] 'Skirmishes of an Untimely Man', s. 45, in *Twilight of the Idols*, in *Portable Nietzsche*, ed. and tr. Kaufmann, 513–56, p. 549.

[4] J. P. Stern, *Nietzsche* (London, 1978), 52, translating a note, from the late 1870s, in *Gesammelte Werke: Musarionausgabe*, 23 vols. (Munich, 1920–9), xvi. 9.

[5] On her Kierkegaardian studies, in Dostoevsky's St Petersburg, see H. F. Peters, *My Sister, My Spouse: A Biography of Lou Andreas-Salomé* (New York, 1962), 54.

[6] See John Powell Clayton, 'Zarathustra and the Stages on Life's Way: A Nietzschean Riposte to Kierkegaard?', *Nietzsche-Studien*, 14 (1985), 179–200, pp. 194–200; but contrast e.g. Gregor Malantschuk, 'Kierkegaard and Nietzsche', in Howard A. Johnson and Niels Thulstrup (eds.), *A Kierkegaard Critique* (New York, 1962), 116–29, pp. 125 ff.

[7] Georges Brandes, *Impressions of Russia*, tr. Samuel C. Eastman (London, 1889), 309.

Nietzsche was more sympathetic. In 1886–7, when browsing in a Nice bookshop, he discovered a copy of *L'Esprit souterrain*. Sensing an affinity, he bought the book, devoured its contents, and went on to read, in French, *The Insulted and the Injured*, *The House of the Dead*, *The Possessed*, possibly *The Idiot*, and probably *Crime and Punishment*.[8] This chapter concentrates on Nietzsche, but it looks beyond Kierkegaard and Dostoevsky to a novelist—Herman Melville—whose history-of-ideas connection with Zarathustra can only be traced circuitously through a common awareness of Emerson, but whose engagement with 'Nietzschean' topics is (repeatedly) apparent in *Moby-Dick*. In the final part of the chapter, the net is cast even wider. There, ideas of repetition are traced from Nietzsche to Freud's *Beyond the Pleasure Principle*, and, on a larger scale, found modulated in that most problematic, yet, for late Nietzsche, most fundamental of theses: the idea of eternal recurrence. At the level of both the Freudian unconscious and of Nietzschean metaphysics, repetition is involved with revenge. As a result, discussion can go further. The motif of repetition is first explored in anti-Platonic mode—i.e. as a mode of repeating forwards, rather than recalling what is gone—in Kierkegaard's philosophical novel, *Repetition* (1843). It becomes, during the nineteenth century, a dynamic of mass production, a principle of intellectual ordering, of control, classification, and generation, and a theory of political unrest[9]— while always (as Raskolnikov's compulsive behaviour suggests) having the potential to register, in crypto-Freudian terms, the rhythm of psychic trauma. Yet repetition also claims what the modernist Paul Valéry would establish for it: a central role in aesthetics. Art consists, for Valéry, 'in a development of sensations tending to repeat or prolong what the intellect tends to eliminate or transcend.'[10] Though this assertion is grounded in late nineteenth-century (indeed, detectably Freudian) assumptions, it defines a view

---

[8] C. A. Miller, 'Nietzsche's "Discovery" of Dostoevsky', *Nietzsche-Studien*, 2 (1973), 202–57, p. 203.

[9] See e.g. Charles Babbage, *On the Economy of Machinery and Manufactures* (London, 1832), esp. pp. 214–15, Siegfried Giedion, *Mechanization Takes Command: A Contribution to Anonymous History* (New York, 1948), pt. III, and, for intellectual contexts, Edward Said, 'On Repetition', in his *The World, the Text, and the Critic* (London, 1984), 111–25, esp. pp. 124–5, Jeffrey Mehlman, *Revolution and Repetition: Marx/Hugo/Balzac* (Berkeley, 1977).

[10] Paul Valéry, 'The Idea of Art' (1935), tr. Ralph Manheim, in *The Collected Works of Paul Valéry*, gen. ed. Jackson Mathews, 15 vols. (London, 1958–75), xiii. 70–9, p. 75; cf. Edward Casey, 'Imagination and Repetition in Literature: A Reassessment', *Yale French Studies*, 52 (1975), 249–67.

of art which runs through symbolism to deconstruction. Repetition has become the trace—if only residual and deferred—of presence, a shadow of transcendence in the material realm of language. In influential literary theory, shaped by Nietzsche and *Beyond the Pleasure Principle*,[11] repetition is enthroned as a condition of narrativity (and so life) itself. In other words, vengeance is intimate with the dynamics of modern textuality—a claim borne out by, for instance, the configuration of Faulkner's post-Nietzschean narratives,[12] and, as this chapter will conclude, by Wallace Stevens's attempts to define, in his reflections on repetition, the poetics of a post-Christian world.

Hostility to retributive thinking shapes Nietzsche's attitude to philosophical problems apparently removed from revenge. In *Beyond Good and Evil* (1886) and *The Genealogy of Morals* (1887), for example, he attacks the Cartesian *cogito* and Kantian thing-in-itself as figments of the 'vengeful cunning of impotence',[13] and rounds on conventional ideas of justice by means of a detour through natural science. 'One should not wrongly reify "cause" and "effect"', he writes in *Beyond Good and Evil*,

according to the prevailing mechanical doltishness which makes the cause press and push until it 'effects' its end; one should use 'cause' and 'effect' only as pure concepts, that is to say, as conventional fictions . . . In the 'in-itself' there is nothing of 'causal connections' . . . there the effect does *not* follow the cause, there is no rule of 'law.'   (s. 21; *BW* 219)

To argue for an interpretative handling of the unknowable plurality of relations which constitute things and events implies a scepticism which is radical enough; but now Nietzsche sails far beyond Hume ('let us clench our teeth!', he cries, 'and keep our hand firm on the helm!' (s. 23; *BW* 221)). 'It is *we* alone who have devised', he declares,

cause, sequence, for-each-other, relativity, constraint, number, law, freedom, motive, and purpose; and when we project and mix this symbol world into things as if it existed 'in itself,' we act once more as we have

[11] e.g. Peter Brooks, *Reading for the Plot: Design and Intention in Narrative* (Oxford, 1982), J. Hillis Miller, *Fiction and Repetition: Seven English Novels* (Oxford, 1982).
[12] Cf. e.g. John T. Irwin, *Doubling and Incest / Repetition and Revenge: A Speculative Reading of Faulkner* (Baltimore, 1975), Donald M. Kartiganer, 'Faulkner's Art of Repetition', in Doreen Fowler and Ann J. Abadie, *Faulkner and the Craft of Fiction: Faulkner and Yoknapatawpha 1987* (Jackson, Miss., 1989), 21–47.
[13] *Genealogy of Morals*, I. 13, in *Basic Writings of Nietzsche*, ed. and tr. Walter Kaufmann (New York, 1968), 482; hereafter, *BW*.

always acted—*mythologically*. The 'unfree will' is mythology; in real life it is only a matter of *strong* and *weak* wills. (s. 21; *BW* 219)

Once seen from this angle, the 'will to power' loses much of its folkloric ferocity. An ardent, but hermeneutical, impulse, 'The will to power *interprets*'.[14] Indeed, *Beyond Good and Evil* presents its assault on natural science and law as a reading-room quarrel, a matter of textual criticism. 'Forgive me as an old philologist', Nietzsche writes,

who cannot desist from the malice of putting his finger on bad modes of interpretation: but 'nature's conformity to law,' of which you physicists talk so proudly . . . It is no matter of fact, no 'text,' but rather only a naïvely humanitarian emendation and perversion of meaning, with which you make abundant concessions to the democratic instincts of the modern soul! 'Everywhere equality before the law; nature is no different in that respect, no better off than we are'—a fine instance of ulterior motivation, in which the plebeian antagonism to everything privileged and autocratic [is] disguised once more. (s. 22; *BW* 220)

Finding a fit between democracy and science, Nietzsche argues that the congruence casts doubt on both. The exercise of a law which claims to punish as the effect of a cause is put in doubt as a fiction willed by dominant interests. A crucial ground of contention in *Crime and Punishment* emerges on just this territory, when the prosecutor Porfiry challenges the claim, in Raskolnikov's article 'On Crime', that conscience should determine the right to kill, and be its own judge (pt. III, ch. 5). Enough of the utilitarian Raskolnikov survives for his article to insist that murders may only be committed in some proportioned relation to the potential of the criminal, and Porfiry, as employee of the Czarist state, cannot simply be said to represent 'democratic instincts . . . plebeian antagonism'. Even so, Nietzsche helps us recognize that Raskolnikov does not just kill the moneylender, as is sometimes implied by critics, in an act of existential absurdity. He does it to vindicate a new legality, to interpolate what he calls 'some *new word*'[15] into the text of the world.

Suddenly opening a trapdoor beneath his argument about philology, Nietzsche adds: 'Supposing that this also is only interpretation . . . well, so much the better' (*BW* 220–1). Given the quagmire

---

[14] *The Will to Power*, ed. Walter Kaufmann, tr. Kaufmann and R. J. Hollingdale (New York, 1968), s. 643.　　　　　　　　[15] *Crime and Punishment*, 282.

of lost footholds into which this pitches us, 'nun, um so besser' has an awesome banality which is positively Dostoevskian. The philosopher proposes an elevation which sounds like Emerson in its interpretative assurance, yet admits that we project our own design upon events. This is 'so much the better' because potentially worse, for, if some cast a mere shadow upon the surface of life, others illuminate at greater depth its circling, meaningless play. 'Nietzsche in Basel', writes Wallace Stevens,

> studied the deep pool
> Of these discolorations, mastering
>
> The moving and the moving of their forms
> In the much-mottled motion of blank time.
>
> His revery was the deepness of the pool,
> The very pool, his thoughts the colored forms,
>
> The eccentric souvenirs of human shapes . . .
>
> The sun of Nietzsche gildering the pool,
>
> Yes: gildering the swarm-like manias
> In perpetual revolution, round and round . . . [16]

The mania of Raskolnikov, after the murder and after that again, shows him failing to reach the self-mastering state in which conscience could gilder the world instead of being dictated to by guilt. Having sought to become a Napoleon, he is doomed to relive what he has done, both inwardly as memory and outwardly in the self-punishing theatre of that return to the scene of the crime, that repetition rewarded by a shock of recognition as the door bell tinkles, which is yet thwarted by those changes to the room introduced by the decorators. The dynamic of revenge tragedy resembles the workings of a guilty conscience when it reconstructs a crime (in retributive *mimēsis*) to stir up guilt or purge it. Raskolnikov internalizes this dynamic, and suffers in *his own* 'Mousetrap'.

There is, however, a turbulence in early and middle-period Nietzsche, set up by the vitality of vengeance and the ambiguities which gather about the term.[17] Even in maturity he can be found conceding that, 'Without cruelty there is no festival . . . and in

---

[16] 'Description without Place', in *The Collected Poems of Wallace Stevens* (New York, 1954), 339–46, p. 342.
[17] See e.g. *Daybreak: Thoughts on the Prejudices of Morality* (1881), tr. R. J. Hollingdale (Cambridge, 1982), s. 18.

punishment there is so much that is *festive!*[18] Revenge might be rancorous, yet it can also release feelings which would otherwise corrupt. As Zarathustra puts it, 'A little revenge is more human than no revenge at all.'[19] If this suggests some confusion about what 'vengeance' might mean, that is also philosophically productive. In *The Wanderer and his Shadow* (1880), Nietzsche notes that 'revenge' comprises so many things that one can neither deny everything it stands for nor believe that its root is what matters:

> The word 'revenge' [*Rache*] is said so quickly, it almost seems as if it could not contain more than one root concept and feeling. And so people are still trying to find this root . . . As if all words were not pockets into which now this and now that has been put, and now many things at once! (s. 33; *BW* 159)

At a time when the evolutionary principle was being applied to language as to every other social phenomenon, Nietzsche, prompted by his thoughts about vengeance, arrives at the older and newer (i.e. Wittgensteinian) view that language expresses the sum of its social uses, that its historical determinates cannot be understood by constructing a line of descent because past usage recedes endlessly into networks of speech.

Let us then not celebrate beginnings, Nietzsche says, for '*the more insight we possess into an origin the less significant does the origin appear*'.[20] To construct a family tree, to isolate the seed of something, is to select, interpretatively, and therefore by means of the will, from the vast reticulation of 'the entire long hieroglyphic record'.[21] That the argument returns to causation is apparent. What *The Genealogy of Morals* asserts is that 'the origin and purpose of punishment' are 'two problems that are separate' because 'the cause and the origin of a thing and its eventual utility, its actual employment and place in a system of purposes, lie worlds apart . . . purposes and utilities are only *signs* that a will to power has become master of something less powerful and imposed upon it the character of a function' (II. 12; *BW* 512–13). So the corollary of Nietzsche's critique of causation is that justice is the exercise of someone's, or some collective, will to power. The retributive code which characterizes nineteenth-century

---

[18] *Genealogy of Morals*, II. 7; *BW* 211.
[19] *Thus Spake Zarathustra: A Book for Everyone and No One*, tr. R. J. Hollingdale, rev. edn. (Harmondsworth, 1969), 94.   [20] *Daybreak*, s. 44.
[21] *Genealogy of Morals*, pref., 7; *BW* 457.

society is not based on absolute principles but is an expression, in the ethical sphere, of the economy of 'repayment and exchange' which dominates the market-place.[22] Meanwhile 'punishment' means so many things that it is 'overdetermined'[23]—Freud will take a hint from this; it is a cultural pun within which no logic can be traced, though certain strands leading from the network of signs which we know as history stand out through it. It is in this context that Nietzsche's attack on *ressentiment*, remorse, and the whole 'Judaic' panoply of pity, guilt, and gratitude must be understood, as must his admiration for the Old Testament, that 'book of divine justice' in which 'the incomparable naïveté of the *strong heart*' is shown in its starkest lineaments.[24] To make more headway with this, however, and return to *Crime and Punishment*, it is necessary to reconsider recurrence in the light of the Book of Job.

*   *   *

Kierkegaard did so in 1843. 'You have surely read Job?', asks the hero of *Repetition*, 'Read him, read him over and over again.'[25] Just why one should, repeatedly, is explained in lines which anticipate yet give one the measure of Nietzsche's originality four decades later. We should read, and re-read, Job because 'he knows that he is innocent and pure in his inmost heart, where he is conscious that God knows it too, and yet the whole of existence contradicts him. The greatness of Job consists in the way that his passion of freedom is not stifled or tranquillized by a false expression' (p. 125). Despite the counsel of his comforters, those agents of guilt and pity, Job protests his purity and is rewarded. Like the Abraham of *Fear and Trembling*, he is a strong heart who, notwithstanding his trials, lives at a pitch of faith which, in the end, brings vindication.[26] 'Time passed, the possibility was there, Abraham believed; time passed, it became unreasonable, Abraham believed.'[27] Time and faith are relevant to Job because his book is plainly not argued to an end. Once God has allowed Satan, the antagonist, to destroy Job's

[22] See e.g. *Human, All-Too-Human* (1878), s. 92; *BW* 148.
[23] *Genealogy of Morals*, II. 14; *BW* 517.
[24] *Beyond Good and Evil*, s. 52; *BW* 255. *Genealogy of Morals*, III. 22; *BW* 580.
[25] *Repetition: An Essay in Experimental Psychology*, tr. Walter Lowrie (Princeton, 1942), 121.
[26] See, however, ibid. 130.
[27] From *Fear and Trembling* (1843), in *'Fear and Trembling' and 'The Sickness unto Death'*, tr. Walter Lowrie, rev. edn. (Princeton, 1954), 32.

children, and to put his hand upon the man himself, the disputations which follow have a spiralling uncertainty which could never
reach conclusion. Not Eliphaz, Bildad, nor Zophar, nor the long-
winded fourth comforter Elihu, can persuade Job of his injustice.
And God's answer, 'out of the whirlwind' (38: 1 ff.), mostly consists
of questions. Indeed, it is Job's admission that, in arguing beyond
his faith, he has 'uttered that I understood not' which precipitates
the divine denouement: 'So the Lord blessed the latter end of Job
more than his beginning: for he had fourteen thousand sheep, and
six thousand camels, and a thousand yoke of oxen, and a thousand
she asses' (42: 3, 12). These numbers double what Job first owned
(repetition at a higher power), and only his 'seven sons and three
daughters' are returned to him—in some sense—singly (42: 13),
'because', as Kierkegaard's young protagonist in *Repetition* observes,
'a human life is not a thing that can be duplicated' (p. 144; cf. 132).

As it happens, this ending is uncertain—and not just because its
reader might wonder (with Kierkegaard's young protagonist) how
complete a restitution new children are for the innocents destroyed.
Like the sublime chapter on wisdom, the verses on Behemoth and
Leviathan, and Elihu's garrulous disquisition, the final 'blessing' of
Job may well be a late accretion.[28] The original Book, nineteenth-
century scholars suggested, dealt with the wretchedness and heroism of a believer who suffers inexplicably yet preserves his faith.
Certainly, *Repetition* only declares its full significance—its closeness,
in this respect, to Nietzsche—when it is realized that doubts of the
kind that surround the coda of Job attached to the novel during its
composition. For its plot reflects the predicament of an author who,
breaking off his engagement with Regine Olsen, wrote *Either/Or*—
known at this stage as *Guilty/Not Guilty*—partly to determine
whether his doubts about marriage had led him into error. In the
novel, *Repetition*, a youth, corresponding with an older man, endures
and explores the consequences of rashly yet purely abandoning a
love affair. Can he undo, re-do, in some way repair through
repetition, the consequences of his action? His correspondent,
Constantine Constantius, establishes by revisiting his own favourite
haunts, in Berlin, that, given the flux of experience, one cannot step
into the same river twice. Even the theatre, that realm of Hamlet-

---

[28] See e.g. Otto Eissfeldt, *The Old Testament: An Introduction*, tr. Peter R. Ackroyd
(Oxford, 1965), s. 64.

esque repetition, disappoints Constantius: 'The next night I was at the Königstäter Theater. The only thing repeated was the impossibility of repetition' (p. 70). Reminded on every side that a broken engagement can no more be unbroken than, say, the harpist outside the theatre be put back into the mixed grey coat that made the other day not now, Constantius can hardly be the young man's redeemer.

This is why Job consoles. The possibility of reparation, including self-restoration, haunts the protagonist of the novel as surely as it did Kierkegaard, and, come to that, Dostoevsky. For *he* read, and re-read, Job, remarking, in 1875, that the book put him into such a condition of 'unhealthy rapture' that he almost wept—like Father Zosima in *The Brothers Karamazov*, moved by the blessing of Job.[29] It induced turmoil and relief in Dostoevsky because it seemed to reconcile the sufferings of the innocent—especially children unjustly 'punished'[30]—with the existence of a benign Deity. In *Repetition*, as we now read it, there is a similar process of reconciliation after doubt. A 'thunderstorm' of relief breaks when the protagonist learns that the woman he has turned away has become engaged to another man. There *is* a redeeming repetition, 'although in the temporal life it is never so perfect as in eternity' (p. 144). When the circumstances of Kierkegaard are recovered, his hero's passion for Job—'For me this narrative contains an indescribable consolation' (p. 133)—takes on an enlarged significance. So close was Kierkegaard to his creation[31] that, when Regine Olsen became engaged to another man, the ending of *Repetition* resolved. After many attempts at atonement in the draft, the hero had, despite Job's consolation, shot himself. Upon hearing of Regine's engagement—re-engagement, in effect—Kierkegaard tore up his ending,[32] rewrote it, and had the young man disappear into a haze of sea imagery: 'My yawl is afloat, the next minute I am where my soul's yearning was, where the ideas foam with elemental rage, where thoughts arise boisterously like the nations in swarmed

---

[29] See Joseph Frank, *Dostoevsky: The Seeds of Revolt 1821–1849* (London, 1977), 52, *The Brothers Karamazov*, tr. David McDuff (Harmondsworth, 1993), 334–6.

[30] See *Brothers Karamazov*, 277–82.

[31] But see Robert Pogue Harrison, 'Heresy and the Question of Repetition: Reading Kierkegaard's *Repetition*', in Mary Ann Caws (ed.), *Textual Analysis: Some Readers Reading* (New York, 1986), 281–8, p. 284.

[32] *Repetition*, tr. Lowrie, p. xxv; for further details see *'Fear and Trembling' / 'Repetition'*, ed. and tr. Howard V. Hong and Edna H. Hong (Princeton, 1983), p. xx.

migration, where at another season there is a stillness like the profound silence of the South Sea . . . there, where one every instant stakes one's life, every instant loses it, and wins it again' (p. 145)

With this existential Job in mind, we can return to Nietzsche on vengeance. 'This, yes, this alone', says Zarathustra in 'Of Redemption',

is *revenge* itself: the will's antipathy towards time and time's 'It was'. . . .

The spirit of revenge: my friends, that, up to now, has been mankind's chief concern; and where there was suffering, there was always supposed to be punishment.

'Punishment' is what revenge calls itself: it feigns a good conscience for itself with a lie. (p. 162)

In the weak will's interpretation of events as 'caused', for Nietzsche, lies the source of that polarity Guilty/Not Guilty, the debased ordering of 'what occurs' into Crime and Punishment:

And then cloud upon cloud rolled over the spirit: until at last madness preached: 'Everything passes away, therefore everything deserves to pass away!'

'And that law of time, that time must devour her children, is justice itself': thus madness preached. (ibid.)

The voice of madness speaks the language of Job's comforters. They understand repetition not as a repeating forwards but as a retributive reinscription of the past. Out of their insistence that the ills which afflict their friend must have a reason, a cause, they invent an evil Job and a correspondingly punitive God. Such a logic would lead to the humanly regretted passage of time itself becoming evidence that wrongs have been done, making even a desired past hateful. But the strong self, Nietzsche declares in *Beyond Good and Evil*, is he who 'has not only come to terms and learned to get along with whatever was and is, but who wants to have *what was and is* repeated into all eternity, shouting insatiably *da capo*' (s. 56; *BW* 258).

This embrace of eternal recurrence contrasts sharply with the Judaeo-Christian desire for escape from punitive time into consoling eternity. Nietzsche's use of 'Erlösung', in the chapter-title 'Of Redemption' (the word partly means 'unloosing'), recalls the German text of Job, where *Erlöser* renders 'redeemer' in the cry,

'I know that my redeemer liveth' (19: 25). In Hebrew, where *go'el* ('vindicator, avenger') is used, Job comes close to succumbing to the language of his comforters. However, a Nietzschean Job would unloose, unbind, in some figurative way remove Lazarus' bandages by not resigning himself to what has happened by deeming it a blight and punishment. In related, more aesthetically oriented terms, 'Tragedy does *not* teach "resignation"', Nietzsche writes in *The Will to Power*: 'Art affirms. Job affirms'—and then, *Erlösung* again, 'How redeeming is Dostoevsky!'[33] In contrast with the affirmation of strong suffering instilled by Job, the fools of Time stall life's 'swarm-like manias' in traumatic repetition—even though this brings with it the corollary that time is the means by which life revenges itself on us for living. Against the ghoulish impulse to atone by reversing time, to redeem or avenge Lazarus by rolling away the stone—that massy stone which by this logic must (compare Raskolnikov) hide a crime—Zarathustra imputes to 'madness' the cry:

'Can there be redemption when there is eternal justice? Alas, the stone "It was" cannot be rolled away: all punishments, too, must be eternal!' Thus madness preached.   (p. 162)

For him, in vital contrast: 'All "It was" is a fragment, a riddle, a dreadful chance—until the creative will says to it: "But I willed it thus!"' (p. 163).

At this point, God's question is worth repeating: 'Canst thou draw out leviathan with an hook? or his tongue with a cord which thou lettest down?' (Job 41: 1). Within a decade of *Repetition*, Melville was answering 'perhaps', in a novel which sets high among its epigraphs, 'Leviathan maketh a path to shine after him; One would think the deep to be hoary' (cf. Job 42: 43). 'Who can open the doors of his face?' God asks out of the whirlwind (41: 14). One of the functions of 'The Sperm Whale's Head', 'The Right Whale's Head', and the other chapters in *Moby-Dick* concerned with cleaning and scraping and boiling Leviathan, is to hollow out, in Nietzschean fashion, the mystery of the *causa sui*, the self-positing immanent idea. 'Now, had Tashtego perished in that head,' we are told, as the whalers gouge out brains, 'it had been a very precious

---

[33] s. 821; 434–5; 'Wie erlösend ist Dostoiewsky!' is dated by Giorgio Colli and Mazzino Montinari (*Friedrich Nietzsche: Sämtliche Werke*, ed. Colli and Montinari, xiii. 214), to Spring 1888.

perishing; smothered in the very whitest and daintiest of fragrant spermaceti; coffined, hearsed, and tombed in the secret inner chamber and sanctum sanctorum of the whale. . . . How many, think ye, have likewise fallen into Plato's honey head, and sweetly perished there?'[34] Here is a lesson for Kierkegaard's young protagonist, 'redeemed' into his quest across a philosophical 'South Sea', and led by the empty cry: 'I belong to the idea. When that beckons me I follow' (p. 145).

In Melville's tragedy of revenge, the will to power which shapes violence cultivates repetition. When Ahab rounds his harpoonists in a circle, and has them swear vengeance on Moby Dick in a scene fraught with echoes of *Hamlet* (ch. 36), he is seeking to roll away the stone 'It was'. He strives to undo by punishing what he wills, what he interprets, to have been an evil-intended act: the white whale's robbing him of a leg. Nothing in the book endorses his will to revenge, as against Starbuck's interpretation that 'a dumb brute . . . simply smote thee from blindest instinct', except the glory in itself of Ahab's will to 'Vengeance' (pp. 261–2). Auden, in *The Enchafèd Flood*—written in Kierkegaard's orbit[35]—dilates on this suggestively. Orestes, he points out, has a task imposed on him which he despatches. Hamlet, however, develops a romantic dimension by secretly cherishing the situation he is asked to resolve, 'and cannot bear to end it, for who will he be then?' 'This conception of revenge as a vocation is made all the clearer', Auden goes on,

when the revenge theme is combined with the quest theme. . . . The revenge as quest brings out the *value* of the hated object to the hero.

The romantic avenger hero, in fact, is a person who is in dread of not having a vocation and yet is unable to choose one for himself . . .

'My injury,' he says, 'is not an injury *to* me; it *is* me. If I cancel it out by succeeding in my vengeance, I shall not know who I am and will have to die. I cannot live without it.' So not only does he cherish the memory of a catastrophic injury, but also he is not lured forward by the hope of happiness at some future date.[36]

---

[34] Herman Melville, *Moby-Dick; or, The Whale*, ed. Harold Beaver (Harmondsworth, 1972), 452.

[35] Cf. George W. Bahlke, *The Later Auden* (New Brunswick, NJ, 1970), 69 ff.; for an extended Kierkegaardian account of the novel, see M. O. Percival, *A Reading of 'Moby-Dick'* (Chicago, 1950).

[36] *The Enchafèd Flood or The Romantic Iconography of the Sea* (London, 1951), 96–7.

Think of Ahab, whose vengeful token (his wooden leg) is the bloody handkercher of traditional revenge drama become integral to the victim. Not only is his injury part of him, and the wooden leg an object arousing passionate feelings of purpose and meaning, but his identity vanishes with his vengeance. Snatched round the neck by a harpoon cable, and swept overboard, he goes down with the whale he has tracked across the South Seas as an object of supreme value for 600 pages.

I have hinted at the ambivalence of Moby Dick. In one of those circling images which run so deeply through the book, Ishmael writes of a 'grey-headed, ungodly old man, chasing with curses a Job's whale round the world, at the head of a crew. . . made up of . . . castaways, and cannibals' (p. 286). Father Mapple's sermon, likewise, offers a benign interpretation of the beast, finding in Jonah's whale a figure of God (ch. 9). For Starbuck, the whale is noble prey and a veritable sump of wealth. 'How many barrels will thy vengeance yield thee even if thou gettest it?' he asks Ahab: 'it will not fetch thee much in our Nantucket market' (p. 261). As the text unfolds, however, typology and commerce alike become inadequate measures of a whale increasingly demonic. The very whiteness of Moby Dick, as a full chapter explains, is deathly sinister (ch. 42). Like a landscape smothered in snow, the milky way hung in interstellar vacancy, a shroud, 'of all these things', Ishmael says, 'the Albino whale was the symbol. Wonder ye then at the fiery hunt?' (p. 296). But if not, then the greater wonder: that a beast could be such a symbol. 'The Whiteness of the Whale', Ishmael's chapter, is (in Nietzsche's sense) a genealogy that traces a tangled skein of concepts, from cultures primitive and contemporary, by sea and land, oriental and American, which inform 'the mystic sign'. So many Ahabs have learned to hate whiteness, and have willed to call it evil, that it has become even for Ishmael awesome in its 'overdetermination'. Out of will comes fate: a topic to which I must now turn, with some help from Freud.

*　　*　　*

For 'overdetermination' is not the only Nietzschean motif to have left its mark on psychoanalysis. At a decisive moment in the history of the discipline, in *Beyond the Pleasure Principle* (1920), we find Freud meditating (in Nietzschean vein) on the '"perpetual recurrence of the same thing" '[37] and the destructive effects of repetition both in dreams and in life's coincidences. Partly with Nietzsche's help, it would seem, the death instinct emerged in Freudian theory, and with it came a pessimistic reorganization of the concept of the ego and its relations with the unconscious. *Beyond the Pleasure Principle* is a major work of tragic literature, however dubious its clinical status, because its intellectual confusions and culs-de-sac witness Freud's efforts to resist the dark conclusions which his argument made inevitable. What the recurrent nightmares of shell-shocked soldiers taught him during and after the First World War was that his old oneiric model, in which bad dreams were punishments for guilty erotic wishes, was inadequate to explain what such men suffered, and that with that model collapsed his belief that the human organism was propelled (however guiltily) towards pleasure and the persistence of life. With his earlier views complicated beyond recovery, Freud returned to Schopenhauer and Nietzsche. When we read in the latter that 'A living thing seeks above all to *discharge* its strength—life itself is *will to power*; self-preservation is only one of the indirect and most frequent results',[38] it is impossible not to think of the new claims in *Beyond the Pleasure Principle*. But what is the more telling is that Freud should have introduced views which ran so counter to his earlier work by thinking of revenge, of repetitive child's play, and the links of both with tragedy.

In chapter 2 of *Beyond the Pleasure Principle*, Freud breaks off his account of 'traumatic neuroses' to discuss a little boy's game. Biographers have shown that, in contradiction to his usual practice, Freud has here been galvanized by events in his own family. The 18-month-old infant who has the habit of flinging a wooden reel over the edge of his cot, crying 'o-o-o-o' (which Freud interprets as *'fort'*, 'gone'), stirs some of the same feelings about danger and loss in the analyst (we can deduce) as the information that this child's 'absent father was "at the front"'. Tragedy comes into question because this boy more often, and repeatedly, threw his reel away crying *'fort'* than he pulled it back on its string with a gratified shout of *'da'*, 'there'. Freud's initial idea that the game rehearses 'the child's great cultural achievement' of letting his mother out of sight without protest, that it shows his 'instinct for

[37] Tr. James Strachey; in *Standard Edition of Freud*, gen. ed. Strachey, xviii. 7–64, p. 22.
[38] *Beyond Good and Evil*, s. 13; *BW* 211.

mastery' in controlling an unpleasant event, begins to run against a
pleasure principle which should have him more often indulging in
'*da*' than '*fort*'. He therefore invokes revenge, accommodating
gratification to violence: 'Throwing away the object so that it was
"gone"', the analyst speculates, 'might satisfy an impulse of the
child's, which was suppressed in his actual life, to revenge himself on
his mother for going away from him.' That his reflections are being
shaped by an economy of vengeance becomes apparent in Freud's
next recalling that, after unpleasant experiences at the hands of a
doctor, a child will reconstruct the events in play but with himself as
the doctor: 'he hands on the disagreeable experience to one of his
playmates and in this way revenges himself on a substitute'. The
tragic relevance of this appears in Freud's then noticing 'that the
artistic play and artistic imitation carried out by adults, which,
unlike children's, are aimed at an audience, do not spare the
spectators (for instance, in tragedy) the most painful experiences
and can yet be felt by them as highly enjoyable'.

The most provocative element in this is not Freud's idea of tragic
spectatorship, nor the way the pleasure principle is briefly rein-
stated despite the dominance of '*fort*' over '*da*', but the emergence of
an argument about sado-masochism[39] which suggests that vindictive feelings can be satisfied through self-punishment. Literature is
not short of characters who, like Shakespeare's Cassius, immolate
themselves on the hostility of another, and who, in doing so and
calling it vengeance—'Caesar, thou art reveng'd, | Even with the
sword that kill'd thee'[40]—seem to confirm and punish a degree of
self-disgust. Symptomatically modern, because psychodramatic, is
the case of Van Gogh's ear, as elaborated by Wyndham Lewis in his
novel, *The Revenge for Love* (1937). Gauguin, he recalls, left the hotel
room he shared with Vincent after waking up to find the latter
crouched beside him with a razor in his hand. 'A few days later',
Lewis records,

he received a small postal packet, and discovered inside, carefully wrapped
up, a human ear. It was a present from his friend. For . . . it occurred to
[Vincent] . . . that having intended to cut his friend's ear off, and driven
him away, by advertising too crudely the intention, the least he could do

---

[39] Cf. Leo Bersani, *The Freudian Body: Psychoanalysis and Art* (New York, 1986), 58.
[40] *Julius Caesar*, v. iii. 45–6.

was to mutilate himself, and sort of give his friend his revenge, but without his being put to the trouble of *taking* it![41]

This story shows how the A/B equivalence which arises from a revenge dynamic can become a psychic tragedy in which vengeance is inflicted without the antagonist being more than a figment necessary to the expression of self-hatred. The agent, driven by him or herself, by the Furies or daemon of the unconscious, is locked into a pattern of behaviour which has the shape of repetition even when it effects for the *first* time what has previously only stirred as a wish.

Thoughts such as these encourage Freud to consider those patients who, unable to remember repressed wishes, act them out repetitively—a line of enquiry which leads him to what ancient tragedy calls the *alastor*. Even among 'normal people', he observes in chapter 3, 'The impression' can be given 'of being pursued by a malignant fate or possessed by some "daemonic" power'. Without anything like a conscious desire being apparent, the relationships of some people repeatedly follow the same destructive course: 'the benefactor who is abandoned in anger after a time by each of his *protégés* . . . or the man whose friendships all end in betrayal by his friend'. More strangely, cases arise in which 'the subject appears to have a *passive* experience, over which he has no influence, but in which he meets with a repetition of the same fatality'. This, for Freud, is evidence that hidden levels of consciousness direct the subject to tragic ends. The obscure operation of the will produces a repetitive pattern of misery which becomes a person's fate.

Before the deep coincidence between this fact of life and of tragedy can be lost sight of, recall how vengeance operates in *Moby-Dick* to assimilate its antagonists. It is not just that, as Auden implies, Ahab needs the whale, but that the monster seems a projection of his need, a sort of daemon. On the third day of the combat with the *Pequod*, as tragedy reaches its final scene and the whale bears down on Ahab, the captain cries 'Oh, his unappeasable brow drives on towards one, whose duty tells him he cannot depart' (pp. 682–3). The magnificence of this inheres in its ambiguity, since, if the captain 'cannot depart', his 'duty' summons Moby Dick. Such is the interchange of retributive anger that the whale takes on Ahab's motives and his death has the self-cancelled completeness

[41] *The Revenge for Love* (Harmondsworth, 1983), 251–2.

of a suicide: atonement in the act (you die for taking a life, though your own) as fully mysterious and convincing as Raskolnikov's 'Was it the old hag I killed? No, I killed myself, and not the old hag,' and the invocation of a daemon which follows: 'I did away with myself at one blow and for good. It was the devil who killed the old hag, not I' (p. 433). 'Retribution,' writes Melville (*not* of Ahab but the whale), 'swift vengeance, eternal malice were in his whole aspect, and spite of all that mortal man could do, the solid white buttress of his forehead smote the ship's starboard bow, till men and timbers reeled' (p. 683). Thus it is that Ahab's relentless quest—ranging circles in search of his destiny—ends. Melville makes us feel the spiralling involve, until 'concentric circles seized the lone boat itself, and all its crew, and each floating oar, and every lance-pole, and spinning, animate and inanimate, all round and round in one vortex, carried the smallest chip of the Pequod out of sight' (pp. 684–5).

Significantly, Ishmael marks his escape from this maelstrom with a quotation from Job. 'AND I ONLY AM ESCAPED ALONE', the 'Epilogue' announces, 'TO TELL THEE' (p. 687). Ishmael has witnessed the destruction of seven sons of Uz, but survived, clinging to a '*coffin*' belched out of the sea. Is he then restored doubly—that is, to himself—like Kierkegaard's hero? Certainly the idea of rebirth from suffering is intimated:

Round and round, then, and ever contracting towards the button-like black bubble at the axis of that slowly wheeling circle, like another Ixion I did revolve. Till, gaining that vital centre, the black bubble upward burst; and now, liberated by reason of its cunning spring, and, owing to its great buoyancy, rising with great force, the coffin life-buoy shot lengthwise from the sea, fell over, and floated by my side. (p. 687)

This is another of Ishmael's circles, within which, 'by a commodius vicus of recirculation',[42] is found the secret of life-in-death. For Melville's narrator stands in a line that (setting aside its Orphic origins) runs from Blake's Enion, weaving her Circle of Destiny, through Emerson's essay on 'Circles', to the gyres and phases of Yeats's Nietzschean *Vision*. The novelist's many images of recurrence are allied, that is, to the mythy orbs and spheres that Wallace Stevens found so prominent in Romantic tradition.[43] And a passage such as this, from a chapter called 'The Gilder', about an ocean as

---

[42] James Joyce, *Finnegans Wake*, 3rd edn. (London, 1964), 3.

[43] Cf. e.g. Georges Poulet, *The Metamorphoses of the Circle*, tr. Carley Dawson and Elliott Coleman (Baltimore, 1966), M. H. Abrams, *Natural Supernaturalism: Tradition and Revolution in Romantic Literature* (New York, 1971), chs. 3–5.

calm as the pool at Basel, in which echoes of Job knit together with Shakespeare, makes Melville's overlap with Nietzsche unignorable. 'Would to God these blessed calms would last', says Ishmael,

But the mingled, mingling threads of life are woven by warp and woof: calms crossed by storms, a storm for every calm. There is no steady unretracing progress in this life; we do not advance through fixed gradations, and at the last one pause:—through infancy's unconscious spell, boyhood's thoughtless faith, adolescence' doubt (the common doom), then scepticism, then disbelief, resting at last in manhood's pondering repose of If. *But once gone through, we trace the round again; and are infants, boys, and men, and Ifs eternally.* (p. 602; my italics)

Part III of *Zarathustra* is what I have in mind. There, the prophet becomes a voyager, questing away from the Blissful Isles, and troubled by the sea's tendency to become, as in Kierkegaard's *Repetition*, a mood-forming image of the mind. Suspicious of what Stevens calls 'The meaningless plungings of water and the wind',[44] Zarathustra responds with an exercise of will. And, like Ishmael, he discovers in the seascape eternity as return. 'To you, the bold venturers', he says to the crew, 'and whoever has embarked with cunning sails upon dreadful seas . . . to you alone do I tell this riddle that I *saw.*' It is his fable of dwarf and gate:

'Behold this gateway, dwarf! . . . it has two aspects. Two paths come together here: no one has ever reached their end.
'This long lane behind us; it goes on for an eternity. And that long lane ahead of us—that is another eternity. . . .
'Behold this moment!' I went on. 'From this gateway Moment a long, eternal lane runs *back*; an eternity lies behind us.
'Must not all things that *can* run have already run along this lane? Must not all things that *can* happen *have* already happened, been done, run past? . . .
—and must we not return and run down that other lane out before us, down that long, terrible lane—must we not return eternally?   (pp. 176–9)

This is a difficult passage, best glossed by Melville's 'If'. In certain accounts of Nietzsche, the fable is discounted as some kind of feint, an impossibility meant to encourage the fullest possible awareness that an individual's life is the only one which he or she can ever live.[45] But a general theory of cosmic recurrence must follow from Nietzsche's attack on causes. An absolute interconnectedness of

    [44] 'The Idea of Order at Key West', *Collected Poems*, 128–30, p. 129.
    [45] See e.g. Alexander Nehamas, *Nietzsche: Life as Literature* (Cambridge, Mass., 1985), 148–69.

things can only be guaranteed by the abolition of a teleology in which beginnings lead to ends; and, in circles, extremes meet. This truth is as valid for philosophical systems as it is for causes, as a congruence with Plato demonstrates. For Nietzsche arrives at his theory of eternal recurrence partly to counter crypto-scientific ideas which would make punishment an 'effect' of crime. Rather similarly, Plato's advocacy of the death penalty for murder makes him, in Book IX of the *Laws*, sympathetic to reincarnation: 'Vengeance for such acts is exacted in Hades,' he reports initiates as fabling, 'and . . . those who return again to this earth are bound to pay the natural penalty,—each culprit the same, that is, which he inflicted on his victim,—and . . . their life on earth must end in their meeting a like fate at the hands of another' (870e-871a).

One virtue of this myth is that it overcomes the problem that retribution requires time but is put in doubt by its passage. The man you hang for murder is not the body and mind which did the deed. His physical constitution will have been changed by what he ate, over several weeks, for breakfast; no memory can be the same before and after a killing. Recent work in philosophy greatly exercises itself with tales of transplanted and split brains, of persons changed cell by cell until they resemble others: can A_1 ever be deemed B? These questions must be awkward for any theory of punishment based on individual responsibility, since, when you are faced with a person who has the memories of a war criminal, and some version of his body, you are required to ask not only whether 'he' can now receive a fair trial but how far that 'he' resembles the person who murdered many Jews. Nietzsche's attack on the *cogito* is immensely important here. It seems natural, for instance, that Derek Parfit's attempt to construct a neo-utilitarian theory facilitated by Humean fluidities of identity, in his celebrated *Reasons and Persons* (1984), should be preceded by an epigraph from Nietzsche which declares: 'the sea, *our sea*, lies open again; perhaps there has never yet been such an "open sea"'.[46] And indeed, if one turns to the earliest reactions to Nietzsche, it is possible to find the question of punishment brought up against his conception of a self which flickers through physical, rather than being secured by spiritual, life.

Jack London's *The Sea-Wolf* (1904) is a useful instance, not just because it meditates early on late Nietzsche but because it sets forth

---

[46] *The Gay Science*, bk. V, s. 343, in *Portable Nietzsche*, ed. and tr. Kaufmann, 448.

on an 'open sea' to support what I have been saying about Ahab's
will to power. Admittedly, unlike Melville's hero, Wolf Larsen is a
perfect Aryan. He is the first of several such in London, summed up
in Ernest Everhard of *The Iron Heel* (1907), 'a superman, a blond
beast such as Nietzsche has described'—his very name echoing
Zarathustra's commandment, 'Be hard'.[47] However, Larsen, in
addition to flaxen hair and strong thews, has a burning desire to
sweep the seas in pursuit of an unattainable goal. It is not clear what
this could be, beyond further pursuit, yet London successfully
conveys a sense that Wolf is, like Ahab, in search of 'vindication'.
Both men are capable of poetic intensity, an amoral force which
baffles them, or shows them incomplete. 'I am filled with a strange
uplift', Larsen will say, 'I feel as if all time were echoing through me,
as though all powers were mine.'[48] Yet these moments standing at
Zarathustra's gate are varied by brutalizing treatment for Larsen's
crew, and by passages of self-contempt unrelieved by the shelf of
books over the captain's bunk: 'Shakespeare, Tennyson, Poe, and
De Quincey. . . . Tyndall, Proctor, and Darwin' (p. 518).

According to London in his Marxist phase, Larsen offers a
critique of the *Übermensch*,[49] and it is true that the novel is wary
of admitting Nietzschean sympathies. In the opening chapter, set on
a ferry crossing San Francisco bay, we hear about a reader of
'Nietzsche and Schopenhauer' (p. 481); but this is a landlocked
friend of the author who spends his time making money in the
city. All that, we are led to think, must be left behind for the plot to
take off. And yet, as the steamer approaches a thick fog bank, a
ruddy-faced man with artificial legs 'stumped across the deck and
back . . . with an expression of keen enjoyment on his face. I was
not wrong', the narrator reports, 'when I decided that his days had
been spent on the sea' (p. 482). This is clearly Ahab on a day outing.
When the ferry is crushed by 'the bow of a steamboat . . . trailing
fog-wreaths on either side like seaweed on the snout of Leviathan'
(p. 484), its rubicund guardian goes down into the maelstrom and
London's hero is taken aboard an ominously named whaler, the

[47] *Jack London: Novels and Social Writings*, ed. Donald Pizer (New York, 1982), 326; cf.
Patrick Bridgwater, *Nietzsche in Anglosaxony: A Study in Nietzsche's Impact on English and
American Literature* (Leicester, 1972), 168.
[48] *Jack London: Novels and Stories*, ed. Donald Pizer (New York, 1982), 538.
[49] Letter to Mary Austin, 5 Nov. 1915, in *The Letters of Jack London*, ed. Earle Labor,
Robert C. Leitz, III, and I. Milo Shepard, 3 vols. (Stanford, Calif., 1988), iii. 1513.

Ghost. What he finds there is, in some ways, Nietzsche himself. Larsen's majestic limbs, lingered over by London with homoerotic fascination, may not be Nietzschean, and his life of strife and combat on the high seas lies beyond the range of the retiring philosopher of Sils Maria. However, he is subjected at the end of the novel to a series of crippling strokes. The narrator, enthusiastic dualist, talks at this point of an unquenchable spirit retreating to its inner recesses. But Wolf, in the wake of *Twilight of the Idols*, insists on the body as absolute. London will have known that, a decade or so earlier, Nietzsche suffered the same affliction. We have Erwin Rohde's and Paul Deussen's accounts from the 1890s, of the great man paralysed down one side, and his speech slurred, heavy, and broken.[50] When Larsen, half paralysed, speaks 'slowly and heavily', or can't utter, and complains that 'Something's gone wrong with my brain' (p. 753), we are close to Nietzsche's decline. And this makes it the more suggestive that the death of the *Übermensch* should be, at least for London's narrator, as he sits by Larsen's bed and consoles him, a 'fearful fate', judged and ordained. 'There was', he writes, 'the awfulness of retribution about it' (p. 753).

It would be wrong, however, to end with the voice of Job's comforters, and leave an aftertaste of revenge. Instead, consider this passage from Wallace Stevens's 'Notes Toward a Supreme Fiction' which overcomes and domesticates the trauma of repetition:

> Whistle, forced bugler,
> That bugles for the mate, nearby the nest,
> Cock bugler, whistle and stop just short,
>
> Red robin, stop in your preludes, practising
> Mere repetitions. These things at least comprise
> An occupation, an exercise, a work,
>
> A thing final in itself and, therefore, good:
> One of the vast repetitions final in
> Themselves and, therefore, good, the going round
>
> And round and round, the merely going round,
> Until merely going round is a final good,
> The way wine comes at a table in a wood.
>
> And we enjoy like men, the way a leaf

[50] See Paul Deussen, *Erinnerungen an Friedrich Nietzsche* (Leipzig, 1901), Ronald Hayman, *Nietzsche: A Critical Life* (London, 1980), ch. 12.

Above the table spins its constant spin,
So that we look at it with pleasure, look

At it spinning its eccentric measure. Perhaps
The man-hero is not the exceptional monster,
But he that of repetition is most master.[51]

Though these wonderful verses question the cult of Napoleon and
would put no roubles into Raskolnikov's pocket, they show, in their
quietly Dionysian way, how repetition can be mastered and pleasure released from self-punishment. To read them is to grasp the
force of Deleuze's perception that Nietzsche 'conceived of repetition in the eternal return as Being'.[52] They do more, in fact, than
show a way of celebrating Being. In the to-and-fro of his lines, the
returns of syntax and stanza-form, Stevens adumbrates something
of that justification of life beyond time which Nietzsche, from his
earliest writings, saw as the aim of existence: 'for it is only as an
aesthetic phenomenon that existence and the world are eternally *justified*'.[53] By willing repetition forwards (to think of Kierkegaard),
against the aftershocks of atonement, Stevens reconciles an ethics
of the quotidian with those patterns of recurrence and prolongation
which writers such as Valéry taught modernity to value in art.

[51] 'Notes Toward a Supreme Fiction', *Collected Poems*, 380–408, pp. 405–6; on
Nietzsche's influence see e.g. Bridgwater, *Nietzsche in Anglosaxony*, 198–201.

[52] *Différence et répétition* (Paris, 1968), 14.

[53] *Birth of Tragedy* (1872), s. 5; *BW* 52

12. 'Of Wars and Rumours of Wars'

THE wrath of Achilles reaches a terrifying climax in the twenty-first book of the *Iliad*. Grief-stricken at Patroclus' death, and cheated of immediate revenge against Hector, the son of Peleus stabs and slashes his way across the Trojan plain. Like a swarm of locusts fleeing a conflagration, his enemies pour into the River Xanthos where they are seized as blood sacrifices or impaled. Most of them die anonymously. Thirty-four lines into the book, however, Achilles comes upon a named son of Priam and the narrative is suspended for one of those passages of retrospection which Homer reserves for especially significant deaths. Once before captured by Achilles, Lycaon broke bread with the Achaean and earned him a sizeable ransom. He is therefore addressed as *philos*, 'friend' (106), even though he belongs to a family responsible for Patroclus' death. But if this encounter involves complicating loyalties, it is also, as Homer presents it, peculiarly stark and direct. Lycaon is unarmed: his spear, helmet, and shield have been lost in the foaming Xanthos. No physical threat to Achilles, he clutches the hero's knees in supplication. Here, if anywhere, the limits of violence are tested. Achilles, however, insists that ransom ended with Patroclus' life. Desire for revenge merges into tragic fatalism. 'Why all this moaning?', he asks Lycaon: 'Patroklos died also, a far better man than you. Do you not see how fine a man I am, and how huge? . . . And yet I tell you death and strong fate are there for me also: there will be a dawn, or an evening, or a noonday, when some man will take my life too in the fighting' (106–12).

In an essay published shortly after the fall of France to Hitler,[1] Simone Weil uses Lycaon's death to characterize a 'poetry of force'. For her the Homeric hero is sustained by a 'power' which turns his victims into things. 'The weak see no relation between themselves and the strong,' she writes, 'and vice versa.' Clad in 'the armour of power', a warrior is exalted above those he betters until Ares turns the tables 'and kills those who kill' (p. 193). We are likely to think at

[1] 'The *Iliad* or the Poem of Force', tr. Mary McCarthy, in *Simone Weil*, ed. Miles, 182–215.

this point—as Weil's early readers must also have done—of the armour and leather of the SS, as they liquidated their prisoners, and of French hopes for a German defeat. But the death of Lycaon reveals more about military violence than its likely moral blindness. For what, in literal terms, is 'the armour of power' described by Homer? When Patroclus rallies the Greeks, as the Trojans threaten their ships, he puts on the armour of Achilles and carries his friend's image into battle. Almost irresistible in this feared equipment, he is tempted to advance too far and meets his match in Hector. It is often pointed out that Achilles' grief over the body of his friend is virtually an act of mourning for his own death, a reaction encouraged by Thetis' prophecy that if he returns to battle—as he now vengefully must—his life will be cut short. Something of Achilles dies when his armour is stripped from Patroclus, and when he kills and strips a Hector dressed in that same brazen stuff (XXII. 306–94) he not only repays his friend's death but destroys his opponent in (yet also in revenge for) what appears a killing of himself. Recognition of this grim economy, which every way spells death, stirs in his words to Lycaon. Men with spears or firearms can be spurred to ruthless violence by a sense of superior force, but equally, at those depths where fear becomes aggression, and is called courage, their own mortality can rouse them pre-emptively to avenge their ends.

The claim that *philos* is, in fact, a word of war, because (as Konrad Lorenz puts it) 'aggression in very many animals and probably also in man is an essential component of personal friendship',[2] has not proved experimentally valid. Few ethologists would deny that 'There is . . . an internal physiological mechanism which has only to be stimulated to produce fighting';[3] but on battlefields, as in the psychologist's workshop, the desire to avoid violence proves strong.[4] Putting troops in a position where attack is the only defence remains the soundest recipe for slaughter. 'We do not fight, we defend ourselves against annihilation,' recalls Remarque, in *All Quiet on the Western Front*: 'we can destroy and kill, to save our-

---

[2] Konrad Lorenz, *On Aggression*, tr. Marjorie Latzke (London, 1966), 239. For evidence against see e.g. Jo Groebel and Robert A. Hinde (eds.), *Aggression and War: Their Biological and Social Bases* (Cambridge, 1989).

[3] John P. Scott, *Aggression*, 2nd edn. (Chicago, 1975), 62–4.

[4] Thus, after an average day of stiff fighting in World War II, 75–85% of allied combat troops would not have fired their weapons. See Samuel Lyman Atwood Marshall, *Men Against Fire: The Problem of Battle Command in Future War* (Washington, DC, 1947), 47.

selves, to save ourselves and to be revenged.'[5] The conscripted, mass uniformity of much twentieth-century warfare might make it easier for soldiers to take life. It is not until sleep after battle that Wilfred Owen is forced to recognize the individuality of his Lycaon, 'the enemy you killed, my friend'.[6] Yet, as the long periods of cursory sniping between trenches in the Great War demonstrate, even the polarities of modern conflict can generate quiescence. 'War is like a fire,' Li Quan said, 'if you do not put it out, it will burn itself out.'[7] Incendiary Achilles, raging across the plain, once more comes to mind. Repeatedly in twentieth-century war literature—as in the rhetoric of Hitler's revanchist speeches[8]—vengeance throws fuel on the flames. Even when the writings in question are memoirs, without epic or dramatic ambitions, a gravitation towards revenge tragedy is clear.

Consider the American accounts of Vietnam. Faced—or, frustratingly, not faced—by attackers who melted away into the jungle and the rice-paddies, GIs were unable to stabilize conflict along clear fronts. Places that were little more than grid references were therefore taken, then abandoned, and 'body counts' became the measure of success. In these circumstances vengeance gave focus to the fighting. Soldiers like those recalled by Michael Herr, with 'AVENGER V' emblazoned on their helmets,[9] changed themselves psychologically from being targets to purposeful protagonists. The enemy was so elusive that battle could rarely condense into the crisp syntax of Tim O'Brien's sardonic 'Johansen was happy. He'd lost many men to the Forty-eighth Viet Cong Battalion. He was getting his revenge.'[10] More often in these memoirs soldiers displace violence onto animals, smash the terrain in 'something like revenge',[11] and shoot civilians. Only a desire to atone for the latter can explain the existence of such books as Philip Caputo's *A Rumor*

---

[5] Tr. A. W. Wheen (London, 1929), 78.

[6] 'Strange Meeting', in *The Collected Poems of Wilfred Owen*, ed. C. Day Lewis (London, 1963).

[7] Quoting the *Spring and Autumn Annals* in Sun Tzu, *The Art of War*, tr. Thomas Cleary (Boston, 1988), 57.

[8] See e.g. J. P. Stern, *Hitler: The Führer and the People*, rev. edn. (London, 1990), 26 and, on the Blitzkreig as Hitler's '"revenge" . . . for the *Fronterlebnis* of thirty years before', 198 (cf. 163–4). For the structuring of French defeat in 1940 as 'revenge for Versailles' (Stern, *Hitler*, p. x) see e.g. Alan Bullock, *Hitler: A Study in Tyranny*, rev. edn. (Harmondsworth, 1962), 590–1.   [9] *Dispatches* (London, 1978), 65, 162.

[10] *If I Die in a Combat Zone* (1973; London, 1989), 101.   [11] Herr, *Dispatches*, 125.

of War (1977), where the author self-punishingly catalogues punitive atrocities. Full of Kennedy-era idealism Caputo joined the Marines and went to Vietnam in 1964. The reality of battle left him scarred but unable to settle away from combat. Withdrawn to base-camp he craved 'Revenge' for the men he had seen killed.[12] After an ambush at Giao-Tri, his troops 'destroy with uncontrolled fury . . . an act of retribution' (p. 110). Attacked near Dieu Phoung, 'I thought, tit for tat. . . . I ordered both rocket launcher teams to fire white-phosphorus shells into the hamlet' (pp. 284–5). Clad in a GI version of Weil's 'armour of power' (he calls it 'a kind of emotional flak jacket'), and gripped by 'urges to destroy that seemed to rise from the fear of being destroyed', his unit ignored 'the cries and pleas' of villagers at Ha Na (pp. 96, 304–5).

Theatrical revengers murder in inset playlets to insulate themselves from what they perpetrate. Caputo updates this when he recalls, of Ha Na: 'Strangest of all had been that sensation of watching myself in a movie. One part of me was doing something while the other part watched from a distance, shocked by the things it saw, yet powerless to stop them' (p. 305). The image is convincingly dangerous. Film is more violently labile than drama. Its killing has the fluency of sight. Technologically related to the revolver and the Gatling gun,[13] a movie camera 'shoots' through sights, off the shoulder like a rifle, often from the angle of an agent in the action. To have film in mind helps a soldier kill. Many Vietnam memoirs recall how such movies as *The Sands of Iwo Jima* (starring John Wayne) provided heroic self-images for the troops, but these remembered projections played across a field already wired for cinema by infra-red detectors, high-voltage searchlights, TV surveillance, and a flow of reconnaissance photographs. High-tech extravagance transformed the traditional theatre of war: flares and tracers making the night brilliant, showers of napalm and phosphorus sending fiery clouds and trails of silver across the screen of the sky. In the flickering scene of revenge tragedy, GIs went on '"vengeance patrols"'[14] with *To Hell and Back* rolling in their heads. On leave in Saigon they were offered such fodder as 'Steve McQueen working through a hard-revenge scenario'.[15] Even

[12] *A Rumor of War* (1977; London, 1978), 231.
[13] Paul Virilio, *War and Cinema: The Logistics of Perception*, tr. Patrick Camiller (1984; London, 1989), 11.   [14] Herr, *Dispatches*, 86.
[15] Ibid. 54.

the intimacies of torture took place in a centre called 'the "cinema room"'.[16]

The Western tragic revenger uses violence to articulate rage. Hieronimo kills in a certain way to express the injuries he has received. War might seem less communicative, but, from the nature of the wounds inflicted, values and meanings can be 'read'. Injuries taken by noble riders, for instance, differ from those suffered in a city-recruited phalanx. Spartans are not wounded in the back. Among GIs in Vietnam, the sign of conflict was mutilation. Bloodily signifying Viet Cong ideology, its Leninist movement among the people in cells too small to fight major battles, mines and booby-traps roused a passionate desire to 'Retaliate' (p. 315) and shaped sensitivities by means of a repeated figuration, or disfiguration, in the language of war. When a man is hit by sniper-fire, Caputo does not think of guns but says, 'One-Three was a corps in the old sense of the word, a body, and Sullivan's death represented the amputation of a small part of it' (p. 163). The psychic dominance of mutilation helps explain why torture became integral. American forces extracted information by a process which parodied the winning of hearts and minds. There was a large vindictive dynamic. You are punishing yourself, the torture said: give the information. The information proves you guilty; now you must be punished. The Viet Cong, lacking firepower, turned bodies into weapons of terror—tactics of mutilation which were peremptorily avenged. In Robert Mason's *Chickenhawk*, an American shoots North Vietnamese prisoners thought guilty of maiming corpses:

'It's murder!' I hissed to the man at my side.
'They cut off Sergeant Rocci's cock and stuck it in his mouth. And five of his men,' said the voice. 'After they spent the night slowly shoving knives into their guts. If you had been here to hear the screams . . . They screamed all night. This morning they were all dead, all gagged with their cocks. This isn't murder; it's justice.'
Another head bounced off the ground. The shock wave hit my body.[17]

It was every GI's nightmare—to be cancelled in the payback of his own flesh—and Mason's prose is correspondingly shuttered. Yet it approaches the condition of tragedy by marking the limits of the tolerable in the tact with which it adumbrates what we cannot hear

[16] Cf. Elaine Scarry, *The Body in Pain: The Making and Unmaking of the World* (New York, 1985), 28.   [17] Robert Mason, *Chickenhawk* (1983; London, 1984), 364.

and could not bear to (for the ellipsis after 'the screams . . .' is authorial), and by refusing to separate the impact of execution on the prisoners from the partly emotional and ethical 'shock wave' which hits the narrator (and then us).

Revenge motives helped US soldiers kill and stopped the war from 'burning out'. Paradoxically, though, the same energies worked against political and racial difference to mesh GIs with the enemy. Before battle along a conventional front the soldier's mind reaches out to gauge 'the other side'. David Jones recalls how the 'malignant opposing' presence of the Germans in World War I produced an almost mystical sense of 'nowness, the pressure of sudden, modifying circumstance—and retribution following swift on disregard'.[18] Lacking clearly divided territory, and 'Like all combat people . . . incredibly superstitious' (as Michael Herr says),[19] GIs projected their fear of 'retribution' into an all-sides awareness of 'Victor Charlie'. The historian and philosopher Michael Walzer has claimed that 'the purpose of soldiers is to escape reciprocity, to inflict more damage on the enemy than he can inflict on them. Soldiers can never be blamed for taking advantage of superior strength.'[20] But the aim of soldiers is less to kill than to avoid being killed, and the retaliation which a successful position attracts can spoil its chances of survival. Hence the troops' not entirely 'superstitious' idea that 'taking advantage' would be as explosively 'blamed' as 'disregard'. 'When Luke the gook zaps you in the back and Phantoms bury him in napalm canisters,' observes Mr Payback in Gustav Hasford's *The Short-Timers*, 'that's payback. When you shit on people it comes back to you, sooner or later, only worse.'[21] This guilt-inducing belief was reinforced when the B-against-A resembles A-against-B infrastructure of revenge tragedy meshed with hostility towards those who ran the war. 'The gooks are grunts, like us,' says another soldier in Hasford: 'They fight, like us. They got lifer poges running their country and we got lifer poges running ours. . . . We kill each other, no doubt about it, but we're tight. . . . Grunts understand grunts.'[22]

The GIs who hardened up and learned to fight like guerrillas felt this most acutely. 'Eating the rice on that desolate hill,' writes

---

[18] *In Parenthesis* (1937; London, 1963), 28.   [19] Herr, *Dispatches*, 16.
[20] 'Moral Judgement in Time of War', repr. in Richard A. Wasserstrom (ed.), *War and Morality* (Belmont, Cal., 1970), 54–62, p. 56.
[21] *The Short-Timers*, rev. edn. (London, 1985), 64.   [22] Ibid. 93.

Caputo, 'it occurred to me that we were becoming more and more like our enemy' (p. 276). In some memoirs the recognition sardonically interacts with the white American myth of virtue recovered in the wilderness, among the injuns. This myth had great appeal because the Hueys and gunships which 'hovered in retributive technology above the green landscape'[23] threatened a cherished image of New World innocence; but the narratives show it being cancelled anyway by the brutality of jungle war. In Robert Roth's *Sand in the Wind* (1973), for instance, a platoon pursues an enemy unit which has taken an American prisoner and killed several marines thanks to a North Vietnamese soldier (it seems) equipped with a captured M-79 grenade launcher. The troops decide that the 'Phantom Blooker' can only be killed if his own type of weapon is fired at him by a Marine called Chalice. This revenge protagonist is a vessel of that frontier virtue which the Blooker represents in corrupt form: for the Blooker and the prisoner turn out to be one and the same. As elsewhere in the tragic fiction of Vietnam,[24] a piece of America splits off, goes native, and comes back at US forces with the kind of vicious competence which a good GI, picking up skills from the enemy, turns against the Viet Cong. Roth's is an extreme version of the anti-myth of spoiled virtue, but its formulation as revenge tragedy is not surprising. In accounts of this war the symmetries of battle repeatedly take shape in a dialectic of awe and hatred, the mutuality of combat. To survive, GIs turn into what the country makes of them, which means the stabbing, shooting, and bombing dealt by war on both sides. As a corpsman at Khe Sanh madly and wisely says, in Herr's *Dispatches*, 'If it ain't the fucking incoming it's the fucking outgoing. Only difference is who gets the fucking grease, and that ain't no fucking difference at all' (p. 32).

*   *   *

Achilles smites Lycaon a mighty blow on the collar-bone, then takes his corpse by the foot and flings it into the Xanthos. 'Now lie there among the fish', he cries: 'They will lick the blood from your wound and give you no loving burial.' Despite the Trojans' gifts to the river,

---

[23] Thomas Myers, *Walking Point: American Narratives of Vietnam* (New York, 1988), 4.

[24] See e.g. 'Sweetheart of the Song Tra Bong', in Tim O'Brien, *The Things they Carried* (London, 1990), 85–107.

he vaunts, 'you [all] will die a vile death, until all of you have paid
for the killing of Patroklos and the ravage of the Achaians'
(XXI. 122–34). Numerous deaths in the *Iliad* are marked by vindictive bitterness. When a warrior sees his brother-in-arms fall, sorrow
mists his eyes and his spear flies in revenge. In Books XIV and XV
especially, the action is criss-crossed by lethal exchanges. It has been
well said that 'doomed' heroes 'engross . . . the poet', that 'Those
who are slain' in Homeric battle 'exist, in many cases, only for the
moment in which they are seen to die.'[25] Impending revenge back-
extends this 'moment', creating that sudden access or realization of
value in loss which is typical of death in tragedy. The value of a
warrior, shown by his killing an enemy, is vindicated by the pathos
of his being 'doomed' to, and taking, a retaliatory death-thrust.
Achilles' wrath, however, pushes beyond even-handedness. He does
not stop at killing, but denies Lycaon the *kleos* or renown which
depends on funeral rites. A tragic motif emerges which, in Book
XXIV of the epic—where Priam supplicates Achilles to release the
abused corpse of Hector—will prove enormously important. For
the slaughter of Lycaon causes less revulsion than the treatment of
his body. The Xanthos itself is stirred, and, provoked by signs of
further havoc, rises up, pursuing the fiery Greek in torrents
(XXI. 136ff.). This strife of stream and warrior could be taken as
metaphorically figuring the mutual annihilation of Myrmidons and
Trojans, in the style of Clausewitz's armies which interact 'Like fire
and water'.[26] But the larger shape of the book shows Homer
intuiting that war which fails to respect the warrior's body will
run to napalm, fire-storms, nuclear weapons, and the environmental tampering outlawed in the *United Nations Convention on . . . Military
or Any Other Hostile Use of Environmental Modification Techniques* (1977). A
sequence which begins with a single sword-blow escalates into a
battle which involves not only a river in pursuit of a hero but a flood
which sweeps across the Trojan plain and the blazing 'counterforce'
of Hephaistos (233–382).

For as long as there has been war tragedy, it has dealt in
elemental destruction. When Gilgamesh and Enkidu attack Hum-
baba in the Mesopotamian epic, they are met with bursts of fire and

[25] Jasper Griffin, *Homer on Life and Death* (Oxford, 1980), 87, 103.
[26] Carl von Clausewitz, *On War*, ed. and tr. Michael Howard and Peter Paret
(Princeton, 1989), 216.

light. The Sanskrit cycle known as *The Mahabharata* is probably based on actual conflict between Dravidian and Aryan warriors in the second millennium BC. Its appalling climactic battle, however, uses projectiles of cosmic power. These mythical exaggerations are now becoming actual. In the century and a half since Clausewitz, weapons of such force have been developed that the great realist sounds naïve when he says, 'the aim of warfare is to disarm the enemy' (p. 77). Most of the weaponry of a modern state (measured by firepower at least) 'disarms' by obliteration. Such devices multiply strength far beyond the reach of Achilles. The gentlest squeeze of a trigger will now destroy a battalion. To all but missile technologists, this must seem like voodoo. Caputo, who joined the Marines believing that Kennedy was 'King of Camelot . . . we were his knights and Vietnam our crusade', discovered that the true resemblance to romance lay in 'magical feats of destruction. Summoned by my voice, jet fighters appeared in the sky to loose their lethal droppings on villages . . . All this by saying a few words into a radio transmitter. Like magic' (pp. 69–70, 3–4). As early as 1914–18, technology had reached a pitch of development which (according to David Jones) thwarted the writer: 'It is not easy in considering a trench-mortar barrage', he reflects, 'to give praise for the action proper to chemicals—full though it may be of beauty. We feel a rubicon has been passed between striking with a hand weapon as men used to do and loosing poison from the sky' (p. xiv). There is plainly a problem for tragedy when the link between action and effect is broken, when the body of Lycaon is shattered by weapons which make valour largely irrelevant as men become adjuncts of their arms.

Betraying the impact of this change upon the language of war, Robert Fisk says, of a Beirut artillery exchange, 'The incoming projectiles arrived with a vengeful clap of sound that had the ambulances wailing through the streets within minutes.'[27] Would those ambulances have come less quickly if the shells had merely landed 'with a crash'? Since Homer, if not earlier, men have infused weapons with the motives of those who use them. The spears of the Myrmidons, for instance, are 'pikra' ('bitter, aggrieved') at *Iliad* XXII. 206 in resentment at Patroclus' death. Almost as often, weapons have been endowed with the effects they are set to

---

[27] *Pity the Nation: Lebanon at War* (1990; Oxford, 1991), 258.

impose. The arrow shot by Pandarus at Menelaus is not only 'pikron' but 'the carrier of black pain' (IV. 117–26). Because revenge is both an overdetermining factor in combat (where simply to have an opponent justifies killing) and a force which pre-shapes retribution, it is adept at generating weapons endowed with purposes and proleptic effect. Fisk's 'vengeful clap' can be taken, from this angle, as the journalistic equivalent of an anthropomorphizing epic formula. But 'clap' is particularly well-put because it hints at the explosive 'clap' of applause claimed by histrionic avengers like Vindice ('When thunder claps, heaven likes the tragedy'[28]), and because, given Fisk's alertness to the way in which modern weaponry dominates and disposes those subject to it, 'vengeful clap' resonates with a sense that falling shells do impend with a force which rivals, then crushes, human will. This explosion belongs to a world of war in which wire-guided missiles tug at their leashes, where rockets are fired in a general direction and left to select, lock onto, and 'take out' the enemy. Pandarus' arrow, loosed in flight, was said to be 'eager to fly on into the mass of men' (IV. 125–6). What hums through the circuits of an intelligent missile as it speeds towards a target is certainly not regret.

How does this relate to tragedy? The speculative General in Norman Mailer's World War II novel, *The Naked and the Dead*, has a real insight when he scribbles in his journal,

> *It's not entirely unproductive conceit to consider weapons as being something more than machines, as having personalities, perhaps, likenesses to the human. . . . The tank and truck like the heavy ponderous animals of the jungle, buck and rhinoceri, the machine gun as the chattering gossip, snarling many lives at once . . .*[29]

The trajectory of a shell, General Cummings notes, follows an *'asymmetrical parabola'*. With a glance towards Spengler he reflects that this is *'the form line of all cultures'*, because *'An epoch always seems to reach its zenith at a point past the middle of its orbit in time.'* However, the paradigm is more than merely collective: *'The fall is tragedy; I should think it a sound aesthetic principle that the growth of a character should take longer to accomplish than his disaster.'* Warming to his theme, Cummings decides that, since the parabola, in which wind resistance joins with gravity to hasten a fall, represents both *'the fundamental curve of love*

[28] *The Revenger's Tragedy*, v. iii. 47.
[29] *The Naked and the Dead* (1949; London, 1964), 479.

. . . *of life*' (a graph of excitation and discharge) and '*the curve of the death missile*', then '*it demonstrates the form of existence, and life and death are merely different points of observation on the same trajectory*' (pp. 480–1). The fascistic (as well as Freudian) General views the asymmetry of this fall as a sign of fatigue or failure, connected with political obstruction—'*the inertia of the masses*'. Further thought would have made him see that, in its swoop from regularity, a shell sacrifices range to speed. Once launched and on its own, it swerves down from its course and plummets to a catastrophe of self-annihilating destructiveness beyond the power of any but the most fabulously vengeful warrior. The '*asymmetrical parabola*' is the tragic '*curve*' of Achilles, who prefers vindictive self-immolation to the long life promised by Thetis. *The Naked and the Dead* is partly concerned with the 'revenge' or 'vindication' (p. 489) sought by Lieutenant Hearn from the General. Pointlessly killed on a mission behind Japanese lines, Hearn fails to secure the satisfaction he seeks. Lacking soldiers born (like Achilles) from sea-nymphs, Cummings must concentrate on shells. His writings show the Clausewitzian mind being led by technological change to switch creative attention from men to arms, from the morale and movement of soldiers to the range and reach of 'projectiles'.

In Andrew Duncan's 'Falkenhain', published in *Cut Memories and False Commands* (1991), the same twentieth-century shift in war tragedy is registered in the voice of a *Wehrmacht* officer retreating from Russia. 'My mortars fill grave-pits', he says:

> The last of the Divine dwells in indirect fire.
> The hand of fatality,
> The mouth of heaven,
> Sift the numb land.
> The Word
> Winnows its dumb subjects.
> That parabola is my parable of the life of man;
> Thought reduced to prayer
> And prayer to sacrifice.
> The epic is the jewel of art, we were taught,
> The hero is the jewel among men.[30]

Harnessing religious language to the flight of mortar-shells, Duncan goes some way towards celebrating (in Jones's words) 'the action

---

[30] Andrew Duncan, *Cut Memories and False Commands* (London, 1991), 57–8.

proper to chemicals'. Those explosive, Achillean trajectories realize an image of fascist heroism, bearing down the will like fate, endowing the warrior by proxy with a touch of the 'Divine' power expressed in the parabolic inevitability of destruction. Yet the verse is rightly confined to measures as abrupt as the shell-flights they adulate. The typical movement of syntax is anadiplotic or more nearly repetitive, with 'Thought reduced to prayer' then 'prayer' taken down to 'sacrifice', 'epic' as a 'jewel' of art, then the 'hero' a 'jewel among men'. Tragic experience is truncated here, its timbre dogmatic and indoctrinated. And a motivating reason for this can be found in the break between the mortar-unit commander's prowess and the might of what he releases. The valour of this soldier is that of his weapon, and he can only be invested with heroism (of a grimly inhuman sort) by subduing his own thought to the sacrificial curve of its action.

Noting the relative success of 'Falkenhain', J. H. Prynne hints at illicit sympathy between Duncan and his officer based on the poet's wanting to counter fascist might with rhetorical force. 'You find the theme of power breaking the forms of human feeling', he writes, 'a primal source of the rage for attention which allows composition'.[31] Such verse, given its subject-matter, displays 'some of that stiff, driven formalism of true tragedy' but, 'feeding more materials into the hopper and matching them up with renewed passions for revenge', it risks substituting iron for wheat (pp. 114, 117). Whatever the justice of this analysis of 'Falkenhain', it points to large difficulties in writing war tragedy given what machines have made of revenge. As Prynne tells Duncan (making an instructive contrast with Homer),

the idea of death is for you a central motor in the revenge-mechanism, the rhetoric which redeems the victim by claiming for him . . . an afterlife of heroic vindication. This motive is thus essentially hyperbolic and retaliatory, only by grim sarcasm and Materialschlacht connected to the classical heroic tradition in which 'death is not the enemy of achievement or creativity but its cause, since the contemplation of death is the single factor which makes us long for immortality'.[32]

It is not just that the actions of modern weapons are less an expression of heroism than the ersatz measure of it, but that killing

[31] 'A Letter to Andrew Duncan', *Grosseteste Review*, 15 (1983–4), 100–18, p. 116.
[32] Ibid. 103, quoting Emily Vermeule, on the *Iliad*, in her *Aspects of Death in Early Greek Art and Poetry* (Berkeley, 1979), 94.

by mortar shells or heavy machine guns ('*snarling many lives at once*')
has a nihilistic randomness which can only be palliated by willing
death to have the meaning endowed by vengeance.[33] The arbitrari-
ness of destruction is heightened as much by long-range accuracy as
by collateral damage, since, selected as a distant mark, the object of
attack becomes a piece of data for machinery to graph in and 'take
out', not a human being engaged. It is hard to find value in 'the
contemplation of death' when its imposition is as heedless as its
effects on the body are ruinous. Hence the desire for vindication,
when every corpse is Lycaon's.

*   *   *

It is impossible to say (the question is hardly rational) just when
weapons began to exercise their 'vengeful' powers through, beyond
and, it may be, upon man. *In Parenthesis* identifies a watershed,
though, by describing a conflict in which soldiers went underground and left battle to heavy weapons. As the Great War
slumped into deadlock, it assumed a posture so dominated by
shellfire that waves of men were swept up on both sides and
consumed by artillery pieces as remorselessly as the munitions,
oil, and grease on which the iron beasts foddered. Dealing with
the early months of battle, Jones's poem registers the pre-shock of
that 'relentless, mechanical' conflict which would be fought after
the Battle of the Somme (p. ix). In these trenches there is still room
for the individual to claim revenge. Just before an attack, 'Joe
looked more set up than ever previous and said outright and before
them all that this is what he had 'listed for and how he would most
certainly avenge his five brethren' (p. 145). Yet the glow of saving
purpose which these negative intentions have is a measure of
emergent chaos:

When Bomber Mulligan & Runner Meotti approach the appointed
channels you can count on an apocalypse, you can wait on exceptional
frightfulness—it will be him and you in an open place, he will look into
your face; fear will so condition you that you each will pale for the other,
and in one another you will hate your own flesh. . . . but more like you'll
get it in the assembly-trench—without so much as a glimpse of his port
and crest. (p. 121)

---

[33] Cf. the fantasy of Duncan's officer that the 'Partisan' who opposes him is his
double—'He has my father's face'—and 'vindication' (p. 62).

The most dreadful interchange remains a face-to-face combat in which hatred expended on the other—whose death anticipates one's own—will pay back in hatred towards the self he threatens; but the field now resembles something from The Book of Revelation. 'Port and crest' is a frail reminder of the possibility of chivalrous combat, lost in shrapnel and sulphur. This is a landscape of war which owes more to 'the day of the Lord's vengeance' described by Isaiah (34: 8) than to Malory.

Nineteenth-century tales of global catastrophe, from Mary Shelley's The Last Man (1826) to Flammarion's La Fin du monde (1893), turn on natural disasters—plagues, the death of the sun. After the Great War, such works are overshadowed by tragic fictions marked by the experience of the Somme:[34] Edward Shanks's People of the Ruins (1920), for example, The Unthinkable (1933) by Francis Sibson, and Joseph O'Neill's Day of Wrath (1936). Pre-1914 stories of impending conflict had been surprisingly optimistic. The secret weapons dreamt up by mad scientists in texts such as Robert Cromie's The Crack of Doom (1895) have the fanciful appeal of gadgets, and do not destroy civilization. Where huge conflicts are described, as in H. G. Wells's The World Set Free (1914), the emphasis is on war so chasteningly destructive that it must end all war. After 1918 the question increasingly was, could one be pessimistic enough? What apocalyptic horrors would be translated from Flanders' fields to civilian centres? The rashly specific title of Neil Bell's novel, The Gas War of 1940 (1931), does not seem so extravagant when read beside Churchill's memo of 6 July 1944, 'It may be several weeks or even months before I shall ask you to drench Germany with poison gas, and if we do it, let us do it one hundred per cent.'[35] It is still more horribly resonant when set beside Mein Kampf: 'At the beginning of the [Great] War, or even during the War, if twelve or fifteen thousand of these Jews who were corrupting the nation had been forced to submit to poison-gas, just as hundreds of thousands of our best German workers . . . had to face it in the field, then the millions of sacrifices made at the front would not have been in vain.'[36]

It was in Nazi Germany, in a militarized state, that technological

[34] See Brian Stapleford, 'Man-Made Catastrophes', in Eric S. Rabkin, Martin H. Greenberg, and Joseph D. Olander (eds.), The End of the World (Carbondale, Ill., 1983), 97–138, pp. 120–4, and, for contexts, I. F. Clarke, Voices Prophesying War: Future Wars 1763–3749, 2nd edn. (Oxford, 1992), ch. 5.

[35] Quoted by Nicholas Humphrey and Robert Jay Lifton (eds.), In a Dark Time (London, 1984), 62.   [36] Mein Kampf, tr. James Murphy (London, 1939), 553.

apocalyptic crystallized as ideology. That Hitler's attack on the Jews
was fuelled by the 'Revenge . . . self-glorification [and] envy' which
D. H. Lawrence diagnosed in The Book of Revelation[37] is evident
across every plane of rhetorical and political construction. The
name of the state, 'The Third Reich', derives from medieval
interpretations of the Apocalypse of St John;[38] and, in the bombas-
tic *Das Dritte Reich* of Arthur Moeller van den Bruck (1923), Nazis
found pseudo-historical grounds for their millenarian project.
Goebbels believed that the thousand-year Reich would be born
out of apocalyptic struggle between good Aryans and Jewish
'demons'. In punishing the Jews, National Socialists were instruments of the divine will and Adolf Hitler an incarnate symbol of
Christ militant and victorious.[39] Consequently, when Reichenau
calls the typical soldier on the Eastern Front—someone like Duncan's mortar-unit commander—an 'avenger of all bestialities
inflicted upon the German people', imposing 'a severe but just
atonement on Jewish sub-humanity',[40] he is using a quasi-biblical
idiom familiar in fascist Germany. The urge to extract a vindictive
new Testament from the supposedly vengeful Old is repulsively
clear in Hitler's speech of 30 January 1942: 'Now for the first
time [the Jews] will not bleed other people to death, but . . . the
old Jewish law of an eye for an eye, a tooth for a tooth, will be
applied.'[41] The power of biblical rhetoric in the script of a social
tragedy has never been more hideously realized. Revenge is discriminate violence; extermination invoked it, rather, for the sake of
its swingeing edge. 'Reprisals' excused the murder of thousands;
'women and children' were liquidated because Himmler did not
feel 'justified in exterminating the men . . . while letting their
avengers in the shape of their sons and grandsons grow up'.[42]
Some Jews in Occupied Europe did, in fact, join armed groups
called 'avengers'; others clung to the prospect of revenge as a
bastard form of hope; others again acquiesced in apocalypse,
saying 'the time of the Messiah is at hand'.[43]

[37] *Apocalypse* (1931; Harmondsworth, 1974), 117–19.
[38] See Ruth Kestenberg-Gladstein, 'The "Third Reich"', *Journal of the Warburg and Courtauld Institutes*, 18 (1955), 245–95.
[39] Claus-Ekkehard Bärsch, *Erlösung und Vernichtung: Dr. phil. Joseph Goebbels . . . 1923–1927* (Munich, 1987), 309–10.
[40] Martin Gilbert, *The Holocaust: The Jewish Tragedy* (1986; London, 1987), 210.
[41] Quoted by Franklin Watts (ed.), *Voices of History 1942–43* (New York, 1944), 121.
[42] Gilbert, *The Holocaust*, 184, 369, 826; Stern, *Hitler*, 196–7.
[43] Gilbert, *The Holocaust*, 188, 811; 266, 285, 636; 262–3, cf. 362.

It is a profound historical irony that the Augustine who resisted literal readings of Revelation should have disseminated a theory of just war based on revenge—'justa bella ulciscuntor injurias'[44]— which, in the massively armed twentieth century, threatened Armageddon. The problem does not just lie in the vengeful basis of Christian war-theory (especially after Aquinas).[45] War's violence differs from that involved in Hamlet's killing Claudius because its 'reciprocal' rhythms—to echo Clausewitz (pp. 77, 139, etc.)—are cumulative. Where no single blow can be conclusive, forces engage in a dialectic through which not merely the wrongs which precipitated conflict must be avenged but a mounting heap of injuries. In the case of World War II that included blitzed cities. When Churchill growled, 'We will mete out to the Germans the measure, and more than the measure, that they have meted out to us' (14 July 1941),[46] he may not have distorted Scripture as wilfully as Hitler, but the biblical resonance of his rhetoric drowned out what Christ had said. Much has been written, with self-righteous hindsight, about how few objected to the vindictive oratory and journalism[47] which encouraged the bombing of Axis civilians. It would be easier to establish that those terrible raids were morally dubious than it would be to demonstrate that (as is often claimed) they had no effect. For punishment can indurate its object. Sustained German resistance is compatible with the Bishop of Wurm's observation, in 1943: 'Our people see the suffering imposed on us by the air raids as an act of punishment for what was done to the Jews.'[48] Measure for measure is a policy which, when expressed in modern firepower, points a thunderous finger of accusation, yet (retributively wiping the slate clean) creates innocence where it smites, and runs from repayment to prepayment.

Edward Bond catches the tragic psychology of this when, in the second of his *War Plays* (1985), a small group of survivors prepares to kill a newly arrived stranger because of what he might do to them:

---

[44] Gratian's *Decretum*, causa XXIII, quaest. II, can. II; see James Turner Johnson, *Just War Tradition and the Restraint of War: A Moral and Historical Inquiry* (Princeton, 1981), 152–3.
[45] For contexts see William V. O'Brien and John Langan, SJ (eds.), *The Nuclear Dilemma and the Just War Tradition* (Lexington, Mass., 1986).
[46] *The War Speeches of the Rt Hon. Winston S. Churchill*, ed. Charles Eade, 3 vols. (London, 1951–2), ii. 25; cf. Matthew 7: 2, Mark 4: 24, Luke 6: 38.
[47] For a remarkable exception (denouncing the attacks as revenge) see John C. Ford, SJ, 'The Morality of Obliteration Bombing' (1944), repr. in Wasserstrom (ed.), *War and Morality*, 15–41.   [48] Gilbert, *The Holocaust*, 591.

FIRST WOMAN: We could be the last people on earth
If we killed him it would be like committing the crime the bombs were
dropped to punish

SECOND WOMAN: Well god knows we were punished so we're entitled to
commit the crime[49]

The intelligence of the exchange lies in its making an audience recognize that, where war is so nihilistic and death so random, survival is not a victory and confers no moral privilege. It cannot justify anything except in the terms of a logic which created destruction in the first place. For it is in punitive retaliation that Bond finds the root of that multi-megaton conflict which provides the backdrop of his trilogy. In the second scene of its first play, *Red Black and Ignorant*, the Monster shows what his life would have been like, in our world, had he not been irradiated and aborted by something like World War III. The scene is set in school. Accidentally spat on by the Boy, who is affecting gawky nonchalance while chatting up the Girl, the Monster at first takes no offence but wanders off to the washroom. There he begins to brood, and the intervention of a Teacher increases confusion and resentment. For he destructively insists that the Boy, Robinson, should be intercepted by the Monster, told that spitting is horrible, against school rules, and that he has risked forfeiting the Monster's friendship. 'Then you will spit on Robinson's sleeve | After that you will both shake hands' (p. 9). It is an allegory of total war, begun by accident and prosecuted on principles which ignore how little will be left for enemies to agree to differ over, but also an analysis, on the most literal level, of how ways of thinking which justify mass destruction are inculcated by authority. To follow the teacher's advice would be to make escalating conflict inevitable by turning Robinson into the kind of *philos* which Achilles finds in Lycaon:

> *The* MONSTER *spits on the* BOY*'s sleeve and then holds out his hand.*
> *The* BOY *automatically shakes it.*
> *A moment's paralysis.*
> *They fight, rolling over and over on the ground.* (p. 10)

Bond's subject is nuclear war. Choric passages, in the style of Greek tragedy, describe the smashing of cities, mighty winds, the melting of stricken crowds into 'one animal with a hundred thousand

[49] Edward Bond, *The War Plays: A Trilogy*, 2nd edn. (London, 1991), 74–5.

legs and arms and one body covered with mouths that shouted its pain' (p. 51). A great deal of what he relates, especially where radiation sickness is concerned, could not belong to any war experienced before 1945. Yet almost as much can be matched to accounts of those 'conventional' raids on Dresden and Tokyo which killed more people than Hiroshima. As Kurt Vonnegut wrenchingly reminds us in *Slaughterhouse-Five*, we shall not understand how atomic bombs could and can be dropped unless we recognize that the first nuclear attacks, while intended to shorten the war, were also, like the raid on Cologne, retributive. The Cold War would not have been so fearful an episode in modern history if its doctrines of 'massive retaliation' and 'mutual assured destruction' had been the product of nuclear weapons alone.[50] The kind of punitive morality blamed by Bond for triggering World War III functioned in the carpet-bombing of Germany and the nuclear assault on Japan—driven, as both actions were, by the schoolyard catch-phrases of opinion. Across America, as Paul Fussell recalls, 'The slogan was conspicuously *Remember Pearl Harbor*':[51] the cry of the ghost in *Hamlet* stripped of elegiac regret. Fussell seems to write with a disabused soldier's bitterness, he is so eager to reduce the purpose of World War II to 'revenge' (e.g. pp. 174, 284–5). Yet anyone's idealism might be dashed to learn that the A-bomb dropped on Hiroshima 'was scribbled over with . . . vengeful and ribald messages to the Japanese'.[52] This is how ready-made rhetoric becomes a weapon, how a mushroom cloud speaks of revenge. In a speech made after the attack, quoted with flat bewilderment by Vonnegut,[53] Truman vaunted, '*The Japanese began the war from the air at Pearl Harbor. They have been repaid many-fold. And the end is not yet.*'

This warns that other bombs are ready, that Nagasaki will follow, but part of Truman's mind is also managing apocalyptic anxiety by recalling Christ's words: 'And ye shall hear of wars and rumours of wars: see that ye be not troubled: for all these things must come to pass, but the end is not yet' (Matthew 24: 6; cf. Mark 13: 7). For tens of thousands of Japanese, however, the end had already come. 'Tragic' can only be the word here if we appropriate Milton's

---

[50] On links between heavy bombing theories and atomic war-plans see Lawrence Freedman, *Evolution of Nuclear Strategy* (London, 1981), ss. 1–2.

[51] *Wartime: Understanding and Behaviour in the Second World War* (Oxford, 1989), 138.

[52] Spencer R. Weart, *Nuclear Fear: A History of Images* (Cambridge, Mass., 1988), 102.

[53] *Slaughterhouse-Five: Or, The Children's Crusade. A Duty-Dance with Death* (1969; London, 1991), 135–6.

308 PART IV. MODERNITY AND POST-MODERNITY

description of The Book of Revelation as 'a tragedy'.[54] 'The whole world was dying . . . the world was ending' was how one survivor recalled Hiroshima.[55] Witnessing the first test explosion, General Farrell said it 'warned of doomsday'.[56] Once the effects of the attack were known, it seemed that the 'last days' had arrived. Preparing for Armageddon became a mainstream occupation. 'Preachers and religious tracts . . . said that the Second Coming of Christ would be heralded by nuclear missiles, fulfilling in plain fact the biblical prophecy of falling stars, scorching heat, rivers of blood, and so forth.'[57] If 'the day of the Lord's vengeance' had dawned in David Jones's trenches, it now threatened to become universal. For who would be the enemy when, in the words of St John, the seventh seal was opened? Even pre-emptive defence would deliver such a payback that 'the fucking outgoing' would be 'fucking incoming', consuming the world in fire. In the wake of Hiroshima, science fiction became a genre of 'chiliastic panic'.[58] From Ray Bradbury's *Fahrenheit 451* (1954) to James Blish's *Black Easter* and *The Day After Judgement* (1968 and 1971) anticipations of the end were worked out. Fantasy was infused with the 'tragic' language of biblical apocalypse, as in Walter M. Miller's *A Canticle for Leibowitz* (1959): 'And a great stink went up from Earth even unto Heaven. Like unto Sodom and Gomorrah was the Earth and the ruins thereof, even in the land of that certain prince, for his enemies did not withhold their vengeance, sending fire in turn to engulf his cities as their own.'[59] A tradition of apocalyptic fiction, involving technological catastrophe, an Antichrist figure, and the survival of a chosen remnant, goes back at least as far as R. H. Benson's *Lord of the World* (1907). In the 1940s, as nuclear research proceeded, the same pattern began to shape such atom bomb stories as 'Lawrence O'Donnell's' 'Clash by Night'.[60] And during the period of the Cold War, it recurred obsessively in popular literature.[61]

[54] Preface to *Samson Agonistes* ('Of that sort of Dramatic Poem which is called Tragedy'), citing David Pareus, *A Commentary upon the Divine Revelation* (1644).
[55] Robert Lifton, *Death in Life* (New York, 1969), 22.   [56] Weart, *Nuclear Fear*, 101.
[57] Ibid. 397.
[58] See James Blish's celebrated essay 'Cathedrals in Space' (1953), repr. in his *The Issue at Hand* (Chicago, 1964), 49–57.
[59] Walter M. Miller, *A Canticle for Leibowitz* (1959; London, 1960), 181.
[60] Henry Kuttner and C. L. Moore (as 'Lawrence O'Donnell'), 'Clash by Night', *Astounding Science-Fiction* (Mar. 1943); discussed by Martha A. Bartter in her essay on 'Normative Fiction', in Philip John Davies (ed.), *Science Fiction, Social Conflict and War* (Manchester, 1990), 169–85, p. 179.
[61] See David Dowling, *Fictions of Nuclear Disaster* (London, 1987), ch. 5.

As the US–Soviet arms race developed, the boundary between sci-fi fantasy and scriptural citation became blurred. This process was encouraged by what Derrida, during the neo-Cold War crisis of the early 1980s, called the *'fabulously textual'* nature of total nuclear war itself—meaning that, in contrast with previous conflicts, the impending one could only be written forward to, not chronicled, since it would devour the means of textual production.[62] St John offered victims of Cold War anxiety credible witness of what would happen, it seemed, not just because his account of the last days sounded so uncannily nuclear but because, by presenting prophecy in the form of a vision experienced and lived through, he could use the past tense, implying the authority of survival: 'and there fell a great star from heaven, burning as it were a lamp, and it fell upon the third part of the rivers, and upon the fountains of waters; And the name of the star is called Wormwood' (Rev. 8: 10–11). The blurring of futurist-fantastic and scriptural-apocalytic modes is perhaps most bizarrely manifest in *The Late Great Planet Earth* (1970), a work by Hal Lindsey (with C. C. Carlson) which had a massive impact on popular attitudes and, especially under Reagan, influenced public policy. In a style at once folksy and grandiloquent, Lindsey proved from biblical sources that the Soviets would soon attack Europe and establish their headquarters in the temple area of Jerusalem (as predicted by Daniel 11: 45). After the defeat of the Red Army (guaranteed by Ezekiel), nuclear war would engulf the world's great cities. At Armageddon, otherwise known as Haifa, Western forces united under the Beast of Revelation would join battle with Oriental hordes. Finally the Lord would destroy the armies of the world and, having converted the Jews, establish his kingdom among one-third of that chosen people. *The Late Great Planet Earth* sold over ten million copies before the Cold War thawed. Perhaps the accumulated royalties reconciled Lindsey and Carlson to the fact that, contrary to their predictions, 'the end' did not come in 1988.

What prevented Armageddon, some say, is 'deterrence'. This word encourages people who would resist retributivism in criminal law to believe that atomic terror somehow derives from utilitarian prudence. But the weakness of the system shows 'deterrence' to be

---

[62] Jacques Derrida, 'No Apocalypse, Not Now (full speed ahead, seven missiles, seven missives)', tr. Catherine Porter and Philip Lewis, *Diacritics*, 14/2 (1984), 20–31, p. 23.

the fig-leaf of revenge. When A fires a dozen missiles at B, retaliation cannot parry the thrust or alleviate B's suffering. Yet B can only keep faith with 'deterrence' by striking back and awaiting another flight of missiles. In his neo-Cold War story 'Bujak and the Strong Force *or* God's Dice', Martin Amis catches this perplexity in argument between the strong, generous New Yorker, Bujak, who came to respect revenge through his experiences in the Polish resistance, and a unilateralist narrator:

> Our arguments always ended on the same side-street. I maintained that the victim of a first strike would have no reason to retaliate, and would probably not do so.
> 'Oh?' said Bujak.
> 'What would be the point. You'd have nothing to protect. No country, no people. You'd gain nothing. Why add to it all?
> 'Revenge.'
> 'Oh yeah. "The heat of battle." But that's not a *reason*.'
> 'In war, revenge is a reason. Revenge is as reasonable as anything.'[63]

This etches the contours of war tragedy at its purest—not just because nuclear vengeance would be so massively *im*pure, irradiating whole populations at the word of mutually fearful leaders, but because it would devour all values except those which would continue the conflict. The process of actively deterring, of giving earnest through nuclear retaliation of what one could do more of if provoked, must shatter the cultural base in which retribution seeks to blast its meanings. A and B could not have enough to punish in each other for their violence to be proportionate to anything but the evil of the other side of the exchange. Behind the complex scenarios of Cold War strategists lay a revenge tragedy in which complementary arcs of violence, initiated by human beings, found their own dynamic.

Nuclear missiles finally put weapons in charge of war. They would be General Cummings's dream-toy did they not make a toy of him. Herman Kahn acknowledged this when he argued that 'deterrence' could be perfected by the construction of a 'doomsday machine'. Costing a mere ten billion dollars (at 1960 prices), this device would be uninterruptably programmed to retaliate against nuclear attack, removing any doubt in A's mind as to B's response.[64] If Kahn's plan entailed an ineluctability and

---

[63] Martin Amis, *Einstein's Monsters* (1987; Harmondsworth, 1988), 39–40.
[64] For analysis see Jonathan Schell, *The Fate of the Earth* (London, 1982), 206–8.

destructiveness scarcely imaginable in earlier tragedy, it simultaneously resisted the tragic by removing altogether the possibility
of individual endeavour and survival. His device in action would
make irrelevant the self-destructive but magnificent anger of
Achilles, by turning warriors into non-combatants and reducing
all to anonymous corpses, or ash. Yet if human error in decision-
making were excluded by the 'doomsday machine', a tragic flaw
might still be located inside it. Novels written at the same time as
Kahn's *On Thermonuclear War* (1960), such as Eugene Burdick and
Harvey Wheeler's *Fail-Safe* (1963)—one of the sources of Kubrick's
Dr Strangelove—begin to notice how war tragedy can turn on
technological *hamartia*. In *Fail-Safe*, a '*tiny knob of burnt carbon on top
of the disabled condenser*'[65] marks the flaw in the system of deterrence,
the source of an error which sends two Vindicator bombers (aptly
named) on an irreversible flight to Russia. Only by bombing New
York can the US President satisfy the Soviets and avoid all-out war:
a perfect fable of deterrent revenge, with A inflicting B's punishment on itself, supplying its own payback.

One symptom of the end of the Cold War is that ironic tragedy of
this sort is no longer written, and hardly could be, since destruction
no longer impends with the same implacable reciprocity from the
East. Nuclear fatalism, that Homeric, tragic certainty (with which I
began) that Ares would turn the tables and kill those who kill, has
been lost at a global level with multiplication of the perceived
sources of danger. This change has been exacerbated by the
replacement of visibility with stealth. The imaginative possibilities
of war tragedy are being modified, and, once again, the pace is
forced by technology. Not the intercontinental ballistic missile but
the flitting, radar absorbent silhouette of the Stealth bomber is the
current icon of Western superiority. The Cold War arms race bred
a secret state, but 'deterrence' ultimately relied on the other side
knowing what one could throw at them. Instead of assuring payback, the new mode of war is covert and elusive, depending on
intelligence-gathering, accuracy of targetting and, above all, on
speed. The directedness of laser weapons and guided missiles
means that victory depends on access. To have the enemy in view
is power.[66] And the control of visual information is crucial at more
than one remove from the theatre of combat. Those TV pictures of
bunkers being smashed by 'smart' bombs during the Gulf War did

[65] *Fail-Safe* (London, 1963), 36.   [66] Cf. Virilio, *War and Cinema*, esp. 4, 88–9.

more to bolster support for the Western campaign than specious
talk of Kuwaiti freedom. Technology shaped morale, as well as the
face of battle, in a conflict which was flashed into the dim rooms of
American and European homes so much in the style of a video-
game that, as massacre, the war did not, until it had been won (and
the Basra Road was filmed), 'take place'.[67]

Looking back from the vantage-point offered by newer, smaller
conflicts to the language of Cold War writers, one finds many signs
of the battle being fought out in fear and reciprocal escalation[68] all
around them. The post-holocaust babble of Russell Hoban's *Riddley
Walker* (1980) is only the clearest instance of novelistic discourse
taking the strain of nuclear experience. Given the presumption
that a certain kind of linguistic precariousness grounded in inven-
tion, a heightened awareness of the contingency of being read as the
product of a culture, is the condition of literature itself, there may
even be some truth in Derrida's claim that 'Literature has always
belonged to the nuclear epoch' and 'that the nuclear epoch is dealt
with more "seriously" in texts by Mallarmé, o[r] Kafka, or Joyce,
for example, than in present-day novels that would offer direct and
realistic descriptions of a "real" nuclear catastrophe'.[69] Certainly
his statement, in 1984, that 'The hypothesis of . . . total destruction
watches over deconstruction'[70] squares with the way this critical
style of anxiety for lost origin, lost presence, for the powerlessness or
lack of instrumentality in words (a tragic vision of language, natural
partner of nuclear crisis) faded with the end of the Cold War. But
what hindsight brings out more sharply still is the approximation
and automatism of words, their clichéd nullity and vagueness, when
writers of the historical moment just gone try to imagine suffering
on a scale far beyond the range of Homer.

Here, for instance, is a defence analyst struggling to make Martin
Amis's point:

We have not found ourselves worrying very much that one side or the other
would simply go countervalue in its first strike, aiming to taking [*sic*] all the

[67] Cf. Jean Baudrillard, *La Guerre du Golfe n'a pas eu lieu* (Paris, 1991).
[68] Cf. William James, on an earlier arms race: 'Every up-to-date dictionary should say
that "peace" and "war" mean the same thing, now *in posse*, now *in actu*. It may even
reasonably be said that the intensely sharp competitive *preparation* for war by the nations *is
the real war*, permanent, unceasing'; 'The Moral Equivalent of War' (1910), repr. in
Wasserstrom (ed.), *War and Morality*, 4–14, p. 6.
[69] 'No Apocalypse, Not Now', 27–8.   [70] Ibid. 27.

purpose out of life for the victims, so that they would somehow be *disinclined* to hit back with their nuclear warheads.[71]

This is not written in a spirit of obfuscation to delude the public, but for like-minded, concerned intellectuals. It is so preoccupied with worry, however, with not having worried enough, that it cannot find room to be troubled about the blandness of such phrases as 'taking all the purpose out of life', and the slipperiness of keywords—'countervalue', for example, meaning 'targetted on civilian centres', but caught between 'counter-' as 'against' (though there is nothing to 'counter' in cities) and as 'reactive' (yet this is a 'first strike'). Above all, there is the small, eloquent absurdity of italicizing '*disinclined*', as though the author were aware that something urgent needed saying but lacked the words to approach it. One merit of Amis's story is that its urgency need neither back away from nor explode into explicit apocalyptic, for, while never missing a chance to point up the nuclear yield of popular speech—the saturation of everyday language with terms of crisis—it has Bujack find himself *disinclined* to exact the revenge he once adhered to in the circumstance of finding the two murderers of his entire family asleep in the home they have gutted. 'Why didn't you kill the sons of bitches?' the narrator urges:

'. . . When I had their heads in my hands I thought how incredibly easy to grind their faces together—until they drowned in each other's faces. But no. . . .
I had no wish to add to what I found. I thought of my dead wife Monika. I thought—they're all dead now. I couldn't add to what I saw there. Really the hardest thing was to touch them at all. You know the wet tails of rats? Snakes?' (pp. 46–7)

These words move slowly, with monosyllabic labour, but at high torque, not flinching from the violence necessary to an imagination which can stop itself from compounding evil by vividly realizing what vengeance would amount to ('until they drowned in each other's faces'), and showing that finely-honed theories of punishment and deterrence blunt on the physicality of bodies, dead and innocent, or sleeping, vulnerable, and repulsive.

[71] George H. Quester (lately Professor at the National War College, Dept. of Military Strategy), 'The Psychological Effects of Bombing on Civilian Populations: Unlimited and Other Future Wars', in Betty Glad (ed.), *Psychological Dimensions of War* (London, 1990), 310–15, p. 314.

The danger was never (fortunately enough) that only Martin Amis stood between us and nuclear catastrophe. It was, and to some extent is, that the experience of atomic cataclysm lies so far beyond what tragic writing about war has shown that thought about it collapses into the clichés of defence experts or escalates into sci-fi apocalyptic. Even at the height of the Cold War the latter did not involve a general belief that the masses of America or Russia deserved to be flung into the nuclear equivalent of brimstone. It did, however, answer to and dangerously assuage the sense of impotence at decisions about mass destruction being taken so far away, by government, that, if the unthinkable happened, it might as well be an act of God. As seductively, apocalyptic thinking offered to destroy the very technologies which threatened destruction. War would end the terrible waiting, consuming fear with fire, and (in the manner of Bond's survivors) make us innocent again, having punished us for creating weapons which could destroy the world. One cannot read far or visit the cinema often without encountering the fantasy in which a chosen remnant or hero—call him Adam— escapes from nuked cities to live in primitive simplicity, or survives to enjoy the thrills of life in the tribe of Mad Max. As I have suggested, the genetics of this motif are not entirely palatable. Indeed, in *The Iron Dream* (1972), Norman Spinrad gives us the text of a sci-fi novel written by a certain Adolf Hitler, who left Germany, and radical politics, when he emigrated to New York in 1919. In Spinrad's piece of ghost-writing—which follows a trajectory entirely generic—a heroic superman destroys the world in saving it from domination by mutants (call them Jews) but succeeds in sending chosen, Aryan seed out into deep space . . . There is, in other words, a dangerous complicity between tragedy and apocalyptic. It lies in their fascination with endings which destructively, yet too redemptively, offer the prospect of a fresh start, for a remnant. Revenge compounds the risk because it promises to undo, to reprise, to absolve, in a crisis of tragic violence. What the world must not forget is that, in Act VI of the nuclear drama, when Adam begins life again, he will ride into a sunrise swathed in radioactive dust, through fields where sheep may not safely graze.

Medea Variations: Feminism

and Revenge

EVEN in Euripides—where her savagery is formidable—Medea is a complex character. Though hostile, arrogant, and brutal, she does not break her word. Her use of poison, and the drugs which she offers Aegeus to relieve (ironically enough) his childlessness, remind us of her reputation, predating the play, for being a dangerously cunning woman, the object of a witch cult in Colchis. Yet audiences cannot mistake Jason's selfishness, and the dishonour which he thrusts upon her. Like Aeschylus' Clytemnestra, Medea provokes divided reactions because of the heightened anxiety which attaches to female violence. Symptomatically, in both ancient tragedies, masculine images characterize the heroine. No doubt the Down Stage Woman in Tony Harrison's *Medea: A Sex War Opera* would take Medea's comparison of herself in Euripides to a charioteer and warrior as evidence that the 'true story' had been overlaid by fantastic male projections (above, p. 89). It quickly becomes apparent, however, that feminist accounts of the role cannot establish what kind of tale the 'true story' ought to tell. Should female revenge be celebrated to stop men assuming that they are as superior to women in the art of murder as they claim to be in the art of motor mechanics? Or would defending Medea's guile discourage us from recognizing that the typical female reaction to ill-treatment—at least in our own time—is slow-burning anger, the battered wife syndrome, not patient, resourceful revenge? For Medea to act against her enemies is for her (the imagery suggests) to act like a man. Should feminism base its ethical claims on equivalence or on difference? Must the former produce a politics which can be tarred with the brush of vengeance?

The boldest recent attempt to justify the actions of Euripides' Medea is, oddly enough, the work of a man. Less oddly, perhaps, his attempt founders. Admitted to St Patrick's Psychiatric Hospital,

Dublin, in 1986, to recover from alcoholism, Brendan Kennelly found himself inspiringly surrounded by 'unutterably hurt' female patients: 'jilted', 'beaten up', and raging against men.[1] He had already been told by a woman who saw a performance of his *Antigone*, 'You understand women's rage. Do *Medea* next.' Writing in hospital, he responded to both encouragements by producing a version of Euripides in which Medea is more furious than cunning and more generalizedly female than particular enough to be dishonoured. 'Medea is the real strength | of woman', he interpolates at one point: 'the strength that | for centuries has been subdued' (p. 55). To explain the heroine's anger, Kennelly heightens Corinthian misogyny. Old men, for instance, reporting the views of Creon, say (as they do not in Euripides),

> Pollution . . . takes many forms,
> and woman is the worst.
> Her stink is natural and inevitable,
> the hot, strong stink of a roused, prowling cat.   (p. 16)

And where the Greek indicates rather tersely how men become possessors of women, Kennelly waxes expansive about the way they use 'Style—that elegant lie' to lure women into the 'lawful barbarisms' of marriage (p. 25). Though a 'yuppified . . . opportunist', Jason is no different in this respect from the abusers complained of in St Patrick's: 'cocky, self-indulgent, plausible "masters" of the house and the pub, the club and the bookie's office, the street and the bed.'

Against the hypocrisy of stylishness, Kennelly sets woman as nature. This makes for contradiction, however, since, while it is apparently misogynistic to compare Medea to a cat, she is praised for her resemblance to 'fox and badger, ferret and stoat'. According to the Nurse, who makes this addition to Euripides, she is also 'the clouds the sun cannot penetrate, | she is the sun the clouds cannot resist, | she is the voices of the rain' (p. 15). This confusion about the weather is not meant to show the Nurse's senility but her understanding of Medea as sharing nature's flux. The heroine's outburst at betrayal is described as 'like | the cry of Nature itself' (p. 21). And, at the heart of the play, at the moment of vengeful decision, there is a related atavism:

---

[1] Preface, in *Euripides' 'Medea': A New Version* (Newcastle, 1991).

Do as you will, Medea,
for your revenge is just,
your rage the cry for justice in your blood.
It is no wonder
that your blood cries out against injustice. (p. 27)

Since these words are attributed to the Chorus, they are not fully Kennelly's. On the other hand, they are added to Euripides and consistent (in their sub-Yeatsian way) with the drift of his adaptation. Wanting Medea to be intuitive and passionate, Kennelly stumbles into simplistic essentialism.[2] He uses a model of 'Nature' to set the moral life of his heroine beyond those activities of language which make it possible for the Chorus to think about what might be 'just'.

In Euripides, Medea manages to be both barbarous and verbally adroit. When she movingly tells the Chorus that she was taken as plunder from a distant land (255–6), the audience must think twice to recall that, in the commonest forms of the story, she eloped willingly and killed her brother in the process. Kennelly omits this passage in an attempt to polarize his heroine against civilized mendacity. 'What is Medea, fierce, true, | trusting, self-willed Medea, to do', the Nurse asks, 'with men-liars, child-liars, | liars unborn?' (p. 19). We are left in no doubt that the heroine's trust in words has been destroyed by Jason's oath-breaking (e.g. p. 23). This motif is Euripidean, but Kennelly develops it so extravagantly that the venomed gifts sent to the Princess of Corinth become veritable emblems of deceit. In his version, Medea turns the 'poison' of lies back upon her enemies (e.g. pp. 44–5). As a piece of thematic recasting this is certainly potent, but it reduces Euripides' ironizing of Greek confidence in the *logos* (above, p. 101) into an opposition between the *logos* and the feminine. For Kennelly's heroine is not just harsh about the arts and crafts of language: she professes no interest in rationality. Her famous lines in the Greek about not bringing up your children to be too clever lest they attract envy (above, p. 95) are suppressed (p. 28). In his preface, Kennelly acknowledges a debt to the 'savage and pitiless and precise' words used by ill-treated women in St Patrick's, and claims the authority

[2] Contrast the subtler views of such post- post-structuralist feminists as e.g. Diana Fuss, *Essentially Speaking: Feminism, Nature and Difference* (New York, 1989).

of their anger. But his version of the play denies the female resourcefulness it rests on.

It is not surprising that, with fellow-travelling of this sort around, some prefer their authors to be female and their feminine revengers to be canny. In the introduction to her Virago anthology, *Revenge*, Kate Saunders argues that

Men have cornered the market in ordinary, bog-standard retaliation; usually hasty and ill-considered stuff, meted out with the first blunt instrument that comes to hand. But for women, revenge is an art form; fine, delicate precision engineering, largely beyond male capabilities. The feminine combination of intense imagination and unlimited patience can transform the whole concept of returning injury for injury into a thing of beauty and a joy for ever.[3]

However, this approach, though initially sympathetic, leads to as many difficulties as Kennelly's, at the opposite extreme. For while Saunders can find enough female-authored stories to support her claim that women enjoy images of this kind, she could find many more by men which misogynistically play up feminine guile. To stay with just the Medean type of 'envenomed or serpentine woman', Margaret Hallissy (in her representative, though limited, survey) discovered only one text by a woman which she felt able to classify as 'a poison-lady story', but plenty written by men.[4] It might of course be argued that Lucretia Borgia and Keats's Lamia are ripe for recovery as feminist heroines, but the old stereotypes die so hard that there are perils in such an approach. It is not so long since Otto Pollak enjoyed acclaim for his theory of female 'masked crime', arguing, in *The Criminality of Women* (1950), that the low rating of women in crime statistics was due to their manipulative skill in getting men to commit offences for them, and to their hiding the wrongs they perpetrated—a pattern of deception which came easily to a sex which specialized in faking orgasms and concealing menstruation. Saunders cannot be put in the dock with Pollak, but her ideas are oddly compatible. Indeed her language is disconcertingly close to that used in Victorian newspapers when they find in female murderers such as Constance Kent 'a *finesse* of cruelty . . . that no man . . . however depraved, could have been guilty of' and

[3] *Revenge* (London, 1990), p. vii.   [4] *Venomous Woman* (New York, 1987), p. xiv.

characterize 'the revengeful act of a woman' as typically 'morbid, cruel, cunning'.[5]

Whatever their bias, criminologists agree that twentieth-century women have made up a small proportion of those found guilty of 'violence against the person'. Nine:one male:female is a routine figure.[6] The pattern of outrage is equally distinctive: the typical female killer is not a gangster but, like Medea, someone damaged by ill-treatment in a close relationship with a man. Given that, what are we to think when a criminologist claims that as many as 30 per cent of female homicide offenders have 'revenge' as their motive?[7] We should, for one thing, sceptically recall that 'revenge' posits cause and effect, making sense for often confused offenders of what they have upsettingly done, while helping judge, jury, and criminologist to categorize a crime. The shapely structures of 'revenge' cannot represent the behaviour of, say, Sara Thornton and Kiranjit Aluwahlia.[8] The wife who suffers abuse over a long period and finally cracks, taking a husband's life without reacting to a sufficient immediate cause, poses difficulties for a system of justice which is keyed up to distinguish the male practice of what Saunders calls 'bog-standard retaliation' (implying provocation, if not self-defence) from premeditated murder. In the case of the battered wife who kills, everything that should palliate the crime is translated, through male-formed law, to the prisoner's disadvantage: 'Any history of previous assaults provides evidence of revenge,' as Sue Bandalli puts it, 'slow burning anger and fear become premeditation and relief that the tormenter will no longer torment becomes lack of remorse.'[9]

So while Kate Saunders strikes a bracing note when she insists that artful and vengeful women be given credit for their guile, the stories which she enjoys obscure—perhaps dangerously—the

[5] Bath Express, 29 Apr. 1865, quoted by Mary S. Hartman, Victorian Murderesses: A True History of Thirteen Respectable French and English Women Accused of Unspeakable Crimes (London, 1977), 126.

[6] See Allison Morris, Women, Crime and Criminal Justice (Oxford, 1987), 20, citing the Home Office Criminal Statistics England and Wales, 1985 (London, 1986).

[7] R. A. Weisheit, 'Female Homicide Offenders: Trends Over Time in an Institutionalized Population', Justice Quarterly, 1 (1984), 471–89.

[8] On these celebrated recent cases see Jennifer Nadel, Sara Thornton: The Story of a Woman Who Killed (London, 1993) and Susan Edwards, 'Battered Woman Syndrome', New Law Journal, 2 Oct. 1992, 1350–1.

[9] Sue Bandalli, 'Battered Wives and Provocation', New Law Journal, 14 Feb. 1992, 212–13, p. 212.

actual shapes of violence. Some recent rewritings of Medea, by contrast, avoid the reductive extremes of Brendan Kennelly and Saunders and relish the ingenious elements in some female vengeance without overlooking the pain and confusion behind it. In Margaret Atwood's 'Hairball',[10] for instance, Kat achieves a finely repulsive fusion of Medea's poisoned gift and infanticide. A Canadian who has worked in London (as a barbarian, from 'beyond the pale'), Kat returns to Toronto to edit a life-style magazine, bringing with her a 'witch'-like capacity to create images, to mould people's looks on the street. Her Jason is Gerald, the bland Canadian who head-hunted her. Conventionally married to Cheryl (the Princess of Corinth), he marks the start of his affair with Kat by sending her a box of David Wood Food Shop chocolate truffles (assuring her that they are the best). Exercising her usual sorcery, Kat makes this Gerald less orthodox, more sexy, more inclined to dress in silk. Later, she goes into hospital for the removal of a large and peculiar ovarian cyst:

> The hair in it was red—long strands of it wound round and round inside, like a ball of wet wool gone berserk or like the guck you pulled out of a clogged bathroom-sink drain. There were little bones in it too, or fragments of bone; bird bones, the bones of a sparrow crushed by a car. There was a scattering of nails, toe or finger. There were five perfectly formed teeth.

Clearly a substitute child, making up for the two (cf. Medea) which Kat had had aborted during earlier affairs, the hairball is pickled in formaldehyde and displayed on the heroine's mantelpiece. During convalescence she even talks to it, a likely enough diversion given that her phone is not often agitated by calls from the magazine. Recognizing the signs of a palace revolution, Kat drags herself into work only to be told by Gerald that he has replaced her as editor of *Felice*. It is a crushing blow, to be ousted by the man she had reinvented. Worse, Kat realizes as the blow falls that she still desires Gerald, and not the 'Ger' of her making but 'the stable, unfashionable, previous, tight-assed Gerald. . . . The Gerald with a house and a small child and a picture of his wife in a silver frame on his desk. She wants to be in that silver frame. She wants the child. She's been robbed.'

[10] In Margaret Atwood, *Wilderness Tips* (1991; London, 1992), 41–56.

Thus far 'Hairball' sounds like one of those tales designed to sap the confidence of career women which Susan Faludi, in *Backlash*, found symptomatic of the 1980s.[11] Like the vindictive 'other woman' of *Fatal Attraction*, played by Glenn Close, Kat falls prey to bitterness and derangement when she sacrifices family life. But Atwood invokes the formula only to challenge it. For one thing, Kat is a victim of her own black magic of fashion, a media Medea who lives by imposing 'grotesque and tortured-looking' images on women until she pays the price of their vacancy by suffering the 'revenge' (as she puts it) of the real. When Kat enters the crazed, hallucinatory state which goes with being the protagonist of a revenge tragedy (but which might, in this case, be the result of a post-operative infection) she enters into communion with her cyst:

sitting here on the rug looking in at it, she pictures it as a child. It has come out of her, after all. It is flesh of her flesh. Her child with Gerald, her thwarted child, not allowed to grow normally. Her warped child, taking its revenge. . . .
Hairball speaks to her, without words. It is irreducible, it has the texture of reality, it is not an image. What it tells her is everything she's never wanted to hear about herself. This is new knowledge, dark and precious and necessary. It cuts.

The passage goes far beyond *Fatal Attraction*, where the Glenn Close figure does not learn but becomes blocked, then murderous. But a still more definitive break with backlash fiction comes in Kat's not being destroyed by her rage but expressing it in a Medean gift. Dusting the cyst with cocoa powder, she wraps it in pink tissue paper and sends it in a box of David Wood Food Shop truffles to Gerald's house, where a party is in full swing. 'Cheryl will not distrust anything that arrives in such an expensive bag', we are told: 'She will open it in public, in front of everyone. There will be distress, there will be questions. Secrets will be unearthed.'

Kat's abortions—which come to feel like infanticide—show how a feminist recasting of Medea can develop Euripidean motifs. Another means of development lies in the way Kat's power as a 'witch' is exercised through a fashion industry which, not content with 'grotesque and tortured-looking' poses, incites anorexia and cosmetic surgery. In Fay Weldon's *Life and Loves of a She Devil* (1983) vast expenditure on the latter allows Ruth to achieve a remarkable

[11] *Backlash: The Undeclared War Against Women* (London, 1992), esp. ch. 5.

permutation of the basic revenge tragedy idea that, when we exact vengeance, we take on our antagonists' characteristics. In Ruth's case it is not that the other's evil acts become her own by her matching them (the rival is more insipidly selfish than wicked). Similarity is not a side-effect of vengeance, a consequence of its being inflicted. Instead, achieving resemblance is virtually the point of the revenge. Ruth, a six-foot-two Medea with fleshy thighs and a bony chin, uses Californian surgery to give herself the body of the novel's Princess of Corinth (a delicate-limbed writer of women's romances, Mary Fisher), having meanwhile got rid of her two noisy brats not by anything so crude as murder but by dumping them on Miss Fisher and Ruth's husband (the Jason figure, Bobbo). Here, certainly, is a heroine whose revenge is (in Kate Saunders's terms) patient and imaginative. Her clever extraction of funds for medical expenses from her husband's accountancy practice, and fiddling of the records so that he goes to prison for the fraud, are (as Saunders puts it) 'fine' and 'delicate'. But though it enables Ruth to achieve a revenge in which 'the whole concept of returning injury for injury' becomes literally—in her remodelled person—'a thing of beauty', it does not prove 'a joy for ever'. By putting on so much of what she hates, Ruth succumbs to the values of a world which treads down plain wives, and she suffers the physical pain which aspiring to a certain kind of beauty inflicts on women.

In her study of film and popular fiction, *Loving with a Vengeance*, Tania Modleski argues that the cheap American novels sold as Harlequin Romances appeal to female readers by taking revenge on men. The sexy and seemingly contemptuous surgeon is humbled by his love for the nurse, as Rochester is punished by blindness and a desperate longing for Jane Eyre. 'A great deal of our satisfaction in reading these novels', Modleski writes, 'comes . . . from the elements of a revenge fantasy, from our conviction that the woman is bringing the man to his knees and that all the while he is being so hateful, he is internally grovelling, grovelling, grovelling.'[12] Modleski accepts that the romances involve such a degree of female 'self-denigration' that they 'can hardly be said to perform a liberating function', but she is determined that their reflection of 'women's anger and hostility' be not overlooked.[13] A glance at the backlist of Mills and Boon confirms that 'vengeance' and 'revenge' are prom-

---

[12] *Loving with a Vengeance: Mass-Produced Fantasies for Women* (1982; New York, 1984), 45.
[13] Ibid. 47.

inent in romance titles. But even if 'anger and hostility' were conceded, there would remain the difficulty (which Modleski half admits) of romantic revenge fantasy encouraging women to put up with horrible partners in the hope that they might turn into Rochesters. Harlequin romances stop where the tribulations of marriage begin, yet they are typically read (for obvious reasons) by the married. Their final pages speak of sunshine and security when, as Ruth can testify, squalling children and infidelities follow. For the lies of Mills and Boon, as much as for stealing her Jason, Ruth loathes Mary Fisher. The opening sentences of the novel make the reader recognize that, as in Kennelly's *Medea*, questions of falsehood will be central: 'Mary Fisher lives in a High Tower, on the edge of the sea: she writes a great deal about the nature of love. . . . She tells lies to herself, and to the world.'[14] Whether or not she indulges revenge in her readers, Mary Fisher deserves to have it thrust upon her (according to Ruth) for promising 'clear water and faith and life when in fact there were rocks and dark and storms out there . . . It is not just for myself that I look for vengeance' (p. 180).

The She Devil assaults disappointing domesticity with more directness than popular romance. When Ruth burns down Jason's palace, for instance—in the tradition of Cherubini's Medea—by turning on every electrical appliance at 19 Nightbird Drive, Eden Grove, she takes revenge on the specious suburban idyll signified by that address. However, there are too many reminders that this Medea is a victim while she triumphs for *The Life and Loves of a She Devil* to be a comfortable read. The attractiveness of Ruth to men, for example, after she has had cosmetic surgery, satirizes not only the superficiality of male desire but also the willingness of women to sacrifice self-directedness in order to become an icon for those who dominate them. When reconstructed she reminds Mrs Black, the wife of her surgeon, 'of an illustration in one of the old *Esquires* of her youth brought back to life: an impossible male fantasy made flesh' (p. 224). One reason, after all, why 'a thing of beauty' cannot be 'a joy for ever' is that images change: the magazines of each generation propose a different feminine ideal. In any case, after writing *Endymion* (from which Kate Saunders's phrases come) Keats said that he 'would reject a petrarchal corona-tion—on account of my dying day, and because women have

[14] Fay Weldon, *The Life and Loves of a She Devil* (1983; London, 1984), 5.

Cancers.'[15] If 'a thing of beauty' takes on flesh, it will only be a joy until it sickens and dies. Such thoughts give Weldon's satire a tragic undertow. *The Life and Loves of a She Devil* has too much compassion for Mary Fisher (who, in lying to herself, is a betrayed woman) for Ruth to settle its tone. Going into decline as the She Devil appropriates her charms,[16] Miss Fisher dies of cancer before Ruth can reclaim Bobbo. The failure, rather than the success, of revenge enhances the sense of tragic waste. In a strangely insecure passage, the She Devil muses on 'the new morning sun', accepts the virtues of her rival's life, and concedes the limits of vengeance. Weldon's Medea contemplates Helios with a difference.[17] 'She is a woman', Ruth concludes, 'she made the landscape better. She-devils can make nothing better, except themselves. In the end, she wins' (p. 230).

*   *   *

Whether this should be the 'end' is quite another matter. If Weldon had been swayed by feminists of the Andrea Dworkin and Catharine MacKinnon school she would have shown Mary Fisher to be guilty of nothing worse than collaboration. Ruth's revenge would have been directed entirely against Bobbo and patriarchy. Instead, Weldon gestures towards the ethos of gender-polarized conflict only to evade it by caricature. In chapter 29, Ruth joins a 'commune of separatist feminists', but even though she is attracted by their Amazonian togetherness, 'she knew that by nightfall . . . someone would fall in love, someone out of it, and that the best looking would suffer least, and the worst looking most, here as anywhere'. Indeed, it turns out that 'the Wimmin' are not really women at all. Like a Victorian physiognomist, Weldon gives the most austere young feminist—the one who bans dried fruit from the muesli—'a pretty, cross face and pale straight eyebrows, which met in the middle as if a line bisected not only her face but her nature'. It is this radically contrary person who gets the most important speech in the chapter, when she finds Ruth surveying her still largely unreconstructed body in an old mirror:

[15] Letter to Benjamin Bailey, 10 June 1818, in *The Letters of John Keats*, ed. Hyder Edward Rollins, 2 vols. (Cambridge, Mass., 1958), i. 292.

[16] This osmosis recalls that central to Weldon's earlier revenge fiction, *Remember Me* (London, 1976).   [17] See above, pp. 97, 107.

you don't have to look in mirrors, you know. Other women's eyes throw back the real reflection. Mirrors can only reflect the body, not the soul, not the woman-spirit. I keep asking them to throw that dirty old mirror out, it's such a temptation, but no one ever gets round to it.

The satire on *Spare Rib* clichés and insinuation of collective vanity ('it's such a temptation') are cattily acute, but they obscure the cogency of the observation that the mirror is meshed in 'male value patterns' (as the eyebrowed feminist puts it), that it reinforces a certain kind of image-anxiety. When the mirror is smashed and Ruth leaves, Weldon shows 'the Wimmin' (or herself) in their true colours: 'They made her pay $27 for her laundry and confiscated her few small belongings . . . They watched her go with hostile eyes.'

Hostility is plentiful in this area, given that a policy of reciprocal antagonism to 'male value patterns' is a contentious topic in feminism. According to Catharine MacKinnon's theory, popularized by the novels and journalism of Andrea Dworkin, the structure of social reality is grounded in the principle, 'man fucks woman; subject verb object'.[18] Pornography is not an incidental feature of this reality. It is an expression of patriarchal politics and an arm of its terror. In such a state of affairs, ideas of sexual difference reinforce oppression because differences are gauged from the male norm rather than perceived as mutual (for A is always as different from B as vice versa). MacKinnon argues against 'treating likes alike and unlikes unlike' (a theme which she traces back to Aristotle) because, 'in a world which men have made in their image', where 'maleness' is held to 'provide an original entitlement', women cannot but be forced by their difference from the norm into something which is called, and which certainly feels like, inferiority.[19] Feminists should therefore not waste time exploring the varieties and potentialities of sexual difference. Recognizing that heterosexual intercourse is a site of subordination, their cry should be 'Out Now'. But MacKinnon surely gives away too much when she ignores the incommensurabilities and surpluses of sexuality, the vagaries of desire uncontained by the notion that 'man fucks woman'. She becomes complicit with dominant values to the

[18] Catharine A. MacKinnon, *Toward a Feminist Theory of the State* (Cambridge, Mass., 1989), 124.

[19] *Feminism Unmodified: Discourses on Life and Law* (Cambridge, Mass., 1987), 37.

extent that she regards sexual experience as constituted by the male perspective which generates that formula. In *Beyond Accommodation* (1991) Drucilla Cornell calls it a 'tragic flaw in MacKinnon's position'[20] that she ignores the capacity of feminine sexuality to free as well as to be freed. Following Irigaray, Cornell argues that, when they adopt a feminine identity, because it is not the (masculine) norm, women start from an exercise of '*mimicry*' that turns 'a form of subordination into an affirmation'.[21] *Mimēsis* of this sort can avoid specular relations of subject and object (which currently equals masculine and feminine) and provide a model of experience in which the subject 'identifies with, rather than identifying as' (p. 148).

The idea of a 'tragic flaw' can be taken further by recognizing that the 'flaw in MacKinnon's position' has consequences for tragedy. 'Without the aesthetic invocation of utopian possibility of feminine difference,' Cornell declares, 'we are left with the politics of revenge to which MacKinnon calls us. Feminism becomes another power-seeking ideology, a reversal that inevitably reinstates the old economy' (p. 185). Yet the point cannot be that MacKinnon's politics entail no aesthetic. It is that the aesthetic disconcertingly resembles that of revenge tragedy. Her desire that the measurement of B against A should be replaced by A against B against A goes with an urge to advance beyond the old, false dream of symmetry (in which the feminine is speculated into existence by the male imagination) for the sake of a symmetry in which differences are equalized by an antagonistic interaction of mutual discounting. It should be said in defence of MacKinnon that Cornell risks sacrificing short-term objectives to long-term possibilities. The strength of MacKinnon's work lies in its analysis of existing deprivation. She sees more clearly than Cornell that, in order to act against anything, feminist politics must operate to a painful extent within the parameters established by dominant value structures. Nor is it so clear that her 'feminist recasting of Marxist materialism', as Cornell puts it (p. 119), lacks what its origins would lead one to expect: a notion of dialectical advance beyond the opposed 'class' interests of men and women. But Cornell's diagnosis of

---

[20] *Beyond Accommodation: Ethical Feminism, Deconstruction, and the Law* (London, 1991), 11.

[21] Luce Irigaray, *This Sex Which Is Not One*, tr. Catherine Porter (Ithaca, NY, 1985), 76, cited by Cornell, *Beyond Accommodation*, 147.

MacKinnon's theory as counselling a 'politics of revenge' finds support in the fact that, when translated into literary practice, it does indeed produce revenge tragedy. Andrea Dworkin's novel *Mercy* (1990) appeared too late to contribute to *Beyond Accommodation*. Yet it shows with stark clarity the aesthetic consequences of MacKinnon's style of feminism.

The heroine of this semi-autobiographical work is called Andrea. On several occasions the reader is reminded that the name means 'courage'. It is a quality much needed in the eighteen years (from 'Age 9' to 'Age 27') during which Dworkin's heroine is exploited and tortured by men. The prose which recounts these experiences is driven, explicit, unparagraphed, traumatic. Like Sade's Justine, Andrea is sustained by a repeatedly betrayed innocence which lasts far beyond the point at which the reader longs for a reaction. In every chapter another kind of trust is broken, another layer of optimism is pierced, torn, smeared with sperm and blood, until (in about 1974) Andrea turns against men collectively, trains herself in martial arts and prepares to kill. 'Justice', she tells herself, 'pushed you into a new womb and outrage, a blind fury, pushed you out of it onto this earth, this place, this zoo of sickies and sadists. You are an avenging angel.'[22] Here is the new Medea: 'sorcerer or assassin or vandal or vigilante; or avenger' (p. 320). And while Sade's account of Justine's misfortunes bristles with philosophical irony, Dworkin keeps Andrea's experiences raw and direct. She puts the narrative in the heroine's voice and guards her tale with a 'Prologue' and 'Epilogue'. Supposedly written by a theoretically inclined feminist, these pages seek to discredit too 'sophisticated' a response to the story. The academic feminist's preference for 'nuance' over 'propaganda' betrays itself as politically evasive, while her arguments in favour of the kind of erotic freedom advocated by Cornell are shown to be excuses for treating her lesbian partner like an oppressed wife. Dworkin writes these framing texts with Swiftian indignation. However, they cannot protect the narrative from the paradoxes which follow from any injured person taking up the injurer's methods. Andrea might dream of an Amazon formation, 'an army for justice, a girls' army, subversive . . . no orders from on high' (p. 317), but her scheme of full

[22] *Mercy* (London, 1990), 166.

retribution is inspired by father figures (Guevara and Whitman), and it rises to phallic fantasies of commanding size and dominance:

> I am writing a plan for revenge, a justice plan, a justice poem, a justice map, a geography of justice; I am martial in my heart and military in my mind; I think in strategy and in poems, a daughter of Guevara and Whitman, ready to take to the hills with a cosmic vision of what's crawling around down on the ground; a daughter with an overview; the big view; a daughter with a new practice of righteous rage . . . (p. 316)

Through films like Tony Garnett's *Handgun* (1983), Ed Sherrin's *Settle the Score* (1989), and Ridley Scott's *Thelma and Louise* (1991), Hollywood has familiarized a mass audience with images of women revenging rape. But the 'deadly dolls' of American cinema (and pulp fiction) are, for the most part, presented as erotic even while they punish those who have treated them as sex-objects.[23] Andrea's 'righteous rage' is 'new' to the extent that it flouts that insidious pornography: there is nothing seductive in *Mercy* about the exercise of violence. Walking the streets in darkness, Andrea picks on drunks, tramps, big men, all judged guilty: 'I fucking smash their faces in; I kick them; I hit them; I kick them blind; I like smashing their faces in with one kick . . . and I like one big one between the legs, for the sake of form and symbolism' (p. 324). Dworkin's stylistic bludgeoning claims—and might even earn—licence from the heroine's outrage. Her talk of 'form and symbolism' mocks the literary decorum breached by her semi-autobiographical satisfaction at Andrea's violence, but it also reduces men to common genital pain, vengefully marking the fact that, to them, 'We're all the same, cunt is cunt is cunt, we're facsimiles' (p. 331).

In terms of the revenge 'aesthetic', this effects a striking variation. The reduction of men and women by mutual violence creates equivalence among those who share a sex as well as those at odds. A and B are collective entities, interchangeably abusive and abused. 'None of them's innocent and who cares?', Andrea says:

> I fucking don't care. It's been justified up my ass. . . . whoever these ones hurt, I'm taking her place, whoever she was, they don't know us apart, cunt is cunt is cunt, I'm taking her place now, when I choose, I'm standing in for her now, when it's good for me; is it good for you? (p. 325)

[23] See Christine Holmlund, 'A Decade of Deadly Dolls: Hollywood and the Woman Killer', in Helen Birch (ed.), *Moving Targets: Women, Murder and Representation* (London, 1993), 127–51.

Andrea's smashing and kicking is as 'justified' by hostile penetration ('up my ass') as by having had to listen to endless male excuses. This kind of black wit makes the heroine's counter-violence appear so much like men's fucking that Dworkin can expose, by reversal, the brutality (as she sees it) of heterosexual intercourse, pitching the question 'it's good for me; is it good for you?' in derisively coital terms. These acid turns of phrase gain political force, however, by defeating themselves ethically. They are apt precisely to the extent that they reproduce the offences (and macho idiom) of patriarchy. When Dworkin's stylistic intelligence is operating at full stretch, her writing is vulnerable to Cornell's warning—apropos of MacKinnon—about 'The mistake of dreaming of a sex-for-itself in which the women are united against men.' Such dreams, Cornell notes, are

> played out in the lives of feminists who can only survive as the "warriors" responsible for keeping the boundaries intact so that men will not violate the border. The Law of the Father is reinstated at the same time that it is supposedly dominated. (p. 175)

*   *   *

An alternative reaction to *Mercy* would highlight the absence of the mother. It is not that Andrea lacks parents, but that sexuality in the novel is divorced from maternal experience. The nearest the heroine gets to bearing and bringing up children is in caring for a dog. Her social relations thus move between the isolated misery of ill-treatment and the (at least notional) collectivity of anger. This range of positions is not offered philosophically, but it more closely resembles those found in liberal-Kantian accounts of identity and community than those adduced in political works which stress family ties, generational links. Despite appearances, Andrea is a familiar type in American fiction: the innocent in search of social justice. She is also a frustrated writer, someone who (as Dworkin understands authorship)[24] must be fiercely individual. In pursuit of both justice and self-expression Andrea's self is scarred, but it remains essentially autonomous. To start from motherhood would change this picture. As the feminist Robin West puts it:

> Women's lives are *not* autonomous, they are profoundly relational. This is at least the biological reflection, if not the biological cause, of virtually all

[24] See e.g. the introduction to *Letters from a War Zone: Writings 1976–1987* (London, 1988).

aspects, hedonic and otherwise, of our "difference". Women, and *only* women, and *most* women, transcend *physically* the differentiation or individuation of biological self from the rest of human life trumpeted as the norm by the entire Kantian tradition.[25]

Of course, this generalizes to the point of being ahistorical, and not so much because women's lives are now much less tied by biology to motherhood than was the case during the lifetime of Kant. On the contrary, what persists as the ideal image of the mother—with her instinctive care for children, self-sacrificing and protective of infant simplicity—developed in the eighteenth century, so that West's notion of 'the counter-autonomous experience of the emotional and psychological bond between mother and infant'[26] is partly a creation of the very period which gave rise to Kantian ideas of autonomy. However, even if the experiences which West describes have a history, and one hedged about and across with ironies, her words help explain why maternal vindictiveness seems more shocking than Andrea's brisk savaging of tramps.

As Adrienne Rich shows in her book on motherhood, *Of Woman Born* (1977), it remains so difficult for women to negotiate the ideal of devoted maternity that a modern Medea could be driven to jealousy and infanticide without a partner's infidelity. Rich begins *Of Woman Born* by quoting from a journal which she kept while bringing up her own sons in the early 1960s. Her 'murderous alternation between bitter resentment and raw-edged nerves, and blissful gratification and tenderness'[27] is vividly displayed. She records the 'Degradation of anger', her 'jealousy even of the child's childhood' and her fear of becoming 'a monster' (p. 22). 'I was Kali, Medea,' she recalls, 'the unwomanly woman in flight from womanhood' (p. 32). Infanticide is no longer the routine, desperate act which it was in the eighteenth and nineteenth centuries.[28] But in Britain at least, those most at risk of being murdered are children under one year old. Of victims in that age group killed in the sample year 1989, three-quarters were murdered by parents, and

[25] 'The Difference in Women's Hedonic Lives: A Phenomenological Critique of Feminist Legal Theory', *Wisconsin Women's Law Journal*, 3 (1987), p. 118; quoted by Cornell, *Beyond Accommodation*, 24–5.   [26] Ibid.
[27] *Of Woman Born: Motherhood as Experience and Institution*, new edn. (London, 1986), 21.
[28] See e.g. Peter C. Hoffer and N. E. H. Hull, *Murdering Mothers: Infanticide in England and New England 1558–1803* (New York, 1981), Lionel Rose, *The Massacre of the Innocents: Infanticide in Britain 1800–1939* (London, 1986).

though men did most of the killing, almost half of the murderers were women: a far cry from their tiny showing in homicide figures overall.[29] Part of us does not want to know this. So the truth is smothered by a myth which appeals not only to men but to feminists who believe that admissions of maternal violence deflect attention from male brutality.[30] 'When we think of motherhood,' Rich remarks, 'we are supposed to think of Renoir's blooming women with rosy children at their knees, Raphael's ecstatic madonnas . . . We are not supposed to think of what infanticide feels like, or fantasies of infanticide, or day after wintry day spent alone in the house with ailing children' (pp. 274–5). To look into the actual lives of mothers, however, is to find 'the embodiment of rage, of tragedy' (p. 279).

One of Rich's own poems, composed while she was working on *Of Woman Born*, seeks to write that tragedy. Entitled 'To a Poet',[31] it might be addressed to Rich's younger self:

> Ice splits   under the metal
> shovel   another day
> hazed light off fogged panes
> cruelty of winter   landlocked   your life
> wrapped round   you in your twenties
> an old bathrobe   dragged down
> with milkstains   tearstains   dust
>
> Scraping eggcrust from the child's
> dried dish   skimming the skin
> from cooled milk   wringing diapers
> Language floats at the vanishing-point
> *incarnate*   breathes the fluorescent bulb
> *primary*   states the scarred grain of the floor
> and on the ceiling in torn plaster laughs   *imago*

Stale tedium and stifled hysteria are memorably registered here. Iced in, deprived of light and a view beyond where she suffers, the mother is bound to thankless labour. The bathrobe which should mean cleanliness is stained with tears of frustration, the dust of

---

[29] See e.g. Allison Morris and Ania Wilczynski, 'Rocking the Cradle: Mothers Who Kill Their Children', in Birch (ed.), *Moving Targets*, 198–217, pp. 200–1.

[30] Cf. the closing paragraph of Rich's 'Ten Years Later: A New Introduction', prefixed to the 1986 edn. of *Of Woman Born*.

[31] Adrienne Rich, *The Dream of a Common Language: Poems 1974–1977* (New York, 1978), 15.

undone housework. Gappy lines and unpredictable enjambing mark the broken rhythm of days fragmented by chores, while insistent participles ('Scraping . . . skimming . . . wringing') enforce the ever-presentness of those demands. This mother has no time to bloom or be ecstatic. Smeared with the waste-stuff of maternity, she washes piss out of nappies. In the real world of motherhood, the fertility of eggs and breast-nourishment of milk are abjected as cruddy waste.

Julia Kristeva's investigation of the links between language and the maternal body in relation to waste substances such as sweat and menstrual blood is relevant here. For her, in *Pouvoirs de l'horreur* (1980), 'abjection' is a fear bound up with the process of expulsion by which the psychic order of the body is stabilized. Associated with vomit, garbage, and sewage it has a charged association with edges, organic surfaces, with Rich's 'eggcrust', soiled diapers, and 'the skin | from cooled milk'. 'When the eyes see or the lips touch that skin on the surface of milk', Kristeva writes, 'I experience a gagging sensation and, still farther down, spasms in the stomach, the belly; and all the organs shrivel up the body'.[32] Kristeva might be describing in this a biologically explicable reaction to the threat of unsafe food. But, for her, the revulsion is extreme because abjection is bound up with the operations of language. As she interprets the evidence, phobia of abjected matter eases the psyche's entry into that signifying domain which Lacanians call the 'symbolic'. In 'To a Poet', however, the mother is stained with what should be expelled. As the stuff of abjection sticks, she who is not a subject in her own life becomes less an object than a site of the abject, a figure of waste (the waste of, as well as in, her life). As a result she is, in no creatively useful way, at the 'vanishing-point' of 'Language', trapped in a place where words 'float' without play or meaning. The nausea of abjection, its visceral mind-blankingness, involves a loss of linguistic capacity, a defeat for the 'Poet'. The word '*incarnate*', in the unnatural glare of fluorescence, rather hints at the 'infleshing' of further pregnancy than an access of the spiritual. This is a life reverting to basics, without the tonal subtleties of art: '*primary*   states the scarred grain of the floor'. And if the symbolic has been lost, what remains is that reflective process, offering yet cancelling self-transcendence, which Lacan dubbed

---

[32] *Powers of Horror: An Essay on Abjection*, tr. Leon S. Roudiez (New York, 1982), 2–3.

the 'imaginary': 'on the ceiling in torn plaster laughs   *imago*'.
Rich describes a self-perception which stiflingly involves incompletion. 'The first effect which appears from the *imago* in the human
being', as Lacan puts it, 'is an effect of *alienation* for the subject.'[33]

'To a Poet' goes on to contrive a related form of dislocation,
shifting 'you' into the register of lyrical Romanticism:

> *and I have fears that you will cease to be*
> *before your pen has glean'd your teeming brain*
>
> for you are not a suicide
> but no-one calls this murder
> Small mouths, needy, suck you: *This is love*

In the loose quotation from Keats, another kind of parturition is
italicized: one which, breeding verse in the brain, allowed that poet,
though his life was cut short 'in [his] twenties', to join the strong,
male tradition of good letters. Rich puts his lines, 'When I have
fears that I may cease to be | Before my pen has gleaned my
teeming brain'[34] into the second person because the subject-
position is not available to her addressee. The young mother is
too busy coping with children, who, made vivid only in their
demand, 'suck' her like leeches, to become an 'I'. Though she is
'not a suicide', she is sacrificing her life to maternity. 'No-one calls
this murder', but that is what it looks like. It is not, however, the
only death in the poem. In a breath-catching swerve towards
Medea and infanticidal tragedy, Rich concludes:

> I write this   not for you
> who fight to write your own
> words   fighting up the falls
> but for another woman   dumb
> with loneliness   dust   seeping plastic bags
> with children   in a house
> where language floats and spins
> *abortion*   in
> the bowl

This surprises the reader by finding new energies in the 'you'. That
part of the landlocked woman which might be the young Adrienne

---

[33] *Écrits* (Paris, 1966), 181.
[34] *John Keats: The Complete Poems*, ed. John Barnard, 2nd edn. (Harmondsworth, 1977), 221.

Rich, or the 'Poet' mentioned in the title of the text, is set apart from the linguistically destitute figure who lives with children and trash. The distinction is perplexed, moreover, because 'I write this not for you' seems to rule out as its addressee anyone capable of reading the poem:[35] anyone, in fact, with the time and energy which exhausted motherhood lacks. Abandoning the informed particularity of 'you' and 'your life', Rich writes of 'another woman'—using a common noun, not a verb-commanding pronoun—who experiences the nullity of total motherhood. Recalling the poetry-as-breeding conjunction in Keats, she insists that it is (after all) the instinct of a young poet to 'fight' her way up to the spawning pools of language. Utterly involved maternity is not, by contrast, so naturally benign that, '*incarnate*' with pregnancy, it will not long for '*abortion*'. In almost every respect the other woman is identical to the 'you' (is what the 'you'-as-chronic-mother would become). She endures the same loneliness and dust, the abjection of 'seeping plastic bags'; but she is 'dumb', and will not be a poet. Language cannot save her, and it might even be responsible (to continue a Lacanian theme) for aborting her *own* nature. In a way which risks suggesting that poetic heroism saves 'you' from thoughts of abortion, Rich identifies this woman's capacity for bearing life as tragically abject.

Citing Kristeva's essay on Bellini, Elizabeth Grosz notes that

Like abjection, pregnancy is a borderline phenomenon, blurring yet producing one identity and an another [*sic*] . . . Like the abject, maternity is the splitting, fusing, merging, and fragmenting of a series of bodily processes . . . Pregnancy betrays any tenuous identity she may achieve as a subject and a woman. In pregnancy, she is positioned as space, receptacle, matter . . .[36]

The maternity of Rich's 'dumb' woman is figured as 'space, receptacle, matter' in those 'seeping plastic bags' and the 'bowl'. She enshrines abjection itself. The vacancy of her condition involves profound verbal vagueness as 'language floats and spins', pausing in a whirl at the line-break until 'spins' becomes transitive and finds an object in '*abortion*'. That '*abortion*' is linguistic (the words of the

---

[35] Cf. Barbara Johnson, 'Apostrophe, Animation, and Abortion', in her *A World of Difference* (Baltimore, 1987), 189–99, p. 196.

[36] 'The Body of Signification', in John Fletcher and Andrew Benjamin (eds.), *Abjection, Melancholia, and Love: The Work of Julia Kristeva* (London, 1990), 80–103, pp. 95–6.

'dumb' die before they are born) but it is also both the name of the act of aborting a foetus and of that foetus itself, imagined as ejected from the womb—by an abortifacient or knitting-needle—into the lavatory bowl. A 'bowl' should be rounded and capable; but this one is built for seepage. It constitutes the coarsest site of abjection in the home, as in the poem, a gap through which a potential child would be voided as fecal waste. In stanza one of 'To a Poet', emblematic eggs and milk become impurity, matter to get rid of. The aborted foetus, glimpsed in a confused vortex (where words waste at 'vanishing-point'), takes this tragic voiding of life to a bloody conclusion.

In Kristeva's work since 1980 there has been an increasing emphasis on the darker aspects of maternity, and especially on the melancholy which she thinks generated by the psychically irresolvable separation between mother and daughter in child-hood.[37] Even so, she has been criticized for having too positive a view of motherhood. What is striking about this quarrel in relation to revenge tragedy is the way arguments so central to feminism quickly lead towards Medea. Drucilla Cornell, for example, cites the 'retelling of the Medea Myth' in Toni Morrison's *Beloved* (1987) to support her own claim that 'The burden of class, racial and national oppression' so alters the experience of motherhood that the 'ideal' which Kristeva 'beautifully evokes', in essays such as 'Stabat Mater' (1977), seems 'only open to middle-class women' (pp. 194, 59). And it is true that when, in *Beloved*, the escaped slave Sethe more or less instinctively kills her baby daughter to save her from falling into the hands of the slave-owners, that killing is compre-hensible. Morrison describes a way of life so grindingly degraded in the plantations of the Old South that the reader must empathize with a mother whose murderous conduct owes nothing to the Mater Dolorosa who attracts Kristeva. Sethe's circumstances make it impossible to measure her crime by the standards of the psycho-analytic consulting-rooms of Paris. Yet, as Cornell recognizes, *Beloved* does not convey the realities of slavery by documentary accumulation. The novel is hospitable to psychoanalytic reading[38] because it has a mythic element, centred on 'the tragedy of Medea'

[37] See e.g. *Soleil noir: Dépression et mélancolie* (Paris, 1987).
[38] As (most relevantly) in the opening pages of Marianne Hirsch, *The Mother/Daughter Plot: Narrative, Psychoanalysis, Feminism* (Bloomington, Ind., 1989).

(p. 195). When placed on a Freudian couch, Sethe could even be seen as 'the castrating mother, who denies . . . the autonomous lives of her children'. What complicates this interpretation, as Cornell says, is the fact that she 'cannot give them . . . an autonomous life' because of slavery (p. 194). Sethe, in short, is a variant of that version of Medea who is pushed into murder by pursuit and fear for her children's fate (above, pp. 89–90). 'It is not her revenge on the Man,' as Cornell puts it, 'but her desire to protect her children from the vengeance of the Father that leads her to kill her children' (p. 194).

Though Cornell's account of Sethe's tragedy is perceptive, it is false in one particular. She keeps referring to the death of 'children', but Sethe only kills one daughter. The infant sons survive their mother's assault yet run away from her in childhood, 'as soon as merely looking in a mirror shattered it (that was the signal for Buglar); as soon as two tiny hand prints appeared in the cake (that was it for Howard)'.[39] It is the dead girl, Beloved, who creates these eery effects, and who fills the gap in Sethe's life by coming back to live with her. Since Cornell is so concerned with Sethe's motives that she mistakes the extent of her infanticide, it is not surprising that she also fails to explore its aftermath. As a result she overlooks Toni Morrison's most remarkable development of the Medea story: her giving Sethe a future—not that recorded in antiquity, which has Medea become Aegeus' lover in Athens, but the more anguished and deprived one of haunted motherhood. The revenant stands for more than Sethe's guilt taking flesh as a grown-up girl; but the power of the novel does partly derive from the return of repressed infanticide. Beloved is not a vengeful ghost in a stagey, Elizabethan way. Yet there is an hostility-in-love between mother and dead-alive child which is resonant in terms of Kristeva's analysis of the haunting psychic damage which comes from bringing up, and being, a daughter. When Sethe sits on the preaching-rock of her dead adoptive mother, Baby Suggs, for instance, not far from the mysterious Beloved, and feels soothing supernatural fingers around her throat begin to strangle her, there is little doubt which dead Baby those hands belong to (pp. 95 ff., 101). By imagining the tragic afterlife of infanticide, Morrison makes us realize more keenly than most Medea adapters how deeply the mother injures

[39] Toni Morrison, *Beloved* (London, 1987), 3.

herself when she destroys a child (even to save it). To live without your children, as surely as caring for them, can be suicide in all but name.

Cornell invokes *Beloved* to discredit Kristevan claims about maternity which are not only dubiously universalized but, in Kristeva's rather incoherent[40] theory of the 'semiotic', associated with a presymbolic realm of libidinal multiplicity. Yet Cornell's antagonism is equally drawn to what Kristeva says about female entrance into the symbolic order. Noting that, according to the psychoanalyst, 'it is only through an imaginary identification with the father that women can successfully enter the symbolic', a process which 'cannot be separated from the abjection of the repressed mother', she construes Kristeva's advice that women tolerate this rejection of the feminine in order to avoid 'crippling depression' as equivalent to Catharine MacKinnon's invitation to adopt the power-seeking of men in a 'politics of revenge'. To enforce this unlikely equation, Cornell introduces a woman poet. 'If the feminine is rejected as we enter "their" world,' she warns, 'we are left with only our masochism and our self-contempt. The terrible psychic cost for women of the abjection of the mother . . . and the corresponding repudiation of the feminine, is portrayed in Sylvia Plath's poem "Daddy"' (pp. 11–12).

What she chiefly has in mind are those lines where Plath imagines Daddy as 'a devil', 'the black man', a Hitler:

> I was ten when they buried you.
> At twenty I tried to die
> And get back, back, back to you.
> I thought even the bones would do.
>
> But they pulled me out of the sack,
> And they stuck me together with glue.
> And then I knew what to do.
> I made a model of you,
> A man in black with a Meinkampf look
>
> And a love of the rack and the screw.
> And I said I do, I do.[41]

In nursery-rhyme, horror-comic style, the father is represented as simultaneously an incitement to suicide and an object of vengeful

---

[40] See e.g. Judith Butler, 'The Body Politics of Julia Kristeva', *Hypatia*, 3 (1989), 104–18, repr. in her *Gender Trouble: Feminism and the Subversion of Identity* (London, 1990), 79–93.

[41] *Sylvia Plath: Collected Poems*, ed. Ted Hughes (London, 1981), 222–4, p. 224.

witchcraft (there is a parting echo of *Macbeth*[42]). Readers of earlier chapters will recognize that Plath contrives by this means not only an arresting image of revenge as retrieval of the past, but an inward and stressed variation on the motif of return as vengeance ('get back . . . to' as getting back *at*). What is distinctive about her treatment of the topic is that she makes it depend on the father's being psychically fabricated: manufactured as a model which terrorizes yet can be impaled with pins—a process which, because of paternal identification, makes the speaker herself take on features of a doll, 'stuck . . . together with glue'.

When Cornell quotes this passage to prove that 'repudiation of the feminine within a genderized world can only come from the side of the masculine in which we make a model of the imaginary father who, as imagined, pushes the feminine under' (p. 12), she seems so immersed in psychoanalytic assumptions as to have lost touch with the language of the MacKinnon she is out to refute. Once again, however, the drift of her critique is borne out by *Mercy*. For on the dedication page of that book is Plath's closing line, 'Daddy, daddy, you bastard, I'm through.' Dworkin appears to take this as meaning 'I've had enough of patriarchy', but the strength of the line comes from its fusing retributive hostility with self-destruction, complicating the poem's movement 'from victimisation to revenge'—as Jacqueline Rose puts it[43]—by reactivating the suicidal impulse and dramatizing it with instant closure (at 'I'm through' the poem is 'through', its voice silenced). In her analysis of 'Daddy' Rose is properly alert to the way 'the final vengeance in itself turns on an identification—"you bastard"—that is, "you father without father", "you, whose father, like my own, is in the wrong place"' (p. 234). Detecting the same complicity with and domination by the father as Cornell, she is sympathetic enough to Kristevan pessimism to find 'Daddy' more than the analysis of one woman's distress. Rose's account suggests how 'Daddy' can be read as a tragedy about the revenge produced in the feminine psyche as it takes shape in our 'genderized world'. The poem 'insists', she says, 'on the speaker's (and reader's) full participation in the most awkward of fantasies, fantasies which the feminist assertion of selfhood can read only as a type of psychic false consciousness, as the internaliza-

---

[42] I. iii. 10.
[43] Jacqueline Rose, *The Haunting of Sylvia Plath* (London, 1991), 223.

tion of patriarchy and mimicry of the eternal behaviour of men' (p. 235). Hence, no doubt, the way its speaker is locked by masochistic defiance into postures of vindictive imprecation, postures forcefully true not by virtue of confessional sincerity—as many admirers of Plath believe—but because they accurately delineate attitudes integral to (though often repressed within) typical 'feminine' identities.

Figures like the speaker of 'Daddy' recur in late Plath. What unites them all—the 'pure acetylene | Virgin' of 'Fever 103°', flame-haired Lady Lazarus and the rest—is a rage of alienating purity ('I am too pure for you or anyone')[44] which refines itself to nothing. The self becomes, in a conjunction of suicide and infanticide, 'The pure gold baby | | That melts to a shriek.'[45] This naturally (if that is the word) means not mothering, or undoing maternity. 'Perfection is terrible, it cannot have children', as Plath writes in 'The Munich Mannequins'. Given these converging strains, it is hardly surprising that, in what seems to be Sylvia Plath's last poem, dated six days before her suicide, Medea comes onstage. What makes this heroine vibrant for Plath is the way her killings can join vengeance with suicide (as in Anouilh's play, or Cherubini's opera), fusing violence against husband and king with a self-immolation which destroys her by and after sacrificing her children while seeking the vacant perfection of death. 'The woman is perfected', the poem, called 'Edge', begins:

> Her dead
>
> Body wears the smile of accomplishment,
> The illusion of a Greek necessity
>
> Flows in the scrolls of her toga,
> Her bare
>
> Feet seem to be saying:
> We have come so far, it is over.
>
> Each dead child coiled, a white serpent,
> One at each little
>
> Pitcher of milk, now empty.

The poem's title must refer to the 'Edge' of sanity and domestic competence to which the poet was driven when, once her marriage

---

[44] 'Fever 103°'.   [45] 'Lady Lazarus'.

to Ted Hughes fell apart, she had to look after two small children (cf., again, Medea) in a chilly apartment, trying to be both poet and mother. She was doubly or trebly subject to the tribulations which Adrienne Rich finds singly sufficient to make any mother dream 'of "going over the edge," of simply letting go, relinquishing what is termed her sanity, so that she can be taken care of for once, or can simply find a way to take care of herself'.[46] How Plath finally took care of herself everyone knows. But a desire to take care of her children preoccupied her almost to the end: she 'left a plate of bread and butter and two mugs of milk' in their bedroom in case they woke up early on the morning of her suicide.[47] Written into 'Edge', the pitchers of milk become painfully ambivalent. They suggest maternal nutrition, a proximity to the female body from which the children are separated in the first half of the poem. However, the milk also seems to have run out (the unproviding breast of the bad mother) and perhaps—in a cunning variation of the Medea story—to have poisoned the children, for they lie dead near the pitchers.[48] This is not the stale, crud-skinned milk which disgusts Kristeva and is abjected in Rich's 'To a Poet'. But 'Edge' is none the less a work of waste. The serpentine children—Plath returns to Cherubini's insight (above, pp. 98–9)—are 'coiled' like excrement, and their corpses are abject. 'If dung signifies the other side of the border,' writes Kristeva, 'the corpse, the most sickening of wastes, is a border that has encroached upon everything. . . . The corpse . . . is the utmost of abjection.'[49] So the poem's title secondarily defines that psychically fraught 'Edge' across which the most coherent, supposedly natural grouping in our culture (that of a mother with her children) fragments in tragic waste. 'Edge' conjures up the powers of horror, disrupting received categories, the order and limits of a world in which it is assumed that mothers mother.

Looking back, it is clear that, while the Medea variations of Fay Weldon and Margaret Atwood explore and partly celebrate the

---

[46] *Of Woman Born*, 279.

[47] A. Alvarez, *The Savage God: A Study of Suicide* (Harmondsworth, 1971), 52.

[48] Cf. Freud's speculation, in *The New Introductory Lectures on Psycho-Analysis* (1933 (1932)), that 'The fear of being poisoned is . . . probably connected with the withdrawal of the breast'; tr. James Strachey, in *Standard Edition of Freud*, gen. ed. Strachey, xxii. 5–182, p. 122.   [49] *Powers of Horror*, 3–4.

heroine's defiance and guile, Plath creates a more disturbing tragedy out of late twentieth-century experience. It is not just that her Medea attempts to reconcile being a good mother with escaping from the role entirely. She also seeks to become more a mother by killing, and perfects herself by reclaiming her (not individuated, not even numbered) infants as more intimately part of herself. This tragically enacts a reversal of that splitting-away of the child-psyche from the maternal body which is (in psychoanalytic theory) the grounds of abjection—as though a reversal, a winding-back of psychic experience, could cure the misery:

> She has folded
>
> Them back into her body as petals
> Of a rose close when the garden
>
> Stiffens and odors bleed
> From the sweet, deep throats of the night flower.

The implication of care in 'folded | | Them', the plosive delicacy of 'petals', and the absorbed internal rhyming ('rose close . . . sweet, deep') lull and draw the reader towards that desperate state of mind in which we can be asked to find something weirdly attractive in the intimated image of dead children lying in pools of blood with their throats cut. Revulsion coexists with beauty, as in the closing lines of the poem:

> The moon has nothing to be sad about,
> Staring from her hood of bone.
>
> She is used to this sort of thing.
> Her blacks crackle and drag.

Plath's final apotheosis of the feminine is cowled with death and draped in night. Unlike 'Daddy' and 'Lady Lazarus', however, 'Edge' manages its iconography with classical decorum. It is the work of someone who has read the Tragedy paper at Newnham[50] and understands the gods. Of all modern Medeas, Plath's is the most painfully grounded in ancient drama. And that makes it the more poignant that 'Edge' should refuse to embrace *anankē*. This Medea is only clad in 'The illusion of a Greek necessity'. In other words, the poem is not tragic because it shows the world what Plath

---

[50] On her preparations see *Letters Home by Sylvia Plath: Correspondence 1950–1963*, ed. Aurelia Schober Plath (London, 1976), 209.

felt she had to do. Its intelligence lies in its perceiving that what the moon is 'used to' does not have to be. That motherhood can be different. And that tragedy, which might be noble, always, just the same, means waste.

14. On Aristotle, Violence, and Dialogue: Revenge Tragedy and Contemporary Philosophy

IN the closing pages of his essay on 'Moral Luck', Bernard Williams describes the mixture of Kantian rule and utilitarian calculation which informs contemporary liberalism as a 'genuine pathology of the moral life'.[1] From Kant descends a vision of autonomous subjects acting in accordance with the categorical imperative,[2] a vision of morality which, radically indifferent to personal endowments and circumstances, discounts virtuous conduct not directed by a sense of duty. Utilitarianism, in different ways, attacks the fabric of personality by so valuing collective welfare that it requires the individual to sacrifice, for the general good, projects and desires which make him or her distinctive. A more valuable approach, for Williams, follows from the acceptance of risk in life, from acknowledging that outcomes can involve 'moral cost' yet not appear wrong to all observers. We may flourish or not, without being able to know in advance what the consequence of our decisions will be, and judgements of the rightness or wrongness of our choices are not dependent on motive or rule but on how our lives turn out. This is a view (it should be noted at once) which, by making the whole experience of the self vulnerable to luck, opens it to tragedy. For I cannot, in these terms, say, if rational deliberation and choice lead to bad results, 'at least I did my duty, and that must always be right'. But it is not a view which harmonizes easily with key tenets of modern liberalism.

This is not to say that Williams's arguments are aberrant. They reveal his affinity with a range of philosophers currently making fresh use of Aristotle. When he praises 'the Aristotelian account' of morality because it 'puts the substantive ethical dispositions into the content of the self',[3] Williams strikes an almost existentialist note;

[1] *Moral Luck: Philosophical Papers 1973–1980* (Cambridge, 1981), 20–39, p. 38.
[2] Above, p. 260.
[3] *Ethics and the Limits of Philosophy*, 50. On the reservations which Williams appends (esp. p. 52) see Julia Annas, *The Morality of Happiness* (New York, 1993), 138–41.

yet a similar appeal to the *Nicomachean Ethics* can be found in a neo-Thomist such as Alasdair MacIntyre.[4] It is obviously not my concern in this chapter to map out the varieties of Aristotelianism which are active in contemporary philosophy. What I want to show, more narrowly, is how a return to Aristotle has revived philosophical interest in tragedy in ways which throw into relief the problem of recompense, atonement, reparation. An important motif in Williams, the latter leads Martha Nussbaum, in her own meditations on 'moral luck', to rediscover, and (as she would see it) discredit, through an 'Aristotelian' reading of Greek drama, the retributive dynamics of Kantianism. Nussbaum's account of Euripides' *Hecuba* is analysed in the second section of this chapter. Partly because of deficiencies which become apparent in her critique, I finish by turning to Jean-François Lyotard (as well as to Shakespeare and Chinua Achebe), a philosophical post-modernist whose discussions of dialogue and judgement—decisively influenced by Aristotle—shed light on tragedy in general, and tragedies of revenge in particular.

The idea of 'moral luck' turns on risk and chance, but it is grounded in a claim that 'an individual person has a set of desires, concerns or projects, which help to constitute a *character*'. As Williams explains in 'Persons, Character and Morality',[5] Kantianism abstracts moral decision-making away from characters in this sense, while 'Utilitarianism strikingly abstracts from their separateness.' Both traditions neglect the 'categorical desires' which, though not necessarily 'grand or large', make an individual's life worth living. If these founding desires (which we all seem to have) were denied scope, an individual would rationally choose not to be, and his attachment to a moral system, whether Kantian or utilitarian, could not be secure, even if he, regardless, chose to live. How, then, would the chances of tragedy impinge on such a person? In 'Moral Luck', Williams instances Gauguin, or at least an artist whose life, in essentials, is that of Gauguin. When this painter leaves his wife and children in the hope of producing major works of art, the rightness of his choice will be hard to measure in Kantian terms because its possibly great outcomes are so obscure yet particular to him that what he is opting for could not be

---

[4] *After Virtue: A Study in Moral Theory*, 2nd edn. (London, 1985), *Whose Justice? Which Rationality?* (London, 1988), esp. 401–3.   [5] *Moral Luck*, 1–19.

generalized as a rule, while even a utilitarian willing to wait for results before judging the choice (not much use to Gauguin about to leave the quayside) would run into difficulties in measuring the value of art against the merits of family life, and also into problems of distinguishing between the waste that would come from the artist's failing in himself and his failing through, say, injury *en route* to Tahiti. Both forms of waste would equally diminish the general good, but could they reasonably be thought morally equivalent?

Williams's position, inevitably, is that, though various kinds of regret are possible, 'agent-regret' is the most crushing and tragic. To bear responsibility for one's own ill-luck is to long for 'recompense or restitution', a desire which easily leads to 'irrational and self-punitive excess' (pp. 28–9). Because deliberation can only see a short distance towards outcomes, regret of this sort is commonplace, grave, and not to be alleviated by appeals to rules or the general good. Williams cites Anna Karenina and Vronsky. In some respects the example is more interesting than that labelled Gauguin. This is partly because it shows how, like other writers given to anti-Kantianism, Williams cannot generate sufficiently embedded 'characters'—persons with complex projects and problems—to illustrate his arguments without appealing to literature.[6] The philosophical return to Aristotle means fewer rules abstracted from reflection and more interest in decision-making in lifelike situations. But Anna Karenina and Vronsky are of interest for more immediate reasons because, through them, Williams is able to demonstrate that tragic ill-luck can involve more than individual choice without turning into the kind of 'extrinsic' misfortune which might injure Gauguin before he arrived in Tahiti.

'Anna remains conscious in her life with Vronsky', Williams notes,

of the cost exacted from others, above all from her son. She might have lived with that consciousness, we may suppose, if things had gone better, and relative to her state of understanding when she left Karenin, they could have gone better. As it turns out, the social situation and her own state of mind are such that the relationship with Vronsky has to carry too much weight, and the more obvious that becomes, the more it has to carry; and that I take to be a truth not only about society but about her and Vronsky, a truth which, however inevitable Tolstoy ultimately makes it

---

[6] For contexts, and a lively defence of Kantian resistance to complex examples, see Onora O'Neill, 'The Power of Example', *Philosophy*, 61 (1986), 5–29.

seem, could, relative to her earlier thoughts, have been otherwise. It is, in the present terms, a matter of intrinsic luck, and a failure in the heart of her project. But its locus is not by any means entirely in her, for it also lies in him. (p. 26)

This lucidly brings out key aspects of the novel. Yet by focusing on a modern and secular predicament—that of tragically inadequate relationships—it neglects the fact that, as Iris Murdoch once put it, with useful exaggeration, Tolstoy is 'immensely, almost dogmatically, *theological*'.[7] Williams shows how, if risks are taken seriously, and not retrospectively demoted as errors, a society such as our own, out of the limited nature of human foresightedness, can still, despite much talk of its death, generate tragedy. But there is another perspective, at odds with Williams's account. For on the title-page of *Anna Karenina* is inscribed: 'Vengeance is mine, and I will repay'.

Pointing several ways at once—towards God's anger against adulterers, for instance, but also Anna's punitive and self-punishing jealousy of Vronsky—this promise, injunction, and threat offers a judgement on Anna's choosing suicide when her life-projects seem to have failed. The fact that, on this evidence, the Tolstoy of 1874–6 would not have approved of Williams's summary is scarcely material. What matters is the not-quite-philosophical thought that the epigraph activates a consolation important to many who operate within the sphere of limited foresight and ethical confidence, that, on the one hand, there is a power which will punish behaviour we might disapprove of, or envy, but cannot reach, and that, on the other, this power will relieve us of the task of deciding whether Gauguin was right and Anna and Vronsky were wrong. This consolation is the more potent because the impulse to respect rules or rule-giving forces seems to draw on feelings grounded in the experience of being nurtured and carried into the life of decision-making through social intercourse—feelings which foster a sense that, when one deliberates in a given situation, one does not start from a position in which only the future of one's own 'categorical desires' is at issue, but in relation to principles which pre-exist one's being in the world, as well as to debts and influences which, always catching up (like divine justice), demand accommodation.

---

[7] 'Existentialists and Mystics: A Note on the Novel in the New Utilitarian Age', in *Essays and Poems Presented to Lord David Cecil*, ed. W. W. Robson (London, 1970), 169–83, p. 170.

The contrast between Williams's account of the novel and that implied by its epigraph valuably highlights his interest in the management of reparation. More worrying is the way in which he offers this example without noticing the fact that fiction is written in language. This leads him to ignore what is said about the characters, and what stories shape their lives. For Williams, inadequate 'understanding' and 'the social situation' make the lovers' relationship go tragically wrong; indeed, as he recalls, Vronsky attempts suicide and Anna takes her own life (p. 27). In the novel, however, Vronsky shoots himself because Karenin tells him that he, the husband, has (as he imagines) been reconciled with his wife. Anna, likewise, flings herself under a train because she mistakenly gathers from a message that she is losing Vronsky. Neither suicide-inciting revelation would motivate in the way it does if it did not belong to a plausible narrative about Anna and about Vronsky: plausible in respect of what has been said in the novel (not least by the lovers) about the shape of their lives. This is not a problem which can be set aside by saying that 'life stories' only exist in fiction, that for people who are not characters in novels the phrase is merely figurative. The degree and kind of Gauguin's success—the grounds for deciding whether his 'moral luck' was good or bad—depend more deeply than Williams concedes (which is not at all) on the sort of story told about him and his work in the discourses of art history and criticism.

Similar reservations bear on the only piece of tragedy actually quoted in 'Moral Luck'. Williams cites a phrase uttered by the blind, ragged Oedipus when, interrogated by the Chorus at Colonus, he describes the actions of his life. Already aware of the exile's story, as something 'told everywhere', the Chorus still wants 'to hear it truly told' from his own mouth (517–18). Oedipus therefore admits that he married his mother and fathered his sisters; but, insisting on the involuntariness of his deeds, he rebuts the word 'erexas'—'You sinned' as the Chicago translation, debatably, puts it (539). 'When Oedipus says "I did not do it",' Williams writes,

he speaks as one whose exile and blindness proclaim that he did do it, and to persons who treat him as quite special because he did. Could we have, and do we want, a concept of agency by which what Oedipus said would be simply true, and by which he would be seeing things rightly if for him it was straight off as though he had no part in it? (These questions have little to do with how the law should be: punishment and public amends are a different matter). (p. 30 n.)

As when discussing Tolstoy, Williams revives respect for the integrity of actions. He heightens the reader's sense of the tragedy of bad outcomes being necessarily attached to persons. Returning to the passage in *Shame and Necessity*, he also refines the question of agency (and thus of regret and recompense) by noting that Oedipus' sufferings are not entirely brought about by his own actions but arise in part 'because of other people's reactions to what he did' (p. 70). Even so, Williams appears reluctant to register the situating capacity of language, of narrative, of dialogue, and thus its role in determining reparation.

These issues are tragically rehearsed in the clash between the Chorus's notion of Oedipus' story and his own perception of what was done. Oedipus acknowledges incest; but the dynamics of a scene in which he already exists, narratively, for the Chorus (as later for Theseus) in ways which, despite Williams's blank word 'proclaim', pre-empt and belie what he would say of himself, push him into the semantic warp of using 'ouk erexa' to mean something like 'In the terms you assume, the language you use, I did not do it.' The broken, urgent movement of the dialogue creates a pressure point in Oedipus' speech where what is said can only gesture, in protest, at what is meant: a situation far removed from assuming 'a concept of agency by which what Oedipus said would be simply true'. Put like that, it is hard to see how such matters have 'little to do with how the law should be: punishment and public amends are a different matter'. The Chorus is already cross-examining and judging Oedipus, starting from narratives in which he figures as one who merely 'did it'. Law, punishment, and the rest do not lie beyond the matter of agency, as supplementary considerations. The justice, or otherwise, of Oedipus' construction by the Chorus starts at the level of language, in the pragmatics of their exchange.

*   *   *

Williams is attracted to *Oedipus at Colonus* because it offers a potent instance of agency being denied yet suffered. He resists the intricacy of the dramatic moment, however, because, as he puts it elsewhere, 'To make [an] example realistic, one should put in more detail; and . . . in moral philosophy, if one puts in the detail the example may begin to dissolve.'[8] Martha Nussbaum, by contrast, welcomes those laden instances which reflect 'the complexity, the indeterminacy, the sheer difficulty of actual human deliberation'.[9] In *The Fragility of Goodness*, where thoughts about 'moral luck' develop into an ambitious account of ancient philosophy and tragedy, she uses literary examples far more freely and expansively than Aristotle, her ethical master.[10] Repeatedly, she gravitates to tragic drama, which, 'unlike a schematic philosophical example making use of a similar story, is capable of tracing the history of a complex pattern of deliberation, showing its roots in a way of life and looking forward to its consequences in that life' (p. 14).

Like Williams, Nussbaum values Aristotle because he helps her resist rule-based morality. She derives from him an emphasis on contingency, particularity, and the non-commensurability of values consistent with certain strains in feminist-influenced liberalism. However questionable this makes her work as historical scholarship, her insistence on the vulnerability of goodness helps reactivate a sense of the tragic. Recalling the words of Pindar, 'But human excellence grows like a vine tree, fed by the green dew, raised up, among wise men and just, to the liquid sky,' Nussbaum observes that persons, like plants, are placed in the world by circumstance, fragile, and open to needs and demands (p. 1). One way of coping with vulnerability is to develop, along with Plato, an ideal of autonomy. Versions of this sufficient self can be found in Stoicism and Kantianism. Nussbaum advocates, by contrast, a practical rationality which respects Pindar's view of personality. Active yet receptive, 'living well within a world in which the external has power', her 'Aristotelian' self trusts in the mutable and seeks the 'good life along with friends, loved ones, and community' (p. 20). In ways which do not square readily with ancient sources,[11] she makes

---

[8] *Ethics and the Limits of Philosophy*, 180.

[9] *The Fragility of Goodness: Luck and Ethics in Greek Tragedy and Philosophy* (Cambridge, 1986), 14.

[10] At *Rhetoric* 1356b, examples are placed in the lowly category of 'rhetorical induction', alongside enthymemes (i.e. apparent syllogisms). In the *Nicomachean Ethics*, Aristotle cites tragic drama informatively but sparingly: 1111a (Merope, in the lost *Cresphontes* of Euripides), 1146a (Sophocles, *Philoctetes*), perhaps 1148a (Niobe and her children), 1150b ('Philoctetes in Theodectes . . . or Kerkyon in the *Alope* of Karcinos').

[11] See A. A. Long's review of *Fragility of Goodness*, in *Classical Philology*, 83 (1988), 361–9, p. 365.

it almost a measure of the merit of such a life that it is open to tragic chance.

Ancient tragedy, as well as philosophy, was familiar with the autonomous ideal, with the notion that goodness could be self-sufficient. Euripides' Hecuba, for instance, hearing of Polyxena's noble demeanour when sacrificed to the dead Achilles, says (in Nussbaum's translation),

Isn't it remarkable (*deinon*), the way that bad soil, receiving opportunity from god, bears a good crop, and good soil, if it fails to get what it needs, will give a bad crop; but among human beings the wicked is never anything but bad, and the noble anything but noble, and is not corrupted (*diephthei*') in its nature by contingency, but stays good straight through to the end? . . . To be nurtured well does offer instruction in nobility. If once one learns this well, one also knows the shameful, learning it by the measuring-stick of the fine.[12]

This speech is often read as shifting—in distressed confusion rather than philosophically—from the aristocratic idea that excellence is innate, to the contrary position, associated with the Sophists, that it can be developed through education. Both claims are consistent with Hecuba's queenly self-image, since, though Polyxena has become a slave, it is a matter of pride to her mother that she was brought up as a princess. For Nussbaum, however, the speech is perplexed for another reason. Too sure of 'the stability of good character under adversity', her Hecuba is perilously reliant on 'fragile things', including 'ethical commitments' supported only by human values (p. 400). The tragedy will dramatize her mistake by showing how broken trust and repeated loss turn the noble, unwise queen into a beast.

It is worth asking whether Nussbaum's vision of Polyxena is preferable to that of Hecuba because her essay on Euripides' play forms the final, in some respects conclusive, chapter of her influential book. From the outset, the Trojan women who make up the central group of protagonists and the Chorus are obsessed with their fall into slavery after the destruction of their city. Polyxena welcomes death as an escape from bondage (356–68), and the nobility which prompts Hecuba's speech lies in her daughter's giving her throat to the sword freely, as one 'of royal blood' who

---

[12] Lines 593–603; *Fragility of Goodness*, 399–400.

'scorn[s] to die | the death of a slave (*doulē*)' (551–2). Determined to identify virtue with social openness, Nussbaum overlooks this assertion of noble autonomy.[13] She even calls Polyxena's modest arrangement of her skirts in death 'astonishing for its display of trust', in that, 'Dying, she does not think to doubt that a group of Greek soldiers will respect, after her death, the chastity of her skirt' (p. 405). That a gesture of containment, of self-protective sufficiency, should be interpreted in this way strains assent, not just because the text has the soldiers say that they admire Polyxena's courage (not her trust), but because Euripides does not need to make explicit what the dead but angry Achilles would do to anyone rash enough to meddle with his bride.

Nussbaum acknowledges the importance of overlapping motives and tacit presences of this kind, but her readings have a way of turning dramatis personae into philosophers. A speech such as Hecuba's can be spoken out of a situation without reflecting upon it. The queen appears to recognize that what she argues is a means to immediate ends—is an attempt to find comfort in Polyxena's death—when she adds, 'But all this is the rambling nothing | of despair' (603–4). Nussbaum omits these words, preferring to leap to the equally famous passage, 200 lines later, in which Hecuba responds to the second crushing blow which tragedy inflicts on her. Hoping to save their youngest son from war, she and Priam had consigned Polydorus to the care of King Polymestor, together with a store of treasure. It is in Polymestor's Thracian kingdom, where Hecuba might have hoped to find more than misery, that the play is set. Once the outcome of the war became clear, however, Polymestor murdered Polydorus and took the Trojan gold. Now the queen must persuade Agamemnon to punish him. 'The gods are strong,' she cries,

> and over them
> there stands some absolute, some moral order
> or principle of law more final still.
> Upon this moral law the world depends;
> through it the gods exist; by it we live,
> defining good and evil.   (799–804)

---

[13] For a comparison with the honour-bound aloofness of Sophocles' Ajax, Antigone, and Electra see R. G. A. Buxton, *Persuasion in Greek Tragedy: A Study of 'Peitho'* (Cambridge, 1982), 176.

Where the Chicago translation gives 'moral order' for *nomos*, Nussbaum's commitment to networks of trust and an 'anthropocentric view' of experience makes her render it 'convention', a 'human and not an eternal *nomos*' (p. 400n.). At some cost to philology,[14] Nussbaum's version of the speech sustains her account of a Hecuba discovering the fragility of goodness; but it neglects, more glaringly than Williams on Oedipus, the inequalities of dialogue—a disproportion registered in the words which introduce Hecuba's claim, and which Nussbaum cuts: 'I am a slave, I know, | and slaves are weak' (798–9). The key point, in other words, is not how free-thinking Hecuba, or Euripides, might be, but what the circumstances of dialogue allow the speaker to mean. Any affront to the gods would permit Agamemnon to reject Hecuba's supplication. In applying moral pressure, she must appeal to a *nomos* more powerful and lasting than those human conventions which a victorious general can ignore.

When the corpse of Polydorus is brought to Hecuba, she laments: 'O child, child | now I begin my mourning, | the wild newly-learned melody (*nomos*) | from the spirit of revenge' (684–7). This, at least, is Nussbaum's translation, calculated to bring out a buried pun on *nomos* as 'melody' and 'convention',[15] and to relate both to 'revenge'. For Nussbaum regards this speech as pivotal, the point at which the heroine's trust gives way to a narrowing of sympathy. 'Revenge, for Hecuba,' she writes,

is a way of placing the world in order, making things habitable. But . . . it will not require a trust in anything outside the thoughts and plans of the avenger. The old *nomos* was a network of ties linking one person with another. The new one will prove a solitary song, for which no confidence in untrustworthy human things is required. (pp. 409–10)

It is true that, at the end of the tragedy, Hecuba will be isolated by transformation into a monstrous hound. But the climax of the play is collective. Hecuba joins with her women in luring Polymestor and

---

[14] Against Nussbaum's interpretation of *nomos* see e.g. Victor Ehrenberg, 'Die Anfänge des griechischen Naturrechts', *Archiv für Geschichte der Philosophie*, 35 (1923), 119–43, pp. 138–43, cited by David Kovacs, *The Heroic Muse: Studies in the 'Hippolytus' and 'Hecuba' of Euripides* (Baltimore, 1987), 144–5 nn. 53, 56, and, on her handling of other key terms in the passage, Malcolm Heath, 'Tragedy and Philosophy', *The Classical Review*, NS 37 (1987), 43–7, p. 45.

[15] *Fragility of Goodness*, 409; on this pun elsewhere, esp. in Plato's *Laws*, see Cartledge *et al.* (eds.), *Nomos*, 12.

his children to her tent, killing his offspring and blinding him. When Agamemnon refuses to punish Polymestor, he expresses doubt that women could take their own revenge (882–3). The play shows that they can, and that, if their violence is coloured by individual experiences of loss,[16] it is their capacity to work together which overcomes their weakness. Judging from Polymestor's vivid account of the assault, indeed, it is the collectivity of their action which helps them put aside moral qualms.

Nussbaum seeks to deny this because she wants vengeance to go with isolation as the dark side of (ultimately Kantian) autonomy. That is why her book climaxes in a reading of revenge drama. For her, *Hecuba* points up the 'vindictive defensiveness' of Platonic/ Kantian/Stoic attitudes. These claims are philosophically eccentric, given Aristotle's acceptance of revenge and Seneca's hostility to it (above, pp. 22, 115); but they are crucial to Nussbaum's argument. For her, the patterns of knowledge and control typical of vengeance correlate with the ethical inflexibility which goes with attachment to rules. Revengers might take physical risks, but they have all the assurance in the world, morally speaking, compared with those who live like Pindar's vine. The 'Aristotelian' life is capable of tragedy because subject to luck; in ways which Nussbaum does not make entirely clear, the autonomous life cannot be tragic, even in revenge tragedy, except in so far as it shows a loss of value in the revenger's life when she or he or simply we recognize that autonomy is not enough. 'If we were able to live an entire life inside the Platonic view that the best and most valuable things in life are all invulnerable,' Nussbaum writes,

we would effectively get revenge, ourselves, upon our worldly situation. We would put the world in good order by sealing off certain risks, closing ourselves to certain happenings. And this world could remain relatively rich in value, since it would still contain the beauty of the Platonic contemplative life. If this is revenge, it may strike us that this is a very attractive and fruitful type of revenge . . . (p. 420)

Treating Euripides and Aristotle as (rather unlikely) partners, Nussbaum argues that *Hecuba* shows how such a life, for all its attractions, could not sustain us through difficult circumstances. When the autonomous self is put under pressure, the result is

---

[16] Lines 905–53; for Nussbaum's attempt to deal with this see *Fragility of Goodness*, 510 n. 45.

solipsism and destruction. Hecuba, in short, becomes a Kantian liberal run wild.

*   *   *

Such a reading of Greek tragedy can only be tendentious, but Nussbaum's account draws strength from its attention to language. Alert to the instrumentality of words, she observes that, for the revenger, 'communication is replaced by persuasive rhetoric, and speech becomes a matter of taking advantage of the other party's susceptibility' (p. 415). Yet while this makes sense of Hecuba's remarkable lines on *peithō*, on how all that matters is eloquence (814–19), it does not provide ways of thinking about that problem of structural advantage which frustrates Oedipus' exchange with the Chorus, and shapes Hecuba's retributive appeal to Agamemnon. This is where Lyotard deserves attention. For, like Williams and Nussbaum, he resists central components of Kantianism, and advocates a return to Aristotle. Like them, though more ambitiously, he identifies points of conflict in contemporary conceptions of agency which shed light on tragic writing; but his approach has been influenced by Derrida's and Levinas's work on language and relations with the other.

Indeed, if one were seeking a point of entry into Lyotard's critique of Kant, it would lie in his meditation, out of Levinas, on the communication problems of two agents.[17] One addresses the other and the other replies, but only by virtue of having been situated by the first speaker. The exchange is asymmetrical, for B has to engage with the terms of A. Dialogue is imbalance. There is, at best, an oscillation of subject and object positions, at worst the violence of two language games at odds:

An addressor appears whose addressee I am, and about whom I know nothing, except that he or she situates me upon the addressee instance. The violence of the revelation is in the ego's expulsion from the addressor instance, from which it managed its work of enjoyment, power, and cognition. It is the scandal of an I displaced onto the you instance. The I turned you tries to repossess itself through the understanding of what dispossesses it. Another phrase is formed, in which the I returns in the addressor's situation, in order to legitimate or to reject—it doesn't matter

---

[17] Lyotard cites Emmanuel Levinas, *Totalité et infini. Essai sur l'extériorité* (The Hague, 1961) and *Quatre lectures talmudiques* (Paris, 1968).

which—the scandal of the other's phrase and of its own dispossession. This new phrase is always possible, like an inevitable temptation. But it cannot annul the event, it can only tame and master it, thereby disregarding the transcendence of the other.[18]

In imagining a human individual, Lyotard contends, we cannot get behind these pragmatics. We cannot reach the realm of will from which general rules might spring without dealing in human beings continuously situated by linguistic acts. So it is not possible to generate out of A, B, and their further interlocutors a general code for equivalently free agents.

On epistemological grounds Kant believed that the moral law could not be deduced from descriptions of experience. We should, however, act *as if* the moral law were a law of nature, so that the rules willed out of our freedom would match, in the human sphere, the regularity and cogency of a universe running on roughly Newtonian lines. Lyotard objects to the tendency to merge the 'you must' of obligation with 'the "I know" of knowledge and . . . the "I can" of freedom'. For, as Geoffrey Bennington notes,

By appealing to the Idea of a "humanity" or a "community of rational beings", Kant is able to annul the asymmetry, in the sentences of obligation, of "I" and "thou" (and posit a "we" into which they are subsumed). It is this argument which gives rise to the notion of autonomy, [implying] that the addressee of the law is also its sender, and, by extension, that the subject of the state is also a member of the Sovereign or legislator. Kant's categorical imperative demands that I be able to place myself in the position of legislator as well as in that of the subject of the legislator's laws . . . But from the perspective of a philosophy of sentences, this involves presupposing a notion of "person" (eventually secured by a proper name) which cannot be established by the sentences being analysed . . . [19]

Through a series of intricate works, from *Instructions païennes* (1977), via *Le Différend* (1983), to *Leçons sur l'analytique du sublime* (1991), Lyotard has resisted the notion of transcendental abstraction of the self given these power relations in language. Williams would not wish to live in a Kantian ethical community. Lyotard, on linguistic grounds, could not conceive of there ever being one.

So what does he want, instead? Equally to the point, how could

---

[18] J.-F. Lyotard, *The Différend: Phrases in Dispute*, tr. Georges Van Den Abbeele (Manchester, 1988), 110–11.   [19] *Lyotard: Writing the Event* (Manchester, 1988), 139.

he tell us? How, that is, can a philosopher suspicious of the power-biases in communication address us without suspending his suspicions? In *Au juste: Conversations* (1979), Lyotard closes the gap between literary and philosophical discourse by enacting his anxieties through a dialogue between versions of himself and Jean-Loup Thébaud. The symmetry between A and B, between J.-F.L. and J.-L.T. is exposed as false by such devices as, for instance, Lyotard using *tu* of his interlocutor and Thébaud the more respectful *vous*. Different linguistic stances and strategies are shown to be inseparable from the authority of the philosopher and Thébaud's subordinate position. The pursuit of truth by dialogue begins to look like the benign aspect of what is also a pattern of domination, that pattern of necessary violence which makes Socrates, at times, seem a bludgeoner in Plato's dialogues. In other words, *Au juste* demonstrates the difficulty of establishing a community of autonomous equals when attempting to define justice. As a step towards alternatives, it presents an epigraph from the *Nicomachean Ethics*, 'The rule of the undetermined is itself undetermined [*indéterminée*]',[20] and proposes that, to avoid rule and prescription—the tradition of Plato, Kant, and Marx—we should adopt the 'pagan' practice of Aristotle and 'judge without criteria. We are in the position of Aristotle's prudent individual,' it is said, 'who makes judgments about the just and the unjust without the least criterion' (p. 14). In support of this Lyotard argues that the Aristotelian 'mean cannot be determined in itself, that is, outside of the situation in which we find it. In fact, regarding this mean, when we speak of it, we really are not saying anything that we can even conceive of, before it is determined in a concrete case. The idea of a mean is not a concept. . . . we just have an idea to guide us. This is characteristic of the judge's position' (p. 27).

How much like Aristotle is this? Despite his subordinate position, Thébaud is quick to query the Greekness of Lyotard's post-modernist-sounding judge, given that Aristotle has in mind élite individuals schooled by a common way of life (*hexis*) into shared values (pp. 26–7). A further doubt must centre on Lyotard's treatment of the mean. As many have noted, Aristotle gets into difficulties when applying the mean to justice. At one point in the *Nicomachean Ethics*,

---

[20] 1137b29–30, in Jean-François Lyotard and Jean-Loup Thébaud, *Just Gaming*, tr. Wlad Godzich (Manchester, 1985).

he goes so far as to claim that 'just conduct is a mean between doing and suffering injustice' (1133b).[21] The same obsession with balance emerges when he defies etymology to argue that '*dikaion* (just) means *dicha* (in half), as if one were to pronounce it *dichaion*; and a *dikast* (judge) is a *dichast* (halver)' (1132a). Aristotle seems drawn to evenness as the static equivalent or resolution of that principle of reciprocity which is so crucial to his account of the virtuous life. In terms of the theory of justice this relates to his tolerance of full retribution,[22] betraying an eagerness to establish symmetry which is in some ways closer to Kantianism than to the 'undetermined itself . . . undetermined' which Lyotard values.[23] And indeed, the epigraph to *Au juste* does not come from Aristotle on justice but from his description of equity. He is talking about the flexibility needed to apply laws fairly to particular cases. Lyotard's attempt to turn Aristotle into something like a Sophist (p. 29) founders on a passage in the *Rhetoric*, where it is said that laws should be firm and clear on every point where definition is possible, leaving 'as little as possible to the discretion of the judges' (1354a).

More interesting than the differences between a post-modernist and the fourth-century Aristotle are the implications of Lyotard's views for tragedy. Think, for example, of *Othello*. This play of multiple revenges opens in dialogue between two characters, Iago and Roderigo, the second of whom has been added by Shakespeare (to source material which he laboured to condense), largely, it can seem, to be abused by his interlocutor. There is hardly an episode in which he appears without Iago, and, though Roderigo is wiser than his cynical manipulator when it comes to judging Desdemona and Cassio, he is, continually, gulled. One reason for his being there, of course, is that the crucial phase of persuasion, played out between Iago and Othello, requires a concentration and celerity which, without the foil of Roderigo's evident naïvety, would make the susceptibility of the Moor to his ensign dramatically intolerable. But recall how much turns, in the great scenes of Act III, on the

---

[21] For discussion see e.g. W. F. R. Hardie, *Aristotle's Ethical Theory*, 2nd edn. (Oxford, 1980), 201.

[22] Cf., again, *Nicomachean Ethics* 1132a, where 'the judge endeavours to make' a murderer 'equal by the penalty or loss he imposes' to the man who has been killed.

[23] On 'Kantian' traits in Aristotle's conception of morality, see the arguments of T. H. Irwin discussed by Nancy Sherman, *The Fabric of Character: Aristotle's Theory of Virtue* (Oxford, 1989), 24.

revenge villain Iago picking up and moulding Othello's side of the dialogue: A's capacity to set the terms of B's speeches, together with Iago's echoing distortions of 'Indeed', 'Honest', 'Think',[24] shape the course of the play. The more Othello and the ensign meet in the common ground of their exchanges, share words, pick up cues and shifts of mind, the more slippage and insinuation is possible. Dialogue is a device of power through which Iago controls the Moor by deflecting his words.

A tragedy full of 'two-handers', whether isolated or overheard, *Othello* has many scenes which explore a similar distortion, the most wrenching being those between the Moor and Desdemona. Such is the distance of the African warrior from the idiom of Venetian chamberers, such the ladylike incapacity of Desdemona to speak of whoring and adultery (even to Emilia, never mind her new husband), that gaps between their language games are inflamed by the action of dialogue, leading to misjudgement, outrage, and wounding repetition. In the 'brothel scene' of Act IV, an audience hears the squeal and grinding of voices which engage in dialogue but not with each other's meaning—'I understand a fury in your words, | But not the words' (IV. ii. 32–3)—until, in the sheer brutality of Othello's rejection, the underlying inequalities of strength and authority become explicit. The stifling of Desdemona's protests, here, ominously anticipates the struggle in the bedroom which will later destroy her.

Desdemona is wronged but cannot prove it. She has not got the words which would reach Othello, cannot speak the language of the camp. This is a problem compounded by the organization of justice in the play. Once the couple are on Cyprus, where Othello is military governor, he is judge and plaintiff in his own adultery case, but also the one-man tribunal where Desdemona's complaint about ill-treatment (vainly aired to Emilia and Iago) might be, but is not, heard. In *Le Différend* Lyotard explains how the asymmetries of A and B translate into legal difficulties when two language games do not coincide. Cases played out between agents in the same linguistic set are 'litigations'. For them, dialogue is disputation. Where there is disequivalence, however, one finds what he calls *différends*.[25] Many apparent litigations turn out to be damaging

---

[24] See esp. III. iii. 94–170.

[25] Cf. Jacques Derrida, 'Force of Law: The "Mystical Foundation of Authority"', tr. Mary Quaintance, *Cardozo Law Review*, 11 (1990), 921–1045, esp. pp. 949–53.

différends, with A disadvantaging B by setting up an exchange in terms alien to him or her. This process of pre-emption deprives B of a voice which signifies before the tribunal, and, even if B is able to translate his or her terms into those of A, that, as often as not, concedes to A what B resists. Lyotard instances the Martinican who feels wronged by being considered a French citizen. His complaint cannot be heard under French law. But to have a case against France in International law, the Martinican would have to be no longer a French citizen. The plaintiff is silenced in both ways. And silence is, in more than one sense, always the end of dialogue. Othello, after all, comes into Desdemona's bed-chamber with legal process, as well as revenge for honour, in mind (v. ii. 1–22). 'It is the cause, it is the cause, my soul', expresses, among other things, his claim to having judged her legal 'cause' and sentenced her for adultery. 'O balmy breath,' he goes on, 'that dost almost persuade | Justice to break her sword!' Much is heard and seen of swords (symbolic and otherwise) in this last scene, but Desdemona's death comes when she keeps trying to speak, to use her 'breath' to engage in dialogue, to 'persuade' Othello across the *différend*, which is (in large part) why the end of dialogue between them involves neither poisoning nor stabbing but his smothering her into silence.

The tragedy of *Othello* is sexual and vindictive. It deals with the deficiencies of heroic character and the self-breeding force of jealousy. But running through it, pervasively, is the question of cultural difference as a dislocating factor in human relations. This is a feature of the play which not only strikes modern audiences as current, because of post-colonial guilt in the West and the problems of living in a multicultural society: it is one which Lyotard's views, partly formed by the war of Algerian independence, illuminate. Consider, more largely, relations between black and white in Chinua Achebe's *Things Fall Apart* (1958). The subject of this tragic novel is the collapse of Ibo systems of religion and justice during the early days of evangelism and colonial government in West Africa. One sign of the book's stature is that it refuses to sentimentalize the old codes. Early in the novel, a daughter of Umuofia is killed in Mbaino and, to avoid war, in recompense, a virgin and a youth of fifteen are given to the clan. This is a peaceful restitution, but not unproblematic, since the fate of the boy, Ikemefuna, has still to be decided. Eventually, without much preparation, the reader, and the hero of the novel, Okonkwo, learn that the Oracle of the Hills and the Caves has pronounced that the boy must die. Okonkwo, harsh, tenacious, and afraid of appearing weak, has been looking after Ikemefuna on his farm, and become fond of him, but, despite warnings not to involve himself in the death of one who calls him father, he ends up killing him to satisfy the oracle. Later, Okonkwo is forced into exile for seven years because, when his gun explodes at a festive gathering, he kills another member of the tribe, and, regardless of his lack of what English language and law calls 'intention', he must be cast out to avoid pollution.

These experiences are cruel but they belong to 'litigation'. Blood payments and purification stem from well-understood and accepted practice. Though it is possible for Obierika, a friend of Okonkwo's, to wonder, after helping destroy the exile's compound, 'Why should a man suffer so grievously for an offence he had committed inadvertently?', he does not challenge the rule of 'The Earth', 'the great goddess', but reconciles himself by recalling one of those proverbs which are the staple of dignified intercourse among the Ibo: 'As the elders said, if one finger brought oil it soiled the others.'[26] Very different is the nature of friction between the tribe and the whites. As the reader is told after Okonkwo's return to Umuofia: 'apart from the church, the white men had also brought a government. They had built a court where the District Commissioner judged cases in ignorance. He had court messengers who brought men to him for trial' (p. 123). This is an almost classical version of the A/B confrontation described by Lyotard, magnified by cultural difference and expressing the asymmetry of law. 'Almost', rather than simply, because many of the messengers of the court are, in fact, tribesmen from 'Umuru on the bank of the Great River, where the white men first came many years before' (p. 123). The pain of the novel lies in the way the indigenous people are divided, until the cogency of old custom is sacrificed to European rules which can turn out, in practice, to be less humane. The chapter which discusses the court messengers (the *kotma*) thus ends with the hanging of Aneto, an account which recalls Okonkwo's exile: 'When he killed Oduche in the fight over the land, he fled to Aninta to escape the wrath of the earth. . . . But the Christians had told the white man about the accident, and he sent his *kotma* to

[26] Chinua Achebe, *Things Fall Apart* (1958; London, 1962), 87.

catch Aneto. He was imprisoned with all the leaders of his family [and] taken to Umuru and hanged' (p. 125).

Revenge tragedy often deals with reciprocal violence between agents in the same language and culture. That is why—despite the inequalities between A/B antagonists which this book has pointed up—its ironies can emerge: B becoming an image of A when, to avenge the wrong done, he injures A as he was injured. What Lyotard's work brings out is that, considered *communicatively*, such equivalence is superficial. The wrong done by A sets the terms for B's response, so that action by the agents cannot have the self-cancelling balance of an equation. When B replies with a left hook which says, 'that is how much your punch grieved me', the statement is in an idiom already chosen by A, however culturally derived the repertoire of blows, gunshots, or rapier-thrusts might be. More interestingly, Lyotard shows how, when A and B belong to different linguistic and cultural fields—as with a missionary and an Ibo—wrongs may be done to B by A without A registering in his own terms that a wrong (such as building a Christian church on the goddess's earth) has been inflicted. Indeed, damage can be done to B's whole sense of the world if he is forced to translate the wrong received into a response which A will comprehend as a reaction to that wrong, for actions might be necessary which dishonour B simply to communicate his sense of outrage to A, a communication which, at best, runs the risk of approximation, and might put B in the wrong by A's standards. In circumstances like these, vengeance is less focused than gestural, more an outburst of rage at the inadequacy of the grounds of exchange than a mode of violent symmetry. Tragedy would then stem from the nature of the *différend*, from the incommensurability of two agents, alienated by their sociolinguistic practices, dealing through a tribunal which can only gauge one fairly.

This is what happens in the novel. When a Christian convert called Enoch unmasks a dancer representing a dead ancestor, an *egwugwu*, Okonkwo and his fellows destroy Enoch's compound and burn down the missionary church. Summoned to what they think will be a parley with the District Commissioner, along traditional lines, Okonkwo and the rest are snatched into custody and required to pay a fine. This subjects them to a code they do not recognize; and when they pay, as they must, it costs them, culturally and emotionally, far more than the couple of hundred bags of cowrie shells exacted. Up to this point in *Things Fall Apart*, even reciprocal violent deaths, such as that of Ikemefuna, have not earned the word 'vengeance'. Now Okonkwo's rage elicits it: 'As he lay on his bamboo bed he thought about the treatment he had received in the white man's court, and he swore vengeance. If Umuofia decided on war, all would be well. But [if] they chose to be cowards he would go out and avenge himself' (p. 141). This unfocused anger is the product of a *différend*, as Lyotard describes it: 'vengeance authorizes itself on account of the plea's having no outcome. Since one is not able to obtain reparation, one cries out for vengeance.'[27] A meeting of Umuofia is called, and Achebe movingly evokes both its elaborate decorum of speech—in contrast to the Commissioner's crisp rationality (p. 137)—and its undertow of insecurity. For 'the clan' has already been 'broken' by recruitment to the church, and those still loyal run the risk of the ultimate disloyalty, that of killing their 'brothers', in order to save 'their fatherland' (pp. 143–4). As messengers sent by the Commissioner approach to close the assembly, Okonkwo confronts them. In a spare few lines, Achebe depicts the show-down, Okonkwo's lashing out with a machete to decapitate the leading messenger, and the tumult in which the dispirited clan 'let the other messengers escape' (p. 144). This loss of will to fight finishes Okonkwo. We do not hear from him again; but, in a bleak two-page final chapter, the Commissioner and his men arrive at the warrior's compound to find him hanged—a gesture largely meaningless to white justice (B does not communicate) and a bitter self-betrayal, in that, as a clansman explains, 'It is an abomination for a man to take his own life. It is an offence against the Earth' (p. 147).

Near the start of *Le Différend*, Lyotard writes of Auschwitz. The subject hardly bears thinking about; but that is part of the point. What Lyotard wants to highlight is that, when revisionist historians such as Faurisson seek to deny the existence of gas-chambers, the absence of millions who could say, 'I was a Jew gassed to death by the Nazis', creates a problem of proof (a crisis for belief) which no amount of documentary evidence can resolve. A historical novel like Achebe's, written in English (not Ibo) by the colonially educated son of an evangelical Nigerian, poses the question of how an artist can bear witness to the fate of victims from an eradicated culture. Of

[27] *Le Différend*, s. 43.

those who seek to answer Faurisson, Lyotard says, 'The victim's vengeance alone gives the authority to bear witness' (ss. 35/42); yet this 'authority' cannot be firm, placed, secure, and capable of seeking credit with readers. Revenge, in this sense, is an uprush of protest, a lost voice clamouring around tribunals which do not acknowledge it. 'Vengeance has no legitimate authority,' he writes: 'it shakes the authority of the tribunals, it calls upon idioms, upon phrase families, upon genres of discourse (any which one) that do not, in any case, have a say in the matter' (s. 44).

Lyotard's 'vengeance' sounds like an outburst of revolutionary energy; but he is careful to distinguish it from the legacy of 1789, the view that all individuals, regardless of linguistic and cultural situation, have the same freedom grounded in automony:

It is wrong to call 'rights of man' that which vengeance calls upon against the law. *Man* is surely not the name that suits this instance of appeal, nor *right* the name of the authority which this instance avails itself of . . . *Rights of the other* is not much better. *Authority of the infinite* perhaps, or *of the heterogeneous*, were it not so eloquent. (s. 44)

There is indeed a risk of eloquence, and perhaps of nebulous rapture. Revenge here invokes a post-modern sublime, losing its traditional base in knowledge, response, retribution. It seems to participate in that 'enthusiasm' which Kant found in the 'presentation of the infinite'.[28] This redefinition is compatible with Lyotard's argument, but the glow of quasi-transcendence is disconcerting. Even without a belief in the inherent 'rights of man', it is easy to sympathize with those such as Habermas who insist that sublimity of this kind is irrational and potentially reactionary.[29]

Lyotard's politics are pessimistic because, in essence, utopian. 'Revolutionary violence' is not necessarily more just than a tribunal exposed by it as concealing a *différend*, he says, because its 'Vengeance' could only issue in a new tribunal, sure to

create new wrongs . . . This is why politicians cannot have the good at stake, but they ought to have the lesser evil. Or, if you prefer, the lesser evil

---

[28] *Critique of Judgement*, tr. J. C. Meredith (Oxford, 1928), 127; cf. Bennington, *Lyotard*, 66, plus Lyotard, *Leçons*, ss. 5–6, and 'The Sublime and the Avant-Garde' in *The Lyotard Reader*, ed. Andrew Benjamin (Oxford, 1989), 196–211.

[29] For contexts see Richard Rorty, 'Habermas and Lyotard on Postmodernity', in *Essays on Heidegger and Others* (Cambridge, 1991), 164–76 and Stanley Raffel, *Habermas, Lyotard and the Concept of Justice* (London, 1992).

ought to be the political good. By evil, I understand, and one can only understand, the incessant interdiction of possible phrases, a defiance of the occurrence, the contempt for Being. (s. 197)

In the urgency of his desire to imagine uncoerced experience, Lyotard strikes an oddly Heideggerean note. Yet his talk of 'possible phrases' concedes that a realm of 'Being' would always, involving language, imply further potential interdictions. Such a view is tragic in a distinctively post-modern way, drawing its despair from the collapse of the grand narratives which supported revolutionary hope, as well as from Lyotard's view of dialogue. Hence the example he chooses, in wondering how far names provide an account of the real:

Reality entails the differend. *That's Stalin, here he is.* We acknowledge it. But as for what *Stalin* means? Phrases come to be attached to this name, which not only describe different senses for it . . . and not only place the name on different instances, but which also obey heterogeneous regimens and/or genres. This heterogeneity, for lack of a common idiom, makes consensus impossible. The assignment of a definition to Stalin necessarily does wrong to the nondefinitional phrases relating to Stalin, which this definition, for a while at least, disregards or betrays. In and around names, vengeance is on the prowl. Forever? (s. 92)

To the historian this would be treacherous if it were taken to mean—as it might, with a little unfairness—that post-Communist accounts of Stalin do 'wrong' to the 'nondefinitional' effusions and evasions of Soviet hagiography. To readers of tragedy, however, and especially to the audiences of plays named after names which stand between history and myth—Shakespeare's *King Lear*, for instance, or those works discussed by Williams and Nussbaum, *Oedipus at Colonus* and *Hecuba*—it sheds light by drawing attention to the provisionality and injustice of those marks which seem to fix identity.

Certainly, when Oedipus reaches Colonus, what he dreads is revealing his name, not because of the mutilating explicitness of its meaning ('swellfoot'), nor (with a name so characteristic) because it might be mistaken for another person's, but because the name itself, so definitely his, will render him mistaken, turn him into what he is not. The effect of pre-emptive narration, of being known in advance of his story, which burdens that exchange with the Chorus touched on by Bernard Williams, is already concentrated in the cry (to them) 'Do not ask my name!' (211) and their assurance, 'Old

man, your name | Has gone over all the earth' (305–6). 'Vengeance'
is literally 'on the prowl' around this name, because the Chorus,
recoiling from Oedipus' disclosure, speaks of God not 'punish[ing]
the man | Who makes return for an injury' (228–9), as though
bracing itself to deny hospitality to an identifiably polluted guest, to
one who has not atoned, while the exile moves from lamenting his
fallen 'name' (259), through the cry 'You . . . cast me out, | All for
fear of a name!' (265), to ask:

> And yet, how was I evil in myself?
> I had been wronged, I retaliated; even had I
> Known what I was doing, was that evil?   (270–2)

As in *Oedipus Tyrannus* (808–12), the protagonist insists that he was
attacked by Laius before striking him at the cross-roads; but who
will spare him for that? These cries of tragic justification, couched
in the language of revenge, are addressed to a tribunal (the Chorus)
too fearful of what a name carries with it to work through
'nondefinitional' accounts of the man before them to something
like justice.

Still more evidently, at the end of *Hecuba*, a revenger's name is
caught up in competing claims centred on a tribunal. For the acrid
exchange between Polymestor and the heroine, in which she claims
indifference to her end now that *dikē* has been taken, is enacted
before Agamemnon as judge. With characteristic boldness, Euripides displaces the usual convention of having a god descend on the
machine to resolve intractable cases. In this play Dionysus speaks,
but only through Polymestor, as he blindly rounds on Hecuba and
vindictively announces to Agamemnon that he will be cut down by
his own wife. The voice of the god, in other words, is not used to
announce in some external, authoritative way what divine justice
requires, but is reported by a plaintiff who, formally judged guilty
by Agamemnon, feels that his language has not been heard in
litigation but broken across a *différend*, and so whirls out with words
of 'vengeance' which claim no legitimacy in the case. That is why
Agamemnon commands that (like Desdemona) he be gagged, and
why he is carried off to some desert island where he will not be
heard.

Before he can be silenced, however, he tells Hecuba that revenge
has earned her the privilege of a name which will establish a sign.
'*When you die*', he says, '*your tomb shall be called* . . . *Cynossema, the*

bitch's grave, a landmark | to sailors' (1270–3). Noting that the word for 'landmark' is *tekmar*—which she translates, rather grandly,[30] as 'a solemn mark, perhaps even a pledge or solemn guarantee'— Martha Nussbaum writes: 'So, too, the possibilities of this play stand in nature: as markers of the boundary of social discourse and as warnings against catastrophe—but also as the pledges or guarantors of a specifically human excellence' (p. 421). What she has in mind is that, without an awareness of what it means for men and women to be transformed (ethically speaking) into animals, we could no longer be human. For most readers of Euripides, however, the denouement of *Hecuba* is more cynical and disturbing than that. Like many liberal critics, Nussbaum seems determined to find comfort in estranging outcomes. Revenge drama is well adapted to facilitating such manœuvres because its victims suffer retributively (so they deserve it) or as agents (however misguided) of justice. Hecuba falls under both headings, and thus her metamorphosis into the bitch which she has, in a sense, become can be, from Nussbaum's perspective, justified.[31] Exiling the queen to a boundary-position, the 'Aristotelian' critic purges revenge from the sphere of the human and defines it (yet again) as a realm of value, trust, and fragility. The merit of Lyotard, by contrast, is that he shows how definition itself, through name-attribution, sign-reading, and dialogue, is inextricable from violence and abuse. He helps us recognize, in Hecuba's fate, an index of the tragic potential which obtains in all the communicative inequalities of life.

Returning, with this in mind, to the starting-point of my book, it becomes apparent that, even before A and B—those agents on the open stage—interact, tragedy is waiting in the wings. Dialogue need not be violent. Unjust namings and narratings can give way to irenic (though ethically unstable) exchanges. For as long as there is difference, however, 'pledges' of conflict are visible. Certainly it is impossible to think about what Bernard Williams calls 'recompense or restitution', about injury, guilt, and retribution, without considering the verbal pragmatics which, in the manner of vengeance, join yet divide A and B. That, of course, is one reason why revenge tragedy has been of lasting cultural importance. We can learn much

---

[30] Cf. Aristotle's more restricted account of the word (*Rhetoric* 1357b), above, p. 75.

[31] On the complexities of canine lore and the heroine's metamorphosis, see Judith Mossman, *Wild Justice: A Study of Euripides' 'Hecuba'* (Oxford, 1995), 194–201.

about human nature by watching a scuffle in the street. When A and B are given voices on stage, however, or have their antagonism explored in a novel, the resulting leap in complexity is greater than anything which could derive from the addition of mere information about their motives, pasts, and futures. The antagonists come alive and into conflict through the articulate operations of a medium which both represents them (divisively) to each other and to the audience or reader. To think about revenge tragedy is to approach an understanding of forces which drive behaviour across many levels—always including the linguistic; forces which, for better or worse, are unlikely to be 'purged' from the human sphere.

Select List of Works Cited

PRIMARY SOURCES

ACHEBE, CHINUA, *Things Fall Apart* (1958; London, 1962).

AESCHYLUS, *Tragedies*, tr. Richmond Lattimore *et al.*, in David Grene and Lattimore (eds.), *The Complete Greek Tragedies*, 4 vols. (Chicago, 1959), i.

―――― *Aeschyli septem quae supersunt tragoediae*, ed. Denys Page (Oxford, 1972).

AMIS, MARTIN, *Einstein's Monsters* (1987; Harmondsworth, 1988).

ANOUILH, JEAN, *'Eurydice' and 'Médée'*, ed. E. Freeman (Oxford, 1984).

ANTIPHON, *The Tetralogies*, in *Antiphon, Andocides*, ed. and tr. K. J. Maidment, Loeb Classical Library Minor Attic Orators, i (London, 1941).

APOLLONIUS RHODIUS, *The Argonautica*, ed. and tr. R. C. Seaton (London, 1912).

AQUINAS, ST THOMAS, *Summa Theologiæ*, gen. ed. and tr. Thomas Gilby, 61 vols. (London, 1964–81).

ARISTOTLE, *The 'Art' of Rhetoric*, ed. and tr. John Henry Freese (London, 1926).

―――― *Nicomachean Ethics*, ed. and tr. H. Rackham (London, 1936).

―――― *Aristotle: 'Poetics'*, ed. D. W. Lucas (Oxford, 1968).

―――― *Poetics*, tr. M. E. Hubbard, in D. A. Russell and M. Winterbottom (eds.), *Ancient Literary Criticism: The Principal Texts in New Translations* (Oxford, 1972).

ATWOOD, MARGARET, *Wilderness Tips* (1991; London, 1992).

BACON, SIR FRANCIS, *The Essayes or Counsels, Civill and Morall*, ed. Michael Kiernan (Oxford, 1985).

BENOÎT DE SAINTE-MAURE, *Roman de Troie*, ed. Léopold Constans, 6 vols. (Paris, 1904–12).

BLAKE, NICHOLAS [= CECIL DAY-LEWIS], *Thou Shell of Death* (London, 1936).

―――― *The Beast Must Die* (1938; London, 1989).

BLAKE, WILLIAM, *The Poems of William Blake*, ed. W. H. Stevenson and David V. Erdman (London, 1971).

BOND, EDWARD, *The War Plays: A Trilogy*, 2nd edn. (London, 1991).

BOUCHAUD, ELISABETH, *Médée* (1993; perf. Cambridge).

BRATHWAIT, RICHARD, *Natures Embassie or The Wilde-Mans Measures: Danced Naked by Twelue Satyrs* (1620).

BRENTON, HOWARD, *Revenge* (London, 1970).

BROWNING, ROBERT, *The Return of the Druses*, in *The Poetical Works of Robert Browning*, ed. Ian Jack and Rowena Fowler (Oxford, 1988), iii.

BURDICK, EUGENE, and WHEELER, HARVEY, *Fail-Safe* (London, 1963).

BYRON, GEORGE GORDON, BARON BYRON, *Byron's Letters and Journals*, ed. Leslie A. Marchand, 12 vols. (London, 1973–82).

—— *Lord Byron: The Complete Poetical Works*, ed. Jerome J. McGann (vol. vi with Barry Weller), 7 vols. (Oxford, 1980–93).

CALDERÓN DE LA BARCA, PEDRO, *The Painter of His Dishonour: El Pintor de su deshonra*, ed. and tr. A. K. G. Paterson (Warminster, 1991).

CALVINO, ITALO, *The Non-Existent Knight*, in his *Our Ancestors*, tr. Archibald Colquhoun (London, 1980).

CAPUTO, PHILIP, *A Rumor of War* (1977; London, 1978).

CHARPENTIER, MARC-ANTOINE, *Médée* (1694), libretto by Thomas Corneille, recorded by William Christie with Feldman, Ragon, Mellon, etc., and Les Arts Florissants (1984).

CHERUBINI, LUIGI, *Medea* (1797), libretto by F. B. Hoffman, tr. Mária Steiner, recorded by Lamberto Gardelli with Sass, Luchetti, Kováts, etc., the Hungarian Radio and TV Chorus, and the Budapest Symphony Orchestra (1978).

CHETTLE, HENRY, *The Tragedy of Hoffman*, ed. Harold Jenkins (Oxford, 1951).

CICERO, MARCUS TULLIUS, *Tusculan Disputations*, ed. and tr. J. E. King (London, 1927).

COLERIDGE, SAMUEL TAYLOR, *The Complete Poetical Works of Samuel Taylor Coleridge*, ed. Ernest Hartley Coleridge, 2 vols. (Oxford, 1912).

—— *The Collected Letters of Samuel Taylor Coleridge*, ed. Earl Leslie Griggs, 4 vols. (Oxford, 1956–9).

—— *The Notebooks of Samuel Taylor Coleridge*, ed. Kathleen Coburn (vol. iv with Merton Christensen) (New York/London, 1957–).

—— *Lectures 1795 on Politics and Religion*, ed. Lewis Patton and Peter Mann (Princeton, 1971).

—— *Biographia Literaria*, ed. James Engell and W. Jackson Bate, 2 vols. (Princeton, 1983).

DAVENANT, SIR WILLIAM, *The Dramatic Works of Sir William D'Avenant*, ed. James Maidment and W. H. Logan, 5 vols. (Edinburgh, 1872–4).

—— and DRYDEN, JOHN, *The Tempest: Or, The Enchanted Island*, ed. Maximillian E. Novak and George R. Guffey, in *The Works of John Dryden*, gen. ed. H. T. Swedenberg, Jr. (Berkeley, 1956–), x.

DE QUINCEY, THOMAS, 'On Murder Considered as One of the Fine Arts', in John E. Jordan, introd., *The English Mail Coach and Other Essays* (London, 1961).

DICKINSON, EMILY, *The Complete Poems of Emily Dickinson*, ed. Thomas H. Johnson (London, 1970).

DICTYS CRETENSIS and DARES PHRYGIUS, *The Trojan War: The Chronicles of Dictys of Crete and Dares the Phrygian*, tr. R. M. Frazer, Jr. (Bloomington, Ind., 1966).

'Dog Bitten by Man is Feeling Ruff', *The Sun*, 11 Apr. 1987.

DORFMAN, ARIEL, *Death and the Maiden* (London, 1991).

DOSTOEVSKY, FYODOR, *Crime and Punishment*, tr. David Magarshak (Harmondsworth, 1955).

—— *The Brothers Karamazou*, tr. David McDuff (Harmondsworth, 1993).

DOYLE, SIR ARTHUR CONAN, *Memories and Adventures*, 2nd edn. (London, 1930).

—— *The Penguin Complete Sherlock Holmes*, pref. Charles Morley (Harmondsworth, 1981).

DUNCAN, ANDREW, *Cut Memories and False Commands* (London, 1991).

DWORKIN, ANDREA, *Letters from a War Zone: Writings 1976–1987* (London, 1988).

—— *Mercy* (London, 1990).

ELIOT, GEORGE, *The Mill on the Floss*, ed. Gordon S. Haight (Oxford, 1980).

ELIOT, T. S., *The Family Reunion* (London, 1939).

EURIPIDES, *Medea*, tr. Gilbert Murray (London, 1910).

—— *Medea*, ed. Denys L. Page, corr. edn. (Oxford, 1952).

—— *Tragedies*, tr. Richmond Lattimore *et al.*, in David Grene and Lattimore (eds.), *The Complete Greek Tragedies*, 4 vols. (Chicago, 1959), iii and iv.

—— *'Medea' and Other Plays*, tr. Philip Vellacott (Harmondsworth, 1963).

—— *Euripidis fabulae*, ed. James Diggle, 3 vols. (Oxford, 1981–94).

—— *Orestes*, ed. C. W. Willink (Oxford, 1986).

—— *Orestes*, ed. M. L. West (Warminster, 1987).

—— *'Medea': A New Version*, tr. Brendan Kennelly (Newcastle, 1991).

EZEKIEL, *The 'Exagoge' of Ezekiel*, [ed. and tr.] Howard Jacobson (Cambridge, 1983).

FAULKNER, WILLIAM, *The Unvanquished* (Harmondsworth, 1955).

GENET, JEAN, *The Thief's Journal*, tr. Bernard Frechtman (1965; Harmondsworth, 1967).

GODWIN, WILLIAM, *Enquiry Concerning Political Justice*, 3rd edn. (1798), ed. Isaac Kramnick (Harmondsworth, 1985).

—— *Caleb Williams*, ed. David McCracken (Oxford, 1970).

GOFFE, THOMAS, *The Tragedy of Orestes* (1633).

GOWER, JOHN, *Confessio Amantis*, in *The English Works of John Gower*, ed. G. C. Macaulay, 2 vols. (London, 1900–1).

HARRISON, TONY, *Theatre Works 1973–1985* (1985; Harmondsworth, 1986).

—— *The Trackers of Oxyrhynchus*, rev. edn. (London, 1991).

HASFORD, GUSTAV, *The Short-Timers*, rev. edn. (London, 1985).

HEGEL, GEORGE WILHELM FRIEDRICH, *Philosophy of Right*, tr. T. M. Knox (Oxford, 1942).

—— *Hegel on Tragedy*, ed. Anne and Henry Paolucci (1962; Westport, Conn., 1978).

HERACLITUS, *The Art and Thought of Heraclitus: An Edition of the Fragments with Translation and Commentary*, ed. and tr. Charles H. Kahn (Cambridge, 1979).

HERBORT VON FRITZLÅR, *Liet von Troye*, ed. Karl Frommann (Quedlinburg, 1837).

HERR, MICHAEL, *Dispatches* (London, 1978).

HESIOD, *Works and Days*, in *The Homeric Hymns and Homerica*, ed. and tr. Hugh G. Evelyn-White, rev. edn. (London, 1936).

HEYWOOD, JASPER, *Jasper Heywood and his Translations of Seneca's 'Troas', 'Thyestes' and 'Hercules Furens'*, ed. H. de Vocht (Louvain, 1913).

HEYWOOD, THOMAS, *The Dramatic Works of Thomas Heywood*, ed. R. H. Shepherd, 6 vols. (1874; New York, 1964).

HOMER, *Homeri Ilias*, ed. Thomas W. Allen, 3 vols. (Oxford, 1931).

—— *The Iliad*, tr. Martin Hammond (Harmondsworth, 1987).

—— *The Odyssey*, tr. E. V. Rieu, rev. D. C. H. Rieu (Harmondsworth, 1991).

HORACE, *Satires*, tr. Thomas Drant, in *A Medicinable Morall* (1566).

INNES, MICHAEL [= J. I. M. STEWART], *Hamlet, Revenge! A Story in Four Parts* (London, 1937).

JAMES, P. D., *The Skull Beneath the Skin* (London, 1982).

JOHNSON, CHARLES, *Caelia; or, the Perjur'd Lover* (1733).

JONES, DAVID, *In Parenthesis* (1937; London, 1963).

JOYCE, JAMES, *Finnegans Wake*, 3rd edn. (London, 1964).

KANT, IMMANUEL, *Critique of Judgement*, tr. J. C. Meredith (Oxford, 1928).

—— *Critique of Pure Reason*, tr. Norman Kemp Smith (London, 1929).

—— *The Moral Law: Kant's 'Groundwork of the Metaphysic of Morals'*, tr. H. J. Paton (London, 1948).

—— *The Metaphysical Elements of Justice: Part I of The Metaphysics of Morals*, tr. John Ladd (Indianapolis, 1965).

KEATS, JOHN, *The Letters of John Keats*, ed. Hyder Edward Rollins, 2 vols. (Cambridge, Mass., 1958).

—— *John Keats: The Complete Poems*, ed. John Barnard, 2nd edn. (Harmondsworth, 1977).

KIERKEGAARD, SØREN, *Repetition: An Essay in Experimental Psychology*, tr. Walter Lowrie (Princeton, 1942).

KIERKEGAARD, SØREN, 'Fear and Trembling' and 'The Sickness unto Death', tr. Walter Lowrie, rev. edn. (Princeton, 1954).

—— Either/Or, ed. and tr. David F. Swenson et al., rev. Howard A. Johnson, 2 vols. (Princeton, 1959).

King Horn, in Donald B. Sands (ed.), Middle English Verse Romances (New York, 1966).

KING, STEPHEN, Carrie (London, 1974).

KYD, THOMAS, The Spanish Tragedy, ed. Philip Edwards (London, 1959).

LACLOS, PIERRE-AMBROISE-FRANÇOIS CHODERLOS DE, Les Liaisons dangereuses, introd. René Pomeau (Paris, 1989).

—— Œuvres complètes, ed. Maurice Allem, 2nd edn. (Paris, 1943).

LACTANTIUS, LUCIUS COELIUS FIRMIANUS, The Works of Lactantius, tr. William Fletcher, 2 vols. (Edinburgh, 1871).

La Mort le roi Artu, ed. Jean Frappier (Geneva, 1954).

La Queste del Saint Graal: Roman du XIIIᵉ Siècle, ed. Albert Pauphilet (Paris, 1923).

LEFEVRE, RAOUL, The Recuyell of the Historyes of Troye, tr. William Caxton, ed. H. Oskar Sommer, 2 vols. (London, 1894).

LENORMAND, HENRI RENÉ, Asie (Paris, 1932).

LEWIS, WYNDHAM, The Revenge for Love (Harmondsworth, 1983).

LINDSEY, HAL (with C. C. CARLSON), The Late Great Planet Earth (1970; London, 1971).

LONDON, JACK, The Iron Heel, in Novels and Social Writings, ed. Donald Pizer (New York, 1982).

—— The Sea Wolf, in Novels and Stories, ed. Donald Pizer (New York, 1982).

—— The Letters of Jack London, ed. Earle Labor, Robert C. Leitz III, and I. Milo Shepard, 3 vols. (Stanford, Calif., 1988).

LYDGATE, JOHN, Troy Book, ed. Henry Bergen, 4 vols. (London, 1906–35).

MAILER, NORMAN, The Naked and the Dead (1949; London, 1964).

MALORY, SIR THOMAS, Works, ed. Eugène Vinaver, 2nd edn. (Oxford, 1971).

MALRAUX, ANDRÉ, Man's Estate, tr. Alastair Macdonald (Harmondsworth, 1961).

MARSTON, JOHN, The Poems of John Marston, ed. Arnold Davenport (Liverpool, 1961).

—— The Malcontent, ed. George K. Hunter (London, 1975)

—— Antonio's Revenge, ed. W. Reavley Gair (Manchester, 1978).

MASON, ROBERT, Chickenhawk (1983; London, 1984).

MATURIN, CHARLES ROBERT, Bertram; Or, The Castle of St. Aldobrand, in Jeffrey N. Cox (ed.), Seven Gothic Dramas 1789–1825 (Athens, Ohio, 1992), 315–83.

MEDWIN, THOMAS, *Medwin's 'Conversations of Lord Byron'*, ed. Ernest J. Lovell, Jr. (Princeton, 1966).

MELVILLE, HERMAN, *Moby-Dick; or, The Whale*, ed. Harold Beaver (Harmondsworth, 1972).

MIDDLETON, THOMAS [or CYRIL TOURNEUR], *The Revenger's Tragedy*, ed. R. A. Foakes (London, 1966).

—— and WILLIAM ROWLEY, *The Changeling*, ed. N. W. Bawcutt (London, 1958).

—— [attrib.], *The Second Maiden's Tragedy*, ed. Anne Lancashire (Manchester, 1978).

MILTON, JOHN, *De Doctrina Christiana*, ed. James Holly Hanford and Waldo Hilary Dunn, tr. Charles R. Sumner, in *The Works of John Milton*, gen. ed. Frank Allen Patterson, 20 vols. (New York, 1931–40), xiv–xvii.

—— *Complete Prose Works of John Milton*, gen. ed. Don M. Wolfe, 8 vols. (New Haven, 1953–82).

—— *The Poems of John Milton*, ed. John Carey and Alastair Fowler (London, 1968).

MORRISON, TONI, *Beloved* (London, 1987).

MOZART, WOLFGANG AMADEUS, *Die Entführung aus dem Serail*, libretto by Gottlieb Stephanie, tr. Peter Branscombe, with Sir Thomas Beecham's 1957 recording with Marshall, Holweg, Simoneau, etc., and the Royal Philharmonic Orchestra (1966).

—— *Il Dissoluto punito, ossia il Don Giovanni*, libretto by Lorenzo da Ponte, tr. Lionel Salter, with Sir Colin Davis's 1973 recording with Wixell, Ganzarolli, Arroyo, etc., and the Chorus and Orchestra of the Royal Opera House, Covent Garden (1973).

—— *Die Zauberflöte*, Capitol Records tr. (1964), with Bernard Haitink's recording with Popp, Gruberova, Lindner, etc., and the Chor des Bayerischen Rudfunks and Sinfonie-Orchestre des Bayerischen Rudfunks (1981).

—— *The Letters of Mozart and His Family*, ed. and tr. Emily Anderson, 3rd edn. (London, 1985).

NICHOLS, GRACE, *Lazy Thoughts of a Lazy Woman and Other Poems* (London, 1989).

NIETZSCHE, FRIEDRICH, *Basic Writings of Nietzsche*, ed. and tr. Walter Kaufmann (New York, 1968).

—— *The Portable Nietzsche*, ed. and tr. Walter Kaufmann, rev. edn. (New York, 1968).

—— *The Will to Power*, ed. Walter Kaufmann, tr. Kaufmann and R.J. Hollingdale (New York, 1968).

—— *Thus Spake Zarathustra: A Book for Everyone and No One*, tr. R. J. Hollingdale, rev. edn. (Harmondsworth, 1969).

NIETZSCHE, FRIEDRICH, *Daybreak: Thoughts on the Prejudices of Morality* (1881), tr. R. J. Hollingdale (Cambridge, 1982).

—— *Sämtliche Werke*, ed. Giorgio Colli and Mazzino Montinari, 15 vols. (Berlin, 1988).

O'BRIEN, TIM, *If I Die in a Combat Zone* (1973; London, 1989).

—— *The Things They Carried* (London, 1990).

OSBORNE, JOHN, *Look Back in Anger* (1957; London, 1960).

OVID, *Ibis*, in P. *Ovidi Nasonis Tristium libri quinque, Ex ponto libri quattor, Halieutica, Fragmenta*, ed. S. G. Owen (Oxford, 1915).

OWEN, WILFRED, *The Collected Poems of Wilfred Owen*, ed. C. Day Lewis (London, 1963).

PASOLINI, PIER PAOLO, script and dir., *Appunti per una Orestiade africana* (1970).

—— screenplay (after Euripides) and dir., *Medea* (1970).

—— *Heretical Empiricism*, ed. Louise K. Barnett, tr. Ben Lawton and Louise K. Barnett (Bloomington, Ind., 1988).

PLATH, SYLVIA, *Collected Poems*, ed. Ted Hughes (London, 1981).

PLATO, *'Lysias', 'Symposium', 'Gorgias'*, ed. and tr. W. R. M. Lamb (London, 1925).

—— *Laws*, ed. and tr. R. G. Bury, 2 vols. (London, 1926).

POE, EDGAR ALLAN, 'William Wilson', in *Edgar Allan Poe: Poetry and Tales*, ed. Patrick F. Quinn (New York, 1984), 337–57.

POUND, EZRA, *The Cantos of Ezra Pound*, rev. edn. (London, 1975).

PROUST, MARCEL, *À la recherche du temps perdu*, ed. Pierre Clarac and André Ferré, 3 vols. (Paris, 1954).

—— *Time Regained*, tr. Andreas Mayor, rev. edn. (London, 1970), 226.

PYKERYNG, JOHN, *Horestes*, in Marie Axton (ed.), *Three Tudor Classical Interludes* (Woodbridge, 1982).

The Quest of the Holy Grail, tr. P. M. Matarasso (Harmondsworth, 1969).

QUINTILIAN, *Institutio Oratoria*, ed. and tr. H. E. Butler, 4 vols. (London, 1920–2).

Raoul de Cambrai, ed. and tr. Sarah Kay (Oxford, 1992).

RAVENSCROFT, EDWARD, *Titus Andronicus: Or, The Rape of Lavinia* (1687).

REMARQUE, ERIC MARIA, *All Quiet on the Western Front*, tr. A. W. Wheen (London, 1929).

RICH, ADRIENNE, *The Dream of a Common Language: Poems 1974–1977* (New York, 1978).

—— *Of Woman Born: Motherhood as Experience and Institution*, new edn. (London, 1986).

RICHARDSON, SAMUEL, 'Six Original Letters upon Duelling', *Candid Review and Literary Repository*, 1 (1765), 227–31.

—— *The Correspondence of Samuel Richardson*, ed. Anna Lætitia Barbauld, 6 vols. (London, 1804).

―――― *Clarissa: Or, The History of a Young Lady*, introd. John Butt, 4 vols. (London, 1932).

―――― *Selected Letters of Samuel Richardson*, ed. John Carroll (Oxford, 1964).

ROBBE-GRILLET, ALAIN, *La Jalousie* (Paris, 1957).

―――― *The Erasers*, tr. Richard Howard (London, 1966).

ROTH, ROBERT, *Sand in the Wind* (1973; London, 1974).

SADE, MARQUIS DE, *Justine, or Good Conduct Well Chastised*, in *The Complete 'Justine', 'Philosophy in the Bedroom' and Other Writings*, ed. and tr. Richard Seaver and Austryn Wainhouse (New York, 1965).

―――― *Œuvres complètes du Marquis de Sade*, ed. Annie Le Brun and Jean-Jacques Pauvert, 15 vols. (Paris, 1986–).

ST PAUL, *Epistle to the Galatians*, ed. J. B. Lightfoot, 10th edn. (London, 1890).

SARTRE, JEAN-PAUL, *'The Flies' and 'In Camera'*, tr. Stuart Gilbert (London, 1946).

SAUNDERS, KATE (ed.), *Revenge* (London, 1990).

SAYERS, DOROTHY L., *Gaudy Night* (London, 1935).

SCHILLER, FRIEDRICH, *The Robbers*, tr. Alexander Tytler (London, 1792).

SENECA, LUCIUS ANNAEUS the younger, *Moral Essays*, ed. and tr. John W. Basore, 3 vols. (London, 1928–35).

―――― *Tragedies*, ed. and tr. Frank Justus Miller, 2 vols., rev. edn. (London, 1929).

―――― *Thyestes*, tr. Jasper Heywood, ed. Joost Daalder (London, 1982).

―――― *Thyestes*, ed. R. J. Tarrant (Atlanta, 1985).

SEXTUS EMPIRICUS, *Outlines of Pyrrhonism*, ed. and tr. R. G. Bury (London, 1933).

SHAKESPEARE, WILLIAM, *The Tragicall Historie of Hamlet, Prince of Denmarke* (1604).

―――― *Hamlet*, ed. John Dover Wilson (Cambridge, 1934).

―――― *The Riverside Shakespeare*, ed. G. Blakemore Evans (Boston, 1974).

―――― *William Shakespeare: The Complete Works*, ed. Stanley Wells and Gary Taylor (Oxford, 1986).

SHELLEY, PERCY BYSSHE, *The Letters of Percy Bysshe Shelley*, ed. F. L. Jones, 2 vols. (Oxford, 1964).

―――― *Shelley's Poetry and Prose*, ed. Donald H. Reiman and Sharon B. Powers (New York, 1977).

―――― *Shelley's Prose: Or, The Trumpet of a Prophecy*, ed. David Lee Clark (1954; London, 1988).

SNOW, TONY, 'Two Years for Fan Who Bit Off Police Dog's Ear', *The Sun*, 27 Oct. 1987.

The Song of Roland: An Analytical Edition, ed. and tr. Gerald J. Brault, 2 vols. (University Park, Pa., 1978).

SOPHOCLES, *The Searchers*, in the Loeb Classical Library Select Papyri, 3, ed. and tr. D. L. Page (London, 1941).

—— *Tragedies*, tr. David Grene *et al.*, in Grene and Richmond Lattimore (eds.), *The Complete Greek Tragedies*, 4 vols. (Chicago, 1959), ii.

—— *Women of Trachis*, tr. Ezra Pound (1956; London, 1969).

—— *Electra*, ed. J. H. Kells (Cambridge, 1973).

—— *Ajax*, ed. W. B. Stanford, corr. repr. (1963; London, 1981).

—— *Trachiniae*, ed. P. E. Easterling (Cambridge, 1982).

—— *Sophoclis fabulae*, ed. Hugh Lloyd-Jones and N. G. Wilson (Oxford, 1990).

SPINRAD, NORMAN, *The Iron Dream* (1972; St Albans, 1974).

STEVENS, WALLACE, *The Collected Poems of Wallace Stevens* (New York, 1954).

STOKER, BRAM, *Dracula*, ed. A. N. Wilson (Oxford, 1983).

SUN TZU, *The Art of War*, tr. Thomas Cleary (Boston, 1988).

TENNYSON, ALFRED TENNYSON, BARON, *The Poems of Tennyson*, ed. Christopher Ricks, 2nd edn., 3 vols. (London, 1987).

TOLSTOY, COUNT LEO NIKOLAYEVICH, *Anna Karenin*, tr. Rosemary Edmonds (Harmondsworth, 1954).

TREMAYNE, PETER, *The Revenge of Dracula* (Folkestone, 1978).

VIRGIL, *Aeneid*, in *Virgil*, ed. and tr. H. Rushton Fairclough, rev. edn., 2 vols. (London, 1934-5).

VONNEGUT, KURT, *Slaughterhouse-Five: Or, The Children's Crusade. A Duty-Dance with Death* (1969; London, 1991).

WEBSTER, JOHN, *The White Devil*, ed. John Russell Brown, 2nd edn. (London, 1966).

WELDON, FAY, *The Life and Loves of a She Devil* (1983; London, 1984).

WILLIAMS, HELEN MARIA, *Letters from France*, facs., introd. Janet M. Todd (Delmar, New York, 1975).

WOLLSTONECRAFT, MARY, *The Works of Mary Wollstonecraft*, ed. Janet Todd and Marilyn Butler, 7 vols. (London, 1989).

WORDSWORTH, WILLIAM, *The Borderers*, ed. Robert Osborn (Ithaca, NY, 1982).

—— *The Salisbury Plain Poems of William Wordsworth*, ed. Stephen Gill (Ithaca, NY, 1975)

—— *Sonnets upon the Punishment of Death*, in Sir Henry Taylor, 'The Sonnets of William Wordsworth', *The Quarterly Review*, 69 (1841-2), 1-52, pp. 39-49.

ZOLA, ÉMILE, *Thérèse Raquin*, tr. Leonard Tancock (Harmondsworth, 1962).

SECONDARY SOURCES

ABRAHAM, KARL, *Selected Papers of Karl Abraham, M. D.*, tr. Douglas Bryan and Alix Strachey (London, 1927).

AHL, FREDERICK, *Sophocles' Oedipus: Evidence and Self-Conviction* (Ithaca, NY, 1991).

ALVAREZ, A., *The Savage God: A Study of Suicide* (Harmondsworth, 1971).

ANDERSON, LINDA, *A Kind of Wild Justice: Revenge in Shakespeare's Comedies* (Newark, Del., 1987).

ANDREW, DONNA T., 'The Code of Honour and its Critics: The Opposition to Duelling in England, 1700–1850', *Social History*, 5 (1980), 409–34.

ARDOIN, JOHN, *Callas: The Art and the Life* (London, 1974).

—— *Callas at Julliard: The Master Classes* (London, 1988).

ASCHERSON, NEAL, 'When Punishment Becomes Revenge We're on the Road to Barbarism', *Independent on Sunday*, 30 Jan. 1994.

ASHCROFT, JEFFREY, '*Miles Dei—gottes ritter*: Konrad's *Rolandslied* and the Evolution of the Concept of Christian Chivalry', in W. H. Jackson (ed.), *Knighthood in Medieval Literature* (Woodbridge, 1981), 54–74.

AUDEN, W. H., *The Enchafèd Flood or The Romantic Iconography of the Sea* (London, 1951).

AVERILL, JAMES R., *Anger and Aggression: An Essay on Emotion* (New York, 1982).

AXELROD, ROBERT, *The Evolution of Cooperation* (New York, 1984).

BACHELARD, GASTON, *The Psychoanalysis of Fire*, tr. Alan C. M. Ross (London, 1964).

BAILEY, F. G. (ed.), *Gifts and Poison: The Politics of Reputation* (Oxford, 1971).

BARBER, PAUL, *Vampires, Burial, and Death: Folklore and Reality* (New Haven, 1988).

BARNES, JONATHAN, 'Proof Destroyed', in Malcolm Schofield, Myles Burnyeat, and Jonathan Barnes (eds.), *Doubt and Dogmatism: Studies in Hellenistic Epistemology* (Oxford, 1980), 161–81.

BARTHES, ROLAND, *Roland Barthes*, tr. Richard Howard (London, 1977).

—— *Sade, Fourier, Loyola*, tr. Richard Miller (London, 1977)

—— *Empire of Signs*, tr. Richard Howard (London, 1983).

BARTON, ANNE, 'The Wild Man in the Forest', 1994 Northcliffe Lectures, 1 (7 Mar. 1994).

BARZUN, JACQUES, *The Energies of Art: Studies of Authors Classic and Modern* (New York, 1956).

BAUDRILLARD, JEAN, *La Guerre du Golfe n'a pas eu lieu* (Paris, 1991).

BEAUVOIR, SIMONE DE, *Privilèges* (1955; Paris, 1964).

BENNINGTON, GEOFFREY, *Lyotard: Writing the Event* (Manchester, 1988).

BENSON, C. DAVID, *The History of Troy in Middle English Literature: Guido delle*

Colonne's 'Historia Destructionis Troiae' in Medieval England (Woodbridge, 1980).

BERGSON, HENRI, 'Laughter', in Wylie Sypher (ed. and tr.), *Comedy: George Meredith, 'An Essay on Comedy', Henri Bergson, 'Laughter'* (New York, 1956), 61–190.

BILLACOIS, FRANÇOIS, *The Duel: Its Rise and Fall in Early Modern France*, tr. Trista Selous (New Haven, 1990)

BILLINGTON, MICHAEL, 'Cruelty and Grief within Reason', *The Guardian*, 6 July 1988.

BIRCH, HELEN (ed.), *Moving Targets: Women, Murder and Representation* (London, 1993).

BLACK, JOEL, *The Aesthetics of Murder: A Study in Romantic Literature and Contemporary Culture* (Baltimore, 1991).

BLOCH, MARC, *Feudal Society*, tr. L. A. Manyon, 2nd edn., 2 vols. (London, 1962).

BLOCH, R. HOWARD, *Medieval French Literature and Law* (Berkeley, 1977).

———— *Etymologies and Genealogies: A Literary Anthropology of the French Middle Ages* (Chicago, 1983).

BLUNDELL, MARY WHITLOCK, *Helping Friends and Harming Enemies: A Study in Sophocles and Greek Ethics* (Cambridge, 1989).

BOEHM, CHRISTOPHER, *Blood Revenge: The Enactment and Management of Conflict in Montenegro and Other Tribal Societies*, 2nd edn. (Philadelphia, 1987).

BONGIE, ELIZABETH BRYSON, 'Heroic Elements in the *Medea* of Euripides', *Transactions of the American Philological Association*, 107 (1977), 27–56.

BOURDIEU, PIERRE, *Outline of a Theory of Practice*, tr. Richard Nice (Cambridge, 1977).

BOWERS, FAUBION, *Japanese Theatre* (Rutland, Vt., 1974).

BOWERS, FREDSON, *Elizabethan Revenge Tragedy 1587–1642* (Princeton, 1940).

BOWLBY, JOHN, *Loss: Sadness and Depression* (London, 1980).

BRADEN, GORDON, *Renaissance Tragedy and the Senecan Tradition: Anger's Privilege* (New Haven, 1985).

———— 'Epic Anger', *Milton Quarterly*, 23 (1989), 28–34.

BRANDES, GEORGES, *Impressions of Russia*, tr. Samuel C. Eastman (London, 1889).

BRECHT, BERTOLT, *The Messingkauf Dialogues*, tr. John Willett (London, 1965).

BRIDGWATER, PATRICK, *Nietzsche in Anglosaxony: A Study in Nietzsche's Impact on English and American Literature* (Leicester, 1972).

BROUDE, RONALD, 'Revenge and Revenge Tragedy in Renaissance England', *Renaissance Quarterly*, 28 (1975), 38–58.

BROWN, COLIN (ed.), *New International Dictionary of New Testament Theology*, 3 vols. (Exeter, 1975–8).

BUCKLEY, THOMAS, and GOTTLIEB, ALMA (eds.), *Blood Magic: The Anthropology of Menstruation* (Berkeley, 1988).

BURKERT, WALTER, *Homo Necans: The Anthropology of Ancient Greek Sacrificial Ritual and Myth*, tr. Peter Bing (Berkeley, 1983).

—— *Greek Religion: Archaic and Classical*, tr. John Raffan (Oxford, 1985).

BURNET, GILBERT, *Some Passages of the Life and Death of Rochester* (1680), in David Farley-Hills (ed.), *Rochester: The Critical Heritage* (London, 1972), 47–92.

BURTON, ROBERT, *The Anatomy of Melancholy*, ed. Holbrook Jackson (London, 1932).

BUTLER, F. G., 'Blessing and Cursing in *King Lear*', *Unisa English Studies*, 24 (1986), 7–11.

BUTLER, JUDITH, *Gender Trouble: Feminism and the Subversion of Identity* (London, 1990).

CAMPBELL, LILY B., *Shakespeare's Tragic Heroes: Slaves of Passion* (London, 1930).

—— 'Theories of Revenge in Renaissance England', *Modern Philology*, 38 (1931), 281–96.

CAMUS, ALBERT, *The Myth of Sisyphus*, tr. Justin O'Brien (1955; Harmondsworth, 1975).

CAREY, JOHN, 'Revenge', *Independent* magazine, 20 Mar. 1993, 20–1.

CARTER, ANGELA, *The Sadean Woman: An Exercise in Cultural History* (London, 1979).

CARTLEDGE, PAUL, MILLETT, PAUL, and TODD, STEPHEN (eds.), *Nomos: Essays in Athenian Law, Politics and Society* (Cambridge, 1990).

CASEY, JOHN, *Pagan Virtue* (Oxford, 1990).

CAVELL, STANLEY, *Disowning Knowledge in Six Plays of Shakespeare* (Cambridge, 1987).

CHESTERTON, G. K., *The Defendant* (London, 1901).

CHURCHILL, WINSTON S., *The War Speeches of the Rt Hon. Winston S. Churchill*, ed. Charles Eade, 3 vols. (London, 1951–2).

CIXOUS, HÉLÈNE, 'Sorties', in Hélène Cixous and Catherine Clément, *The Newly Born Woman*, tr. Betsy Wing (Minneapolis, 1986), 63–132.

CLAUSEWITZ, CARL VON, *On War*, ed. and tr. Michael Howard and Peter Paret (Princeton, 1989).

CLAYTON, JOHN POWELL, 'Zarathustra and the Stages on Life's Way: A Nietzschean Riposte to Kierkegaard?', *Nietzsche-Studien*, 14 (1985), 179–200.

CLÉMENT, CATHERINE, *Opera, or the Undoing of Women*, tr. Betsy Wing (London, 1989).

COHEN, DAVID, *Law, Sexuality, and Society: The Enforcement of Morals in Classical Athens* (Cambridge, 1991).

COLLINS, JACKIE, *et al.*, 'Revenge', in *Elle*, June 1993, 63–9.

CONRAD, PETER, 'Revenger's Comedy', *Observer Magazine*, 15 Dec. 1991, 34–9.

CORNELL, DRUCILLA, *Beyond Accommodation: Ethical Feminism, Deconstruction, and the Law* (London, 1991).

CRAWFORD, PATRICIA, 'Attitudes to Menstruation in Seventeenth-Century England', *Past and Present*, 91 (1981), 47–73.

DAVY, MARIE-MADELEINE, 'Le Theme de la vengeance au Moyen Âge', in Raymond Verdier and Jean-Pierre Poly (eds.), *La Vengeance: Études d'ethnologie, d'histoire et de philosophie*, 4 vols. (Paris, 1980–4), iv. 125–35.

DAWSON, P. M. S., *The Unacknowledged Legislator: Shelley and Politics* (Oxford, 1980).

DEANE, SEAMUS, *The French Revolution and Enlightenment in England 1789–1832* (Cambridge, Mass., 1988).

DELACROIX, EUGÈNE, *The Journal of Eugene Delacroix*, tr. Walter Pach (New York, 1937).

DELEUZE, GILLES, *Différence et répétition* (Paris, 1968).

DE ROMILLY, JACQUELINE, *Magic and Rhetoric in Ancient Greece* (Cambridge, Mass., 1975).

DERRIDA, JACQUES, 'No Apocalypse, Not Now (full speed ahead, seven missiles, seven missives)', tr. Catherine Porter and Philip Lewis, *Diacritics*, 14/2 (1984), 20–31.

—— 'Force of Law: The "Mystical Foundation of Authority"', tr. Mary Quaintance, *Cardozo Law Review*, 11 (1990), 921–1045.

DEVEREUX, GEORGE, *Dreams in Greek Tragedy: An Ethno-Psycho-Analytical Study* (Oxford, 1976).

DODDS, E. R., *The Greeks and the Irrational* (Berkeley, 1951).

—— *The Ancient Concept of Progress and Other Essays on Greek Literature and Belief* (Oxford, 1973).

DONALDSON, IAN, 'Jonson and Anger', *Yearbook of English Studies*, 14 (1984), 56–71.

DOUGLAS, MARY, *Purity and Danger: An Analysis of the Concepts of Pollution and Taboo* (London, 1966).

—— *Implicit Meanings* (London, 1975).

DUBY, GEORGES, *The Chivalrous Society*, tr. Cynthia Postan (London, 1977).

EAGLETON, TERRY, 'Angry 'Un', *London Review of Books*, 15/13 (8 July 1993).

EASTERLING, P. E., 'The Infanticide in Euripides' *Medea*', *Yale Classical Studies*, 25 (1977), 177–91.

ECO, UMBERTO, and SEBEOK, THOMAS A. (eds.), *The Sign of Three: Dupin, Holmes, Peirce* (Bloomington, Ind., 1983).

EDEN, KATHY, *Poetic and Legal Fiction in the Aristotelian Tradition* (Princeton, 1986).

ELIADE, MIRCEA, *The Myth of the Eternal Return*, tr. Willard R. Trask (London, 1955).

ELIOT, T. S., *Selected Essays*, 3rd edn. (London, 1951).

—— *On Poetry and Poets* (London, 1957).

ELLIOTT, ROBERT C., *The Power of Satire: Magic, Ritual, Art* (Princeton, 1960).

FALUDI, SUSAN, *Backlash: The Undeclared War Against Women* (London, 1992).

FANTHAM, ELAINE, 'ZHΛΟΤΥΠΙΑ: A Brief Excursion into Sex, Violence, and Literary History', *Phoenix*, 40 (1986), 45–57.

FEINBERG, JOEL, *Doing and Deserving: Essays in the Theory of Responsibility* (Princeton, 1970).

FISK, ROBERT, *Pity the Nation: Lebanon at War* (1990; Oxford, 1991).

FORTUNA, JAMES LOUIS, JR., *'The Unsearchable Wisdom of God': A Study of Providence in Richardson's 'Pamela'* (Gainesville, Fla., 1980).

FRANK, JOSEPH, *Dostoevsky: The Seeds of Revolt 1821–1849* (London, 1977).

FRAPPIER, JEAN, 'Vues sur les conceptions courtoises dans les littératures d'oc et d'oil au XIIᵉ siècle', *Cahiers de civilisation médiévale*, 2 (1959), 135–56.

FREUD, SIGMUND, *The Standard Edition of the Complete Psychological Works of Sigmund Freud*, gen. ed. James Strachey, 24 vols. (London, 1966–74).

FUSSELL, PAUL, *Wartime: Understanding and Behaviour in the Second World War* (Oxford, 1989).

GARLAND, ROBERT, *The Greek Way of Death* (London, 1985).

GILBERT, MARTIN, *The Holocaust: The Jewish Tragedy* (1986; London, 1987).

GIRARD, RÉNÉ, *Violence and the Sacred*, tr. Patrick Gregory (Baltimore, 1977).

GOODHART, SANDOR, 'Ληστὰς ῎Εφασκε: Oedipus and Laius' Many Murderers', *Diacritics*, 8/1 (1978), 55–71.

GORER, GEOFFREY, *The Life and Ideas of the Marquis de Sade*, rev. edn. (London, 1953).

GREEN, ANDRÉ, *The Tragic Effect: The Oedipus Complex in Tragedy*, tr. Alan Sheridan (Cambridge, 1979).

GREENAWALT, KENT, *Conflicts of Law and Morality* (New York, 1987).

GREENE, NAOMI, *Pier Paolo Pasolini: Cinema as Heresy* (Princeton, 1990).

GREG, W. W., 'Hamlet's Hallucination', *Modern Language Review*, 12 (1917), 393–421.

—— *Biographical Notes 1877–1947* (Oxford, 1960).

GRIFFIN, JASPER, *Homer on Life and Death* (Oxford, 1980).

GRIFFIN, SUSAN, *Pornography and Silence: Culture's Revenge Against Nature* (London, 1981).

GROSZ, ELIZABETH, 'The Body of Signification', in John Fletcher and Andrew Benjamin (eds.), *Abjection, Melancholia, and Love: The Work of Julia Kristeva* (London, 1990), 80–103.

HALL, EDITH, *Inventing the Barbarian: Greek Self-Definition Through Tragedy* (Oxford, 1989).

HALLETT, CHARLES A., and HALLETT, ELAINE S., *The Revenger's Madness: A Study of Revenge Tragedy Motifs* (Lincoln, Nebr., 1980)

382 SELECT LIST OF WORKS CITED

HALLISSY, MARGARET, *Venomous Woman* (New York, 1987).

HANSON, ANTHONY TYRRELL, *The Wrath of the Lamb* (London, 1957).

HARDIE, W. F. R., *Aristotle's Ethical Theory*, 2nd edn. (Oxford, 1980).

HARRIS, JOCELYN, 'Richardson: Original or Learned Genius?', in Margaret Anne Doody and Peter Sabor (eds.), *Samuel Richardson: Tercentenary Essays* (Cambridge, 1989), 188–202.

HART, H. L. A., *Punishment and Responsibility: Essays on the Philosophy of Law*, rev. edn. (Oxford, 1970).

HARTMAN, MARY S., *Victorian Murderesses: A True History of Thirteen Respectable French and English Women Accused of Unspeakable Crimes* (London, 1977).

HELLER, AGNES, *Beyond Justice* (Oxford, 1987).

HERRICK, MARVIN T., *Tragicomedy: Its Origin and Development in Italy, France, and England* (1955; Urbana, Ill., 1962).

HERTZ, ROBERT, 'Contribution à une étude sur la représentation collective de la mort', *Année sociologique*, 10 (1907), 48–137.

HILDESHEIMER, WOLFGANG, *Mozart*, tr. Marion Faber (London, 1983).

HILL, CHRISTOPHER, 'Clarissa Harlowe and her Times', *Essays in Criticism*, 5 (1955), 315–40.

HIRSCH, MARIANNE, *The Mother/Daughter Plot: Narrative, Psychoanalysis, Feminism* (Bloomington, Ind., 1989).

HITLER, ADOLF, *Mein Kampf*, tr. James Murphy (London, 1939).

HOBBES, THOMAS, *Leviathan*, ed. C. B. Macpherson (Harmondsworth, 1968).

HONDERICH, TED, *Violence for Equality: Inquiries in Political Philosophy*, rev. edn. (Harmondsworth, 1980).

HUME, DAVID, *A Treatise of Human Nature*, ed. L. A. Selby-Bigges, 2nd edn., rev. P. H. Nidditch (Oxford, 1978).

HUMPHREY, NICHOLAS, and LIFTON, ROBERT J. (eds.), *In a Dark Time* (London, 1984).

HUMPHREYS, S. C., *The Family, Women and Death: Comparative Studies*, 2nd edn. (Ann Arbor, 1993).

HUNTINGTON, RICHARD, and METCALF, PETER, *Celebrations of Death: The Anthropology of Mortuary Ritual*, 2nd edn. (Cambridge, 1991).

HUXLEY, THOMAS H., *Collected Essays*, 9 vols. (London, 1894–1908).

IRIGARAY, LUCE, *This Sex Which Is Not One*, tr. Catherine Porter (Ithaca, NY, 1985).

JACOBY, SUSAN, *Wild Justice: The Evolution of Revenge* (London, 1985).

JANOUCH, GUSTAV, *Conversations with Kafka*, tr. Goronwy Rees, 2nd edn. (London, 1971).

JOHNSON, BARBARA, *A World of Difference* (Baltimore, 1987).

JOHNSON, LEE, *The Paintings of Eugène Delacroix: A Critical Catalogue*, 6 vols. (Oxford, 1981–9).

JOHNSON, SAMUEL, *Selections from Johnson on Shakespeare*, ed. Bertrand H. Bronson and Jean M. O'Meara (New Haven, 1986).

JONES, EMRYS, *The Origins of Shakespeare* (Oxford, 1977).

JONES, JOHN, *On Aristotle and Greek Tragedy* (London, 1962).

KAHN, HERMAN, *On Thermonuclear War* (Princeton, 1960).

KAPPELER, SUSANNE, *The Pornography of Representation* (Cambridge, 1986).

KERÉNYI, CARL, *The Heroes of the Greeks*, tr. H. J. Rose (London, 1959).

KERNAN, ALVIN, *The Cankered Muse: Satire of the English Renaissance* (New Haven, 1959).

KLEIN, MELANIE, *Love, Guilt and Reparation* (London, 1975).

—— *Envy and Gratitude and Other Works 1946–1963* (London, 1975).

KNOX, BERNARD, *Oedipus at Thebes* (New Haven, 1957).

—— *Word and Action: Essays on the Ancient Theater* (Baltimore, 1979).

KOSMAN, ARYEH, 'Acting: Drama as the *Mimēsis* of *Praxis*', in Amélie Oksenberg Rorty (ed.), *Essays on Aristotle's 'Poetics'* (Princeton, 1992), 51–72.

KRISTEVA, JULIA, *Powers of Horror: An Essay on Abjection*, tr. Leon S. Roudiez (New York, 1982).

—— *Soleil noir: Dépression et mélancolie* (Paris, 1987).

KUHN, THOMAS, *The Essential Tension: Selected Studies in Scientific Tradition and Change* (Chicago, 1977).

LACAN, JACQUES, *Écrits* (Paris, 1966).

LAWRENCE, D. H., *Apocalypse* (1931; Harmondsworth, 1974).

LEFKOWITZ, MARY R., *Women in Greek Myth* (London, 1986).

LEVENSON, J. L., 'The Narrative Format of Benoît's *Roman de Troie*', *Romania*, 100 (1979), 54–70.

LEWIS, WYNDHAM, *The Lion and the Fox: The Rôle of the Hero in the Plays of Shakespeare* (London, 1927).

LIFTON, ROBERT, *Death in Life* (New York, 1969).

LLOYD, G. E. R., *Magic, Reason and Experience: Studies in the Origins and Development of Greek Science* (Cambridge, 1979).

LONG, A. A., *Hellenistic Philosophy: Stoics, Epicureans, Sceptics* (London, 1974).

LORENZ, KONRAD, *On Aggression*, tr. Marjorie Latzke (London, 1966).

LOWE, DAVID A. (ed.), *Callas As They Saw Her* (London, 1987).

LYOTARD, JEAN-FRANÇOIS, *The Differend: Phrases in Dispute*, tr. Georges Van Den Abbeele (Manchester, 1988).

—— *The Lyotard Reader*, ed. Andrew Benjamin (Oxford, 1989).

—— *Lessons on the Analytic of the Sublime*, tr. Elizabeth Rottenberg (Stanford, Calif., 1994).

LYOTARD, JEAN-FRANÇOIS, and THÉBAUD, JEAN-LOUP, *Just Gaming*, tr. Wlad Godzich (Manchester, 1985).

MACDOWELL, DOUGLAS M., *The Law in Classical Athens* (London, 1978).

MCFARLAND, THOMAS, *Coleridge and the Pantheist Tradition* (Oxford, 1969).

MACKINNON, CATHARINE A., *Feminism Unmodified: Discourses on Life and Law* (Cambridge, Mass., 1987).

—— *Toward a Feminist Theory of the State* (Cambridge, Mass., 1989).

MACKINTOSH, JAMES, *Vindiciae Gallicae: Defence of the French Revolution* (London, 1791).

MARCH, JENNIFER, 'Euripides the Misogynist?', in Anton Powell (ed.), *Euripides, Women, and Sexuality* (London, 1990), 32–75.

MARSHALL, SAMUEL LYMAN ATWOOD, *Men Against Fire: The Problem of Battle Command in Future War* (Washington, DC, 1947).

MAUSS, MARCEL, *The Gift*, tr. Ian Cunnison, corr. edn. (London, 1969).

MILLER, C. A., 'Nietzsche's "Discovery" of Dostoevsky', *Nietzsche-Studien*, 2 (1973), 202–57.

MILLER, WALTER M., *A Canticle for Leibowitz* (1959; London, 1960).

MILLER, WILLIAM IAN, *Bloodtaking and Peacemaking: Feud, Law, and Society in Saga Iceland* (Chicago, 1990).

MIOLA, ROBERT S., *Shakespeare and Classical Tragedy: The Influence of Seneca* (Oxford, 1992).

MODLESKI, TANIA, *Loving with a Vengeance: Mass-Produced Fantasies for Women* (1982; New York, 1984).

MONTI, RICHARD C., *The Dido Episode and 'The Aeneid': Roman Social and Political Values in the Epic* (Leiden, 1981).

MORKAN, JOEL, 'Wrath and Laughter: Milton's Ideas on Satire', *Studies in Philology*, 69 (1972), 475–95.

MORRIS, COLIN, *The Discovery of the Individual 1050–1200* (1972; London, 1973).

MURDOCH, IRIS, 'Existentialists and Mystics: A Note on the Novel in the New Utilitarian Age', in W. W. Robson (ed.), *Essays and Poems Presented to Lord David Cecil* (London, 1970), 169–83.

MYERS, THOMAS, *Walking Point: American Narratives of Vietnam* (New York, 1988).

NEHAMAS, ALEXANDER, *Nietzsche: Life as Literature* (Cambridge, Mass., 1985).

NOLAN, BARBARA, *Chaucer and the Tradition of the 'Roman Antique'* (Cambridge, 1992).

NOZICK, ROBERT, *Philosophical Explanations* (Oxford, 1981).

NUSSBAUM, MARTHA C., *The Fragility of Goodness: Luck and Ethics in Greek Tragedy and Philosophy* (Cambridge, 1986).

O'NEILL, MICHAEL, *The Human Mind's Imaginings: Conflict and Achievement in Shelley's Poetry* (Oxford, 1989).

OUSBY, IAN, *Bloodhounds of Heaven: The Detective in English Fiction from Godwin to Doyle* (Cambridge, Mass., 1976).

OVERING, JOANNA, 'Images of Cannibalism, Death and Domination in a

"Non-Violent" Society', in David Riches (ed.), *The Anthropology of Violence* (Oxford, 1986), 86–102.

PADEL, RUTH, *In and Out of the Mind: Greek Images of the Tragic Self* (Princeton, 1992).

PAINE, TOM, *Rights of Man*, ed. Henry Collins (Harmondsworth, 1969).

PARKER, ROBERT, *Miasma: Pollution and Purification in Early Greek Religion* (Oxford, 1983).

PATER, WALTER, *Greek Studies: A Series of Essays* (1895; London, 1928).

PATRIDES, C. A., *Milton and the Christian Tradition* (Oxford, 1966).

PAZ, OCTAVIO, *The Labyrinth of Solitude*, tr. Lysander Kemp (1961; Harmondsworth, 1985).

PEACE, RICHARD, *Dostoevsky: An Examination of the Major Novels* (Cambridge, 1971).

PERISTIANY, J. G. (ed.), *Honour and Shame* (London, 1965).

POLLAK, OTTO, *The Criminality of Women* (1950; New York, 1961).

POLLARD, ALFRED. W., *et al.*, *Shakespeare's Hand in the Play of Sir Thomas More* (Cambridge, 1923).

PORTER, DENNIS, *The Pursuit of Crime: Art and Ideology in Detective Fiction* (New Haven, 1981).

PRATT, NORMAN T., *Seneca's Drama* (Chapel Hill, NC, 1983).

PROSSER, ELEANOR, *Hamlet and Revenge*, 2nd edn. (Stanford, Calif., 1971).

PRYNNE, J. H., 'A Letter to Andrew Duncan', *Grosseteste Review*, 15 (1983–4), 100–18.

PUTTENHAM, GEORGE, *The Arte of English Poesie*, ed. Gladys Doidge Willcock and Alice Walker (Cambridge, 1936).

QUESTER, GEORGE H., 'The Psychological Effects of Bombing on Civilian Populations: Unlimited and Other Future Wars', in Betty Glad (ed.), *Psychological Dimensions of War* (London, 1990), 310–15.

RAHEJA, GLORIA GOODWIN, *The Poison in the Gift: Ritual, Prestation, and the Dominant Caste in a North Indian Village* (Chicago, 1988).

RAWLS, JOHN, *A Theory of Justice* (Oxford, 1972).

READE, WINWOOD, *The Martyrdom of Man* (London, 1872).

ROBERTS, SIMON, *Order and Dispute: An Introduction to Legal Anthropology* (Harmondsworth, 1979).

ROBINSON, HENRY CRABB, *Henry Crabb Robinson on Books and Their Writers*, ed. Edith J. Morley, 3 vols. (London, 1938).

ROE, NICHOLAS, *Wordsworth and Coleridge: The Radical Years* (Oxford, 1988).

ROSE, JACQUELINE, *The Haunting of Sylvia Plath* (London, 1991).

ROSENMEYER, THOMAS G., *Senecan Drama and Stoic Cosmology* (Berkeley, 1989).

SAID, EDWARD, *The World, the Text, and the Critic* (London, 1984).

SANDEL, MICHAEL J., *Liberalism and the Limits of Justice* (Cambridge, 1982).

SARTRE, JEAN-PAUL, *Sartre on Theater*, ed. Michel Contat and Michel Rybalka, tr. Frank Jellinek (London, 1976).

SAYERS, DOROTHY L., *Unpopular Opinions* (London, 1946).

SCARRY, ELAINE, *The Body in Pain: The Making and Unmaking of the World* (New York, 1985).

SCHAFFER, SIMON, 'Self Evidence', *Critical Inquiry*, 18 (1992), 327–62.

SCHLEINER, LOUISE, 'Latinized Greek Drama in Shakespeare's Writing of *Hamlet*', *Shakespeare Quarterly*, 41 (1990), 29–48.

SCOTT, JOHN P., *Aggression*, 2nd edn. (Chicago, 1975).

SEGAL, ERICH (ed.), *Euripides: A Collection of Critical Essays* (Englewood Cliffs, NJ, 1968).

——— (ed.), *Oxford Readings in Greek Tragedy* (Oxford, 1983).

SHAPIN, STEVEN, 'The House of Experiment in Seventeenth-Century England', *Isis*, 79 (1988), 373–404.

——— and SCHAFFER, SIMON, *Leviathan and the Air-Pump: Hobbes, Boyle, and the Experimental Life* (Princeton, 1985).

SHAW, GEORGE BERNARD, 'Art Corner', in *Our Corner*, 1 June 1886, 370–3, repr. in *Shaw Review*, 15 (Jan. 1972), 35–8.

SHOWALTER, ELAINE, *Sexual Anarchy: Gender and Culture at the Fin de Siècle* (London, 1991).

SHUTTLE, PENELOPE, and REDGROVE, PETER, *The Wise Wound: Menstruation and Everywoman* (London, 1978).

SICILIANO, ENZO, *Pasolini*, tr. John Shepley (London, 1987).

SIMONDON, MICHÈLE, *La Mémoire et l'oubli dans la pensée grecque jusqu'a la fin de Vᵉ siècle avant J.C.* (Paris, 1982).

SIMPSON, JAMES, 'Genius's "Enformacioun" in Book III of the *Confessio Amantis*', *Mediaevalia*, 16 (1993), 159–95.

SINGER, ISIDORE (gen. ed.), *The Jewish Encyclopedia*, 12 vols. (New York, 1901–6).

SINGER, PETER, *The Expanding Circle: Ethics and Sociobiology* (Oxford, 1981).

SORABJI, RICHARD, *Necessity, Cause and Blame: Perspectives on Aristotle's Theory* (London, 1980).

STAPLEFORD, BRIAN, 'Man-Made Catastrophes', in Eric S. Rabkin, Martin H. Greenberg, and Joseph D. Olander (eds.), *The End of the World* (Carbondale, Ill., 1983), 97–138.

STASSINOPOULOS, ARIANNA, *Maria: Beyond the Callas Legend* (London, 1980).

STEINER, GEORGE, *The Death of Tragedy* (London, 1961).

STENDHAL, *Love*, tr. Gilbert and Suzanne Sale (London, 1957).

STERN, J. P., *Nietzsche* (London, 1978).

——— *Hitler: The Führer and the People*, rev. edn. (London, 1990).

STEWART, J. I. M., *Myself and Michael Innes: A Memoir* (London, 1987).

TAMBIAH, S. J., 'The Magical Power of Words', *Man*, NS 3 (1968), 175–208.

TAPLIN, OLIVER, *The Stagecraft of Aeschylus*, corr. repr. (Oxford, 1989).

—— *Comic Angels and Other Approaches to Greek Drama through Vase-Paintings* (Oxford, 1993).

TAVRIS, CAROL, *Anger: The Misunderstood Emotion*, rev. edn. (New York, 1989).

THOMAS, KEITH, *Religion and the Decline of Magic* (1971; Harmondsworth, 1973).

TILL, NICHOLAS, *Mozart and the Enlightenment: Truth, Virtue and Beauty in Mozart's Operas* (London, 1992).

TODOROV, TZVETAN, *The Poetics of Prose*, tr. Richard Howard (Oxford, 1977).

TRELAWNY, EDWARD JOHN, *Records of Shelley, Byron and the Author*, ed. David Wright (Harmondsworth, 1973).

TRENDALL, A. D., and WEBSTER, T. B. L., *Illustrations of Greek Drama* (London, 1971).

TREWIN, J. C., *Peter Brook: A Biography* (London, 1971).

VALÉRY, PAUL, 'The Idea of Art', tr. Ralph Manheim, in *The Collected Works of Paul Valéry*, gen. ed. Jackson Mathews (London, 1958–75), xiii.

VANCE, EUGENE, *Reading 'The Song of Roland'* (Englewood Cliffs, NJ, 1970).

VERNANT, JEAN-PIERRE, *Myth and Thought Among the Greeks*, tr. Janet Lloyd (Boston, 1983).

—— and VIDAL-NAQUET, PIERRE, *Myth and Tragedy in Ancient Greece*, tr. Janet Lloyd (New York, 1988).

VIRILIO, PAUL, *War and Cinema: The Logistics of Perception*, tr. Patrick Camiller (1984; London, 1989).

WALCOT, PETER, *Envy and the Greeks: A Study of Human Behaviour* (Warminster, 1978).

WALLACE, JOHN M., '*Timon of Athens* and the Three Graces: Shakespeare's Senecan Study', *Modern Philology*, 83 (1985–6), 349–63.

WALLACE-HADRILL, J. M., *The Long-Haired Kings and Other Studies in Frankish History* (London, 1962), 121–47.

WASSERSTROM, RICHARD A. (ed.), *War and Morality* (Belmont, Calif., 1970).

WATSON, LINDSAY, *Arae: The Curse Poetry of Antiquity* (Leeds, 1991).

WATTS, FRANKLIN (ed.), *Voices of History 1942–43* (New York, 1944).

WEART, SPENCER R., *Nuclear Fear: A History of Images* (Cambridge, Mass., 1988).

WEIL, SIMONE, *Simone Weil: An Anthology*, ed. Siân Miles (London, 1986).

WHITE, STEPHEN D., 'Feuding and Peace-Making in the Touraine Around the Year 1100', *Traditio*, 42 (1986), 195–263.

WILLIAMS, BERNARD, *Moral Luck: Philosophical Papers 1973–1980* (Cambridge, 1981).

—— *Ethics and the Limits of Philosophy* (London, 1985).

—— *Shame and Necessity* (Berkeley, 1993).

WILSON, JOHN DOVER, *The Manuscript of Shakespeare's 'Hamlet' and the Problems of its Transmission*, 2 vols. (Cambridge, 1934).
—— *What Happens in 'Hamlet'* (Cambridge, 1935).
WINE, HUMPHREY, *et al.*, *Tradition and Revolution in French Art 1700–1880: Paintings and Drawings from Lille*, Catalogue of a National Gallery Exhibition (London, 1993).

INDEX